Ron Bates
12-25-76
Gift of MLC

ORGAN BUILDING AND DESIGN

POUL-GERHARD ANDERSEN

Organ Building and Design

TRANSLATED BY JOANNE CURNUTT

New York
OXFORD UNIVERSITY PRESS
1969

FIRST PUBLISHED IN 1969
SECOND IMPRESSION 1976

Translated from the Danish
ORGELBOGEN

Printed in Great Britain by
Biddles Ltd, Guildford, Surrey

PREFACE

Danish is a very difficult language, and it is particularly difficult to translate a Danish technical book into English. I am therefore much obliged to Dr. Curnutt for the admirable courage she showed when six years ago she began, on her own initiative, to translate my book, and I am no less thankful now that the great task she took upon herself has been fulfilled.

I also tender to Mr. Ralph Downes, London, my heartiest thanks for the meticulous care he took in reading this translation and checking the English technical terms, but I must also record my obligations to Dr. Eugene Selhorst, Rochester, Professor Fenner Douglass, Oberlin, Mr. J. E. Knott, London, and my daughter Inger-Lise Andersen, M. A., Copenhagen.

FOREWORD

My work on this book was begun at the request of the Royal Danish Conservatory of Music in Copenhagen. Originally it was intended as a course in tonal and technical design of the organ and in organ history; but during my work I was also asked by the Danish National Museum to write about organ architecture and the location of the organ.

Although I received financial support from *Statens almindelige Videnskabsfond* (The National Science Foundation), the condition was a strict limitation of this comprehensive subject, and for that reason less essential matters had to be omitted and everything essential to be concentrated as much as possible.

The tonal design of the organ has been dealt with in detail, the technical design has been discussed as far as necessary for understanding how the technical parts of the organ determine the tonal character and the general structure and division of an organ. Furthermore, the technical details which determine the understanding of the historical organ types have been discussed.

In the chapters on organ history, my chief intention has been to characterize the tonal design of organs from different countries and epochs. I have had neither the time nor the opportunity for greater research into the archives. This may be unfortunate, yet the archives do not contain the most interesting sources of organ history; they are to be found in the extant instruments, regardless of their present state. During a historical investigation of an organ the organ builder may have some preference over the historian; anyway there is no harm done when for once an organ builder writes history.

Circumstances have forced me to use a concentrated form but I have attempted to give as detailed information as possible. I know that an organ can only be poorly described by a specification, and this is why I have also discussed scaling technique, voicing, compositions and repetitions of mixtures, and quoted historical advice for registration.

The visual aspect is an essential part of the description, and the plates will help to show the close connection between tonal and optical architecture; in many instances they will emphasize the tonal character.

Furthermore, I have sought to give a survey of the capabilities of the different organ types, for instance by showing how the organ has been a "culture barometer" of West European history, even of our own time.

This brief account contains only part of the basic knowledge which every organist should acquire and which would be useful to the Church Board and the ecclesiastical authorities when an organ is being built or rebuilt. But it will also be a useful ballast to those who want to read the numerous specialized works on organ building.

Copenhagen 1966
Poul-Gerhard Andersen

CONTENTS

1

The Proportions of Sound

When we consider the multiple variations of sound – music, speech, noise, etc. – it is remarkable that the vibrations in the air which transmit the sound oscillations from the sound source to our ears can be altered in only two ways: in amplitude and frequency.

We know from our school-days that irregular vibrations are perceived as noise, while regular vibrations, of which the single oscillations maintain a constant duration or fixed period, are perceived as pitches. The pitches rise or fall in relation to the frequency of vibration, indicated by cycles (abbreviated c.), that is, the number of complete vibrations per second. A complete vibration may be defined as the movement from one extreme position to the opposite and back to the point of origin.

The range of vibrations which can be perceived by the human ear extends from 16 to 16,000 c., but the sensitivity to the high frequencies is reduced with increasing age, and frequently the threshold of hearing for older persons does not go beyond 8,000 c.

The amplitudes of the oscillations determine the size of the compression waves resulting from the movements and thereby also the intensity of the tone. These compression waves are minute. They are measured in phons (1 phon = 1 microbar = *ca.* 1:1,000,000 atmosphere), and sound-intensities as low as 0·0001 phon can be distinguished; at about 500 phons the intensity annoys. This limit is referred to as the threshold of pain.

The phon scale is, however, no practical measure for the intensity, because the ear is, comparatively, much more sensitive to weak than to strong tones. In most instances the decibel scale is preferred. It has a logarithmic relation to the phon scale and approximately corresponds with the increasing sensitivity of the ear.

The zero point of the decibel scale correlates with 0·0002 phon and with such a weak intensity of a tone at 1000 c. that the ear just cannot hear it. The threshold of pain, at 500 phons, corresponds to 130 decibels.

The sensitivity of the ear varies in relation to different frequencies, and this is the reason why the zero point on the decibel scale is set in connection with a specific pitch. In the diagram (Fig. 1) the curved lines indicate how much intensity is required in order that perception can be constant throughout the various frequency ranges. The lowest curve, the zero curve, shows, for example, that a tone of 330 c. must have an intensity of above 65 decibels in order to be heard. This curve also demonstrates that the ear is most sensitive to frequencies between 3000 and 4000 c. Within this range the threshold of hearing lies at 0·0001 phon, below the zero point of the decibel scale. To weaker tones, the sensitivity of the ear is rather dissimilar. An intensity of 70-80 decibels is necessary to make a wave of the same amplitude continually perceptible throughout the frequency ranges.

Since the vibrations of sound can be varied with regard to frequency and amplitude, both pitch and intensity can be varied, and these are the two resources required for producing not only music, but also timbres, which are very important components of musical sounds.

In studying the intervals used in music, we see that their frequencies have simple reciprocal relations. For each ascending octave, the frequency

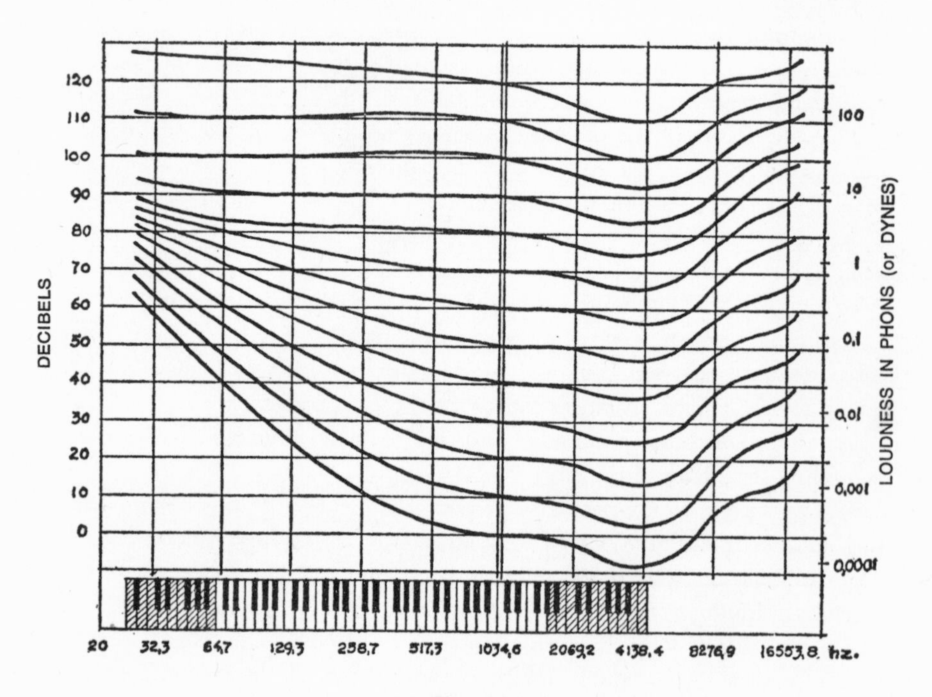

Fig. 1.

is doubled; for intervals of a major third, the frequencies have the ratio of 4:5; for the interval of a fourth, 3:4, and for the interval of a fifth, 2:3.

These tonal proportions were known and used several centuries before frequency was studied and measured, not only because they are instinctive or natural, but because they can be located with the aid of a taut string. If the string is held firmly in the middle, and one-half is allowed to vibrate, it will produce a tone located an octave higher than when the full length of the string vibrates and produces the so-called fundamental. If the string is divided into three parts, and two-thirds of it are allowed to vibrate, the fifth above the fundamental is obtained. If it is divided into four parts, and three-fourths vibrate, it produces the fourth. And if it is divided into five parts, the major third is produced with four-fifths of the string vibrating, and with three-fifths of the string vibrating, we will get the sixth. In other words, the frequency is inversely proportional to the length of the string, as long as the same tension is maintained in the string. The monochord, as such a single string is called, thus became the theoretical basis for the development of our tonal system, whose origin is attributed to the Greek mathematician and philosopher Pythagoras (or his school), *ca.* 500 B.C.

We know that the Pythagorean diatonic scale (c-d-e-f-g-a-b) fulfilled its function in the culture from which it sprang. It also served the early church and was further developed in the Christian Europe of the Middle Ages, eventually becoming the basis of our music up to the present time. We recognize its possibilities of variation in the church modes, and later in the major and minor keys, but there is particular reason to note that it is a small link in a far greater entity.

The fact that this scale originates with Pythagoras indicates that it was a matter for the consideration of philosophers, persons who studied mathematics and geometry, because they saw the principle of life and the harmony and regularity of existence in the proportions of the numbers.

We encounter the proportions both in music and in the architecture of the church, where this philosophy of numbers is clearly exemplified; and we see how these principles, just as the Pythagorean scale, were further disseminated via the Roman Church during the Middle Ages.

In architecture, four relations appear repeatedly; they are the simple relations of 1:2, 1:3, 2:3, and the so-called Golden Section (sectio aurea).

The first three ratios are intimately associated when considered geometrically.

The AC line segment is divided at B into two parts in such a way that AB becomes twice as long as BC. Point B therefore divides the AC line segment in the ratio of 1:2. However, a line segment can also be divided "externally". Point C externally divides the AB segment into sections AC and BC, and it appears from the sketch that this ratio is 1:3. In the same way, point A externally divides the BC segment into the ratio of 2:3.

The Golden Section is the ratio which divides a line segment so that the smaller segment is related to the larger as the larger is to the entire line.

Therefore AB:BC = AC:AB. Later we shall see how this ratio also concerns pipes and organ-cases.

To return to Pythagoras: how did he construct his diatonic scale? We only know that he employed fifths and that his practice even in the Middle Ages and up to the close of the eighteenth century formed a basis for the computation of pipe lengths and widths.

Applying this system to the monochord, we know that the fundamental, which we can call C, is obtained when the full length of the string is vibrating. We have the octave above this (c), when one-half of the string is vibrating. Within this octave, we shall try to produce the pitches D -E -F -G -A and B.

If we divide the string in the relation of 1:2, one part being twice as long as the other, the longer section will produce the fifth, G, above the fundamental, and the shorter will produce the octave above that, g, the fifth of the second octave.

If we reverse the operation by using the string length of the second octave as a basis (half the original string length) and increase this by one-half to make three-fourths of the total length, we arrive at F, the fifth below c or the fourth above the fundamental C. In other words, both octaves and fifths can be constructed by means of the ratio 1:2.

In the preceding operations, we found the fourth and the fifth. If we now divide the string length of the fifth, G, in the proportions of 1:2 and permit the larger segment to vibrate, we arrive at the fifth above the first fifth, d, and by doubling its string length, we attain the octave below, D.

By the same process we can advance from D to A, from A to e, from e to E, and from E to B.

Pythagoras stops here. He might have continued from B to f#–F#, from F# to c#–C#, from C# to G#, from G# to d#–D#, and from D# to A#. Thus our chromatic scale would have existed, the so-called circle of fifths would have been traversed and concluded with the octave, yet with one small deviation, the "Pythagorean comma".

We can assume that Pythagoras was aware of this continuation. We know that it was recognized by Aristoxenos (*ca.* 350 B. C.), and we know that the twelve-tone chromatic scale was known in ancient Egypt; and Pythagoras may have studied it during his exile there.

Why then restrict the building material to seven pitches?

Perhaps it was satisfactory to the mathematical philosophers that the total of pitches was precisely seven, the sacred number that we encounter in so many other places. But there is another reason for stopping at the seventh pitch. This is perhaps best understood, if one further restriction is made. If the fifth and sixth links are omitted in the progression of fifths described above, the pitches E and B drop out. This means the loss of the two half-step intervals of the scale (seen in relation to the neighbouring tones), and the result is the ancient five-tone or pentatonic scale whose smallest intervals are whole steps. Pythagoras extended this scale with two more pitches and acquired the two half-step intervals and thereby a multitude of new possibilities for expression.

When going farther in the circle of fifths (beyond the seven pitches), a new feature enters the scale. The Pythagorean half-steps were not adjacent, but already in the next link, when F# is added, we have half-steps lying next to each other, and the remainder of the circle of fifths provides the missing half-steps. Through this process we have attained the chromatic scale that certainly contains all possibilities, but which in itself is neutral and provides no guidance.

History of music teaches us that first the Greek scales and centuries later the church modes were derived from the Pythagorean scale. Its authority was maintained, not only in the centuries of unison music, but for a long time thereafter.

Polyphony began, in a modest way, about 900 A. D.; at first, two voices in parallel fifths, later developing into the well-known polyphony of the Middle Ages. The concept of harmonic relations created new problems.

The fifths were pure, but the major third caused some trouble. When using the Pythagorean method to reach this third, the following string lengths are obtained (assuming a string length of 1′ for the fundamental, C): $G = {}^2/_3$, $d = {}^2/_3 \times {}^2/_3 = {}^4/_9$, $D = {}^4/_9 \times 2 = {}^8/_9$, $A = {}^8/_9 \times {}^2/_3 = {}^{16}/_{27}$, $e = {}^{16}/_{27} \times {}^2/_3 = {}^{32}/_{81}$, $E = {}^{32}/_{81} \times 2 = {}^{64}/_{81}$.

As we know, the pure third should have had a string length of ${}^4/_5$, that is ${}^{64}/_{80}$; thus the Pythagorean third is a little too high, a little too large.

Perhaps you wonder that there could be any problem, as the pure, or harmonic, third had been known almost as long as that of Pythagoras (Archytas, 408 B. C.). The pure third was naturally the better one, but the question of which third was employed had no really practical significance in unison music. Even in polyphonic music the listeners could tolerate the impure third, because they were predisposed more to the linear than to the harmonic aspect. At any rate, it is a fact that the Pythagorean third was held in high esteem until the sixteenth century.

Homophonic music and the use of the triads were gaining widespread acceptance, and the church modes, which were not created for the purpose of this development, were gradually reorganized into the major and minor keys.

Paul Hindemith describes the church modes as "rails which compel the musical thoughts to move in a specifically linear direction", and the entire development which took place after 1500 must be seen in connection with the universal emancipation from archaic tradition brought on by the Renaissance.

The pure third was a foreign element in the Pythagorean system, but in a triad, it was decidedly superior in tonal beauty to the Pythagorean third, and was accordingly preferred.

Not only the new musical orientation, but also the development of keyboard instruments with their fixed tuning made it necessary to consider these problems. As long as it was a question of unison music, vocal music, and instruments without fixed tuning, the small flaws within the tonal system had no practical importance; but with keyboard instruments there is no way to conceal these imperfections; everything is revealed with mathematical precision.

The real development of these instruments begins at the close of the Middle Ages, and about 1400 we find keyboards of a somewhat normal size and with twelve half-steps in every octave.

The first keyboard instruments had Pythagorean tuning, and the "comma" of "wolf" was customarily placed on the interval f♯–b. This interval was so impure that it was unusable. The performer had to contend with the thirds, and if he did not go too far from the starting point on the circle of fifths, music could be performed quite satisfactorily.

The real problems appeared when the pure thirds were introduced. A mutual balance of the intervals could no longer be achieved, and the only possibility was either to insert some extra pitches in the octave or to place the intervals which became too impure at the least annoying places. Both procedures were attempted, but since it was impractical to have more than twelve tones in each octave, the so-called "tempered" tuning was finally chosen.

By this method it was endeavoured to keep the most used keys as pure as possible at the expense of those less used. There were many ways of doing this, but the basic principle was the same in all of them, and so it is sufficient to refer to a few examples.

The first has been taken from Praetorius' *Syntagma musicum* and is probably connected with Esaias Compenius, the master-builder of the Frederiksborg Castle organ (Denmark). Here, f′ is the starting point, and thereafter the tuning is done in the sequence given below. The last-named pitch on each line is tuned to the first one. The operation proceeds in this way: the fifths are made a little too small, and the impurities are regulated and distributed so that the thirds at the check-points remain pure. Only the fifth g#–d#′ remains too large and so impure that it cannot be used; this is the "wolf".

1. f′–c″
2. f′–a′ tuned pure
3. c″–c′ " "
4. c′–g′
5. c′–e′ " "
6. g′–d″
7. g′–b′ " "
8. d″–d′ " "

After this, the fifth d′–a′ is checked to hear if it has the correct impurity, i. e., if it is tempered correctly in relation to the preceding fifths.

9. d′–f#′ tuned pure
10. a′–e″

The third c″–e″ is checked for purity.

11. a′–c#″
12. c#″–c#′

13. c#′–g#′

The third, e′–g#′, must be checked.

14. f′–f″ tuned pure

15. f″–b♭′

The third, b♭′–d″, is checked.

16. b♭′–d#′

The third, d#–g′, is checked.

17. d#′–d#″ tuned pure

The lower and higher pitches on the keyboard are tuned in octaves according to the established pitches, but the thirds must be checked constantly.

Dom Bedos mentions another method in *l'Art du facteur d'orgues* (1766). In reality, we find the same method in Schlick's *Spiegel der Orgelmacher und Organisten* (1511), and it was, to all appearances, the method most employed in both Germany and France until the last half of the eighteenth century.

The principle is the same as before. The fifths are made smaller than pure fifths, making it possible to have the pure third instead of the Pythagorean one. Nevertheless, four slightly impure thirds cannot be avoided, but eight remain pure. The starting point is c″.

1.	c″–c′	tuned pure
2.	c′–g′	
3.	g′–d″	
4.	d″–d′	
5.	d′–a′	
6.	a′–e″	
	c″–e″	checked
7.	e″–e′	tuned pure
8.	e′–b′	
	g′–b′	checked
9.	b′–b	tuned pure
10.	b–f#′	
	d′–f#′	
11.	f#′–c#″	
	a′–c#″	" "
12.	c#″–c#′	" "
13.	c#′–g#′	
	e′–g#′	checked

14. c″–f′
    f′–a′ checked
15. f′–b♭
    b♭–d′ ”
16. b♭–b♭′ tuned pure
17. b♭′–d♯′
    d♯′–g′ checked
18. d♯′–d♯″ tuned pure

In compensation for the pure thirds, some keys acquired such impure intervals that they could not be used. Again the "wolf" (g♯–d♯) created the troubles; c♯ and f♯ were so affected that nothing could be built upon them. In the lowest octave, the pitches C♯, D♯, F♯, and G♯ were useless and therefore omitted. The so-called "short octave" was derived from this practice. C was moved to the position of E, and D and E became black keys in the positions of F♯ and G♯ respectively, in this way:

C F ^{D} G ^{E} A $^{B♭}$ B

Several attempts were made in order to procure some further usable keys; the four impure thirds could be augmented to five, and these thirds could then be placed in different ways according to need. At the end of the eighteenth century the so-called Kirnberger tuning appeared; it has been named after Johann Philipp Kirnberger, a pupil of J. S. Bach, and it has 8 impure and only 4 pure thirds; but with this tuning all of the keys may be used, as the impurity of the intervals has been reduced to a moderate degree. In addition, this tuning is characterized by 9 pure fifths, that is, an approach to the Pythagorean tuning. The Kirnberger tuning undoubtedly won an extended application, and it is still a very suitable tuning for any kind of music up to the later Baroque; even in our own time it has again been debated by people concerned in keys and tuning.

Because of the varying purity of the intervals these systems of tuning were called unequal temperament in contrast to the equal temperament; the latter had attained a degree of prominence in the middle of the eighteenth century and at last entirely superseded the unequal temperament.

Equal temperament was no new discovery. Even before 1500, it was a matter of interest. Bartolo Ramis (Spain) had described and advocated it in 1482, and Mersenne in *Harmonie universelle* in the year 1637; but the theory had no importance, until musical development a hundred years later demanded free and unrestrained access to all keys.

The principle of equal temperament is this: the twelve tones of the octaves are arranged in half-steps of equal size; this is achieved by distributing the same degree of impurity among all of the fifths; this impurity is sufficient to ensure that the circle of fifths can be completed with the starting pitch. By this means, the fifths become a little larger and purer than in unequal temperament, but the thirds remain impure, although not so impure as in Pythagorean tuning.

In laying a temperament (for organs, at least) the usual method of procedure is the following: the concert-pitch a′ is used as the starting point. It is tuned to the tuning fork, and then e′ is tuned to a′ with the intention of making e′ a little lower than pure. The interval of the fourth, the inversion of the fifth, therefore is slightly enlarged. After this, b′ is tuned to e′, so that b′ is also a little lower than pure. The interval of the fifth then will be somewhat diminished; f♯′ is then tuned to b′, with a slight augmentation, and the process is continued throughout the octave with slightly augmented fourths and slightly diminished fifths in this order: a′–e′–b′–f♯′–c♯′–g♯′–d♯′–b♭′–f′–c,–g,–d,–a.

The fourths are usually made a little more impure than the fifths, but in general the impurities must be regulated and distributed evenly to make certain that d′, the end of the series, has the proper ratio to the starting tone, a′.

The thirds were the decisive point when a choice had to be made between the two methods of tuning. When the issue was debated in the eighteenth century, the instrument builders insisted on the old method for the sake of good sound, and the musicians insisted on the equal temperament. For example, J. S. Bach had many heated discussions with the organ builder, Gottfried Silbermann. The two men were equally stubborn, and both had good arguments to support their opinions, but as is well known, Bach was the winner.

With this, the subject was fully debated, and there are no reasons to-day to resume the discussion. When we hear an old instrument tuned with pure thirds, we can possibly imagine renouncing certain keys in order to obtain the remarkable harmony of these thirds. But no matter how we consider the problem, we cannot avoid a compromise, and we are obliged to distribute the impurities in such a way that they will cause the least possible annoyance.

The pitch used as a basis for tuning has varied a great deal in the course of several centuries. Until the invention of the tuning fork in 1711, the determination of pitch was fairly arbitrary. It depended very much on what range of pitches was most suitable for the human voice, and it was possible for the pitch to shift several half-steps from one period to another and from place to place. Certain established criteria in the building of instruments also played a part; but in spite of everything, the variations were kept within rather narrow limits.

In a letter dated 1772, Johann Andreas Silbermann, the organ builder, wrote that four different pitches were in use. The highest of these was the *Cornett-ton* (cornet-pitch, D, used by town musicians for tuning brass instruments), which was very common in Germany. This permitted an economy in both the length and width of pipes. While this was convenient for the organ builders, it was difficult to sing with these organs. *Chorton* (choir-pitch) was preferred, and it lay a half-step lower, C#. The *Kammerton* (chamber-pitch), used by the majority of musical instruments, was another half-step lower, C. It was also called the "Italian" pitch since the Italians used it almost universally. This pitch was slightly lower than our present concert-pitch (435 c.).

In 1859 the French tuning was established at a′ = 435 c., and this pitch was recognized and accepted at an international tuning conference in Vienna in 1885. However, orchestral practice has constantly forced the tuning upward. The official tuning for the State Radio Orchestra, Copenhagen, is 440 c., and the majority of organs are now tuned to this pitch.

According to the Viennese tuning (a′ = 435 c.), the frequencies for the range of the organ are as follows when computed in equal temperament:

		C	C#	D	D#	E	F	F#	G	G#	A	B♭	B#
32′	C_2	16,2	17,1	18,2	19,2	20,4	21,6	22,9	24,2	25,7	27,2	28,8	30,5
16′	C_1	32,3	34,3	36,3	38,5	40,7	43,2	45,7	48,4	51,3	54,3	57,6	61,0
8′	C	64,7	68,5	72,6	76,9	81,5	86,3	91,5	96,9	102,7	108,8	115,2	122,1
4′	c	129,3	137,0	145,2	153,8	162,9	172,6	182,9	193,8	205,3	217,5	230,4	244,1
2′	c^1	258,7	274,0	290,3	307,6	325,9	345,3	365,8	387,5	410,6	435,0	460,9	488,3
1′	c^2	517,3	548,1	580,7	615,2	651,8	690,5	731,6	775,1	821,2	870,0	921,7	976,5
½′	c^3	1034,6	1096,1	1161,3	1230,4	1303,5	1381,0	1463,2	1550,3	1642,3	1740,0	1843,5	1953,1
¼′	c^4	2069,2	2192,3	2322,6	2460,7	2607,1	2762,1	2926,3	3100,3	3284,7	3480,0	3686,9	3906,2
⅛′	c^5	4138,4	4384,5	4645,2	4921,5	5214,1	5524,6	5852,6	6200,7	6569,4	6960,0	7373,9	7812,3
1/16′	c^6	8276,9	8769,1	9290,5	9842,9	10428,3	11048,3	11705,3	12401,3	13138,7	13920,0	14747,0	15624,7

For further guidance, the pitch of a′ of a few well-known organs will be given. It is impossible to decide if these pitches are identical with the original ones, but there is no reason to expect important differences.

1. Frederiksborg Castle Church (1610) – Esaias Compenius – 460 c.
2. St. Jacobi, Hamburg (1688) – Arp Schnitger – 489 c.
3. Strassburger Münster (1713) – Andreas Silbermann – 393 c.
4. Trinity College, Cambridge (1759) – Father Smith – 395 c.

OVERTONES (partials)

Beside the diatonic and the chromatic scales, there is also a scale of harmonics, that is, a series of pitches whose frequencies lie in whole multiples in relation to the frequency of a given fundamental. If this fundamental has a frequency of 100, the following tone in the series has the frequency of 200, the next 300, the succeeding one 400, etc. Or, if we transfer the system to the monochord and use the entire string length as the fundamental, the next tone uses half the string length, the following $^1/_3$ of the string length, the next one $^1/_4$, and so on. For this reason, these pitches are also called "fractional tones" or partial tones, and the simple relations in the frequencies signify that they are interrelated harmonically; thus the derivation of the term, the scale of harmonics.

This scale has naturally no direct musical importance and was a little known concept until the nineteenth century. The turn of the century marked the beginning of a purely scientific interest in sound and pitches, although organ building centuries before had experimentally discovered its most important intervals.

The tones in this scale are produced automatically in musical instruments, in the sounds of speech, and wherever they appear; for this reason, they are also referred to as natural tones.

With C as the fundamental, the series has the following pitches and string lengths on the monochord:

1	$^1/_2$	$^1/_3$	$^1/_4$	$^1/_5$	$^1/_6$	$^1/_7$	$^1/_8$	$^1/_9$	$^1/_{10}$
C	c	g	c′	e′	g′	b♭′	c″	d″	e″

C is considered as the first partial, c as the second, etc. The series can be continued into infinity.

Timbres are created by grouping these partials in different combinations and in variations of intensity. In such a combination the partial tones will not be heard individually, but they blend into a single tone whose pitch is perceived as the pitch of the fundamental. The development of this complex tone can best be seen by a graphic illustration.

The movement represented in the basic form of sound waves corresponds to ordinary pendulum oscillations, steadily decreasing in speed toward the outer limits of the movement and moving with greatest speed when the resting point is passed. If we suppose that the lowest point of a swinging pendulum traces a line on a piece of paper which is moved vertically at a constant speed behind the pendulum, we obtain a graphic picture of the sequence of the pendulum oscillations. The vertical line at the axis of the curve indicates the resting position, and its longitudinal divisions show the lapse of time. A period is the time which is consumed by a double oscillation from one outer position to another and back again; in the case of curve A, four temporal units. The amplitude of oscillation determines the intensity of the sound, and the point of greatest amplitude is called the loop of oscillation. In the same way, we speak about the "node" (knot), referring to the place where the curve intersects the axis, and where the vibration is consequently nil.

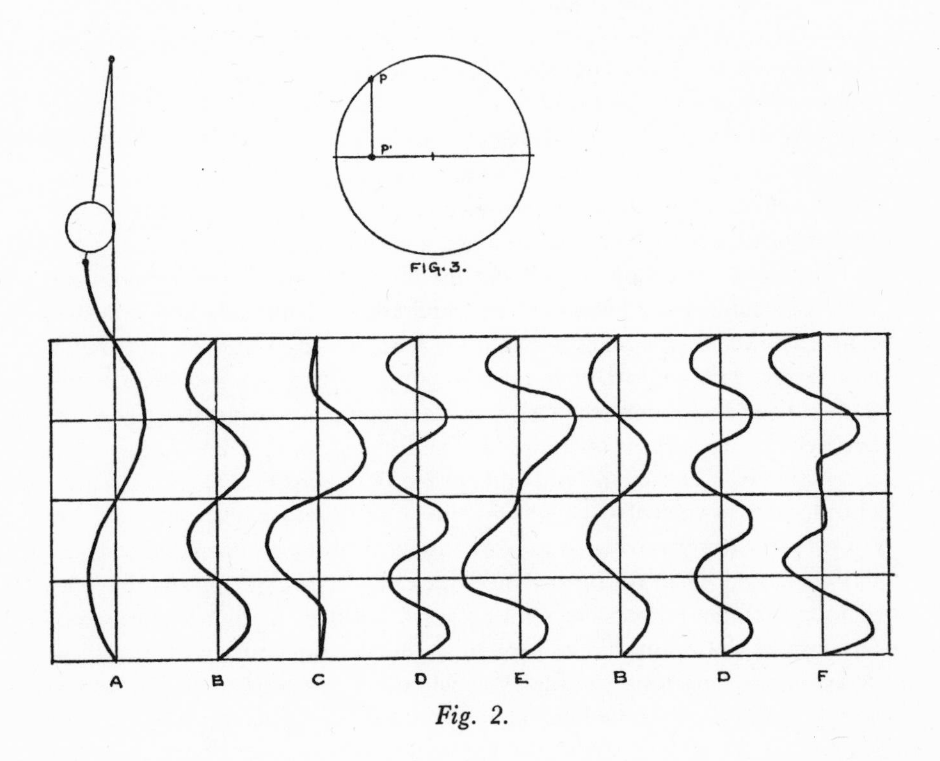

Fig. 2.

We would get the same curve if we used a tack, at the end of a vibrating tuning fork, to sketch the movement as in the case of the pendulum. This is the so-called sine-curve, which corresponds to the sinusoidal function in trigonometry.

If we imagine that point P (in Fig. 3) traverses the arc of the circle with constant speed, its projection (P′ on the diameter) will execute a movement forwards and backwards completely corresponding to the pendulum oscillations.

At B (Fig. 2) a pitch with twice as many vibrations per time unit is depicted, that is, it lies an octave higher than curve A and is therefore the second partial tone in relation to A. When the curves of these two pitches are combined, the effect is similar to curve C, which is called the resultant.

Curve C is produced by adding (or subtracting) the simultaneous amplitudes of curves A and B, since the curves now are constructed in relation to the resting position. We see that the curve C has retained the frequency of the fundamental (A), though with increased amplitude, and that it likewise contains the higher frequency (B). In the event that the two tones are not synchronous, there will be some divergence in the curves; a phase displacement results, and thereby a somewhat different resultant curve appears, but nevertheless, a curve with the same characteristic timbre. Consequently, the difference is not audible.

With the same method as before, we now add curve D, representing the third partial. The resultant (E) shows more intervening oscillations, but the periods of the fundamental are retained and intensified.

When we combine the second and the third partials (B and D) we note that the resultant (F) has two large amplitudes at both ends, which means that a vibration with a lower frequency than B and D has resulted; more specifically, with the same frequency as curve A. This is a so-called combination tone (or differential tone), because its frequency is just the difference between the frequencies of B and D. The frequencies of B and D have the proportion of 3 and 2, and the difference is 1. Summation tones also exist, but they are so weak that they have no practical significance.

Our ears discern with great certainty if two tones are harmonic or dissonant, and when we further investigate the matter, it appears that the vibrations of the harmonizing tones "beat" together, so that simultaneous crossings of the resting position occur at regular intervals. With tones an octave apart, one tone executes two vibrations, while the other executes one; with two tones at the interval of a fifth, one tone makes two vibrations, while the other makes three; with tones a major third apart, four and five vibrations take place in the same space of time, etc.

If we now assume that we have two tones tuned as an octave and thereafter make one a little higher, the oscillations will no longer agree, and we have the same phenomenon that is present when two church bells do not coincide in their strokes. At a specific interval, the strokes of the bells are precisely synchronized, then they separate until the alternations are quite regular. Then the strokes become more synchronous, and at last they coincide exactly, after which the separation begins again.

Sound vibrations occur at a faster rate, and when they cease to agree, the separations are observed as the periodic increase and decrease of the loudness with very distinct points of culmination, the so-called "beats" or "waves". These beats are therefore a very exact test of whether two tones harmonize with each other (are in tune); and with tempered tuning, beats can be used as a test for the degree of deviation from pure tuning, because the beats become faster as the two tones become more dissonant. In the case of complete dissonance, the beats are so fast that they are indistinguishable – they can only be perceived as an irritation.

2

The Acoustics of Buildings

Gottfried Silbermann, the organ builder, was accustomed to throw his cane on the floor when he wanted to judge the acoustics in a church. This test could be so conclusive that he refused to build the organ if the acoustics did not please him.

Even less temperamental persons know the inspiration of a good room and the oppressiveness of a bad one. But it is difficult to define what enhances the quality of sound and what detracts from it, ignoring the case of the entirely "dead" room. A long echo can be flattering and can give an impressive feeling of spaciousness, but the intimate quality of a small room has its special charm, too.

Modern electro-acoustical methods of measuring have made it possible for us to penetrate the mysteries of space acoustics. The main value in these methods is that, with the aid of a sound filter, they permit us to listen to (and measure) the desired frequency and to exclude temporarily all other frequencies. In this way we can dissect a sound and ascertain the details of its composition, and we can follow the echo through all its phases and frequencies.

When sound-vibrations strike a solid body – a wall for example – a more or less complete reflection occurs. The direction of reflection is determined by this general rule: the angle of incidence is equal to the angle of reflection, and the amount of the reflection depends on the stability of the body concerned and the nature of its surface. Especially in the case of more complicated vibrations, a complete reflection is uncommon. The surface absorbs a part of the energy of the vibration, and this absorption usually varies in the different tonal ranges, according to the form and texture of the surface. The variations are innumerable.

When sound waves are reflected and collide, on their return, with the succeeding waves from the sound source, a reciprocal effect is produced (interference), which may result in "standing" waves. The stipulation is a simple numerical relation between the wave length and the distance between the sound source and the reflecting surface. This causes loops and nodes to stabilize themselves at fixed places in the room.

For example, if one of the deepest Sub-bass tones of the organ is speaking, its intensity will be observed to vary from place to place in the room, depending on whether we listen within the loops or the nodes of the standing waves. If the fundamental of the pipe is very pronounced and the overtones are very weak, the intensity can vary between nothing and a tone stronger than that of the pipe when heard close by; we only have to move about a pipe length ($^1/_4$ of the wave length) to observe this. Thus interference can both weaken and intensify the sound.

Another product of reflection is the echo, the reverberation. With repeated reflections, especially in a larger room, the sound waves may be protracted to such an extent that a certain time must elapse before they are absorbed or dissolved. In this complicated wandering from surface to surface, the vibrations are consequently affected by the phenomena of reflection, absorption and interference of the room in question. The structure of the original sound combination is gradually changed.

We can get an impression of this change if we measure the reverberation period in various frequency ranges. The reinforcement for the primary

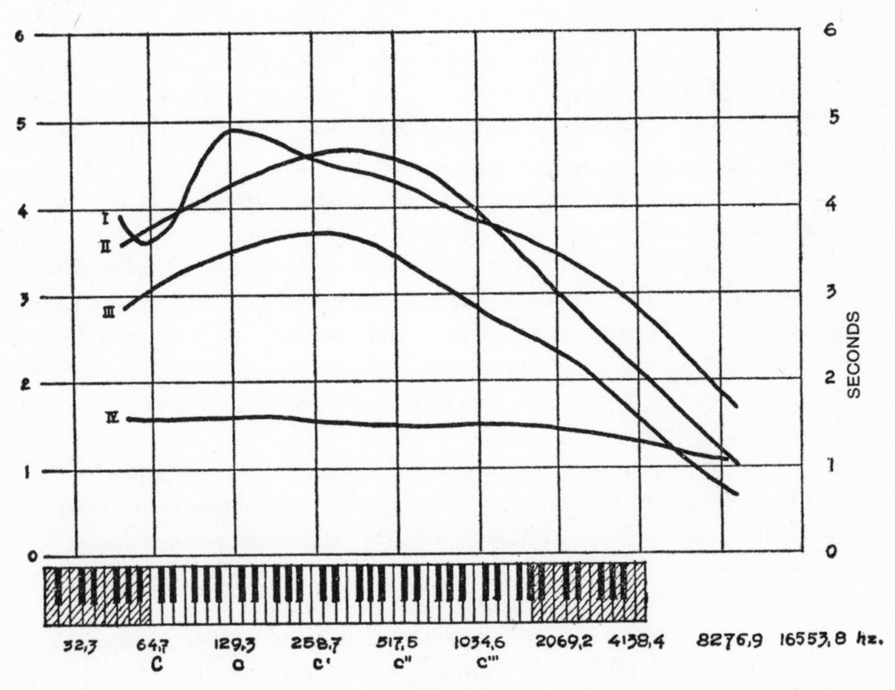

Fig. 4.

tonal spectrum of the sound corresponds in intensity to the reverberation period. In relation to the reverberation period, the extent of this reinforcement of the upper partials can vary somewhat in different rooms, but we nevertheless get a general idea of the change in the harmonic balance.

In Fig 4, the curves for four different rooms appear in diagram form. The reverberation period is indicated in seconds on the ordinate (vertical), while the frequency ranges are indicated in logarithmic division on the abscissa (horizontal). The unshaded part of the keyboard corresponds to the normal organ keyboard.

Curve I. Our Saviour's Church, Copenhagen
Curve II. Oscar's Church, Stockholm
Curve III. Bethlehem Church, Copenhagen
Curve IV. Concert Hall of the State Radio House, Copenhagen

However, the curves do not provide a complete impression of the acoustical character of the room. Two rooms may have the same reverberation period and still create quite different effects. A smaller room with hard, smooth walls can reflect the sound so strongly and so quickly that the reverberation period is just as long as it would be in a larger, more normally absorbing room.

A curve only indicates the duration of the sound in a room and not its way of expanding and contracting. It does not reveal the basic difference between a smaller room with many echoes (and the resulting confusion of interference) and a larger room with a less complicated and more natural sound-development. In comparing large and small rooms, the basic difference is the fact that the natural loss of intensity in the air occurs more unhindered in the large room; thus the reverberation period must always be considered in relation to the size of the room, to the cubic content. The shape and division of the room also merit attention in an evaluation of the acoustical properties.

By measuring various rooms and by making experiments with changes of the reverberation period in the same room, the problem of quality has been proved to be closely associated with the balance of frequencies in the reverberation period. A general solution will scarcely be found, because each room and every purpose requires its own solution.

Music needs a longer reverberation period for the lower frequencies, since the sensitivity of the ear decreases rapidly in this range. This lengthening of the reverberation period is common in larger rooms, because the air-absorption is most effective in its repression of high frequencies (from 3000 c. and upwards); but large, sound-absorbing surfaces can change this relationship. To-day such surfaces are one of the most important means in the control of room acoustics.

In general, we distinguish between four types of absorbents: (1) the well-known *porous absorbents,* soft rugs, an audience, and similar objects, which are most effective against high frequencies. (2) *A layer of material absorbents,* which are only employed when a very effective deadening of standing waves must be achieved (a "dead" room and similar instances). But it is difficult to employ these absorbents in churches and concert-halls, as they must be mounted at a distance of ¼ the wave length from the wall. The *membrane absorbents* (3), consisting of a tight surface, oilcloth for example, with a stratum of air behind it. Both the weight of the fabric itself and the stratum of air isolated by the coating will prevent the vibrations. This method is particularly effective in curbing the low frequencies. The most common method is based on *resonance absorption* (4), known from ancient times. It was theoretically developed by Helmholtz, the nineteenth century physicist. Today it is practised by arranging a resonance chamber behind some thin, hard surfaces of wood or fibre perforated with grooves or holes. The chamber absorbs the frequencies which are "in tune" with it. By varying the depth of this posterior chamber and possibly by using porous absorbents in the chamber, these surfaces can be adapted for deadening any frequency range that must be reduced. The degree of absorption is regulated by the area of the surface. By this admittedly negative means, the disadvantageous high points of a reverberation curve can be removed, and the curve can be balanced according to the purpose.

It is important to distinguish between this *qualitative* regulation and the purely *quantitative type,* known from office and factory rooms, where it is primarily a matter of muffling irritating noise. Also in school rooms, lecture halls, theatres, and other places requiring an acoustically neutral space, the deadening is carried out mainly from this quantitative point of view.

The exaggerated deadening of a large room is an entirely different matter, because this alteration produces an unnatural effect without creating favourable conditions for speaking.

When we enter a large room, we have a natural desire to perceive, also through the ear, that it *is* a large room. Obviously, the visual character of the room is closely connected with the aural impression; we do not expect the same acoustics in a high-vaulted church and in a theatre, even if the cubic content is the same. Our auditory habits know quite well how to take the "furnishings" into consideration. If invisible muffling is used to a greater extent, we inevitably get an aural surprise – an unpleasant surprise in the case of music.

In churches, which must be used both for speaking and for music, the problem is difficult but not insoluble. In the few instances where acoustical regulations have been attempted, there has been an unfortunate inclination to exaggerate the deadening, possibly from a misconceived deference to the clergy. The understanding of the nature of sound has still an extensive development ahead.

The present opinions are, to a predominant degree, conditioned by the microphone. This is not surprising, because the microphone is indeed an important tool in modern acoustical research; but a microphone listens in a way which is essentially different from the way of two human ears, one reason being the lack of the stereophonic effect. As long as this disparity prevails, our ears should be regarded as the highest authority.

Our ears tolerate far more reverberation than a microphone, and this is a great advantage. When regulating the acoustics of a church, it is important to pay attention to the musical aspect. The organ, comprising all frequencies, is of course extremely dependent on the acoustics of the room – and on an imprudent regulation, too.

Our experiments in this area have not yet passed the primary stage. There is much work to be done with measurements of good rooms and studies of these measurements, before we really can use the possibilities available to us, and before we know something exact about this problem of quality.

3

The Organ Pipes

The pipes are divided into two main groups according to construction and function: the flues (labials) and the reeds (linguals).

Flue Pipes (labials).

The flues are constructed as shown in Figs. 5, 6, and 8 which show a pipe partly in perspective, and partly in a vertical cross-section. The lower tapering part is called the *pipe foot* (B) and the upper cylindrical part the *pipe body* (F). Between the foot and the body, there is a horizontal partition, the *languid* (D), which, seen from above, is circular with a straight cut on one side. Where the languid is cut off straight, the wall of the foot is bent in toward the languid, so that a narrow slit remains, called the *flue,* between the foot and the languid. In a similar way, the wall of the body is pressed flat above the languid, and into this surface, which is called the *upper lip,* the pipe mouth is cut; the height of the pipe mouth is called the *cut-up.* The flattened surface in the foot is called the *lower lip.* At the top, the body can be open or closed. The operation of the closed or "stopped" pipe will be studied first.

Air enters the pipe through the opening in the bottom of the pipe foot, and this air flows upward like a flat wind sheet, passing through the flue and on toward the upper lip, where eddies of vibration are formed, starting the real action of vibration. As the wind is directed chiefly within the upper lip, the air column in the body will be somewhat compressed, like a spiral spring. The compressed air will "rebound" quickly and force the wind out, most of it passing outside the upper lip. This is accompanied by the expulsion of air from the body of the pipe, and the ensuing rarefaction causes the wind sheet to be sucked back into the pipe. Then the process is repeated.

The wind sheet from the flue accordingly oscillates in and out on both sides of the upper lip, and the air column in the body is respectively compressed and expanded like a spiral spring. At the languid, the air molecules make upward and downward vibrations, depending on the effect of the vibrating wind from the flue; but at the top of the pipe, near the stopper, the air molecules are hindered in executing these movements, and therefore the air is, instead, alternately compressed and rarefied. In other words, these pressure alterations near the cover are caused by vibratory action farther down in the body of the pipe. Nearer to the stopper, the vibrations gradually decrease, because the stopper acts as an impediment. This produces a complementary increase in the pressure alterations.

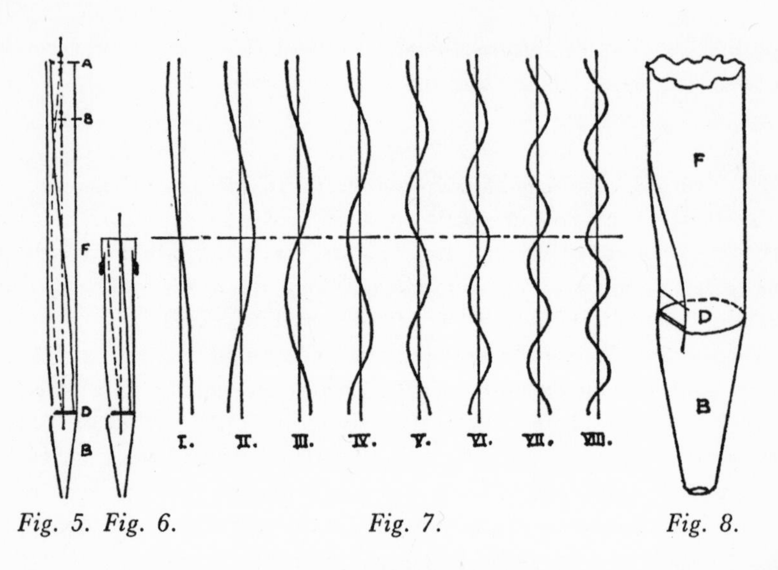

Fig. 5. Fig. 6. *Fig. 7.* *Fig. 8.*

It is easy to understand how the vibrations can be started in a stopped pipe. But it is not immediately obvious how vibrations can arise without a stopper to restrict the vibrations of the wind stream from the flue.

The process may be clarified by imagining an experiment with a relatively long, and slack spiral spring with open turns. When such a spring is held at one end and permitted to hang down freely and vertically, the entire spring can be moved up and down without it changing its length or form, if the movement is slow enough. But if the speed is increased, the spring cannot keep pace with the movements; it is expanded or/and contracted. If regular movements can be produced at the point of suspension in a rhythm corresponding to the weight and tension of the spring, loops will be formed with energetic movements up and down, and nodes between the loops. Nodes develop at the points where the turns of the spring do not move at all, because they are counteracted by equally energetic movements from the two nearest loops.

The same is true of the air column in an open pipe. The vibrations take place so quickly that the inert air column is subdivided into two equally large parts. They move toward each other, collide in the middle of the pipe, and a node is formed. The contrary vibrations from the upper half of the pipe have the same effect as the stopper of a closed pipe.

Of course it must be assumed, as in the case of the spiral spring, that the air column is affected in a rhythm corresponding to its elasticity and inertia; but since the action comes from the vibrating wind stream at the flue, the reactions of the air column itself govern the inward and outward vibrations.

It is difficult to illustrate the vertical vibrations of the air column, the so-called lengthwise or longitudinal vibrations. If we want to form a visual image of these vibrations, we must mark off the oscillations at right angles to their direction of movement. The vertical movement of the points A and B, indicated by arrows, is marked horizontally to the left of the middle line, and when this has been done for all points of the middle axis, the solidly drawn curves appear, shown in Figs. 5 and 6. These curves thus indicate the vibrations, while the broken lines indicate the pressure alterations.

These curves show only the basic form for the oscillations in the air column, the fundamental pitch. The majority of pipes have a considerably more complicated pattern of vibration. The air column also makes partial vibrations corresponding to one-half, one-third, one-fourth, etc. of its length. In other words, it produces larger or smaller series of partial tones beside the fundamental pitch. The fundamental and six of these partials are indicated by the curves in Fig. 7, and these curves show that only the odd-numbered partials (1-3-5-7, etc.) have a node in the middle of the pipe. The even ones have loops at this point.

Since the cover in a stopped pipe prevents the formation of a loop (that is, maximum molecular activity) at the cover, such a pipe can only contain the partials 1-3-5-7, etc. (in relation to the pitch C they are C, g, e′ b♭′, d″, etc.). Therefore, stopped pipes are incapable of producing partials that correspond to the octaves of the fundamental.

So much for the theory. In practice this is less categorical, because the lengthwise vibrations in organ pipes have proved to be somewhat larger at the pipe's walls than in its middle; and in the lowest part there is, in addition, a considerable distortion of the vibrations due to the influence from the mouth.

This causes various exceptions to the rules; in practice the stopped pipes can, for example, have quite weak, even partials.

Two factors are decisive for the timbre of the pipe; first, the shape and the dimensions of the pipe body, and second, the method used for activating the air column in the body (cautiously or energetically). The latter depends partly on the wind pressure used for voicing the pipe, partly on the height and the width of the pipe mouth, and finally, on the width of the flue. The length of the flue is usually the same as the width of the mouth.

In this connection, the aids to voicing must also be mentioned. In the first place there are the so-called "ears" or "beards", which are applied at the pipe mouth. They can have various forms (Fig. 9 "sidebeard", 10 "boxbeard", 11 "rollerbeard", 12 "frontbeard", 13 "sidebeard with rollerbeard", 14 "harmonic bridge"), but they all have the same purpose: to separate the vibrating wind stream from the surrounding air. Especially the so-called overblowing must be prevented: i.e. the pipe losing its foundation pitch and breaking into an upper partial.

In the same drawing, various tuning devices are illustrated. They serve to lengthen or shorten the functioning pipe length. Figure 9 shows the common tuning slot which is cut from the upper edge of the pipe. The pipe can also be tuned by means of an adjustable cylinder above, a so-called

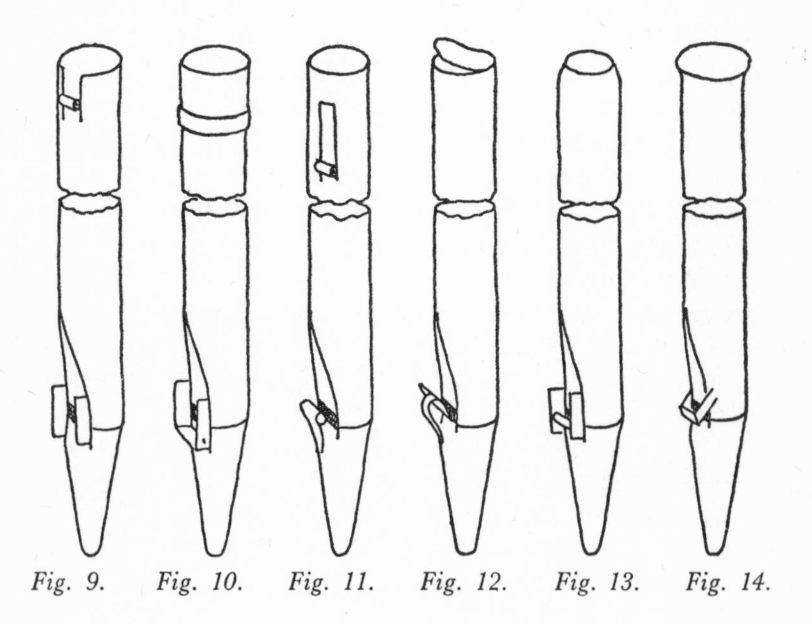

Fig. 9. *Fig. 10.* *Fig. 11.* *Fig. 12.* *Fig. 13.* *Fig. 14.*

"tuning-slide" or "sleeve" (Fig. 10). For stopped pipes this tuner is sealed above with a soldered cover, or the cover is soldered on the pipe itself. The pipe, in this case, is provided with large sidebeards, and it can be tuned by bending the sidebeards more or less in toward the mouth. Figure 11 shows the Reuter tuning slot, which is placed at a short distance below the upper edge of the pipe. The pipe in Fig. 12 is tuned with a flexible cover, a method which is, however, most used with wooden pipes. Pipes can also be tuned by narrowing or widening the upper opening (Figs. 13 and 14). This method is restricted to the smaller pipes, and the operation is performed with a tuning "horn", which has a conical point at one end for broadening the opening, and an inner cone in the other end for compressing it.

Among the voicing devices are the "nicks", quite small, vertical grooves at right angles to the flue. Nicks are cut with a sharp knife into the front edge of the languid or, with a double-edged knife, both into the front edge of the languid and the inner side of the lower lip. These nicks increase the breadth of the wind stream, and this means a more sensitive influence on the air column, a softer attack, and fewer overtones, especially of the non-harmonic type.

It is a common misunderstanding that the material of pipes, metal or wood, determines the quality of the sound, and that this material even creates the vibrations, like a string or a bell. This is not true. The tone is produced by the air column which is confined in the body of the pipe, and the sole function of the pipe walls is to enclose the air column and provide it with the correct dimensions. Of course we cannot entirely ignore the fact that the pipe wall vibrates at the same time, and such vibrations can involve some very weak non-harmonic overtones, which may be advantageous in certain cases. But in principle, the pipe wall must be neutral, and that is why lead-alloys are so common. When the pipe material is selected, consideration must also be given to purely practical matters such as manufacture, stability and price; and just because the air column in the pipe and not the pipe wall is the sound-producing element, practical considerations will often have a decisive influence on the choice of pipe materials.

In the course of time, pipes have been made of many different materials: glass, porcelain and stiff cardboard, for example. But in practice, alloys of tin and lead are chiefly used, and the tin content generally varies between 30, 50, 60, 75 or 90 per cent. Since modern rolling mills can produce sheets of harder metals at a moderate price, copper or zinc have also been used for larger pipes. And now as before, wood is an excellent pipe material.

The difference in tonal quality between wooden pipes and metal pipes is more dependent upon the form of the body than upon the material. The rectangular cross-section of the wooden pipes produces vibratory conditions that are unlike those associated with the circular cross-section of the metal pipe, particularly at the nodes. The circular form offers a more effective resistance to the pressure alterations than the rectangular one, depending on the amount of deviation from the quadratic.

Thus the dimensions of the pipe, the "scale", are by far the most conclusive for its sound. Generally, pipes with a large cross-section in relation to the length have a dominating foundation pitch and weaker harmonics, that is, a soft and flutelike sound, while pipes with a small cross-section in relation to the length have stronger harmonics and a weaker foundation pitch, that is, a brighter and more "stringy" sound.

The shape of the pipe body can also affect the structure of the harmonic series. By closing the pipe at the upper end we can exclude half of the partials, but if the body is conical, tapering upward toward the stopper, the even-numbered partials will be present, although rather weakly. If, on the other hand, we make the body of an open pipe taper upward, the even-numbered partials are weakened, and the sound resembles that of the stopped pipe. In rare cases the body can also have a larger diameter at the top than at the bottom. The effect is tantamount to a weakening of the harmonics without the foundation tone becoming correspondingly stronger, as would occur with an ordinary enlargement of the diameter.

These are the main characteristics of the tonal variations that can be obtained by changing the shape of the body, but the function of the mouth must also be considered (a constant wind pressure is assumed). A narrow mouth with a high cut-up signifies mild action on the air column, that is, weak harmonics. A broad mouth with a lower cut-up produces a stronger influence which promotes the harmonics at the expense of the fundamental, and the tone becomes steadier, more brilliant, and stronger. The width and opening of the flue also determine the force with which the air column will be attacked, since a broad flue naturally emits a larger air stream than a narrow one. Another important matter is the adjustment of the languid in relation to the upper and lower lip, that is, how the wind stream hits the upper lip. And one more thing must be remembered: the wind pressure in the pipe foot.

These last relationships in particular belong to the concept of voicing, and the voicer's only task is to produce the sound that is natural for the pipe in question, according to its construction and its scale. By means of voicing, he can make a pipe sound in many different ways, but the natural sound lies within rather narrow limits, and it is the voicer's craft to find it.

This outline has attempted to emphasize the factors that determine the tonal physiognomy of the single pipe, but when dealing with the rank of pipes corresponding to the entire keyboard, a question arises concerning the development of the scale throughout the pipe series, both the length scale and the width scale.

The length scale is the least complicated of these two questions, because the theoretical pipe lengths are governed by the same laws (already mentioned) that we know from the monochord.

From the diagrams for simple vibrations in open and stopped pipes (Figs. 6 and 7) it can be seen that the theoretical pipe length is half of the wave length in the open pipe, and one-fourth of the wave length in the stopped one. To obtain the wave length, the velocity of sound (*ca.* 340 metres per second) must be divided by the doubled frequency of the pipe in question.

However, for various reasons, the practical pipe length is somewhat shorter than the theoretical one, and it is, in addition, dependent on the scale and mouth relation of the pipe. Figure 123 demonstrates the effect of these relations on the pipe length. All of the pipes in the picture have the same pitch. The narrow pipes are longer than pipes with a wide scale, and pipes with narrow mouths are shorter than pipes of the same width with broad mouths. When pipes are voiced with greater intensity, they must also have a greater length in order to compensate for a rise in the pitch, and besides, various relations at the mouth play a part. For example, the length must be reduced if beards or other voicing aids are employed, or if the space in the organ makes it necessary for the pipes to stand close together.

In the course of time, many methods of calculation have been tried, and many formulas have been proposed for the computation of the pipe lengths. One of the simplest of these methods was stated by Cavaillé-Coll, the French organ builder. He arrived at the actual pipe length after reducing the theoretical pipe length by twice the depth of the pipe, measured horizontally from the flue to the backwall. This is simply a formula of experience, but it is a good one, because both the diameter of the pipe and the width of the mouth are included in the calculation.

For conical, open pipes, tapering upward, there is a correspondingly simple length correction: the theoretical pipe length is reduced by an amount which equals the sum of twice the lower diameter and one-half the upper diameter ($2D - \frac{1}{2}d$).

Naturally, the results obtained with these methods are not entirely exact, among other reasons because the conditions stated earlier play a part. In practice the pipes are therefore made with some extra length, which is then regulated in connection with the voicing and the tuning.

Here it should be mentioned that the wave length and consequently the tuning are largely dependent on the temperature of the air. When the temperature rises, the specific gravity of the air is decreasing, and consequently the wave length for tones with fixed frequencies increases. In organ pipes, the wave length is determined by the length of the pipe and is thereby invariable, and therefore the pitch must rise when the air in the pipe body is heated. During the heating the pipe itself certainly expands in a counteraction, but this expansion is so infinitesimal that it is negligible.

In practice this relation is not particularly disturbing, because the pitch of all flue pipes rises proportionally, so that the reciprocal tuning of the flue pipes is not upset. The circumstances are different concerning the reeds, but more about this later.

At 32°F and with a′ = 435 c., the theoretical pipe lengths have the following measurements in centimetres:

	32′	16′	8′	4′	2′	1′	½′	¼′	⅛′
C	1053,4	526,7	263,4	131,7	65,8	32,9	16,5	8,2	4,1
C♯	994,3	497,2	248,6	124,3	62,2	31,1	15,5	7,8	3,9
D	938,4	469,2	234,6	117,3	58,7	29,3	14,7	7,3	3,7
D♯	885,8	442,9	221,4	110,7	55,4	27,7	13,8	6,9	3,5
E	836,1	418,0	209,0	104,5	52,3	26,1	13,1	6,5	3,3
F	789,2	394,6	197,3	98,6	49,3	24,7	12,3	6,2	3,1
F♯	744,9	372,4	186,2	93,1	46,6	23,3	11,6	5,8	2,9
G	703,1	351,5	175,8	87,9	43,9	22,0	11,0	5,5	2,7
G♯	663,6	331,8	165,9	82,9	41,5	20,7	10,4	5,2	2,6
A	626,4	313,2	156,6	78,3	39,2	19,6	9,8	4,9	2,4
B♭	591,2	295,6	147,8	73,9	37,0	18,5	9,2	4,6	2,3
B	558,0	279,0	139,5	69,8	34,9	17,4	8,7	4,4	2,2

At C, an ordinary open foundation stop in the manual has the theoretical length of 263.4 cm., that is, a good 8 feet, and the practical pipe length, which is indeed somewhat shorter, will vary in the vicinity of 8 feet. This is the reason why such a foundation stop is called an 8′ stop, a term which is almost as old as the organ itself.

With the use of the monochord principle, the successive octave c's will have the following foot lengths:

C″ 32′, C′ 16′, C 8′, c 4′, c′ 2′, c″ 1′, c‴ 1/2′, c⁗ 1/4′, c′′′′′ 1/8′.

These are of course no exact measures, but venerable pitch designations. For the intervening fifths the foot lengths are:

G″ 21 1/3′, G′ 10 2/3′, G 5 1/3′, g 2 2/3, g′ 1 1/3′, g″ 2/3′, g‴ 1/3, g⁗ 1/6′.

And for the thirds:

E 6 2/5′, e 3 1/5′, e′ 1 3/5′, e″ 4/5, e‴ 2/5′, e⁗ 1/5′.

The length scale thus deals with rather simple proportions, and the pitch of the pipe is not so great a problem as the phenomena connected with its timbre: the width scale and the mouth scale. It is no wonder that the evolution in this area extended over centuries.

It took a long time before the width scale received any attention. From the ninth to the twelfth century there obviously was no interest in that subject, because all pipes, from bass to treble, had the same diameter. According to a description taken from a twelfth century source, the diameter had the size of a pigeon's egg, between 24 and 30 mm. However, with this constant diameter, it was only possible to extend the pipe series to a good two octaves, because the pipes became too narrow in the bass and too wide in the treble to be capable of producing a consistent tone.

It would be difficult to establish whether the desire for a greater keyboard compass or purely tonal considerations caused the fourteenth century organ builders to introduce ranks of pipes with decreasing diameters toward the treble. Both reasons are possible: if the keyboard compass should be made larger, the reduction of diameters was a necessity; and with the constant diameters there had indeed been a remarkable difference in timbre between bass and treble; the bass was very "stringy" and the treble very "fluty". Above all, the organ builders had begun to work with the decrease of diameters toward the treble in order to produce a more homogeneous sound throughout the rank.

We have no certain information about the solutions which were first brought to light. No pipe material has been preserved, and the available archive material is of a later date. Our knowledge actually commences in the middle of the fifteenth century; but concerning the next three centuries, we know that the octave relation of 1:2 was the basis for the calculation of the width scale. Probably there will be no error in assuming that it has been like this from the beginning.

Now we cannot, as a matter of course, employ the relation of 1:2 without some modification; the bass would be too wide and "fluty" and the treble too narrow and "stringy". On the other hand, the diameters of the second octave (the fifteenth) can be given the ratio of 1:2, and instances are known. Some records from Burgundy, representing the middle of the fifteenth century (National Library, Paris) are the oldest evidence at present, but de Caus (1615) and Kircher (1650) also discuss this scale. It may be illustrated with a figure which shows squares combined with a succession of inscribed and circumscribed circles (Fig. 15). As it appears from the figure, the octave ratio becomes $1: \sqrt{2}$.

However, this scale was not really good. Of course it could be used through 4-5 octaves, especially in stopped pipes, but the bass became rather narrow in relation to the treble. At any rate, other proportions were also employed, mostly derived from geometry. As known from ancient times, the right-angled triangle of which the sides are related 3:4:5 (Fig. 16), furnished such appropriate ratios as 3:4 and 3:5; and the Golden Section (sectio aurea), which was also very near the ideal, could be deduced from the regular pentagon and its diagonals (Fig. 17: the ratio between one side and a diagonal, or the ratio at which the diagonals intersect each other). Many other later-recognized octave ratios were closely akin to these: 4:7, 5:9, 5:8, 5:7; for open pipes, especially 3:5 and sectio aurea gave a satisfactory, constant timbre. For stopped pipes, 2:3 and 5:7.

This entire development was connected with the contemporary development of different stops and stop families, which created the demand that a rank, as far as possible, preserved its timbre, its "equality", from bass to treble.

Do the numerical relations and the geometrical figures, which are found in the archives, imply that the scales of the late Middle Ages have had a consistent pattern? In other words, has the octave ratio been the same throughout the entire rank? There is reason to doubt this. The pipe material which can be studied is so sparse and distorted that it provides very few clues; only a small number of constant scales are to be found in the available material. The majority are variable and similar to the practice of later periods.

Constant scales are usually to be found in stopped or half-stopped pipes. For example, the Bordun 16′, Gedackt 8′ and Rørquint $2^2/_3$′ in the Petri organ at Malmö, Sweden (*ca.* 1500) follow the octave ratio of 2:3, while the Principal group has the so-called fixed-variable scale.

The basis for these fixed-variable scales is most often the octave ratio of 1:2, supplemented by a corrective, which, in all its simplicity, provides an infinite number of possibilities. The procedure is that we add an appropriate (according to the case) constant amount, a so-called additive constant, to all of the values in a progressive basic scale with the octave ratio of 1:2. With this system we can let the scale be narrow in the bass and wide in the treble, or the reverse, if this is desired (comparable to the scaling sequence of 3:5). If a large additive constant is used, the treble becomes wide in relation to the bass, and with a small additive constant the bass becomes wide and the treble narrow, still in comparison with the course of the scale of 3:5.

Of course other ratios can also be used for the basic scale. The use of 3:5, for example, is almost as old as the use of 1:2; and we can even work with a negative additive constant, that is, a reduction of all of the values in the basic scale by a constant amount. Fundamentally, the result is the same: no constant ratio can be maintained between the different octave values.

These fixed-variable scales are sometimes called curve-scales, because they usually appear as curves in a co-ordinate system. Then the fixed scale is naturally represented as a straight line with the zero point placed on the abscissa.

Organizing these scales in this manner may be useful, if we want to form a picture of their tonal characteristics from bass to treble, but it is wrong to believe that the scales resulted from ingeniously calculated curves. As mentioned, their origin is much more simple, and these scales also appear as straight lines in the system where they were generated.

For the basic scale of 1:2, a scale table can be made in the following way (Fig. 18). Point c is established as the midpoint of a horizontal line, CO. The segment cO is bisected at point c′; then the segment c′O is halved at point c″, and point c‴ is produced in a similar manner. Through these points, right angles are constructed. Every oblique line which extends through point O and intersects these right angles will isolate line segments having the ratio of 1:2 to the adjacent segment.

For example, if NC represents the basic scale for a C pipe, the basic scale for its upper octave, c, will be the segment nc. This is a constant scale with the same octave ratio throughout, and since this ratio is 1:2, the progression may be regarded as a diminutive representation of the pipe lengths. (For the sake of clarity, only the C's have been indicated; the intervening pitches can be located by means of the circle of fifths – the old method – or by logarithms.)

Such constant scales can be changed into fixed-variable scales by adding the same segment to all of the values; in the drawing it is the segment AC, which is the same as OB.

With the same procedure, a scale table can be constructed for the octave ratio of 3:5. The line cO will then be related to CO as 3:5, and when continued, c′O and cO, c″O and c′O, c‴O and c″O must have the same proportions.

A legitimate objection to this system of scaling is the fact that, in itself, it produces no exact or definitive method for scale calculation. A dabbler would not be successful in using it. But the fact is that just this method and the basic scales of 1:2 and 3:5 have been used in the majority of European instruments built in the period from *ca.* 1500–1800. This span of nearly 300 years includes the most prolific eras of organ building, with names like Compenius, Scherer, Schnitger, Dom Bedos, Riepp, the Netherlanders, and many others.

In Fig. 19 are shown some examples of how different an 8′ Principal can be developed on the basic scale of 1:2, both as for relative width and for scaling sequence. The values given in the diagram represent the diameters in half their natural size. These examples have been taken from outstanding organs from western Europe, and they cover the period mentioned before. Moreover, they have been selected entirely at random. The constant, so-called normal scale (see p. 48) has been indicated by the dotted line for the purpose of comparisons. Sketched into this system it appears as a curved line.

The entire operation may give the impression of being a matter of chance, with the exception of the additive constants, of which the deviations are extremely small in the quoted examples. The breaks of the scale lines occur at the C's, because the majority of scale tables comprised only one octave and had in principle been established as shown in Fig. 20, which is merely a copy of Fig. 18, with the omission of the right angles c′, c″, c‴. Equally good results are obtained, and Fig. 20 represents the same scale as Fig. 18.

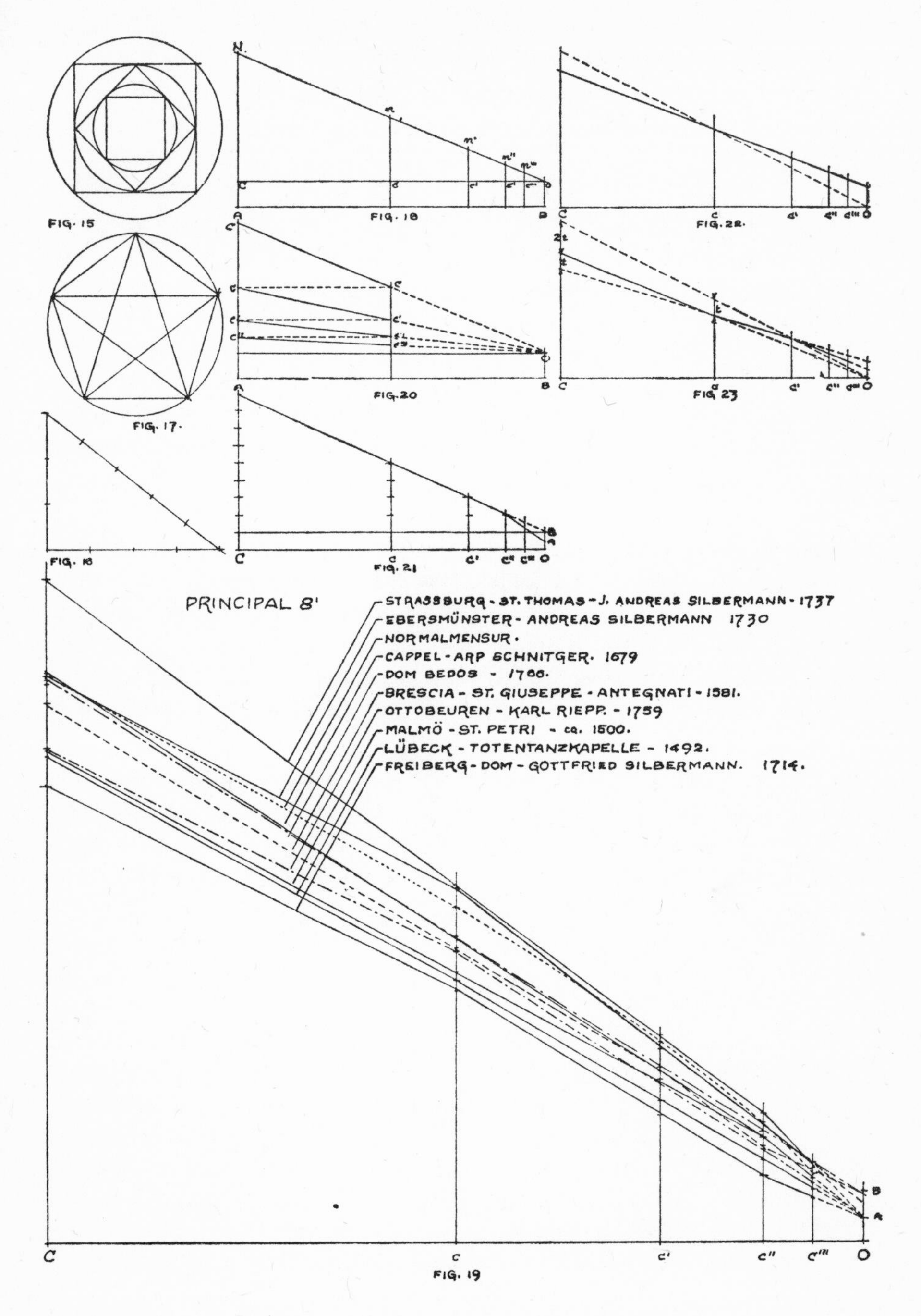

FIG. 15 FIG. 16 FIG. 17 FIG. 18 FIG. 19 FIG. 20 FIG. 21 FIG. 22 FIG. 23

From earliest times, the custom has been to use a certain pipe in the rank as a point of departure, the measuring pipe, and to establish its diameter or circumference in a simple numerical ratio to its length. Naturally, this ratio changes at the very next pipe, because diameter and length do not increase porportionally, but sometimes the octave values are established with simple proportions, that is, the additive constant is given a certain ratio to the basic scale.

A remarkably fine example of this is demonstrated in the three lowest octaves of the Principal in the Petri organ at Malmö. At c″, the ratio between the diameter of the pipe and its length is the well-known 1:8, and the diameter at c″ is twice the constant OB, which means that this constant enters into the basic scale as a module. Consequently, the diameter at c′ must be three times the additive constant; c is five times the diameter, and C nine times (see Fig. 21). Moreover, the additive constant is $^1/_{16}$ of the length at c″.

In both theory and practice, organ builders are usually more concerned with the circumference of the pipe than with its diameter; this is chiefly due to the process used in manufacturing pipes. The pipe metal is cast or rolled out in sheets, which are cut out, after which the curved pieces are bent and soldered together. For this reason, the pipemaker would prefer to work from the circumference instead of the diameters, and besides, the results are more exact.

Mersenne mentions a 4′ Gedackt-scale with a geometrical composition similar to that of the Malmö Principal. The circumference is stated in feet:

C $-^1/_4 + ^1/_4 = {}^1/_2$	i. e.	51,7	mm.	diam.
c $-^1/_8 + ^1/_4 = {}^3/_8$	"	38,8	"	"
c′ $-^1/_{16} + ^1/_4 = {}^5/_{16}$	"	32,3	"	"
c″ $-^1/_{32} + ^1/_4 = {}^9/_{32}$	"	29,1	"	"
c‴ $-^1/_{64} + ^1/_4 = {}^{17}/_{64}$	"	27,5	"	"

This is not a good scale. Mersenne can scarcely have taken it from practice; the treble is far too wide for use. Nevertheless, it proves that northern Europe was not alone in associating geometrical puzzles with scales. This does not mean that the problem of scaling was solved with such methods, or that a geometrically amusing or well-proportioned solution provided the best tonal result. The nine principal scales in Fig. 19 indicate that geometry was not paramount.

Where, then, can we find reliable information about the art and procedure of scaling? Or, we may ask, have the fixed-variable scales any relationship whatever to a scientific truth concerning the tonal problems, an "arcanum" as the ancients called it?

Fortunately, we have statements from competent persons like Werckmeister (in his "*Orgelprobe*") and Bendeler, the son-in-law of Arp Schnitger (in "*Organopoia*"). Both were opposed to the secrecy, the "alchemy", and the long-winded arguments that certain organ builders employed to give the impression of great wisdom. Werckmeister says that when this type of trick is exposed, it is just as simple as Columbus' famous egg-trick (according to anecdote, Columbus made an egg stand on end by simply breaking the lower end).

With some examples, Bendeler shows the main ideas and the simplicity with which they can be treated. The basis is the "musical proportions", that is, 1:2. Using the diameter of the measuring pipe as the standard, a small amount is subtracted from the diameter of the pipe an octave below; then one-half of this amount is added to the pipe representing the octave above the measuring pipe. From Fig. 22, it is easy to see that this, in principle, is the same as in the previously shown constructions.

Bendeler gives nothing more than approximate directions concerning the amount to be added or subtracted. On the other hand, he calls attention to the fact that this method is not entirely satisfactory, because it produces a *merkliche Inæqualität* (marked inequality), particularly in the cases where the bass must be kept relatively narrow. The art of scaling requires a more complex method for the attainment of the proper *unbetriegliche und unumstössliche* (unmistakable and irrefutable) fundament. He then describes the operation shown in Fig. 23. With the usual ratio of 1:2, the horizontal line is divided at points C, c, c′, c″, c‴. The dotted line through the zero point cuts off progressively doubled segments which lie at right angles to these c-points. The diameter of the measuring pipe is marked out at c′, and the c-segment – which is twice as large – is reduced by the amount of t, thus providing the diameter at c. The two end points for these diameters are connected, and the line is extended to the right angle at O, where a segment having the same length as t is cut off; t is the additive constant for the diameters c–c′. After that, Bendeler assigns one-half of the additive constant to the two upper octaves and none whatever to the C-octave.

The amount of the constant is not specified in this instance, and in general, neither Bendeler nor Werckmeister gives any concrete directions, not because any secret must be concealed, but because such universal instructions are simply impossible. Each particular case must be independently resolved in accordance with the prevailing conditions.

Figure 24 shows some examples of scaling with the basic scale of 3:5. With one single exception the examples have been taken from Andreas Silbermann's organ in Maursmünster.

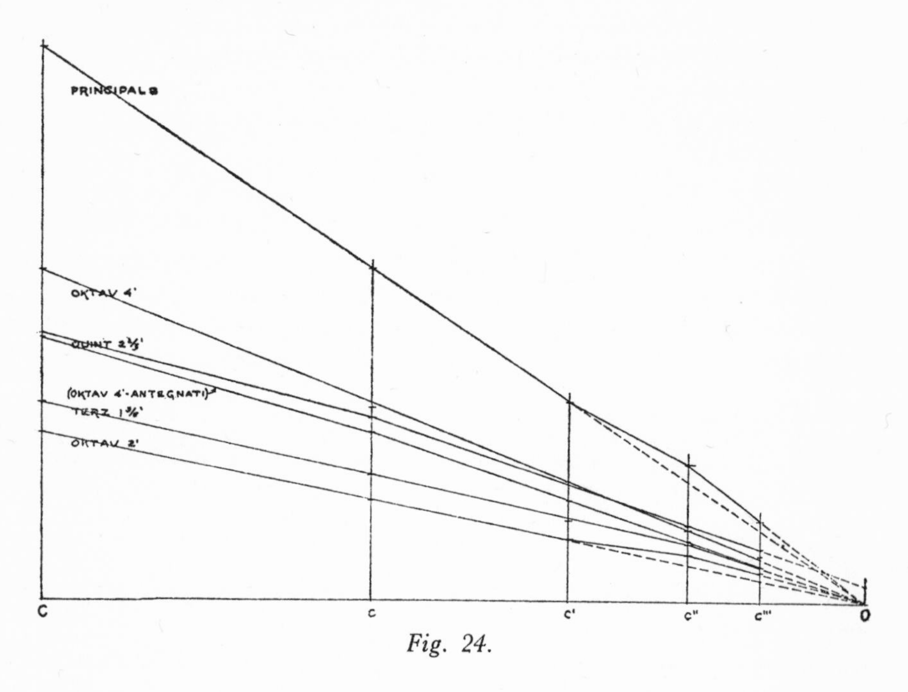

Fig. 24.

During the organ reform movement in the 1930s, interest in Baroque methods of scaling was awakened. The methods were credited with certain distinctive features such as the promotion of clarity in polyphonic music. The explanation of these characteristics was generally believed to reside in the often mysterious scaling curves, especially mysterious when the scale lines of a principal group of 16′, 8′, 4′ and 2′ were compared. The so-called "depth-points" of the curves, the places where the scale was most narrow, were special objects of attention, but these reflections did not lead to any really well-founded theory.

Neither Werckmeister, Bendeler, nor any other of the old organ theorists refer, by one single syllable, to the idea of polyphonic clarity, nor did they have any "normal" scale to use as a standard for judging their scales. Depth points and similar items were not included in their considerations. But they were principally concerned with *Æqualität,* and surely all breaks in the scale line are related to this quality.

Many of the Baroque organs really had outstanding polyphonic qualities, but the sequence of the width scale was only one of several reasons for this. The mouth scale is also a very important matter, affecting both timbre and intensity, and the specification and the voicing are factors of equal significance.

The normal mouth for principals is $^1/_4$ of the circumference of the pipe, and the height of the mouth is $^1/_4$ of its width; but frequently a somewhat narrower mouth is combined with a wide scale, when a fuller sound is desired without an increase in intensity. Mouth widths exceeding $^1/_4$ of the circumference are found only in exceptional instances, and ordinarily the minimum width is $^1/_7$. The interplay between the width scale and the mouth scale produces the final result and determines the tonal development throughout the rank.

Above and beyond these considerations, one very important factor remains: the acoustics of the room.

None of our sources furnishes specific information about these problems, for good reasons, because it is a matter that cannot be solved in "scale keys" or by scientific calculations. They must be delegated entirely to the organ builder, and he must develop his ability to judge what he wants and what he can accomplish in the various situations. In reality, the fixed-variable scales must be regarded as scales of experience, regulated and equalized by a certain geometrical system. The secret, the "arcanum", was the organ builder himself.

A basic change in scaling technique occurred in the latter half of the eighteenth century, at the same time as the equal temperament was taken into use. In Sorge's book, *Der in der Rechen und Messkunst wohlerfahrene Orgelbaumeister* (1773), he violently attacks the time-honoured fixed-variable methods, which, from a mathematical-scientific point of view, were rather easy to ridicule. Just at that time logarithmic calculation had become widely known and organized with the requisite tables. For organ building it meant all intervening values in the course of a *constant* scale could be found by a relatively simple calculation, when the highest and lowest tones were given. An organ builder could select the pipe in a rank which was to have one-half the diameter of the lowest pipe, and then compute not only the intervening values, but thereafter the entire sequence of the scale. Mathematically, all progressions were possible; he was no longer dependent on the "coïncidences" involved in the old system. Equal temperament had provided free access to all keys, homophonic music was gaining admittance at the expense of polyphonic music; the theory of the different keys was explained, etc. In brief, this was a period of change.

Sorge arrived at this result: "the width must not be sought in the length, but must be independently determined, so that the ratio of 1:2 is given either to the ninth or the minor tenth or the major tenth." He regarded the scale of the ninth as the best of these progressions, as a kind of normal scale.

During the nineteenth century, scientific research in the field of acoustics gradually penetrated some of the mysteries in the world of sound. Now it was possible to measure tonal values technically, and with the aid of resonators a tonal structure to a certain degree could be dissected.

It was quite natural to anticipate that science now would "set things in order". "It is of the utmost importance for organ building to possess established measures, theoretically based and computed, in preference to being governed by rules gained from experience, where capriciousness and uncertainty depreciate the result," writes the Rev. Allihn (1888) in his adaptation of the book by the organ theorist Töpfer: *Die Orgelbaukunst nach einer neuen Theorie dargestellt und auf mathematische und physikalische Grundsätze gestützt* (published 1833).

Töpfer's effort in the field of scaling technique was to find an actually "normal" scale with the same timbre and intensity from bass to treble. The problem was not new, but the novelty was his desire to solve it rationally with the newly available devices. He had the greatest respect for Dom Bedos' large treatise *l'Art du facteur d'orgues,* but he admitted that Sorge was right in his criticism of it. It was logical that the scale progression had to be constant, but there must also be logic in the choice of the progression. In that respect, Sorge contributed nothing.

Töpfer's contribution as an innovator was first and foremost the fact that he worked with the cross-sectional area of the pipe and not with the pipe diameters. Actually, Töpfer had not discovered it; this idea was discussed already at the close of the seventeenth century; Bendeler, among others, strongly opposed it in *Organopoia.* However, Töpfer was the first to implement the idea.

The tonal action of a pipe has obviously more to do with the cross-sectional area than with the diameter; and when we work with tonal relations, the square of the diameters – and not the diameters alone – supplies the correct ratios.

Another point of departure for Töpfer's work was the idea that the amount of air used by a pipe must be an indication of and be in proportion to the sound-energy produced. Through the study of numerous ranks and by experiments with shortening a test pipe, he discovered this rule: the quantity of air increases in direct porportion to the cross-sectional area and is inversely proportional to the square root of the pipe length. In accordance with this he deduced that the quantity of air in most ranks will be divided in half for each octave leap.

Töpfer now experimented with the areal scale of 1:3 (which is very close to Dom Bedos' scale), but it did not satisfy him. "Then I tried to find another," he reports, "and finally, by the application of Chladnis' principles concerning the intensity of tone, and by my own speculations and conclusions in which a distinction was made between the penetration and the resonance of sound, I found that the ratio of 1: $\sqrt{8}$ corresponded to a perfectly even penetration and resonance." We have no more detailed account of Töpfer's line of deduction, but he must have judged the results by the ear alone, since no measuring instruments capable of recording the implicated details were available at that time.

On the other hand, we know that he made comparisons with other scale progressions. The scale of 1:3, his point of departure, has half the diameter at the minor tenth (the 16th half-step); with the sequence of 1: $\sqrt{8}$, the half-diameter occurs at the major tenth (the 17th half-step). As mentioned, Sorge had already suggested these two scales. After that, Töpfer experimented with placing the half-diameter at the 18th, and later at the 19th half-step, and thus again obtained tonal shiftings within the pipe series.

Töpfer gained further support for the validity of the scale of 1: $\sqrt{8}$ from the fact that the amount of air according to the previously mentioned formulas had the exact ratio of 1:2 at the octave leap.

$$\left(\frac{1}{\sqrt{8}} \cdot \frac{\sqrt{2}}{1} = \frac{\sqrt{2}}{\sqrt{8}} = \frac{\sqrt{2}}{2\sqrt{2}} = \frac{1}{2}\right)$$

There is still another way of finding and verifying Töpfer's normal scale. It may be stated as follows: the limits of achievement in scaling are determined by the ratios of 1:2 and 1:4 (that is, the areal scale). The "most correct" scale should then appear as the average of these two ratios, that is, the square root of their product, which is exactly 1: $\sqrt{8}$.

With regard to the mouth scale, Töpfer establishes that the area of the pipe mouth must be directly proportional to the area of the cross-section of the pipe, that is, this ratio must also be $1:\sqrt{8}$ at the octave. Consequently, if we choose an ordinary mouth width of $^1/_4$ of the circumference, and the cut-up $^1/_4$ of the mouth width, the area of the mouth will be directly proportional to the cross-section of the pipe, and in this way it will also have the proper octave ratio.

When judging Töpfer's work today, various objections may be raised concerning his methods and measures, which are not sufficiently accurate to merit a result to several decimal places. We would also be able to object that the normal scale was no new discovery. A half-century earlier, Sorge had suggested the same progression (although he preferred the scale of the ninth), and the slight difference between this and the two very old scales of 3:5 and the Golden Section, would be imperceptible in practice. And even if it can be detected with contemporary measuring instruments, it is difficult to decide which of the three scales is the most "normal" one. Numerically, the octave ratios are thus: (a) Töpfer, converted to cross-sectional scale: $1:\sqrt[4]{8} = 1:1.682$. (b) $3:5 = 1.667$. (c) The Golden Section $= 1:1.618$.

All of this is less essential than the fact that the organ builders now began to know why, whereas before they had only known how. And Töpfer attempted to get to the bottom of his subject. The normal scale was not the only matter with which he was occupied. With genuine German thoroughness, all details of the organ were carefully treated, explained and converted into formulas and rules. With exceptional competence, with unlimited industry, and with great personal sacrifices, he accomplished this project, the work of a lifetime.

The future consequences were entirely different from what Töpfer had planned and deserved. Töpfer himself acknowledged that the normal scale was not absolutely suited for practice and that, in many instances, it was better to have a scale sequence the timbre of which was not constant from bass to treble.

This was overlooked by the organ builders. Now the standards of excellence had been scientifically established, and consequently there was no reason either to think or to hear any more. The normal scale was the ideal scale (so was the opinion). There was nothing else to be done except making shapes according to it, working with diligence and accuracy, using good materials, and so on.

The reaction came in the early 1920s and resulted, as already mentioned, in attention being directed toward Baroque scaling techniques, both with regard to types of stops and to scaling sequences. Undeniably, the new experiments were sometimes accompanied by a "museum romanticism" and an exaggerated faith in the Baroque masters, which were not advantageous.

This, however, is a thing of the past. Organ builders now take a more realistic view of these matters, and they work pragmatically as well as theoretically with such problems. No actual scientific truth has been found in the Baroque masters or in their systems. But they have taught us to treat the work in a natural manner and to use our ears.

Reed Pipes (linguals).

The second main group of the speaking parts of the organ, the reeds or linguals, function according to the principle that a vibrating metal tongue alternately opens and closes the passageway for a wind stream. This wind stream is admitted as small, fast, regular puffs into a resonating body, of which the air column is transformed into standing vibrations.

Figure 25 shows the construction. The *shallot* (A) consists of a tube

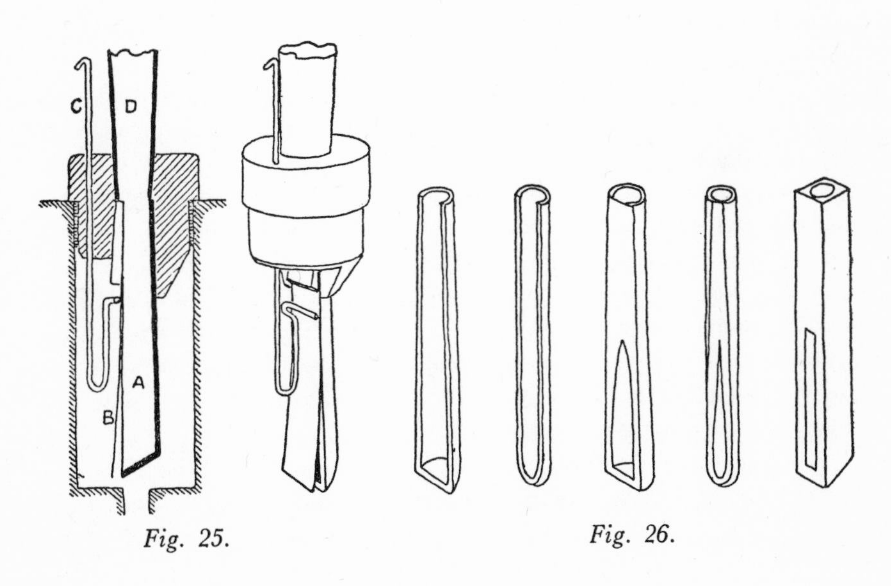

Fig. 25. *Fig. 26.*

which is closed at the lower end and planed flat on one side so that a throat-shaped opening is produced. A *metal tongue* (B) of the same size as the planed surface is mounted in such a way that it covers the throat-shaped opening, as shown in the drawing.

At the top, a wedge in the *block* maintains a firm grip on the shallot and the tongue. The tongue has a gradual outward curving, so that it bends away from the shallot at its lower end. The *tuning spring* or tuning wire (C), which clips the top of the tongue against the shallot, can be shifted up and down, thereby lengthening or shortening the lower free part of the tongue. A *resonating body* (D), the "resonator", is mounted in the block as an extension of the shallot, and the tongue and the shallot are encased in the *boot,* which fits tightly at the top into the block.

When wind is admitted through the opening at the bottom of the boot, the wind sheet, which continues through the shallot and the resonator, will first press the tongue against the shallot; this stops the wind stream. Next, the elasticity in the tongue, in connection with a rebound from the air column in the resonator, causes the tongue to snap back and reopen for the wind. Then the tongue is again pressed in toward the shallot, etc.

By knocking the tuning spring downward and thereby shortening the vibrating length of the tongue, faster vibrations and a higher pitch are obtained. Conversely, raising the tuning spring results in a lower pitch. The pitch is determined by the vibrations of the tongue, but the supplementary resonance of the resonator also has a certain influence on the frequency of the tongue.

This influence is mainly dependent on the length of the resonator. Short resonators, which reinforce the upper partials, have only a relatively small effect on the reed tone; but long resonators, which are generally tuned to the wave length of the first or second partial, have such a strong resonance that the reed tone and the resonator tone must work together, that is, reed tone must be tuned in agreement with the vibrations of the resonator. The latter may be so powerful that they displace the reed tone by several half-steps or completely smother it, if it is tuned to a frequency for which there is no resonance. If the tongue is tuned toward the correct pitch, it will be observed that the resonator tone begins to support the reed tone and finally gives it complete resonance.

The reed tone (the tone produced by the tongue) contains very little foundation but a large number of overtones, both harmonic and inharmonic (that is, tones foreign to the harmonic series), depending on the scale ratio of the tongue and shallot. Thin, broad, stiff tongues generally provide more overtones than thick, narrow and soft tongues, but the wind pressure in the boot also plays a vital role here, and the curvature of the tongue is equally important. As a rule, the tongue is given a decreasing radial curve at its lower end. When this curve is increased, the sound is softer; when the curve is decreased, the overtones are more prominent. Furthermore, the overtones may be enhanced by reducing the width or the thickness (possibly both) of the tongue at its lower end, or the bottom of the tongue.

The shape of the shallot, cylindrical or conical, and particularly the width and length of the throat-opening in relation to the scale of the tongue are also important for the formation of overtones. Flat, cylindrical shallots with a large throat-opening in relation to the tongue scale promote the overtones, while deep, conical shallots, tapering upward and with a small throat-opening hinder the formation of overtones. In addition, the weight and material of the shallot play a role, as it must counteract the attack of the tongue. A very effective means of neutralizing the formation of overtones is to cover the surface of the shallot with a parchment cushion. Fig. 26 shows some different examples of variations in the shallot.

As for the tongue scale, the possibilities of variation are so far-flung that it is difficult to formulate general rules. Some examples from practice will best illustrate the manipulation of the relevant dimensions (where two numbers are given, the tongues do not have the same thickness or width at the top and the bottom. The upper number states the thickness and width at the top; the lower, the thickness and width at the bottom).

The purpose of the resonator is to adjust and regulate the reed tone's large selection of partials, partly by providing resonance and emphasizing the tones desired, and partly by failing to provide resonance and thereby suppressing the remaining tones. The general rule concerning stopped pipes is valid for the shape of resonators too: the conical (funnel-shaped) ones emphasize all partials; the cylindrical ones, chiefly the odd-numbered partials.

As stated, we distinguish between short, untuned resonators and long, tuned resonators which are computed according to half the wave length of the first or second partial. However, as with labial pipes, the resonator length is not exact; it can be varied within certain narrow limits, and the pitch can be adjusted by the aid of the reed tone.

The timbre is affected by these modifications of length, especially in the

	Width of tongue					Thickness of tongue				
	C	c	c′	c″	c‴	C	c	c′	c″	c‴
NS according to Mahrenholz	15,4	11,0	7,9	5,6	4,0	0,57	0,41	0,29	0,21	0,15
Compenius-Ranket 16′	8,7/11,9	7,7/9,2	6,2/7,5	5,7/6,5	5,0/5,9	0,29/0,27	0,27/0,21	0,15/0,23	0,13/0,17	0,06/0,08
Compenius-Krumhorn 8′	9,0/9,5	7,8/8,2	5,4/6,1	4,7/5,5	4,3/5,2	0,30/0,32	0,24/0,27	0,23/0,13	0,16/0,12	0,11/0,09
Compenius-Sordun 16′	14,5/16,4	9,2/10,5	7,3/8,5			0,48/0,38	0,38/0,28	0,22/0,18		
Schnitger-Basun 16′	29,3	20,5	16,0			0,90	0,64	0,41		
Schnitger-Dulcian 8′	15/17,0	10,9/12,3	6,6/7,4	6,2	5,9	0,56	0.40	0,22	0,15	0,11
Cahmann-Trompet 8	11,4/13,4	9,0/10,4	7,0/8,0	7,0/7,9	6,0/6,0	0,45	0,25	0,17	0,16	0,11
Toledo-Vox Humana	11,0	8,6	6,9	6,3	6,1	0,30	0,21	0,16	0,13	0,08
Cavaillé-Coll-Trompette Harmonique	8	6,25	6	4,74	3,7	0,50	0,34	0,20	0,18	0,12

case of the tuned resonators. Shortening the resonator stimulates the overtones, and conversely, the foundation tone is intensified by a lengthening of the resonator. If the resonator becomes too long, the fundamental suddenly disappears, and the tone breaks into the octave above (it overblows); and an excessive reduction in the length will cause the tone to become ugly and rough, and it may be entirely smothered.

Of course, we can also give tuned (tonal) lengths for the short-resonator reeds when these lengths are calculated in relation to one of the partials. But then the lengths must "repeat", that is, leap back, at certain places in the scale, to lengths corresponding to lower partials. Or else the resonators in the upper range will become too short, resulting in a treble that is too weak.

The resonator length at C for a tuned 8′ stop may be from 1 to 3 half-steps shorter than the ordinary length for a principal at the same pitch, but the sequence of the length scale through a rank does not correspond to the length sequence of the labials. Here, the width scale is an important factor, but generally it can be said that the resonator length is proportionally larger in the treble.

Nor is the scaling sequence for resonator widths governed by the same laws as the labial stops. The reed maker has a considerably freer hand, because so many extrinsic factors play a part: the shallot and tongue scales as well as the length scale.

Since reeds have a tendency to be strong in the bass and weak in the treble, this must be counteracted with the width scale, by making it fairly large in the treble and narrow in the bass (compared with the fluework). For example, an octave ratio like 5:7 or 10:13 is quite normal in conical resonators; in cylindrical resonators the treble must be still larger in proportion to the bass. The customary octave ratio is 5:6.

The timbre and pitch of the reeds is consequently a complicated interplay of many factors: the shape, length and width scale of the resonator; the material, form and scale of the shallot; the shape and elasticity of the tongue; the wind pressure; and finally, the scale and construction of the boot.

While the reeds are speaking, simultaneous vibrations will arise in the boot, and in some ways they are linked with the actual vibrations in the shallot and resonator. Often they are very pronounced, especially in short-resonator stops which are not controlled by the strong supplementary vibrations of the resonator. To obtain the proper resonance, either the boot lengths must be regulated, or the vibrations in the boot must be altered or neutralized.

With this diversity of resources for determining timbre, the scale ratios of the reeds become extremely complicated. Definite rules are almost out of question, because the many tonal resources are so mutually dependent that they can be used in a different manner each time and in an endless succession of combinations.

We know a great deal about the laws that govern vibrating metal tongues; we are also well-informed about resonance in tubes, etc. But concerning the interaction of all these details, vast numbers of additional factors assert themselves, and the theory becomes hopelessly inadequate for any practical application.

A well-known organ theorist expresses himself in this way (and this is only a reflection on a theory about resonators): "With an experience coefficient, the formula might have been corrected and put to some use, if it was not already so complicated that it was unsuitable for any practical purpose."

4

The Stops of the Organ

LABIALS (flues)

At the close of the Middle Ages the possibilities offered by the various pipe forms and scales were already classified in specific stop families, whose grouping and types are the same today, with only a few additions.

However, the development of individual stops has been so closely connected with period and locality that the stop names do not indicate any exact identity, but merely refer to the general character of the sound, in the same way as the colour designation "red" includes many nuances within limits. Moreover, many stop names are used indiscriminately or employed incorrectly; thus it would not be difficult to find exceptions to the groupings and descriptions mentioned later.

In the table given below, the labials are divided into main groups, and within each group the most important stop names are given in the order of their scale width, starting with the widest scales.

Open Pipes		
Cylindrical	Conical	Funnel-Shaped
Hohlflöte Nachthorn Prinzipal Überblasende Flöten Traversflöte Various String Stops	Spitzflöte Gemshorn Blockflöte Flachflöte Waldflöte Spitzgamba	Dulzianflöte

Stopped Pipes		
Cylindrical	Conical	Funnel-Shaped
Gedackt (Stopped Flute) Gedacktpommer Quintatön Überblasende Gedackt	Spitzgedackt Überblasende Spitzgedackt	Trichter-Gedackt

Half-Stopped Pipes		
Cylindrical with a cylindrical chimney	Cylindrical with a conical top	Conical with a cylindrical chimney
Rohrflöte Rohrquintatön	Spillflöte Koppelflöte	Rohrflöte

For the sake of simplicity and clarity in the following discussion of width scales for the individual stop families, the normal scale (hereafter indicated by NS) adopted at the *Freiburger Tagung für deutsche Orgelkunst* has been stated below. This scale assumes a diameter of 155.5 mm. at 8′ C, and thereafter progresses according to the Töpfer octave ratio of $1:\sqrt{8}$.

	32′	16′	8′	4′	2′	1′	$^1/_2$′	$^1/_4$′	$^1/_8$′	$^1/_{16}$′
C	439,7	261,5	155,5	92,2	54,9	32,6	19,3	11,5	6,8	4,0
C ♯	421,2	250,4	148,9	88,5	52,6	31,3	18,6	11,0	6,5	3,9
D	403,2	239,8	142,6	84,7	50,4	29,9	17,8	10,5	6,3	3,7
D ♯	386,2	229,6	136,5	81,1	48,2	28,4	16,9	10,1	6,0	3,6
E	369,9	219,9	130,7	77,7	46,2	27,4	16,3	9,7	5,7	3,4
F	354,1	210,6	125,2	74,4	44,2	26,3	15,6	9,3	5,5	3,3
F ♯	339,1	201,6	119,9	71,3	42,3	25,2	14,9	8,8	5,2	3,1
G	324,7	193,1	114,8	68,2	40,5	24,1	14,3	8,5	5,0	3,0
G ♯	311,0	184,9	109,9	65,3	38,8	23,1	13,7	8,1	4,8	2,8
A	297,8	177,4	105,3	62,6	37,2	22,1	13,1	7,8	4,6	2,7
B♭	285,2	169,5	100,8	59,9	35,6	21,1	12,6	7,4	4,4	2,6
B	273,1	162,3	96,5	57,4	34,1	20,2	12,0	7,1	4,2	2,5

Principal. The term "Principal" is encountered in the first primitive organs, where the pipe ranks had not yet been developed into different and characteristic timbres; instead, many ranks of "flutes" at various pitches, at the interval of the octave, fifth and fourth, were sounding in chorus as a constant combination. The lowest of these flute ranks, producing the fundamental, was called "Principal" or "Vox principalis", and thus the term had nothing to do with the timbre of the rank.

As the scale sequence was developed, and as the organ builders attained a more unified timbre with the individual ranks, they also learned how to make the entire scale of the rank wider or more narrow, so that they obtained, in the first case, a more decided flute quality, and secondly, a more stable sound with a good fundamental and a more nearly equal structure of the partials. This stop type, the Principal, now becomes the most important voice of the organ, because its firm and supporting qualities formed the backbone in the tonal structure of the organ, and because it could be used throughout the compass of audible pitches without changing character. Principals appear at all pitches, 32′, 16′, 8′, 4′, 2′, and only at the 1′ stop, in the normal manual compass, do we reach the limit of what can be attained in the upper range.

The Principal scale can be varied within certain limits, so that the timbre becomes lighter or darker. The diagram on p. 43 gives an idea of the possibilities. Generally, the mouth width is $^1/_4$ of the circumference, and the cut-up is $^1/_4$ of the mouth width. But the mouth width is sometimes decreased as far as $^2/_9$; in such a case, particularly when the width scale is also small, the cut-up must be somewhat higher, up to $^1/_3$ of the mouth width.

Wider Principal scales, possibly in connection with narrow mouth scales, are now and then indicated as "Italian Principal" because the soft and vocal quality of sound produced by this scaling is especially characteristic of the old Italian Principals. In a similar way, the more narrow Principal type is called "German Principal", because its fresh, solid sound is typical of the North European conception. In both countries, however, narrow and wide Principals are used, depending entirely on the need, and the difference in tonal character is due to many other factors than the width scale. Nowadays, we have been inclined to consider these two indications in connection with the width scale, but it would be more correct if the terms were applied to the tonal character, thereby taking the mouth scale and the voicing technique into consideration.

The Principal pipes are usually made of metal. The oldest Principals and organ flutes were made of copper hammered out into sheets, but soon copper was replaced by tin-lead alloys, of which the tin content could vary from 100 to 30 per cent. Principals most often have a fairly high percentage of tin (60 or 75 per cent), because it provides a fresher sound, and because Principal pipes are often mounted in the organ front, where the appearance is of importance. Wood can be used in the 16′ octave and sometimes, for economical reasons, in the 8′ octave. In rare cases, where a mild and distinctive character is desired, the entire rank is made of wood. For this purpose the harder and less porous kinds of wood, for example maple, are preferred. Wooden Principals appear both in the 8′ and 4′ range, as in the Compenius organ at Frederiksborg Castle; but small wooden pipes are rather costly and relatively unstable in tuning. This explains why wooden Principals are rarities, especially in the 4′ range and higher.

At the close of the previous century, the use of zinc became increasingly common in the 16′ and 8′ octaves, and occasionally in the 4′ octave. This was due to economy and to the fact that the large tin-lead pipes were apt to collapse under their own weight, because, in the course of time, the metal softened. About thirty years ago, a considerably better but somewhat more expensive solution was found, when the organ builders began to use copper pipes. With regard to both tonal quality and stability, copper is an excellent pipe material which can be used not only for the large pipes in the bass, but throughout the entire rank.

Various names are used for Principal stops, depending on the pitch and placement of the rank in the organ. A Principal mounted in the front is often called *Prestant* (also *Montre* in France), and a 16′ Principal in the pedal is called *Untersatz,* referring to its position in the oldest pedal Werks. The 8′ Principal in the pedal is called *Octave 8′,* if there is already a 16′ Principal, just as a 4′ Principal in the manual is called *Octave 4′,* when there is already a Principal 8′. If there is also a 2′ Principal, it is called *Superoctave 2′*. Besides, the terms *Principal 4′* and *Principal 2′* appear, when there are no lower Principal ranks in the same Werk. A narrow Principal, rich in overtones ("stringy"), is sometimes called *Violinprincipal,* and finally, the slightly wider *Schwegel* ought to be mentioned. It has a narrow mouth, between $^1/_4$ and $^1/_5$ of the circumference, and has a higher cut-up and a weak sound, not especially rich in overtones.

The *Hohlflöte* has a very vide scale, 4–7 HT (= half-tones or half-steps) above NS (normal scale), a broad mouth, about $^1/_4$ of the circumference, and a fairly high cut-up. This flute is either made of a lead-type alloy (only 30 % tin) and used at the pitches from 8′ to 1′, or it is constructed of wood and then appears in the 16′, 8′ and possibly the 4′ ranges. Concerning the high stops, the wide scale must decrease toward the treble, since it otherwise exceeds what is expedient for the voicing. Sometimes other names are used in the low range, for instance *Thunbass, Offener Subbass, Oktavbass;* and for the higher stops, *Thunflöte, Tibia, Koppel* or *Waldflöte*. The sound is full-bodied, steady and solid.

The *Nachthorn* has a width similar to that of the Hohlflöte, but can be still wider, especially in the higher stops, with a decreasing scale, however, toward the treble. The mouth is distinctly narrow, and the cut-up is greatly varied, according to the intensity desired. The rank is built almost exclusively of metal (lead-tin alloys of about 30 % tin are best) and can be found at the pitches from 8′ to 1′. We distinguish between this open Nachthorn and the stopped one (see p. 66). The open Nachthorn comes from the Netherlands, and the origin of the name is probably *Nachsatz* or *Nassat* (later, it acquired another meaning), which means, one of the ranks that stood behind the Vox principals. At any rate, the name has nothing to do with night or a horn.

The *Transverse Flutes* are stops which overblow at the second partial, the octave. This is due to a narrow scale, a low cut-up, and sometimes also a narrow mouth. This second partial then becomes the fundamental, and the real fundamental, which corresponds to the pipe length, completely disappears.

These stops are already encountered at the close of the fifteenth century, and probably they have been inspired by the transverse flute which had become popular just at that time, particularly in Germany and the Netherlands. The phenomenon of overblowing was scarcely new to the organ builders. Especially in the difficult Schwegel scales, it was hard to avoid overblowing in the voicing, and when this tonal phenomenon proved to be usable, it was quite natural to utilize the "disadvantage".

Many different names are used for this type of stop. Frenchmen, who made its acquaintance in Germany, called it *Flûte allemande. Querflöte, Traversflöte* or *Schweizerpfeife* were most common in Germany. In the eighteenth century, the overblowing flute is found in France under the name of *Basse de Viol;* in the nineteenth century as *Flûte harmonique, Flûte octaviante* and *Flûte traversière. Harmonic flute* may be the most natural English name.

While the overblowing flutes went out of use in the course of the seventeenth century in North German and Nordic organ building, they were retained in France and the Netherlands, although to a rather modest extent. In the middle of the nineteenth century occurred a renaissance of these flutes in French organ building, not in their original form, but usually with a significantly wider scale and stronger voicing. Today, they appear at all pitches from 16′ (hence with 32′ length pipes) up to 1′.

The wider scales which had come into use were dependent on a little voicing trick which Sorge had described in 1773. Two small holes are bored opposite to each other and somewhat below the middle of the pipe body. This permits the release and destruction of the vibrations occurring at the node of the fundamental. With this overblowing, the octaves are strongly emphasized in the overtone structure. The sound, especially in the wide scales, can be very intense and concentrated in spite of its decidely flute-like character.

String stops. We have already observed that the narrowest Principal has been called Violinprincipal because of its stringy character. If the scale is diminished even more, the result is the group of stops called string stops. The prominence of the overtones creates a resemblance to the tone of the string instruments. The first indications of this stop group in organs are found at approximately the same time as the string instruments asserted themselves in the Baroque orchestra. The actual reason for the development is a change of tonal ideal, not merely the fact that string stops were "discovered" at that time. Long ago the organ builders were already sufficiently experienced in the art of scaling and voicing that they could control their results. From overblowing, narrow-scaled flute pipes they have certainly known the string-like sound that occurred when these pipes did not overblow. The connection between the overblowing stops and the string stops can be seen, inter alia, from the fact that the *Salicional* (willow-flute) was originally an overblowing flute and later became a string stop. The French term *Basse de Viol* points in the same direction. Regardless of the evolution, it has not been any great problem for the organ builders to obtain the string character.

The scales of the earliest string stops were not much narrower than the Principal scale (2–4 HT under NS), and for that reason the sound was rather mild and full. The new tendencies after the middle of the eighteenth century bring a more extensive development in this field; by means of narrower scales a more direct imitation of the string instruments is aimed at. Sorge suggests 9 HT under NS, and examples of still narrower scales are known, especially in South German instruments. The imitative tendencies of the nineteenth century continued this development, and the organ builders deliberately sought the most successful imitation of orchestral instruments. By making further reductions in the scale and by employing various tricks (diverse forms of "beards") they were able to stimulate the overtones without losing the foundation tone; thereby a balance of partials was obtained which somewhat corresponded to the string instruments of that period. It is scarcely necessary to add that a tonal difference still remained.

The narrow scaling of the string stops places a limitation on their upper range. For the most part, these stops occur at the 16′, 8′ and 4′ pitches, and quite exceptionally as 2′ stops.

In the course of time, the commonly known stop names have been used so much at random that any classification relating to the specific scaling groups is a very difficult task. Logically, the name *Salicional* (willow-flute) would be associated with the widest scale. *Fugara* (shepherd's flute) would indicate a slightly narrower scale. Next, in terms of scale, should be the *Viola da Gamba* (knee-violin), with a full, but absolutely stringy sound (as a pedal stop it is called *Cello*). Beyond these, we have the more modern stops: *Orpheon, Physharmonika, Vox angelica* and *Aeoline*. The *Vox celeste* should also be mentioned here. It consists of two string stops having the same pitch, or possibly at the interval of an octave. One rank is purposely tuned a little too high, or too low, and this produces slow interference vibrations ("beats"). Obtaining a tremolo in this way was already known in Italy in the sixteenth century and is found in Germany at the beginning of the eighteenth century; first in association with flute stops, later with string stops. The use of such "beating" ranks was not prevalent in the north until the nineteenth century.

Cone-shaped flutes appear as early as the close of the Middle Ages, but this stop group is not developed completely until the Baroque. Apparently, *Spillflöte* is the earliest term for a conically shaped stop, but the *Spitzflöte* also appears at the beginning of the sixteenth century. The Spillflöte had then a relatively wide scale, while the Spitzflöte had nearly a Principal scale at the languid, and the upper diameter of the body was $^1/_3$ to $^1/_5$ of the lower. The mouth was broad, and the sound fairly subdued, yet rich in overtones.

Gradually, the name of Spillflöte went out of use, and instead, the term *Blockflöte* was applied to the widest of the conical stops and the *Gemshorn* to those of medium-wide scale. The Gemshorn could be 4–6 HT over NS, and the upper diameter from $^1/_3$ to $^1/_2$ of the lower. The mouth was relatively narrow and the cut-up low; the sound was somewhat muted, but round. The lower diameter of the Blockflöte ranged from 8 to 11 HT over NS, and the ratio between the upper and lower diameters was similar to that of the Gemshorn. The sound of the Blockflöte was gentle and nasal, but rounder and more solid than the narrower Gemshorn.

Toward the end of the sixteenth century, the *Flachflöte,* a name inspired by its very broad, flat mouth, the breadth of which could be as much as 1/3 of the circumference, was developed as a variant of the Spitzflöte. The cut-up is very low, and the sound is free and fresh, but still flute-like. The lower diameter is about 2 HT above NS, and the upper diameter is approximately 2/3 of the lower.

The *Waldflöte* has a similar width and cone, but the mouth width and cut-up are normal. In character, this stop is more flute-like than the Flachflöte; the quality resembles the tone of the cylindrical Nachthorn.

Only two of these stops, the Gemshorn and Spitzflöte, are found in all pitches from 16′ to 1′. The Blockflöte can be found in the 8′ range, but is most common as a 4′, 2′, or 1′ stop, and the same is true of the Flachflöte and Waldflöte.

As these string stops gradually developed in the eighteenth century, cone-shaped structures in the narrow scales also became more common, especially in middle Germany. Transitional shapes like the narrow-scaled Spitzflöte, usually called Viola da Gamba or Spillflöte, had been known for many years, but the actual *Spitzgamba* first appears in the eighteenth century. Its scale was relatively wide, 4–6 HT under NS, and its upper diameter was 1/3 or 1/2 of the lower. The mouth width was usually a little less than 1/4, and the cut-up was low. With these conditions, the sound was relatively full, somewhat muted, and slightly stringy.

Soon after the Spitzgamba, another conical stop with narrow scale was developed: the *overblowing Traversflöte,* inspired by a contemporary "vulgar" flute in France. However, this stop has never been used to any great extent.

Funnel-shaped open stops are rarities in spite of the fact that they have been known since the sixteenth century. The earliest of these stops had the ratio of 4:3 between the upper and lower diameters and had the dimensions of a Principal at the bottom. The mouth was broad and the cut-up rather low; the sound resembled a resonant Principal, at the same time with a certain stringy character. Later, the scale variations favoured either the string or the flute quality, with names such as *Portunalflöte, Dolzan, Viola da Gamba, Salicet,* and *Vox retusa.*

STOPPED PIPES

Stopped, cylindrical pipes have been present in the organ just as long as open pipes; stopped pipes are even found in the Panpipe.

We may doubt that the Gedackts were incorporated in the organs of the early Middle Ages, but they are traceable from the middle of the fourteenth century. At first, the scale for these Gedackts seems to have corresponded to the scale of the Principals, but according to Praetorius, there are also instances of wider Gedackt scales.

These Gedackts which Praetorius mentions were rather soft and lacking in overtones when compared with the later Gedackts of the Baroque, the sound of which was bright and clear as a result of narrower scaling. French organ building has always adhered to the wide Gedackt-scales, while Germany and North Europe have worked with highly varied scales, depending on the situation. The mouth scale can be greatly varied, and so can the cut-up. For example, it is not uncommon that Gedackts with a narrow mouth have a cut-up of $^1/_2$ the mouth width.

Due to the endless modifications and to purely external reasons, many names are associated with the stopped pipes. Without doubt, one of the oldest designations is *Bordun* (Bourdon). The early organ builders, strangely enough, used this term for open flutes, especially the long bass pipes, which resembled burdones (pilgrims' staves) because of their narrow scales. The word burdones thus acquired the meaning of bass pipes, and since the Gedackts have presumably often been used in this range because of their half-length, Bordun has gradually become identical with Gedackt, particularly when it concerns a 16′ stop.

The hollow sound characteristic of the Gedackts, which is due to the lack of even partials, was the reason for the name given to wide Gedackts: *Hohlflöte* or *Hohlpijp*. In many cases, these stops were simply called *Flöte* (in French references to the 4′ range, *Flûte* is traditional).

The large side beards, which are often fitted to stopped pipes, inspired the name *Bartpfeiffe*. Other names are *Bauernflöte, Blockflöte,* and for pedal stops, *Untersatz* (32′) and *Subbass* (16′).

Both wood and tin-lead alloys have been used as materials, chiefly the latter and generally with a low tin-content (30%). Recently, copper has become more utilized, particularly in the low range, where it is an excellent material.

When the partials in the very narrow Gedackts are further stimulated by a low cut-up and a plentiful supply of wind, the third partial (the fifth) stands out strongly and gives the sound the special colour which is characteristic of the *Quintatön*. Praetorius writes that this stop originated in the Netherlands and came into general use about 1500, but more recent studies indicate that the stop dates from the fourteenth century. Curiously enough, it does not appear in French organs until the nineteenth century, although it was known and discussed by both Mersenne and Dom Bedos. The possibilities of the Quintatön scale lie within rather narrow limits (10–14 HT under NS), and the usual mouth width is $^1/_4$ of the circumference and the cut-up $^1/_4$ of the mouth width, but a narrower mouth width can also be used along with a higher cut-up. In certain cases, box beards are necessary for strengthening the fundamental. Just like Gedackts, Quintatöns appear in all ranges, from 32′ to 2′.

The *Gedacktpommer,* also called *Nachthorn,* has a somewhat wider scale than the Quintatön, but is rather "quinty" in the sound because of its low cut-up. The width scale runs 5–8 HT under NS.

The *overblowing Gedackt.* In a narrow Quintatön pipe, the overtones may be activated to such an extent that the fundamental disappears and the pipe overblows at the third partial, the fifth. When the fundamental is shifted in this manner, from the octave to the fifth, the remaining partials and the fundamental will have a relationship which is unlike that in any other stop. In a Quintatön having C as the fundamental, we find the following partial series: C, g, e′, b♭′, d″. In overblowing, C is omitted and g becomes the fundamental. If we imagine shifting this new fundamental to C, the partial series becomes this: C, A, d♯, g. The partials are closer together, and only g is common to the partials of other stops.

Praetorius refers to the overblowing Gedackts as a new discovery, which means that they date from approximately the year 1600. They did not achieve any great adoption, but nevertheless, they were not forgotten in the succeeding period. In 1754, Snetzler, an English organ builder, constructed an *overblowing Rohrflöte,* and a *Traversflöte,* as an overblowing Gedackt is known from the Netherlands.

Conical Gedackts contain all of the partials and therefore avoid the hollow sound that is so characteristic of the cylindrical Gedackts. When a round and clear flute sound is desired, the use of Spitzgedackts with wide scale is natural, but a stringy quality is also possible with this body shape. In this case, the scale must be reduced, and the upper diameter must be small in relation to the lower *(ca.* 1:5). In the more flute-like stops the ratio is about 2:3 or 1:2.

The Spitzgedackts date from the close of the sixteenth century and are described in the "Syntagma musicum". Today they are found in the

Compenius organ (1610, made entirely of wood), where all of the stopped pipes (except the Quintatön) taper slightly upward.

Praetorius also mentions an overblowing type, which (in contrast to the cylindrical Gedackts) overblows at the octave, like an open pipe.

No historical information concerning funnel-shaped Gedackts is available, but some contemporary examples are known.

HALF-STOPPED PIPES

The term half-stopped pipes refers to Gedackts having a larger or smaller opening in the stopper, into which a top is soldered, usually a cylindrical tube. These *Rohrflöte* (chimney flutes) appear in the sixteenth century, but probably they were originated in the previous century.

The oldest names are *Hohlflöte* and *Bauernflöte,* the identical names that are used for Gedackts. For this reason, there is no clue from specifications as to the actual debut of the Rohrflöte. Apparently, it was invented in the Netherlands, but at any rate, it quickly won acceptance in the neighbouring countries.

The function of the inserted tube is to reduce the vibrations at the pipe cover and to provide resonance for the desired partials; naturally, the length, width and form of the tube are decisive in that respect. The mounting of the tube also plays a certain role. It can be located on the outside of the stopper or inside the pipe under the stopper; it can be partly inside, partly outside with a properly proportioned ratio, and finally, two or three tubes of different lengths can be mounted in the lower ranges and especially in the middle range. In the 16′ and 8′ octaves, the tubes must be relatively narrow, since a wider tube reduces the fundamental too much. The tubes are often entirely omitted in this range, or they are closed at the upper end (presuming that they are outside). Covered tubes may also be used in the upper ranges, but in such cases a relatively wide tube scale must be used, up to $^1/_2$ of the pipe scale.

The width and mouth scale adhere, fundamentally, to the practice known from the Gedackts, and the diameter of the tube is usually proportional to the diameter of the pipe. The tube diameter varies between $^1/_3$ and $^1/_8$ of the pipe diameter, while the length of the tube is most often proportional to the length of the pipe. But there are some instances in which the tube length is in direct ratio to the pipe diameter; this can, however, be practised only in comparatively short tubes.

The Rohrflöte has many variants, but they can be classified into certain main groups.

In principle, long, narrow tubes produce only a small deviation from the completely stopped pipe. The sound is perceived as somewhat freer and brighter than in the Gedackts, but because of the slenderness of the tube, vibrations cannot be formed active enough to make a noticeable effect on the partial structure. For this reason, the *Rohrgedackt* is the most appropriate name of this type, whose tube may be as long as $^1/_2$ of the pipe length.

When the tube is shortened, resonance is supplied for certain high partials, but since the node at the cover of the pipe is weakened, the air column in the pipe will function in a different way. Indeed, the wider the tube is, the freer the "working" of this air column, and the more resonance produced by the tube.

In this connection these factors are important: (1) the strength of the tones produced by the pipe itself; (2) the width scale (wide or narrow); (3) the mouth scale (broad or slender); (4) the cut-up (high oı low). In a narrow, quinty pipe the fifth can be further emphasized by an appropriate tube scale (this is the so-called *Rohrquintatön*). But also the third (the fifth partial) can be emphasized without the quint sound disappearing, and this accentuated third is the most characteristic quality in the ordinary *Rohrflöte.*

By utilizing two or three tubes of various lengths, an emphasis is placed on the partials corresponding to the tube lengths. Nevertheless, practice is considerably more complicated than theory, and the result is seldom the desired one. With this method and the aid of certain interference phenomena, it has also been tried to add inharmonic overtones. Especially the *overblowing Rohrflöte* seems to be suited to that, but the formation of overtones is precarious and results in strange phenomena during the attack (the initiation of the tone). This type of stop (with only one tube) dates from the close of the eighteenth century and is, in addition, very rare.

In Rohrflötes with conical bodies, all of the overtones are represented just as in the conical Gedackts. This Rohrflöte type is also rare, but there is a remarkable example in the Compenius organ in Frederiksborg Castle. The entire rank is made of wood. It is called *Bauernflöte* and is found as a 1′ stop in the pedal. Rohrflötes with funnel-shaped tubes can be made, but, to our best knowledge, they are never employed in practice.

On the other hand, half-stopped ranks with conical chimneys are very common; yet this is done in such a way that the lower diameter of the cone is always the same as the diameter of the pipe body. In other words, the cylindrical part of the pipe extends above into a cone-shaped section, of which the extreme point is missing, so that a larger or smaller opening results. Numerous variants of this construction are possible, but in practice, two types are paramount: one with a narrow scale and a long cone, the so-called *Spillflöte;* and another with a wider scale and a shorter cone, the *Koppelflöte.* These two types are depicted by Praetorius (1618–19), and hence they were known at the beginning of the seventeenth century.

The Spillflöte scale may drop to 4 HT under NS, and the diameter of the opening at the top comprises from $^1/_3$ to $^2/_3$ of the diameter of the pipe. The conical section can be equal to, or a little shorter than, the cylindrical portion, and the mouth is relatively narrow with a comparatively high cut-up.

For the Koppelflöte, the scale is 2–6 HT over NS, and the upper diameter is between $^1/_3$ and $^1/_5$ of the lower. The mouth is also rather narrow, but the wider scale permits a lower cut-up. The cone length can be varied somewhat, from $^1/_5$ to $^1/_2$ of the length.

The *stopped Koppelflöte* is a variation of this stop. It has the same shape as the open Koppelflöte, but is entirely closed at the top and is thus a combination of a Spitzgedackt and an ordinary Gedackt.

DOUBLE STOPS AND MUTATIONS (Aliquots)

Besides pipe construction and scale variation, the previously described methods for creating varied timbres, also the harmony between two or more pipes is used to a great extent in the creation of timbre. In the "double" stops, two ranks of the same pitch (usually 8′) are correlated, while the ranks in the mutation stops are situated in some reciprocal partial-relation, resulting in "synthetic" timbres.

Based on the Latin "bifarium", the double stops are often called *Bifaria, Tibia bifaris* or *Piffero.* Stops bearing such names are often found in the Italian Renaissance organ (*ca.* 1500). They are single stops intended to be used together with an 8′ Principal. The two ranks are tuned "in beats" in order to simulate the vocal tremolo. For that reason, the term *Vox humana* is also found in this connection.

Among the double stops, the treble doubling of the 8′ Principal (from c′ as a rule) must also be mentioned. It was practised in the sixteenth century and could still be found in the middle of the eighteenth in the Netherlands. The original purpose was undoubtedly to strengthen the treble in contrast to the bass; indeed, primitive organs had more ranks in the treble than in the bass. Later, the doubling was exploited in order to obtain a special tonal effect. Concerning this, Schlick in *Spiegel der Orgelmacher und Organisten* (1511) writes that one rank must have a "long" scale (that is, a narrow scale, which certainly means that the pipes must be longer), and the other must have a short (wide) scale, because "the long one thus imparts its sweetness to the short one, and the short one helps the long one in blending." The intention was to achieve both sonority and the refined sharpness of the narrow scales, and the same idea has inspired the use of more than one 8′ Principal for the same Werk in large organs. Curiously, the two ranks did not always have different scales. In the Principal 8′ in the old Petri organ from Malmö, Sweden, the doubling is carried out with the same scale in both ranks.

Doubling is familiar practice in string stops to achieve a round and still stringy sound, possibly with "beats". From the eighteenth century and later periods, there are, especially in southern and south-eastern Germany and Austria, examples of the combination of a Quintatön and a string stop, an open Flute and a Gedackt, and so on, all having the two ranks at the same pitch. At the distance of an octave, the following pairs may appear: Gemshorn 4′ and 2′; Gedackt 4′ and 2′; Superoktave 2′ and 1′; Nachthorn 2′ and Rohrflöte 1′, etc.

The *mutation stops* represent pitches that correspond to the partials in foundation stops. If an 8′ foundation stop is taken as a point of departure, the foot lengths appear as stated below for the mutations. In the table, the diatonic intervals, as used with mutations in England and America, have been combined with the corresponding Italian terms.

1.	Principale	8′ : 1	=	8′	C
8.	Ottava	8′ : 2	=	4′	c
12.	Duodecima	8′ : 3	=	$2^2/_3$′	g
15.	Quintadecima	8′ : 4	=	2′	c′
17.	Decimasesta	8′ : 5	=	$1^3/_5$′	e′
19.	Decimanona	8′ : 6	=	$1^1/_3$′	g′
		8′ : 7	=	$1^1/_7$′	b♭′
22.	Vigesimaseconda	8′ : 8	=	1′	c″
		8′ : 9	=	$^8/_9$′	d″
24.	Vigesimaquarta	8′ : 10	=	$^4/_5$′	e″

With the exception of the seventh and the ninth, all of these mutations were known and employed long before scientific understanding of their function as sound components had been arrived at, and long before it was possible to ascertain the partials in the organ stops and other musical instruments.

In spite of their application as timbre-producing materials, the origin of the mutation stops is due to other circumstances. We see this from the fact that the earliest mutation ranks in the position of the fifth (i. e. the twelfth above the fundamental) were not at the $2^2/_3'$ pitch; on the contrary, they were an octave lower, at the $5^1/_3'$ pitch, a fifth above the fundamental. This brings to mind the early vocal polyphony in parallel fifths that we meet in Hucbald's "organum". But even if there was some confusion in the first assumptions concerning mutations, experiences gradually brought practice into the proper development.

As soon as the higher fifth-mutations ($2^2/_3'$ and $1^1/_3'$) came into use, it was possible to study the blending of two tones and the new character that the high tone gave to the low one. Soon the fifth mutations were designed with this objective in mind. For instance, it can be seen from the fact that the low were used by preference in connection with 16′ stops, which is theoretically correct.

The first third-sounding stops or Tierces ($3^1/_5'$ pitch) are to be found in France at the beginning of the sixteenth century. Again, the pitch could suggest that the origin was due to harmonic reasons and not to an aural impression. One of the reasons was the contemporary transition from the Pythagorean third to the pure third. On the other hand, this low third was usually used in connection with a fifth, $5^1/_3'$, and a 16′ stop (correctly aligned with regard to the partials). Regardless of the origin, the tonal effect was based upon a natural foundation.

These third-stops soon advanced to the higher ranges ($1^3/_5'$ and $^4/_5'$). In French organ building, Tierces became one of the characteristic features. Acceptance of the Tierces came at a rather late date in north European organ building. Tierces were consistently linked with series of fifths in a high range until new concepts were brought into prominence at the close of the eighteenth century.

The first attempts at using the seventh ($2^2/_7'$) were also made in France at that time, but the experiments were not successful, because the rank was started an octave too low. The seventh based on the normal 8′ pitch is $1^1/_7'$, but this was not realized until scientists had explained the concept of partials and thereby cleared the way for a more constructive understanding of the mutations. However, in Spanish organ building, the seventh had been used satisfactorily in mixtures since the seventeenth century.

An immediate and spontaneous development of synthetic timbres might have been expected as a consequence of the accessible theoretical knowledge and first-hand experience. But, in reality, the number and extent of possible innovations was strictly curtailed. The use of the fifth and the third, in mutation stops and in the formation of difference tones, was so conventional and well-executed that an original contribution was almost out of question. The only novelty was the seventh; and, in some cases, the ninth. Of course, experiments were also made with more extreme mutations, but they attained no practical significance.

A second and more critical aspect of the matter was the gradual deterioration of the organ builder's ability to select the correct pipe forms and scales for mutations, the particular art which had been carried to such great perfection during the Baroque era. The entire understanding of mutations had disappeared – the tonal ideal had changed.

The pipe forms and scales are the determinants of the mutations since these stops do not only function at their nominal pitch, but also exert considerable influence by means of their overtones.

At C in a Quint $2^2/_3'$, the fundamental is g, and if this is an open pipe, some natural overtones are also present: g', d'', g'', b'', d''', f''', g''', a''', etc. With a stopped pipe, the overtones are: d'', b'', f''', a''', etc. If we imagine a rank of Quintatön pipes, the ninth (from C to d'') is very prominent. Thus some of the overtones involved in the mutations do conform to the normal overtone series; others do not.

The possibilities for mutations are almost innumerable. In practice, nearly all pipe shapes and scales are used, with the exception of the string stops, because the latter do not blend well with other stops. The first rule is that mutation stops with a strong fundamental are most capable of blending. Relatively wide scales are best in this respect, and the Principal scale generally represents the minimum in width.

Mutation names most often originate from the interval designations, fifth, third, seventh, especially in the case of mutations with Principal scale. When unique pipe forms are used, the interval name is added to the ordinary name for the stop; for example, *Gemshornterz, Rohrquint, Spitzquint,* etc. Today, the old name *Nasat,* a derivative of Nachsatz which may be traced to the oldest organs, is still attached to fifth mutations, both alone and in association with other stop names, for instance, *Gedacktnasat, Rohrnasat,* etc. In French organ building, the name *Larigot* denotes the high Quint $1^1/_3'$.

The mutations are of course determined by their foot length. In former times, this was often expressed in whole numbers, or approximate figures: Quint 3′, instead of $2^2/_3'$; Terz 2′, instead of $1^3/_5'$; and Nasat $1^1/_2'$, instead of $1^1/_3'$. This does not mean that the early organ builders were unable to arrive at the proper numbers and fractions; but probably, they did not find it convenient to use these complicated numbers, since the measurements were inexact, after all.

MIXTURE STOPS

The parallel fifths in medieval polyphonic music presumably led to the first quint stops in the organ. In all likelihood, these quints were inseparable from the related octave stops; for instance, the combination 8′, $5^1/_3'$, 4′, $2^2/_3'$, 2′ from the primitive organs. However, the 8′ rank, *Vordersatz,* could be played independently, while the remaining ranks, *Hintersatz* or *Nachsatz,* could not be isolated.

These multi-rank, mixed stops, the mixtures, are closely allied with the early history of the organ in Europe. In other words the organ, in its early years, was like a large mixture stop having one or more fundamental ranks that sometimes could be used individually.

Such mixture organs could have tremendous dimensions. Praetorius mentions an example where the 8′ pitch had 2 ranks; the 4′ pitch, 3-4 ranks; the $2^2/_3'$ pitch, 4-5 ranks; the 2′ pitch, 6 ranks; the $1^1/_3'$ pitch, 7 ranks; the 1′ pitch, 8 ranks; and the $^2/_3'$ pitch, 10 ranks, a total of 42-44 pipes on every key. In addition to this Hintersatz, there was a Vordersatz containing a Principal 32′, Octave 16′, Octave 8′, and Quinte $5^1/_3'$, but we do not know how many of these ranks were joined to the Hintersatz or which ones could be employed independently. The presence of the Principal 32′ certainly indicates that an unusually large organ was concerned. In most instruments, the total of ranks was a good deal smaller, although there were often as many as 20-24 ranks.

With technical advances, an increasing number of single stops was separated from the Hintersatz, but the multi-rank mixtures were characteristic of north European organs until late in the sixteenth century. In the Praetorius period, the total of ranks was greatly reduced, and the mixtures were essentially as we know them to-day. Progress in this direction is understandable, because a tonal blending to a reasonable degree was increasingly desirable. Polyphony and part-singing could not be cultivated with *solch ein tieffes, grobes brausen und grewliches grümmeln* (such a deep, rough roaring and horrible grumbling), as the big, deep mixtures produced, according to Praetorius.

In practice, the maximum pitch for flue pipes is taken as 12,000 - 13,000 cycles (the fundamental), which means that a 1′ rank can be extended from bass to treble, as the g‴ has a frequency of 12,401.30 cycles. With ranks of higher pitch, this maximum pitch occurs at some point within the normal keyboard range. But instead of letting the rank stop at this point, a "repetition" (or "break") is customarily made, that is, the continuation is permitted to leap back to a lower pitch: in octave repetition, an octave lower; in fifth repetition, back to the nearest fifth; thus, the interval of a fourth when the octave leaps back to the fifth, and the interval of a fifth when a quint "breaks" back to the octave. In fifth repetition, an octave series is continued with a fifth series, and a fifth series with an octave series.

We must admit that these repetitions were a necessary evil, but in time the organ builders learned to exploit their positive qualities. Certainly there was no obligation always to take a rank to the limit of the upper range; the repetition could easily occur sooner if this was found to be expedient. When octave repetition or frequent fifth repetitions were exercised, a mixture stop could start in the bass with high-pitched ranks and terminate in the treble with relatively low ranks. Or, if the repetitions were used sparingly, the course might begin with a fairly low rank in the bass and conclude with a high one in the treble. A judicious selection from the two types was an important technique for balancing the mixtures.

Another circumstance left its mark on the evolution of the mixtures. The large churches absorb much of the high frequencies, and the common treble doubling for the Principal 8′ has already been mentioned. In the Grossmixtur described by Praetorius, the ascending line shows progressively larger numbers of ranks, and many later mixtures have similar increases in the number of ranks.

The number of ranks, their pitches, and the repetition schemes employed (not to mention the scaling of the pipes) are the basic elements in mixture construction. The methods and some variants will be illustrated here by some typical examples.

The oldest type of repetition is the octave "break", which could be applied to a four-rank mixture in this way:

C–B	$1' - {}^{2}/_{3}' - {}^{1}/_{2}' - {}^{1}/_{3}'$
c–b	$2' - 1^{1}/_{3}' - 1' - {}^{2}/_{3}'$
c′–b′	$4' - 2^{2}/_{3}' - 2' - 1^{1}/_{3}'$
c″–f‴	$4' - 2^{2}/_{3}' - 2' - 1^{1}/_{3}'$

This mixture repeats only at c and c′, and at the repetitions, all ranks drop down an octave, so that the C, c, and c′ become a unison. When the lowest rank in the c octave is indicated as a 2′ (line 2 in the diagram above), this does not mean that the c pipe has a length of 2′; in such a case it would belong to a 4′ stop. On the contrary, this indicates that the rank is a part of a 2′ stop, of which the largest pipe would be 2′ if the rank were started at C.

Since both octaves and fifths in the composite tone are lying at the distance of an octave, we can also picture the octave repetition like this: the two highest ranks are omitted, while the two lowest continue. A fifth and an octave are added, being an octave lower than the two ranks which continue.

The abruptness of such an octave leap is not without significance for the melodic lines. "Breaks" create an important change in the quality from bass to treble. Consider the following example of a low-pitched mixture, of which the highest rank in the C octave is ${}^{1}/_{2}'$, and which, in the c″ octave, contains both 8′ and $5^{1}/_{3}'$ pitches. In other words, a 16′ combination tone.

C–c♯	$2' - 1^{1}/_{3}' - 1' - {}^{2}/_{3}' - {}^{1}/_{2}'$
d–b	$2' - 1^{1}/_{3}' - 1' - {}^{2}/_{3}' - {}^{1}/_{2}' - {}^{1}/_{2}'$
c′–b′	$4' - 2^{2}/_{3}' - 2' - 1^{1}/_{3}' - 1' - 1'$
c″–f‴	$8' - 5^{1}/_{3}' - 4' - 2^{2}/_{3}' - 2' - 2'$

Thus the highest rank is doubled from d.

In the course of the seventeenth century, fifth repetitions came into frequent use, especially in north European organ building. In this form of repetition, only the highest rank is omitted, and it is replaced by a rank which lies below the lowest rank. Using the same ensemble on C as in the first example, the following result is obtained with fifth repetition:

C–B	$1' - \frac{2}{3}' - \frac{1}{2}' - \frac{1}{3}'$
c–b	$1\frac{1}{3}' - 1' - \frac{2}{3}' - \frac{1}{2}'$
c′–b′	$2' - 1\frac{1}{3}' - 1' - \frac{2}{3}'$
c″–f‴	$2\frac{2}{3}' - 2' - 1\frac{1}{3}' - 1'$

Although there are three repetitions instead of two, the treble of this mixture is higher than the first example. Consequently, its brilliance is more consistent from bass to treble, and at the same time the repetitions are less noticeable. The alternate use of the highest or lowest rank in octave and fifth positions has been considered a disadvantage of fifth repetition, because, historically speaking, octave repetition yielded very slowly, and never completely, to fifth repetition. The reason that this alternation between octaves and fifth plays such a minor role is the lack of any appreciable change in the combination tones of the mixture ranks. This is also true of mixtures having an uneven number of ranks, where fifths and octaves are alternately in the majority.

In larger mixtures, this ratio is naturally more favourable, but, by the way of compensation, the repetition problem is more complicated, because the multiple ranks cover a wider tonal range. One of Schnitger's mixtures may serve to illustrate this point:

C–B	$1\frac{1}{3}' - 1' - \frac{2}{3}' - \frac{1}{2}' - \frac{1}{3}' - \frac{1}{4}'$
c–f#	$2' - 1\frac{1}{3}' - 1' - \frac{2}{3}' - \frac{1}{2}' - \frac{1}{2}' - \frac{1}{3}'$
g–b	$2' - 1\frac{1}{3}' - 1' - 1' - \frac{2}{3}' - \frac{2}{3}' - \frac{1}{2}'$
c′–f#′	$2\frac{2}{3}' - 2' - 2' - 1\frac{1}{3}' - 1' - 1' - \frac{2}{3}'$
g′–b′	$4' - 2\frac{2}{3}' - 2' - 2' - 1\frac{1}{3}' - 1' - 1' - \frac{2}{3}'$
c″–f#″	$4' - 4' - 2\frac{2}{3}' - 2\frac{2}{3}' - 2' - 2' - 1\frac{1}{3}' - 1'$
g″–c‴	$4' - 4' - 2\frac{2}{3}' - 2\frac{2}{3}' - 2' - 2' - 1\frac{1}{3}' - 1\frac{1}{3}'$

The basic procedure is the repetition of fifths, but many of the doublings can be construed as octave repetitions of single ranks. If reasonable tonal limits are to be retained, the doubling of ranks and frequent fifth repetitions are necessary in multiple rank mixtures.

In spite of the many variations of the mixture stops, there are very few names for distinguishing the various types. The formulation of general rules is difficult because the meaning of these names has changed from one place to another and from one builder to another. For example, one type, such as the previously cited Schnitger mixture, appears under two names,

Mixtur and Scharff, even in Schnitger's own organs. The only explanation is that, in the one case, the mixture's relation to the other stops justifies one designation, and in a second case, the other.

At present, *Scharff* indicates a high mixture stop with as many as four ranks, while the name *Mixtur* is reserved for the lower mixtures. The Scharff is regarded as a supplement to the Mixtur, as a stop which continues and completes the superstructure of the Mixtur. Praetorius describes an identical concept in the "Syntagma musicum"; he differentiates between (1) the low *Grossmixtur* without repetitions, (2) the common, repeating mixture, and (3) the *Klein-Mixtur.*

Concerning the mixture, he writes that it may have four to nine ranks, and that it usually has a 2′ or 1′ as the lowest rank. The Klein-Mixtur, or *Scherp* as the Netherlanders call it, has either three or four ranks in the customary fifth-octave arrangement; or it may consist of three octave ranks and a fifth-sounding rank (at C, for instance, 1/2′, 1/4′, 1/6′, 1/8′); or, as the third possibility, it may employ octaves exclusively. For example:

C–B	1/2′ – 1/4′ – 1/8′
c–b	1′ – 1/2′ – 1/4′
c′–b′	1′ – 1′ – 1/2′
c″–c‴	1′ – 1′ – 1′

Praetorius describes a fourth type of mixture, the *Zimbel,* and mentions six varieties: (1) *Klingend Zimbel,* a three-rank mixture consisting of an octave, a fifth and a third with octave repetition; (2) *Zimbel II,* fifth and octave ranks with frequent repetitions; and (3) *Kleiner Zimbel I,* repeating in fifths, so that it alternates between octave position and fifth position. The Compenius organ at Frederiksborg Castle has a Zimbel of this type (with wooden pipes), and Praetorius, who collaborated very closely with Compenius, presumably assisted in its composition. It is laid out in this fashion: C–A, 1/6′; B♭–e, 1/4′; f–a, 1/3′; b♭–d♯, 1/2′; e′–a′, 2/3; b♭′–d♯′, 1′; and e″–c‴, 1 1/3′. The three remaining types are: (4) *Zimbel-Bass* (pedal-Zimbel), with 1/2′ as the lowest rank and one or two repetitions; (5) *Repetierende Zimbel,* which is not described in detail; and (6) *Grober Zimbel III,* also lacking detailed information. The name suggests that it had very low ranks.

A typical example of a Klingend Zimbel from that period is found in the organ of the Jacobi Kirche in Hamburg. Undoubtedly, this stop is the work of Scherer. The following ranks are included:

C–E	$\frac{1}{6}' - \frac{1}{8}' - \frac{1}{10}'$
F–B	$\frac{1}{4}' - \frac{1}{5}' - \frac{1}{6}'$
c–e	$\frac{1}{3}' - \frac{1}{4}' - \frac{1}{5}'$
f–b	$\frac{1}{2}' - \frac{2}{5}' - \frac{1}{3}'$
c′–e′	$\frac{2}{3}' - \frac{1}{2}' - \frac{2}{5}'$
f′–b′	$1' - \frac{4}{5}' - \frac{2}{3}'$
c″–e″	$1\frac{1}{3}' - 1' - \frac{4}{5}'$
f″–c‴	$2' - 1\frac{3}{5}' - 1\frac{1}{3}'$

Praetorius mentions the *gar kleine, subtile und junge Pfeifflin* (quite small, subtle and delicate pipes) which make up the Scharff, and in defining its relation to the Mixtur, he uses the expression *vor seine rechte Mixtur gesetzt und geordnet* (composed and planned with reference to its own particular mixture). But he adds that the Scharff is used independently in the Brustwerk of some large organs. Such independent applications gradually changed the Scharff into a larger and lower-pitched mixture.

The pitch difference between the Zimbel and the Scharff is sometimes difficult to define. However, in terms of scaling, the difference is more clear-cut. A wide Principal scale, possibly a Gemshorn scale, is often found in the Zimbel, while a Scharff always has a narrow scale. In the north European tradition, the presence of a third-sounding rank was a trade-mark of the Zimbel, but at the close of the Baroque, the opposite situation prevailed: the Scharff had a third, and the Zimbel had a fifth.

The French *Cymbale,* as treated by Dom Bedos, is always a fifth mixture. Its range of ranks and repetitions are specified as follows:

C–B	$4'-2\frac{2}{3}'-2'-1\frac{1}{3}'-1'-\frac{2}{3}'-\frac{1}{2}'-\frac{1}{3}'-\frac{1}{4}'$
c–e	$5\frac{1}{3}'-4'-2\frac{2}{3}'-2'-1\frac{1}{3}'-1'-\frac{2}{3}'-\frac{1}{2}'-\frac{1}{3}'$
f–b	$8'-5\frac{1}{3}'-4'-2\frac{2}{3}'-2'-1\frac{1}{3}'-1'-\frac{2}{3}'-\frac{1}{2}'$
c′–e′	$10\frac{2}{3}'-8'-5\frac{1}{3}'-4'-2\frac{2}{3}'-2'-1\frac{1}{3}'-1'-\frac{2}{3}'$
f″–b′	$16'-10\frac{2}{3}'-8'-5\frac{1}{3}'-4'-2\frac{2}{3}'-2'-1\frac{1}{3}'-1'$
c″–e″	$21\frac{1}{3}'-16'-10\frac{2}{3}'-8'-5\frac{1}{3}'-4'-2\frac{2}{3}'-2'-1\frac{1}{3}'$
f″–c‴	$32'-21\frac{1}{3}'-16'-10\frac{2}{3}'-8'-5\frac{1}{3}'-4'-2\frac{2}{3}'-2'$

For the *French mixture, Fourniture,* Dom Bedos arranged the ranks in this manner:

C–e	$4' - 2\frac{2}{3}' - 2' - 1\frac{1}{3}' - 1' - \frac{2}{3}' - \frac{1}{2}'$
f–e′	$8' - 5\frac{1}{3}' - 4' - 2\frac{2}{3}' - 2' - 1\frac{1}{3}' - 1'$
f′–c‴	$16' - 10\frac{2}{3}' - 8' - 5\frac{1}{3}' - 4' - 2\frac{2}{3}' - 2'$

The fifth in the Cymbale thus repeats six times, and there are two octave repetitions, but the lowest of the numerous ranks illustrated here were never adopted for practical use. In a large organ with a 16′ manual Principal, the lowest rank of the mixture was usually a 2′, and the total of ranks could extend to five. The Cymbale could be four-rank, with a $^{2}/_{3}$′ as the lowest one. In small instruments, the total of ranks was reduced by the omission of one or more of the low ranks. The French Cymbale is a parallel to Praetorius' Scharff, but in exceptional instances the Cymbale can also extend over a pitch range which is not only higher but also lower than that of the mixture. This type of Cymbale has a double function: 1) to extend the mixture in the upper range, and 2) to supplement the ranks of the mixture.*

Although Dom Bedos does not discuss the matter, the Tierce Cymbale did exist in early French organ building. The third is customarily reserved for the *Cornet,* whose origin may be traced to the sixteenth century. From the latter half of the seventeenth century, the Cornet has been almost a permanent feature in French organs, and on some occasions, several Cornets are specified, one for each manual. The Cornet is composed of 8′, 4′, $2^{2}/_{3}$′, 2′, and $1^{3}/_{5}$′ ranks (the 8′ and 4′ may be omitted), and hence it has a complete series of partials up to the third (the fifth partial). It does not repeat, but its downward range is only to c′ or f. Its 8′ is constructed as a Rohrflöte or Gedackt and the remaining ranks as wide Principals, graduated in scale in relation to the stops with which they are supposed to function. The purpose of the Cornet is to reinforce the reeds in the treble and to act as an independent solo stop. For these reasons, the lower pitches are not included.

Recently, experiments have been made with other combinations of partials. The 8′ and 4′ series, which can be borrowed from single stops, are omitted in most cases. The three remaining ranks may be supplemented by a seventh ($2^{2}/_{3}$′–2′–$1^{3}/_{5}$′–$1^{1}/_{7}$′), or an octave ($2^{2}/_{3}$′–2′–$1^{3}/_{5}$′–1′), possibly with both an octave, a seventh and a ninth ($2^{2}/_{3}$′–2′–$1^{3}/_{5}$′–$1^{1}/_{7}$′–$^{8}/_{9}$′). When placed in the pedal or in the manuals of large organs, the Cornet can be based on a 16′ and thus have $5^{1}/_{3}$′–4′–$3^{1}/_{5}$′ ranks, perhaps with the addition of the seventh, $2^{2}/_{7}$′.

In brief, the Cornet is an autonomous combination of ranks. It belongs

* Dom Bedos clearly states that the Furniture and Cymbale were to be used together for the *Plein Jeu.* The effect of double ranks was indeed present.

to a group of mixed stops called "instrumental imitators", because these stops bear resemblances to certain wind instruments and have been named after these instruments. They originated in the sixteenth century, and at that time the *Rauschpfeife,* a kind of oboe, was a favourite imitation.

The Rauschpfeife, or *Quartian,* is composed of octave and fifth ranks, with the octave as the lowest rank ($4'$–$2^2/_3{}'$ – or $2'$–$1^1/_3{}'$) or with the octave on top ($2^2/_3{}'$–$2'$ or $1^1/_3{}'$–$1'$). As a three-rank mixture, the ranks are usually $4'$–$2^2/_3{}'$–$2'$; when it is a four-rank mixture, they are $4'$–$2^2/_3{}'$–$2'$–$1^1/_3{}'$, or perhaps $2^2/_3{}'$–$2'$–$1^1/_3{}'$–$1'$. The Rauschpfeife or *Rauschquinte,* still another designation for this stop, can be scaled in several ways. In many cases, a wide Principal scale is employed, but even a wider scale is used. The fifths and the octaves can be differently scaled; for instance, the fifth as a Flachflöte and the octave as a Principal. The $4'$ rank can be scaled like a Rohrflöte. There are no repetitions.

Zink was the original name for the $2^2/_3{}'$–$1^3/_5{}'$ pair of ranks, but gradually, as the Zink as a reed stop came into use, the term *Sesquialtera* was preferred. Thus, the Sesquialtera is a Cornet which has lost its octave ranks. The name Sesquialtera has occasionally, and somewhat deceptively, been applied to the small Cornet ($2^2/_3{}'$–$2'$–$1^3/_5{}'$); the deception lies in the fact that the octave ranks produce the specific difference in character between the Cornet and Sesquialtera. Like the Rauschpfeife, the Sesquialtera can take either a Principal scale or a wider scale. The fifth and the third are often divergent in their scaling, at least with regard to the mouth scale. Although the Sesquialtera is primarily a solo stop, an octave repetition is usually made at c, possibly with regard to the fifth only. In the latter case, the ranks in the C octave are $1^3/_5{}'$–$1^1/_3{}'$. On some occasions, two repetitions are used, for example at A and g, and then the ensemble is this:

C–G♯, $^2/_3{}'$–$^2/_5{}'$; A–f♯, $1^1/_3{}'$–$^4/_5{}'$; g–c‴, $2^2/_3{}'$–$1^3/_5{}'$.

The purpose of these repetitions is to avoid the low ranks that do not blend well and to facilitate a mixture-like, not soloistic, use of the Sesquialtera.

The *Terzian,* with $1^3/_5{}'$–$1^1/_3{}'$ ranks, is closely related to the Sesquialtera; it has the same scaling, and repetitions are not encountered in this stop.

Finally, the *Piffero* and *Schreipfeife* ought to be mentioned. Both consist exclusively of octave ranks; the Piffero in a low range ($8'$–$4'$–$2'$), and the Schreipfeife in a higher one, partly repeating, somewhat like an octave cymbal.

The sound of tinkling bells that can be simulated by combining very high ranks with lower ones at the distance of more than an octave, has resulted, particularly in German organ building, in a variety of stops named after percussion instruments with a similar sound. Names like *Glöckleinton, Glocken-Zimbel, Hölzern Gelächter* (Xylophone), *Faberton* (the sound of hammer strokes on the anvil) disclose the imitative realism of this stop group. The ensemble of ranks and scales were extremely varied, and for the high ranks, frequent repetitions were mandatory. In the bass, the octave ranks should have an interval of three octaves; in the treble, two octaves will suffice. When the effect of bells must be obtained, the fifth and octave ranks should have a distance of $2^1/_2$ and $1^1/_2$ octaves. Thirds also work excellently in this arrangement.

Through these examples, the most essential types of mixtures have been illustrated. Their manipulation within different stylistic periods will be given a more detailed treatment in connection with the instruments representing each country.

THE REED STOPS

No authoritative date has been determined for the first appearance of reeds in the organ. In the thirteenth century, an organ in Dijon is said to have had a stop named *calami deicustodientes,* probably a type of Schalmei, but reeds did not achieve widespread acceptance until the fifteenth century. During this period, the so-called Regals came into use. They were small, portable keyboard instruments, with one or more ranks of reed pipes, designed for use in church services and processions.

An amazing development of reeds occurred after the turn of the fifteenth century. The numerous wind instruments of the period inspired the organ builders to create a great number of new types. In 1619, Praetorius (in the *Syntagma musicum*) was able to print such a complete and descriptive list of reeds that recent years have had very little to add.

As mentioned earlier, reeds may be separated into two main groups: those with long, tuned resonators; and those with short, untuned resonators. It has also been mentioned that the form of the resonator, cylindrical or conical, makes a decisive difference in tonal quality.

The *Trompete,* the "Principal" of the reeds, should be given first place in a discussion of the reeds with full-length resonators. It has a funnel-shaped resonator (Fig. 27 A) with a very small diameter at the bottom

(12–16 mm. at C). The diameter at the top (also at C) is usually between 85 and 165 mm. With regard to the length, Praetorius mentions 5 feet (however, with a tuning higher than our concert pitch), but he recommends 6 feet length (which corresponds to approximately 200 cm. in our tuning), *wenn es pralen, prangen und gravitätisch klingen soll* (if the sound must be ostentatious, sparkling and pompous). He claims that shorter resonators produce a *flachen und plattwegfallenden Klang* (a shallow and colourless tone). Today, lengths varying between 190 and 230 cm. are customary, but the width scale exercises a substantial influence in this matter. In narrow scales, the resonators must be correspondingly shortened.

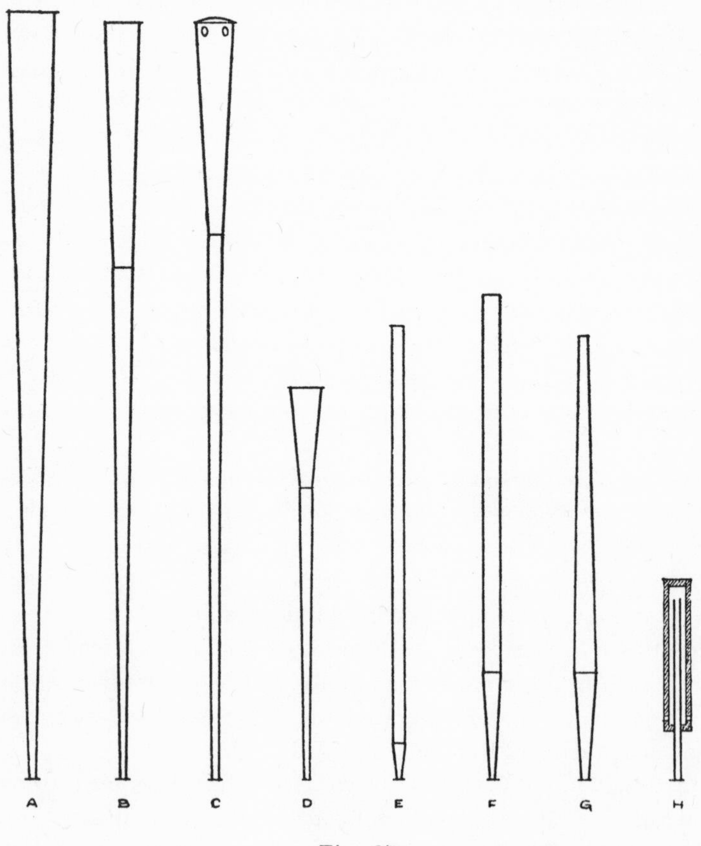

Fig. 27.

For emphasizing the fundamental and reducing the overtones, we have one very effective method besides lengthening the resonators: overblowing. The conditions are nearly the same as in flue pipes. To make the pipe overblow, a double resonator length and forced voicing are used. Due to the increased intensity, overblowing is limited to the upper range, from c′ upward, in order to procure a favourable balance of intensity between bass and treble.

The Trompete is found at 32′, 16′, 8′, and 4′ pitches, and in addition, in the pedal at 2′ pitch. The 4′ pitch can, when necessary, be extended throughout the normal keyboard compass, but flue pipes are usually preferred to the reeds in the upper octave, for tonal reasons and for the sake of stability in the tuning.

Traditionally, the name Trompete is reserved for the 8′ stop. In the pedal, the 16′ Trompete is called *Posaune* (Trombone), and the 32′ Trompete, *Contra-Posaune* or *Posaunenbass*. The 4′ stops are sometimes named *Kornett,* a designation which can be appropriated for the 2′ range if the French term *Clairon* is not preferred. In France, the 16′ Trompete is called *Bombarde,* both on the manuals and in the pedal, and the overblowing Trompete, *Trompette harmonique*. In Germany, the very narrow-scaled 16′ Trompete may be known as *Fagott* (Bassoon).

The French *Oboe* is another reed with full-length resonator. In the bass, it is built as a narrow Trompete, but from c, f, or c′, the resonator is composed of two conical sections, a very narrow lower section and a more funnel-shaped upper section (Fig. 27 B). In the joint between the upper and lower cones, there is a small slit that can be opened or closed, and this tiny "leak" contributes some upper partials to the sound. These partials create a timbre that is similar to the orchestral oboe. In recent decades, French organ building has developed this stop and given it the double name *Basson-Hautbois* because of the two resonator shapes.

Contemporary German organ building has exploited a similar type of construction. From bass to treble, the resonator is double-conical; it is closed at the top, but four holes are bored through the pipe wall, immediately below the cover (Fig. 27 C). The slit-shaped opening that characterized the French Oboe is absent, and for this reason, the sound is round, soft, and restrained.

The *Schalmei* (Fig. 27 D), as described by Praetorius, resembles the French Oboe, but its resonator is cut to half-length, and the sound is very bright and clear. Considerable experimentation has been applied to this stop. The double-conical form permits innumerable alterations in scaling, both as to the width and length and as to the length ratio between the upper and lower cones.

The name Schalmei (Calami) was, indeed, associated with some of the first French reeds, but they did not have double-conical resonators. Their resonators were cylindrical with the same diameter from bass to treble, like the earliest ranks of flue pipes. It was only later that the organ builders discovered the secret of diminishing the diameters toward the upper range.

As these French reeds gradually entered the Netherlands and Germany, the name Schalmei went out of use and was supplanted by *Cromorne* or *Krummhorn* (Fig. 27 E). The diameters varied between 28 and 33 mm., and in the comparatively rare *Grosse Krummhorn,* the diameter could broaden to 55 mm. at C. Frequently, the resonators were widened at the top by pressing the metal outward into a rounded funnel-shape; or a short cone was soldered on at the bottom. With these exceptions, the authentic Krummhorn has a cylindrical resonator with a tuned half-length. This resonator shape is more than a symbol of the first organ reeds; it has played a continuous role in organ history.

The names of this resonator shape have been changed periodically. In the Renaissance, it was called *Schalmei, Chalumeaux,* or *Zink,* and later (when the Krummhorn had retired from the orchestra) Oboe. With the emergence of the new "organ oboes", northern Europe lost interest in the Krummhorn, and only the more conservative French organ builders preserved both the stop and the name up to the present. Krummhorns normally appear at 8′ pitch, but can be found at 16′ and 4′ pitch.

The *Dulcian* is closely related to the Krummhorn (Fig. 27 F). Like the Krummhorn, it has tuned cylindrical resonators of half-length, but, at the bottom, these resonators have a conical point, of which the lower diameter is approximately that of the Trompete, and of which the length can vary from $^1/_4$ to $^1/_2$ of the entire resonator length. The scale for the cylindrical section is a little wider than in the Krummhorn, the total length somewhat greater. These dimensions imply a resonant and softer sound. The Dulcian is one of the early reeds and was already in widespread use about 1500. It is found regularly in the 16′ and 8′ ranges; the 16′ is often named *Fagott* (Bassoon). When the 16′ is a manual stop, shortened resonator lengths, usually $^1/_4$ length, are sometimes employed in the C octave. The width scale, unaffected by this shortening, continues with the normal progression.

The *Musette* (Fig. 27 G), a variant of the Dulcian, is a reed with a well-established position in French organ building of the eighteenth century. Here, the upper cylindrical section of the resonator is replaced by a conical tube, tapering upward; for this reason, the tone is weaker and more muted.

The name *Zink,* which is applied to both the Sesquialtera and various reeds, is used in Praetorius' reference to a variant of the Dulcian 8′, which produces a hollow and sensitive sound by means of a very wide scale and thick, narrow tongues. This tonal ideal probably caused the Zink (on the manuals) to become an 8′ treble stop beginning at f or c′. In the bass, a snarling sound is extremely difficult to avoid.

Also the *Sordun* may be classified with the reeds having tuned resonators. A double resonator, consisting of an inner resonator and an outer one, is the distinctive characteristic. The inner resonator is open at the top in the usual manner, but it is enclosed in the outer resonator, which is closed at the top and open at the bottom. Thus the two resonators function as a curved resonator with the aggregate length of the components. The transition from one resonator to the other is seldom worked out as a continuation of the width scale. On the contrary, a leap in both scale and resonator size is usually intended, a scale "coupling". Figure 27 H supplies an example of this stop. The example represents the Sordun 16′ in the pedal of the Compenius organ.

The reed group with the short, untuned resonators, the *Regals,* offers such endless prospects for variations in resonator forms and scales that there is really no tonal basis for a distinction of types. Organ regals were intensively cultivated in the course of the sixteenth century. The period had a strong predilection for the sound of wind instruments, and here were infinite opportunities for imitating not only the wind instruments, but almost any sound. Fresh and remarkable sounds, original "creations", were the order of the day.

The new stop names from that period allude to the resonator forms and to some curious tonal effects. German organ builders had a particularly exuberant and vivid selection of names: *Trichterregal, Apfelregal, Knopfregal, Harfenregal, Singend Regal, Jungfrauen Regal, Rankett, Sordun, Bärpfeife, Zooglossa* (Animal Voice), and *Kälberregal,* for example. In France, we could find *Falsetto* and *Baby's Voice,* and in Spain, it was not uncommon to have *Old Man's Voice* and *Old Woman's Voice.* The *Vox humana* was inevitable – in fantastically altered shapes and with resonators of all possible types. One thing they had in common: their lengths and widths were fairly large, and the sound, compared with the usual Regal, was rich and full-bodied. Not all Vox humana types have a connection with the sound of the human voice; whether the objective was imitation, whether it was a case of an "unsuccessful" experiment leading to some positive results, or whether the stop was a completely unique creation – we must be content with conjecture.

The important thing is that these fuller and more "refined" Regal types were intended as concertizing solo stops. And perhaps it is no coincidence that the name Vox humana emerges in about 1600, at the same time as the solo recitative (with accompaniment) was being introduced.

But the Regals could be used for other purposes than solos. Their luminous sound, rich in overtones, blended excellently with other stops, especially with mixtures and mutations. One of the most conspicuous traits in the Renaissance and early Baroque organs was the brilliance, the "humour", or the mysterious quality that the Regals often possessed.

In attempting a more detailed sketch of the Regals, a few simple and universally recognized resonator shapes can serve as the basis for comparison. The width scale is extremely variable, and the length scale (in spite of large variations) commonly stays within the scope of a short, untuned length in the bass, whereas frequently a tuned length, $^1/_4$ or $^1/_2$, in some cases the whole length, is incorporated in the upper treble range.

The partial cover at the top of the Regal resonators is very important, especially in the wider scales. The purpose of the cover is not only to moderate the intensity, but also to shape and mould the sound, in the same way as the human voice is shaped by different positions of the mouth and tongue. In regard to the balance of intensity between bass and treble, the cover is always tightest in the bass and is opened gradually toward the treble.

The cover also has many variations. It is customary to use a metal cap, which is soldered over ⅓ to ½ of the opening above and opened as desired (Fig. 28 A). Or, the cover may be soldered all the way round and supplied with a hole in the middle or an adjustable flap (Fig. 28 B).

The cap may be completely sealed. In this case, the opening, consisting of holes or a slit, is placed in the resonator itself, immediately below the cap or at a suitable distance from it (Fig. 28 C and D). Further, the cover can be formed like a cone (Fig. 28 E), a hemisphere (Fig. 28 F), or a cap with a chimney like the Rohrflöte (Fig. 28 G).In addition, this type of cover can be varied by placing the tube inside or partly inside and partly outside the resonator. Finally, the length and width of the chimney may be varied, and even a conical chimney is conceivable.

The quite short, cylindrical shape is undoubtedly the simplest and oldest type of Regal resonator (Fig. 29, type 1). Often the resonator length does not exceed the length of the tongue. With narrow scaling, the resonator is usually uncovered, and the result is a thin sound with an abundance of overtones; the name may be *Harfenregal* or *Geigenregal,* or merely *Regal.* This type of stop is also found with slightly conical resonators or with resonators that are cylindrical in the bass (perhaps still with narrowing above) and increasingly funnel-shaped in the treble. A wider scale usually requires a rather effective covering for the top of the resonator.

The second of the basic Regal forms is the *Trichterregal* (Funnel-regal) Fig. 29, type 2. Its resonator is strongly reminiscent of the treble resonator

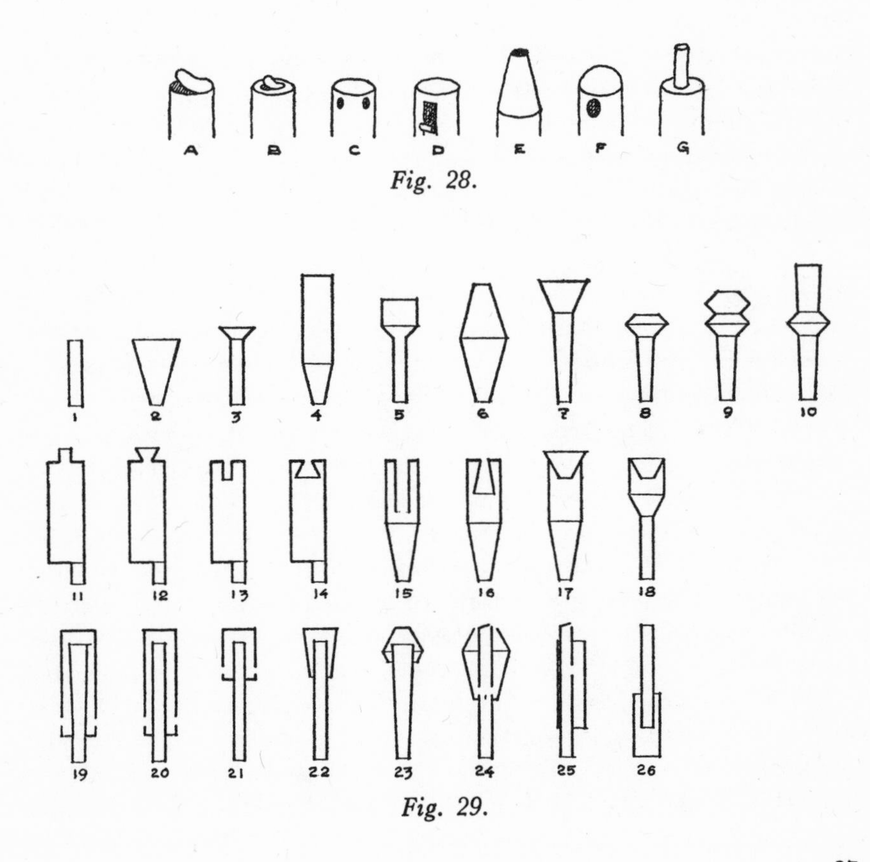

Fig. 28.

Fig. 29.

for the Trompete. At C, the resonator length for this Regal may vary from 30 cm. to 5 cm., and the diameter at the top, from 50 mm. to 25 mm. To prevent the tone from becoming rough and noisy, an adequate cover is necessary; this is often a cap with a flap in the middle. Stops with this type of resonator may be called Vox humana. The Spanish *Voz viejos* and *Voz viejas* ("Old Man's Voice" and "Old Woman's Voice") are frequently constructed in this way. On the whole, this resonator form is much used in Spain.

In the *Kornett,* we find another funnel-shape, with narrow scale and longer resonator. Sometimes its length scale is tuned at $^1/_4$ length.

The combination of a cylindrical resonator with a small, funnel-shaped upper section (Fig. 29, type 3), like the Krummhorn, represents one of the earliest inventions and a first step in the direction of the later funnel-shaped resonators. The result was a freer sound and a somewhat greater intensity, but it seemed more practical to place the cone under the cylindrical section (Fig. 29, type 4), as in the Dulcian. This produced better speech and provided both tonal and practical means of introducing a wider scaling in the cylindrical section.

The very early *French Vox humana* has this construction, with diameters ranging from 27 mm. to 36 mm., and with $^1/_8$ to $^1/_6$ of full length at C. The resonator-covers have openings, usually in the form of a flap.

Type 3 can also be extended with a small cylinder at the top, and this produces an increased resonance space (type 5), imparting a certain sonority to the thin tone. With an appropriate covering, the length and width scales can be rather large. Although this model is sometimes called Vox humana, the current designation is *Knopfregal.* The shape of the resonator's "knopf" (knob) can be changed without notable influence on the sound, which is largely dependent on the cubic content of the knob and the degree of covering. For example, the knob may be composed of two cones (type 8), or it may be ball-shaped.

The coupling of two conical resonator sections (type 6) was an early phenomenon representing a further step in the evolution of the Trichter-regal. The upper cone serves as an extension of the length scale and as a cover (with opening). Usually the cover must be reduced in the treble range. This is accomplished in two ways: first by changing the length ratio between the upper and lower cone in favour of the lower, and secondly by progressively enlarging the opening above. The resonator may be long (60 - 80 cm.) and tuned, or short with a wide scale. At first, the long type went under the name of Krummhorn, although the cylindrical Krummhorn was to be found at the same time. Another designation for this stop is Dulcian, but in the middle Baroque and later the short form often assumed the name Vox humana. Strangely enough, this characteristic stop has never acquired a name of its own.

Although the double-conical Schalmeis (type 7) were known during Praetorius' lifetime, this type of resonator does not make an appearance among the Regals until a later date. The length of these Schalmeis is approximately 30 cm. at 8′ C, increasing to a half or a whole tuned length in the upper range. The bass resonators have covers which, however, are discarded in the high range.

If the cover is made with a cone, as in the double-cone Regal *(Doppelkegelregal),* we arrive at type 8, which, with longer, tuned resonators, is known in French organ building as the *Basson.* A double cone is sometimes even added to this form in the low range in order to make the covering more complete (type 9), but in general, more simple and equally effective methods are preferred, a flap, for instance.

The muting can also be achieved with a slender, conical tube (type 10) which, in scale, may be regarded as an extension of the narrow shaft below; or, the whole resonator may be viewed as a narrow, slightly conical tube with a double cone inserted near the middle. Besides the short Regal, the same type with a tuned half-length is found toward the end of the eighteenth century under the name of *Oboe,* or under the name of *Viola da Gamba,* if the upper section is extended with a cone (like the Schalmei).

A variant of type 10 has a conical resonator with an inserted cylindrical section, analogous to the double-cone in the Oboe mentioned above. The cylinder can be equipped with small holes if a brighter and clearer sound is desired.

The typical Rohrflöte covering (type 11) is generally associated with very wide-scaled resonators. Such resonators produce resonance for comparatively low partials, in addition to the very high ones; in this way, the sound maintains restraint and sonority, coupled with some brilliance and clarity. In Germany, this stop has the name *Bärpfeife,* or, in some of its variations, Vox humana again. Of course this resonator form can be modified within very wide limits, with particular reference to changes in placement, form, and scale of the tube, as shown in the examples 12 - 16. The tube scale can be so ample that it is nearly the equivalent of an inner resonator (types 17 and 18).

Inner resonators play a large role in the Regal family, especially in the *Ranketts,* which are often patterned after the Sordun (see p. 85). Here, the basic component is the inner resonator, which is directly connected to the shallot; the outer resonator functions as a continuation of the inner one (types 19 - 23). The outer resonator, in the majority of cases, has a cylindrical shape, but the effectiveness of its form and scale clearly depends on how much space the inner resonator occupies and, therefore, subtracts from the internal volume. If, for instance, the inner resonator is conical (type 19), the most effective form for the outer resonator is also conical, since its cross-sectional area is augmented to the same extent as the cross-section of the inner resonator is decreased. The scaling of the two resonators can be controlled so that no scale-break occurs at the transition between the resonators, but this is seldom the case, for particularly in this resonator form, there is an opportunity to work with the special tonal effects which can be obtained by the coupling of two resonance bodies. The external resonator, which must normally have its sound openings at the bottom, is sometimes also equipped with some small "vents" at the top, if it is desired that the resonance from the inner resonator shall assert itself at the expense of the external one.

The location of the sound openings is of vital importance in the composition of timbre. For example, an ordinary, cylindrical resonator, closed at the top, can be divided into two resonance spaces by placing the opening so that it divides the resonator length proportionally. When the shapes of the resonators have already divided them into several resonance spaces, the placement of the sound openings provides an important means for the control of sound coupling and tonal balance.

Type 24 illustrates a newer Vox humana construction, consisting of an inner cylindrical resonator that is partly covered at the top with a flap. The upper half of this resonator is encased in a double-conical resonator which receives its vibratory impulses through two holes in the middle of the inner resonator. The external resonator will then add a strong upper octave to the somewhat weakened resonance tone of the inner resonator. At C, the complete length can be an $^1/_8$ tuned length.

In type 25, the inner resonator again consists of a cylindrical tube with $^1/_8$ tuned length, but this time, the location of the opening causes it to divide the resonator length in the ratio of 1:2. The outer resonator is a wider, cylindrical tube, of which the length is $^2/_3$ of the inner resonator length. Both ends of the external resonator are open. The external resonator is mounted in such a way that the opening in the inner resonator also divides the external one in the ratio of 1:2. This combination creates four resonance spaces having the relation of fifths. Furthermore, the even partials, the octaves, are suppressed by the cylindrical form. The so-called *Rohr-Krummhorn* (type 26) works according to quite similar principles.

In all of the preceding resonator types, construction in metal is assumed, most often tin alloy. Wood is another excellent and commonly used material for Regal resonators, and even though the technique associated with wood turning requires different and simplified forms for the exterior, the tonal technique is unchanged.

5

The Technical and Tonal Design of an Organ Werk

From the beginning of organ building, the ensemble of many stops, especially those of different pitches, has been, and still is, one of the most essential tonal resources of the organ, not only for the sake of intensity, but primarily for the creation of synthetic timbres and the tonal qualities which are mandatory for polyphonic music.

As a parallel to the development of individual stops with varying structure and balance in their respective series of partials, groups of stops can be constructed with distinctive tonal characters, depending entirely on the selection and design of the chosen stops. The development of the individual stops must emphasize the qualities which condition the collaboration with other stops, because the unique possibilities of the organ are inherent in this collaboration or ensemble of stops.

A complex of stops, composed of a unified tonal ensemble and connected to the same keyboard, is called a *Werk* (division). The balance between foundation stops, mutations, and reeds determines the character of the Werk, which is further defined by the selection of stops within these groups and by their scaling and voicing.

The Principals, or the Principal chorus (ranks), as they are usually called, are basic. Their lowest ranks and their scales indicate the essential features in the character of the Werk. We speak of a 16′ Werk as well as 8′, 4′, or 2′ Werks; and these expressions refer to Werks of which the lowest Principal stop is 16′, 8′, 4′, or 2′ respectively, and of which the remaining Principal stops are developed in accordance with the law of partials. These Principals are then supplemented with stops from the remaining groups, always preserving and underscoring the tonal character of the Principal ranks.

Just as a Werk is composed of various stops, several Werks of different character can unite in a larger, total ensemble, another of the special resources of the organ.

When the tonal structure is analyzed, with regard to both the historical development and contemporary problems, certain elements in the technical design of the organ must first be considered, since the tonal and technical matters have always been closely associated. This is true of pipe construction and also for the entire mechanical action.

For manipulating several ranks in different combinations as well as singly, two controls are required: one, at right angles to the ranks, that connects each key on the keyboard with the pipe that produces the corresponding tone; and another, parallel to the ranks, that connects or disconnects the single ranks from the action of the key.

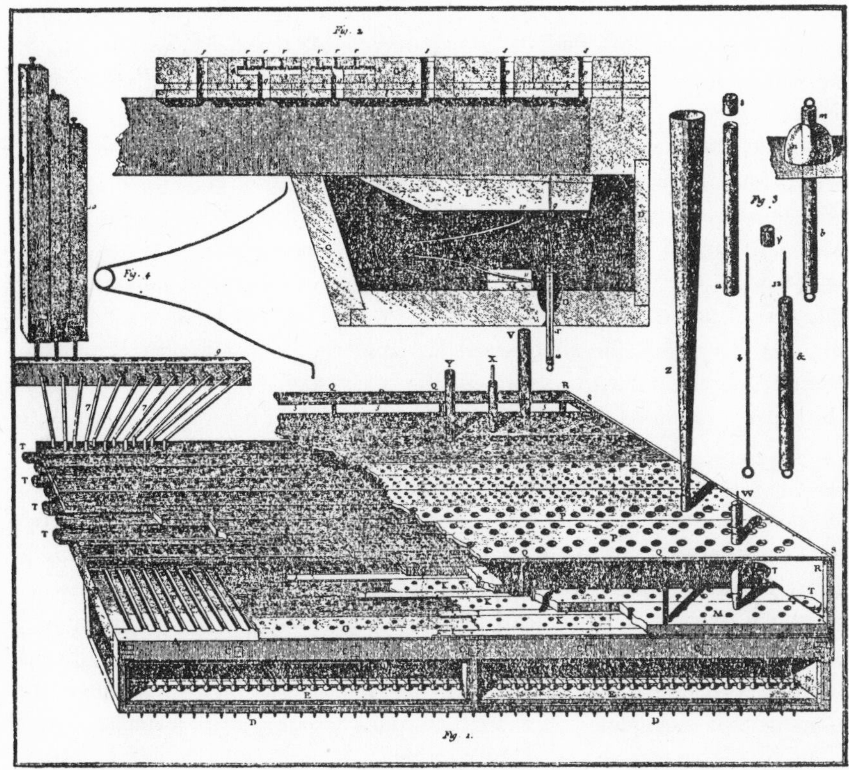

Fig. 30.

For more than six centuries the key mechanism, the action, has been made in this way: every key is coupled to a *pallet* (valve) which controls the flow of wind from a wind chamber into a channel, or *groove;* the grooves are laid out at right angles to the ranks, and thus, the pipes served by a groove and its pallet represent the same pitch of the various ranks mounted on that chest. Between the grooves and the toe holes of the pipes, a stop-action valve, or *slider,* is installed parallel to the ranks (one for each rank). The slider (by regulating the passage of wind from the groove up through the toe holes) can connect or disconnect the entire rank from the grooves.

The wind chamber with its pallets, grooves, and sliders – this whole appliance – is called the wind chest and the universally accepted type of construction, the slider chest, is shown in Fig. 30. (The illustration has been taken from Dom Bedos' *l'Art du facteur d'orgues.* At the top, we see a vertical section through the wind chest; below, the wind chest in perspective.)

In the lower half of the illustration, there is a sketch of the uncovered wind chamber, which makes it possible to see the front edge of the pallets. The grooves are located above the pallets. In making groove partitions, the flat chest, above the wind chamber, is divided into just as many spaces or channels as there are keys. (The channels (grooves) are visible in the lower left corner of the drawing, because the "table" has been removed.) When a pallet is opened, the compressed air from the wind chamber flows into the groove, and thereafter, through the borings in the top board and into the pipes – provided that the slider does not prevent it.

The sliders in the slider chest function in this way: the slider, a very thin board, is inserted between the top board (that is, the board on which the pipes are standing) and the table, or cover, of the wind chamber. A lengthwise shift in the slider's position will completely obstruct the borings leading from the groove, through the slider, and into the top board. All windways from the grooves to an entire rank are opened or closed by moving the slider longitudinally. The two mouldings (bearers) that support the top board are situated on each side of the slider, and these mouldings are thicker than the slider, just enough to allow freedom of movement.

As simple as this arrangement may seem, it is actually the most vulnerable point of the slider chest. The slider must glide smoothly, and at the same time, form an air-tight juncture with both the wind chest and the top board. This means that the slider, along with the table of the wind chamber and the lower side of the top board, must be executed and matched with the greatest precision. Extreme care is required in the selection of materials.

However, wood has the unpleasant habit of "working". While drying, it shrinks in the direction across the grain, and when absorbing dampness (from a humid church, for example), it swells. The situation is still worse when the wood twists, causing a flat-planed surface to warp and leak. This also happens as a result of changes in humidity.

These defects can be counteracted by choosing the most appropriate varieties and qualities of wood and by carefully seasoning and drying it before manufacture. But there is no way to prevent wood from absorbing moisture from the air, or to keep it from exuding this dampness again.

If an organ stands in a church where the heating causes the degree of humidity to be lower in the winter than in the summer (and this is not uncommon in churches where there is continual and strong heating during the winter months), the wood, in spite of its age and seasoning, will expand in the summer and contract in the winter.

The sliders and the top boards are very sensitive to such changes in humidity. For instance, if a top board warps and bulges in the middle (crosswise), a space remains between the slider and board, so that the wind streaming upward to the pipes through one or more borings, partly escapes through this leak and partly travels to some of the neighbouring pipes, causing them to speak softly at the same time. This is called a "run". Such leaks may be the reason for an unsteady wind stream, and the result is an unstable tone. The leaks can become so serious that the pipe receives insufficient wind. Then the tone is not only shaky, but also too weak and too low in pitch – the pipe goes out of tune. If the top board warps in the other direction, the slider will jam and be difficult, or impossible, to move.

These are serious disadvantages. However, unheated churches, with small fluctuations in humidity, have enabled the slider chest, in spite of its frailties, to maintain a dominant position in European organ building for nearly five centuries. The wood in these instruments has not changed, appreciably, since it was first acclimated to the churches. Naturally, good materials and reliable workmanship have been of significance. At any rate, the slider chest must have given satisfactory results, because it managed to supersede the older spring chest. Here, instead of sliders, a small pallet was placed in the groove under each pipe, and all pallets belonging to a single rank were connected to a guide rail, which permitted them to be opened and closed by a stop knob. On each pallet there was a little spring that closed the pallet when the stop was uncoupled. With this type of construction, leakage between the groove and the pipe was impossible; and in this respect, the spring chest was superior to the slider chest. But the stop action was more complex and occupied more space than the sliders. For these reasons, this system was inappropriate for small wind chests with narrow, crowded grooves; besides, the operation was much more difficult. The pressure of approximately fifty pallet springs had to be overcome when pulling a stop knob, and these springs snapped back into their original positions when the stop was uncoupled – hence the name "spring chest".

The spring chest went out of use in most places by the start of the seventeenth century, and after that the slider chest held its ground until well into the nineteenth century. Contemporary trends and intensive church heating finally caused its weaknesses to be subjected to a critical examination.

Warped sliders and top boards were by no means the only lamentable features. One of the greatest annoyances was the inadequacy of the wind supply for the stops on a chest; or, the distribution of the wind was imperfect – one stop "robbed" another. These conditions led to a diminished intensity and "coughing" (or "consumption", as it was often called). Of course, this shortcoming became a cardinal point at a time when exact tuning was reckoned as one of the first criteria for a tone. Imperfection was intolerable in the "age of accuracy".

At length, someone struck at the root of the matter. Each pipe was given its own pallet. This system corrected the apportionment of wind and the tuning, and sliders immediately became superfluous. With the new system, the wind chest was partitioned lengthwise into stop grooves (like the spring chest) instead of crosswise into tone grooves. For each stop, there was a groove containing the pallet series that belonged to the pipes of the rank in question. By connecting or disconnecting these stop grooves from the wind chamber (in this case the so-called stop action channel), the stops were made operative or inoperative. Naturally, all pipe pallets belonging to the same pitch had to be controlled by the same key. This was somewhat more complicated than the slider chest, but the difficulties were not insuperable.

Figure 31 shows a section through the stop channels in a typical cone chest, the first modern form of the stop channel chest. Cone chests probably originated at the close of the eighteenth century, but they did not appear in practical use until the middle of the nineteenth century. The name derives from the cone-shaped pallets lying in the bottom of the wind chest. Due to their weight and to the wind pressure when the stop has been pulled, they drop into the pallet seats and close the borings which admit wind to the pipes. The mechanism under the wind chest is controlled by

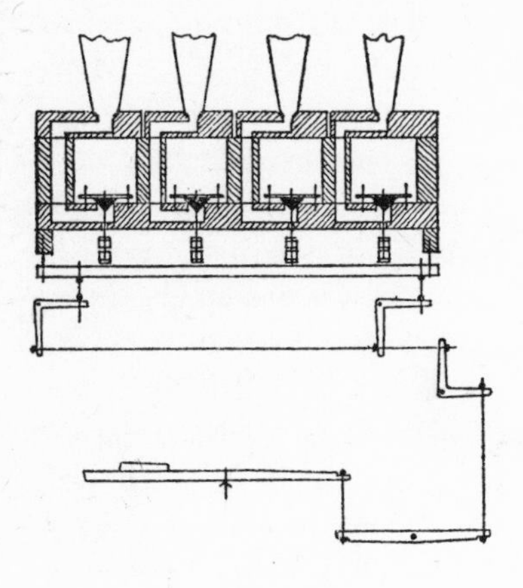
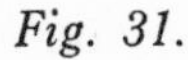

Fig. 31.

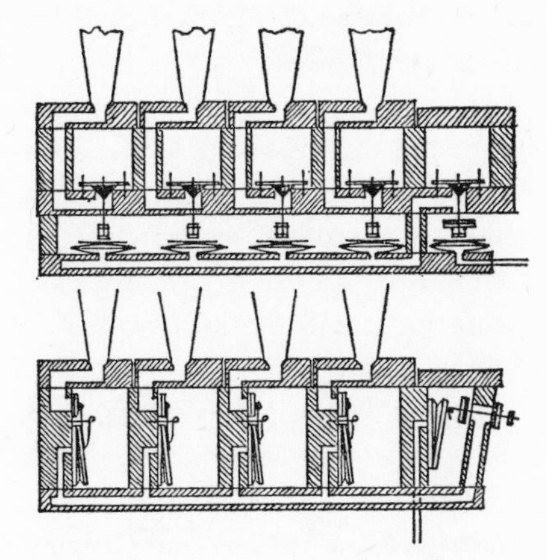

Fig. 32 (above). Fig. 33 (below).

the keys and opens all pallets for the same pitch in every rank, regardless of whether there is wind in the stop channels. The cone chest has eradicated the technical imperfections of the slider chest, and the immediate result, for organists and organ builders, was a much improved stop action.

With the advent of tubular pneumatic action, playing became still more effortless. Instead of lifting the cone pallets with the strength of his fingers, transmitted through a complicated mechanism, the organist relinquished this task to the compressed air inside the instrument. A small pouch of thin leather (a "diaphragm" or membrane) was placed below each pallet pin under the wind chest, and the membranes for the pallets belonging to the same key were supplied with wind from a joint relay valve, which was also operated by a leather membrane (Fig. 32).

The relay valves were double-acting; that is, they were capable of closing the conveyance of wind to the membranes while simultaneously opening for the immediate release of the wind that they had contained. This was necessary for a quick repetition of the action. At the key, only a very small pallet was needed (also double-acting), whose sole function was to provide wind for the relay valve membrane; the minute amount of wind required was conducted through a very thin lead tube. The relay valve could also be operated by a magnet, governed by a contact under the key.

The only disadvantage of the pneumatic cone chests was that they were rather noisy. When a single, soft stop was played, it was irritating to have an "accompaniment" supplied by the pallets for all of the other stops on the same wind chest.

This was avoided by the use of several types of "bellows chests". According to the theory, the pipe pallets were mounted on small bellows lying in the stop channels (as shown in Fig. 33). While in the rest position, these bellows were under wind pressure from the relay valves. When a stop was pulled, the pressure in the bellows and the channel was equalized. A small spring then held the bellows in the position at which the pipe pallet was closed.

When a key was pressed down, the double-acting relay valve opened to admit the wind from the pallet bellows. In the channels which were supplied with wind because the stops were pulled, the wind pressure compressed the bellows and thereby opened the pallets. Thus the functioning pallets were limited to those in the stops which were pulled.

For the sake of sheer convenience, it is reasonable that these systems would have their day of victory. However, one vital matter was ignored when the stop channel chests came into use: the wind chest is more than a piece of machinery for conducting the proper amount of wind to the proper pipes; it has a decisive influence on the tone quality. In other words, the vibrations in the pipes react upon the wind conveyed to them through the pipe foot, and this means that the wind in the wind chest to some extent takes part in these vibrations.

In a slider chest the pipes representing the same pitch in different ranks are connected with the same groove so that they can work as a unit. When the vibrations of these pipes are transmitted into this groove, a vibration coupling results, which, to a considerable degree, promotes the blending. The pipes on the same groove are well-suited for coupling, because their frequency is a multiple of the frequency of the fundamental.

In the cone chest and other systems with stop channels, this vibration coupling is impossible; stop channels isolate the pipes which should collaborate. When vibration coupling of any significance occurs in large stop channels, it occurs in the wrong direction, that is, parallel to the ranks. This has a negative influence on polyphonic music.

Every organ builder who has worked with both systems knows that the tone groove chest is best suited to the natural method of sound production in the organ, and that the tone groove chest, basically, offers better technical arrangements for voicing than the stop channel chest. In making a choice, however, some practical aspects must be considered.

If the slider chest is to be used to day, it must be rid of its old flaws, "consumption", "runs", etc., and it must be able to endure the sizeable fluctuations of humidity resulting from present-day heating systems.

More specifically: pallets and grooves must be scaled so that each pipe receives an adequate supply of wind; the stop arrangement and the wind chest must be constructed in such a way that the wood can warp, within reasonable limits, without disturbing the action.

Experience has proved that this can be done. A properly built slider chest is superior to all other wind chests, with respect to both reliability and durability. The costs of production are somewhat higher, but favourable, nevertheless, when actual years of service are a condition.

All arguments support a return to a modernized form of the slider chest, and the contemporary trend is moving rapidly in that direction. In Denmark, the problem was settled some time ago – the stop channel chests have had their day. Many excellent slider chests are now in existence to meet all demands.

Wind Supply. The compressed air which enables the pipes to speak, comes from the bellows, which have a double purpose: to compress the air, and to maintain a steady wind pressure. Organ pipes are very sensitive to changes in the wind pressure, which affects the voicing as well as the tuning.

The oldest wind systems simply consisted of two or more wedge-shaped bellows, mounted horizontally and resting on the lower board. The upper board could be lifted, rotating on one of the narrow sides, where it was fastened with a leather hinge to the lower board. Each bellows had an intake or suction valve. This valve allowed wind to enter the bellows when the upper board was raised, but it also prohibited wind from escaping. In the wind trunk leading from the bellows to the organ, there was a valve of the same design, which caused the compressed wind to leave the bellows and to enter the organ. The same valve prevented the entry of wind from the neighbouring bellows when the first pair of bellows was raised for the intake (Fig. 35).

The weight of the bellows' upper board, and the load placed upon it, determined the wind pressure. For measuring the wind pressure in organ bellows, we employ a U-shaped glass-tube, half-filled with water (water manometer). One end of the tube is connected with the bellows or the wind trunk. The difference in the water levels for the two prongs of the tube represents the amount of pressure. In different cases, this may vary between 40 and 130 mm. Water Column ($1^3/_5''$–$5^1/_5''$). In theatre organs and high pressure reeds, wind pressures may range from 300 to 450 mm. Water Column ($11^4/_5''$ - $17^3/_5''$).

The wedge bellows had various defects, resulting in a wind pressure that did not remain entirely steady. This obstacle was overcome with the chest bellows invented by the Danish organ builder Marcussen (1814). The chest bellows consists of a small chest, which moves vertically, like an air-tight piston, inside a larger chest. Its intake and exhaust valves are like those of the wedge bellows. This design also requires at least two bellows, so that one may be raised for the intake, while the other exhausts its supply of wind.

Both systems have the great disadvantage of occupying much space. For this reason, they must be installed at a certain distance from the organ, and then fairly long wind trunks (or conduits) are necessary, even in the best situations. The wind in the trunks is both inert and elastic. If the wind consumption varies greatly, the wind in the long trunks must suddenly be forced into motion and abruptly brought to a stop. This cannot be done without producing blasts of wind, which can be very annoying.

Even in Bach's time, the demands for the big tutti effects began to be heard, but not until the nineteenth century did these demands cause the wedge bellows to be demoted to a feeder bellows, supplying wind to a large reservoir and regulator bellows placed inside the organ, as near the wind chests as possible.

This was a great step forward, and the next followed shortly after; first in the form of various attempts to operate the feeder bellows by machinery, and finally by the replacement of the feeder bellows with an electric centrifugal blower. Here was the perfect solution. The regulation of the wind, supplied by the blower, could easily be achieved with a throttle valve, which was controlled by the reservoir bellows and located in the trunk, between the latter and the blower. As the wind was used, the bellows fell, and the throttle valve opened just enough so that the air being admitted was equal to the recession. When no more wind was needed, the bellows were reinflated until the throttle valve closed.

The Tracker Action. A direct connection from key to pallet is possible for only very small and primitive organs. In such cases, the pipes must be arranged in the same succession as the keys, that is, chromatically. The wind chest, in conventional practice, is considerably longer than the width of the keyboard. To accommodate this extra width in the wind chest, the first step in a pallet-to-key connection is a lateral shifting of the levers *(trackers)* from the pallets, in order that they come to agree with the arrangement of the keys.

A lateral shifting of a tracker is achieved by the aid of a *roller,* a rotating axis equipped with two arms, whose ends are joined to the tracker rods. Figure 34 shows an example of a "roller-frame", the system of rollers which brings the pallet trackers into alignment with the keys. When it is necessary for a tracker to change direction, a *square* (Fig. 34 C) or a *backfall,* or "rocker" (Fig. 34 D) is employed. If the tracker not only changes direction but also moves sideways, a roller is used, of which the arms do not lie in the same plane; they form the necessary angle (Fig. 34 E).

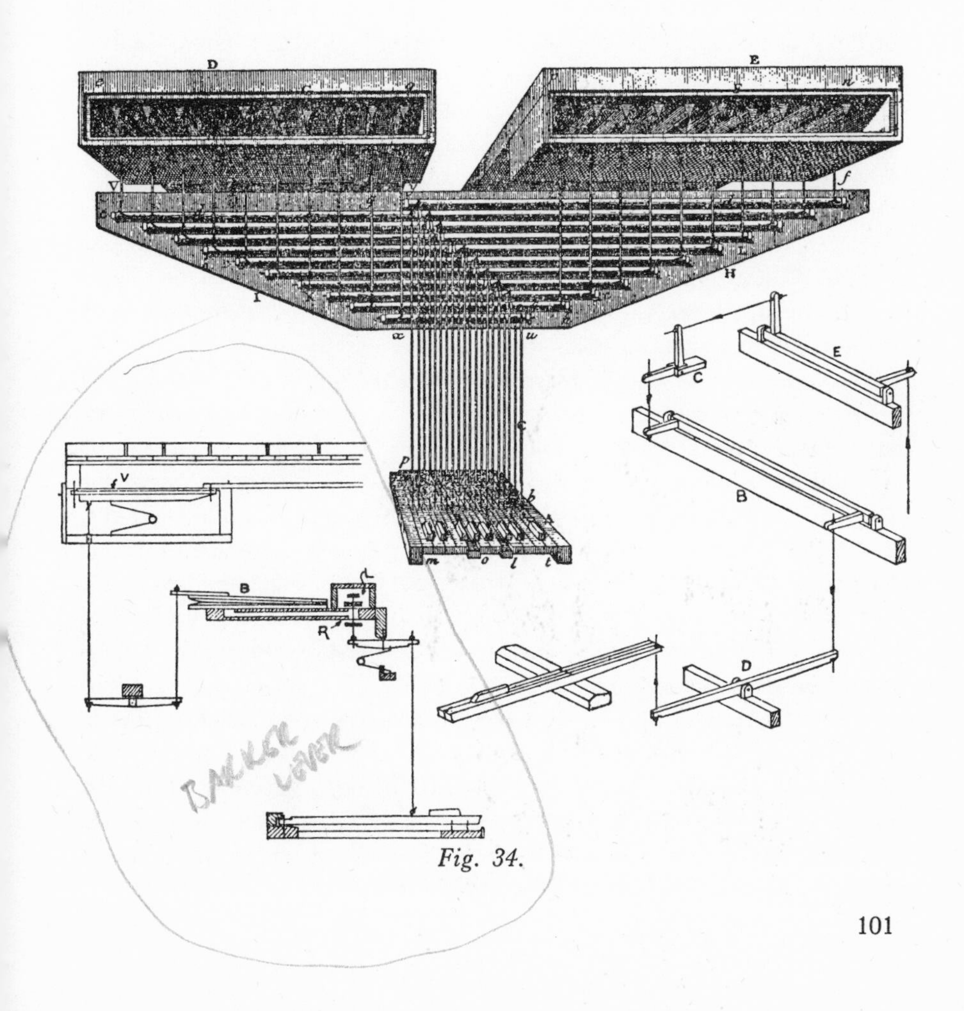

Fig. 34.

The tracker rods ("pull-downs") are usually made of wood and resemble very thin mouldings (cross-section 1×8 mm. or $1^1/_2 \times 10$ mm.). At the ends, these mouldings are fitted with hooks or adjusting screws and threaded wires in order that they can be attached to the arms of the rollers or those of the squares.

For all movable parts of the mechanical action, the weight must be kept to a minimum, and all joints must function with the least possible friction and noise. Proper methods are also important in the suspension and bracing of the stationary parts of the action. One of the most difficult, if not insoluble, problems in building an organ is the retention of an absolutely fixed distance between the wind chests and the manuals, because this distance is seriously affected by the wood and its "working". The constant change in the adjustment of the mechanism was a fundamental weakness in the old tracker-action organs, and this required subsequent regulation. The normal depth of the key action is 11 mm., but drying the wood could easily reduce the drop of the manual keys so much that the pallets of the wind chest failed to open sufficiently, and too little wind passed into the groove. This resulted in "consumption", and the pipes went out of tune. Or the opposite might happen: the wood could expand while moist, thus making the action too tight and preventing the pallets from closing.

These disadvantages can be eliminated, through effective bracing following the action from keyboard to wind chest, and through the use of a variety of compensatory devices. Such matters require the professional skill of the organ builder, and he must not neglect them.

In gigantic organs with several large Werks and great distances to the Werks, direct mechanical action can become so unwieldy that the insertion of a subsidiary lever is inevitable. The Barker Lever Action (patented in 1839) is the best known and operates on the principle shown at the left in Fig. 34. The wind chest pallet (V) is regulated by a secondary bellows (B), which uses wind from the primary bellows and is controlled by a relay valve (R) joined to the key. The Barker Lever is placed as near as possible to the keyboard; it is inserted in the tracker at a point where the latter is still in alignment with the keyboard. Regardless of the uncomfortably small spaces between the trackers, this location is preferable, since the couplers can also be attached to the Barker Lever. In such a case the Barker Lever operates not only its own manual Werk, but also those coupled to it. Otherwise, they would make the action much heavier. The Barker Lever is restricted, generally, to the largest of the manual Werks, the remaining Werks operating with direct action from their respective keyboards. These Werks, of course, are assisted by the Barker Lever, when they are coupled to the largest Werk.

In unique circumstances, the keyboard may be so far removed from the organ pipes that the installation of a completely mechanical action is impractical. Even where the distance is more reasonable, the available space may not be well-disposed for a mechanical action. In such cases,

Fig. 35.

electric action would be preferable. The operative principle (as discussed previously) is the following: the key is connected to a simple contact, and when the key is pressed down, the switch completes a low tension circuit (12–15 volts) to a magnet that controls the relay of the wind chest. When a slider chest is to function with electric action, the first step is to plan an auxiliary bellows for the pallets, and this bellows must be controlled by a double valve coupled to the magnet.

Both the Barker Lever and the electro-pneumatic action interrupt the direct key-to-pallet connection. Even if a completely satisfactory degree of rhythmic precision could be attained with these actions, the living contact with the instrument has been lost. This contact, unconscious though it may be, is present when the organist, through the direct connection, "feels" the pallets.

Recent years have given organists and organ builders ample opportunity for drawing comparisons between different actions. In fact, the problems have been thoroughly discussed and elucidated from every point of view, particularly in the Netherlands, Germany and Denmark, and without risk of exaggeration, we may say that there is general agreement on one issue: the practical, tonal, and technical conditions for playing clearly justify a revival of traditional organ construction, that is, tone groove chests with completely mechanical action.

Similar tonal-technical problems do not arise in conjunction with the stop action. It may be entirely mechanical, electro-pneumatic, or pneumatic (with an auxiliary motor at the sliders), depending on what seems most appropriate in each particular case.

In choosing a certain stop action, due consideration must again be exercised with regard to space. The auxiliary bellows at the sliders require some space, and in small organs it may be impossible to provide this space without upsetting some of the basic conceptions in acoustics and architecture. However, small organs certainly do not necessitate the use of pneumatic stop action. There is little opportunity for fundamental conflicts.

Presumably, the discussion about aids for registration will be resolved, by degrees, as experiments are made with the most essential aid to registration: a well-planned distribution into as many and characteristic Werks as possible in relation to the given total of stops. In the case of large organs, certain arrangements may be necessary for easy control of the pedal stops, either a division into groups with cut-off valves, or some free combinations.

6

The Organ in the Middle Ages

Although the European church organ has always employed tone groove wind chests, the stop channel chest is older. Vitruvius in *De Architectura* (*ca.* 50 A. D), gives a highly detailed description of the oldest known organ with a number of stops, the water organ or "hydraulos"; the name is derived from its wind supply system, a kettle-shaped "wind chest", submerged in water; two pumps compressed the air that was regulated and stored in this chest. The hydraulos could have as many as eight stops, each of which was mounted on its own channel. A top board was placed over the channels; then sliders, at right angles to the channels and in connection with a kind of key, were inserted between the channels and the top board. Springs attached to the sliders returned them to a closed position. The wind chest was cast in bronze, and each channel had a faucet-shaped, rotating stop pallet.

Basically, the primitive organ had attained its complete development by the time of Christ, but organs are described as early as *ca.* 100 B. C. in the *Pneumatica* by Hero of Alexandria. These instruments, of course, had only one rank of pipes, but they were not restricted in size. For example, there is discussion of an instrument that required a windmill for the operation of its bellows.

Tertullian mentions a certain Ctesibius, who is reputed to be the inventor of the organ; he refers to Archimedes as having perfected the organ. Evidently organ building was of interest to the advanced scientists.

After Vitruvius, there is no information for quite a long period, and it seems most probable that the art of organ building vanished from Europe after the decline of Roman culture and the upheavals and disturbances of the great migrations.

According to the Spanish bishop Julianus (*ca.* 450 A. D.), the organ was well-known in Spanish churches, but in France, the first report concerning an organ dates from 757 when Emperor Pepin the Short (king of the Franks) received an instrument as a gift from the Byzantine emperor. Then bits of information slowly begin to appear.

Obviously, organ building had hibernated outside of Europe. The increase in commerce with foreign countries or the pilgrimages to the Holy Land may have brought the isolated Europe of the Middle Ages into contact with the outer world; at any rate, the craft of organ building was restored to its former status.

This naturally occurred within the walls of the Roman Church (there was not even a remote possibility of anything else). By virtue of the powerful organization and firmly established unity of the Church, the larger part of Europe was affected at approximately the same time. In a Latin poem by Wulstan (or Wolstan), a monk, we find a colourful description of one of the large cathedral organs, the organ at Winchester. The poem is dedicated to the Bishop Elphegus Calvus (the tenth century). In free translation:

> Nowhere at all can be seen / such organs as here you have built them,
> Organs designed in pairs / built on a double ground.
> On the tier above / there are twelve bellows in number,
> Moreover, fourteen below / follow arranged in rank.
> These by alternate use / enormous wind are supplying,
> When they are pumped by a crowd / of seventy powerful men.
> Those with their arms are at work / all covered with much perspiration,
> Eagerly each calls out / encouraging all of his mates;
> And they of all their might / work up the pressure of wind
> Making the instrument / sing at the top of her voice.
> Four times hundred in all / is the content of pipes,
> All these an organist / governs with skilful hand.
> Listen! He opens the closed / again he closes the opened,
> Just as the nature of song / and the various sounds will require.
> Most concordant of heart / two brothers are sitting together;
> Each of the learned men / governs an alphabet (= a key board).
> Moreover, hidden holes / are found in the forty tongues (= slider pallets)
> And to each of the tongues / ten pipes in group are connected.
> Hither some of them run / whilst thither the others are running;
> Carefully each will serve / the proper time for its note.
> Shouting with joy they begin / singing the seven keys,
> Blending into their song / the lyrical semitone.
> Boldly as thunder-storm / the steely voices are singing,
> So that the stricken ear / no other music perceives.
> Powerful echo is heard / everywhere widely resounding,
> Making the listener soon / cover his ears with his hands.
> No one dares to approach / knowing quite well that he cannot,
> Not being able to stand / music so complex of sound.
> Through the entire town / the pipes are singing and booming;
> Reputation has flown / far away over the land.
> You commended this church / to God, the Master of Thunder,
> Built it to honour the Saint / Peter who has the keys.

This could give the impression of exaggeration, but another report describes a hydraulic organ, built during the reign of Pope Silvester II (d. 1003) for a church in Rheims, and the instrument was to be operated with *aqua calefactae violentia,* that is, very hot water – more accurately, steam.

Such turbulence does not seem altogether improbable after reading Praetorius' description of the Halberstadt organ. It was built in 1361, to a specification already referred to. The façade pipes were composed of a Principal 32′; behind this was an Octave 16′, 2 Octave 8's, Quint $5^{1}/_{3}'$, 3–4 ranks in the 4′ range, as well as 4–5 ranks at $2^{2}/_{3}'$, 6 ranks at 2′, 7 ranks at $1^{1}/_{3}'$, 8 ranks at 1′, 10 ranks at $^{1}/_{2}'$. The sound is described in these words: "... ein solch tieffes, grobes brausen und grewliches grümmeln; auch wegen der vielheit der Mixtur-Pfeiffen / ein überaus starcken schall und laut / und gewaltiges geschrey" (such a deep rough roaring and horrible grumbling; and due to the large number of mixtures / an extremely violent sound and tone / and an atrocious screaming).

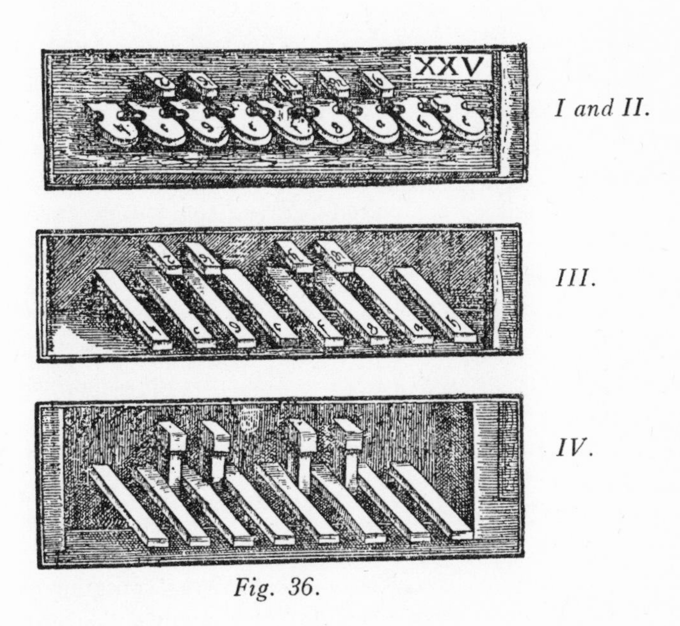

Fig. 36.

This is in perfect agreement with what a French Cistercian monk writes toward the end of the twelfth century: "D'ou vient, je la demande, tant d'orgues, tant de montres, tant de cymbales dans l'églises? Pourquoi – je vous prie – ce souffle terrible qui exprime plutôt le fracas du tonnerre que la douceur de la voix" (Where have they come from, I ask, so many organs, so many Principals, so many Cymbals in the churches? Why this terrible blast – I pray you – it is more like the rumbling of thunder than the sweetness of the voice).

If we imagine the workers at the bellows, as at Winchester, competing to produce the highest possible wind pressure, we are fully convinced that the result was a tremendous noise – and nothing more. The stability of the wind pressure and the tuning would be thrown into absolute chaos by that type of bellows operation.

Praetorius publishes a sketch of the Halberstadt keyboard. It is reproduced in Fig. 36, and it is clearly seen that the keys are intended for fists, for organ beaters. The upper row of keys (I) is called treble and is coupled to the complete instrument. The next keyboard (II) is a mate to the first, but it controls only the Octave 8′. The following row of keys (III) is a bass manual, which may be operated with the hands or with the knees, as required. Manual III is connected to the largest bass pipes, standing in the towers, and thus it corresponds, in some ways, to our pedalboard. The actual pedalboard (IV) operates the bass for the entire instrument.

As for the appearance of the organ, we are told that the twelve largest pipes were placed in the two side towers. The smaller pipes (the continuation of the rank) were placed between the towers, "nach der Mensur geordnet" (arranged scalewise), that is, according to length (see p. 268-69 with reference to the Norrlanda organ).

On the two middle keyboards, the Prestant therefore could be played alone (Octave 8′); a two-part composition could be performed with both fists or with one fist and one knee. With the upper keyboard and pedalboard, a three-part composition could be executed "Zum gantzen Werck und vollem geschrey" (on the whole organ and with full volume), according to Praetorius.

Understandably, most of the available historical information pertains to these giant organs. The usual organ of the Middle Ages was decidedly smaller. There were two types: (1) the *positives,* consisting of flue stops up to 4′ pitch, possibly with a stopped 8′ (for instance, the Norrlanda organ); and (2) the *portatives,* a smaller and more transportable version of the positive; and finally the *regals* which have already been discussed on p. 85. They belonged to the portatives.

For the regals, the specification could be an 8′ rank, an 8′ and a 4′, or perhaps 16′, 8′ and 4′. In the larger regals, an additional high-pitched flue stop was conceivable, a 1 or 2 rank Cymbel, for example, or a stopped 2′, a $1^{1}/_{3}'$, or a 1′.

An illustration of such a regal, from the *Syntagma musicum,* is reproduced in Fig. 37. The reed stop is seen at the very edge of the keyboard, and above that, a flue rank with what seems to be 1′ length. The largest pipes are mounted horizontally in the top of the instrument. At the treble end of the keyboard, two "tongues" are visible; they are stop sliders. Figure 38 shows a smaller type of regal without flue stops.

Fig. 37 above Fig. 38 below

The regals were of paramount importance in the performance of vocal music, not only in churches, but wherever there was music. They were the favourite chamber instruments, and they could even be used in processions, either transported by a wagon or carried by one person (who also operated the bellows) and played by another.

A similar use was made of small portable organs with fluework and a small keyboard compass, the portatives. Next, in the order of size, were the positives, so large that they could not be transported. They had their natural position in, or in the vicinity of, the choir of the church.

Very little is known about the specifications of the first positives, but judging from the few preserved remains, they were comparable to the large organs that Praetorius discusses, that is, the Mixtur-block organs, with two bass-sections at the extremes and the treble-section erected in the middle, "according to scale". (For more details, see p. 267/8 concerning the Swedish organs on the island of Gotland.)

About 1400, these organs assumed more "normal" forms, especially the keyboard. The gradual acquisition of stop control valves facilitated the independent use of an increasing number of ranks. At the same time, stops with different timbres were being developed, and some preliminary work was being done with an ensemble of stops. Organ building was more than the production of the required pitches at the requisite degrees of intensity; timbres and tonal contrasts now merited critical judgment.

The antiphonal use of choir and organ (especially the choir and the large organ when one was present) had been practised for a long time; but gradually it became the custom for the main organ and the positive to alternate. This proved to be impractical if the two instruments stood too far away from each other. Consequently early in the fifteenth century the positive was moved up to the main organ loft and mounted on the gallery railing behind the organist; the positive was now a Rückpositiv ("back-positive"). Its keyboard was placed immediately below the keyboard of the main organ. This was most natural for the mechanical action.

A similar procedure was applied for incorporating the regal in the main organ (this happened a short time prior to the annexation of the positive). In the base of the main organ, between the wind chest and the keyboard, there was an unoccupied space, the minimum height of which was determined by the roller-frame (in most cases a space of about 1 metre). This space was just adequate for a regal chest and its keyboard which, for that reason, got its logical place above the keyboard of the Hauptwerk (the Great). This integrated regal Werk came to be known as the Brustwerk.

In the Netherlands, the thin Brustwerk was not satisfactory. One reason, among others, was that the Hauptwerk was built as a block-Werk without individual stop action, and this construction was maintained up to the middle of the sixteenth century. Instead of enlarging the Hauptwerk with flutes and reeds, etc., as in other countries, the Dutch assembled these stops in one large Werk, located above the Hauptwerk (due to the lack of space below it). This new Werk was called a Bovenwerk (in German: Oberwerk), and the characteristic design later spread to North Germany, but without superseding the conventional German Brustwerk.

This coalescence of the Werks was begun in the course of the fifteenth century and occurred almost simultaneously in the Dutch, French (Burgundian), and German territories. There is some doubt concerning the date of the earliest Rückpositiv, because the oldest accounts do not differentiate between a Rückpositiv and a Brustwerk; but at any rate, we know that the church of Our Lady in Zwolle (the Netherlands) had a Rückpositiv in 1447. In 1463, at the Cathedral of Toulouse (France), the combination of five Werks was attempted, permitting them to be played from one manual; and the famous organ at Strassburg Münster, whose façade is intact (see Fig. 56), was constructed in 1498–92 with Hauptwerk/Pedal, Rückpositiv and Brustwerk.

The type of pedalboard used in the Halberstadt organ (a pedalboard connected to the main organ) was a well-established tradition. This kind of pedal was partially coupled to the bass of the manual, and the remainder served as an extension of the bass range (in France, the latter is named "*ravalement*"). By degrees, this extension was converted into independent stops. The first completely independent pedal Werks can be found in North-European organ building of the seventeenth century.

In the course of the concluding century of the Middle Ages, and especially in the later part of this century, a fantastic amount of progress had been achieved. From primitive positives and crude mixture organs, the instrument had advanced to a stage where, with the exception of the narrow-scaled string stops and overblowing flutes, all stop types were recognized: the Principals, both wide and narrow-scaled; Gedackt, Quintatön, Rohrflöte, Spitzflöte; various mutations, including the recently discovered Tierce; several mixture compositions; and last, but not least, a generous selection of reeds.

This development was like an explosion when viewed against its background of nearly uniform, simple, and stable traditions that had controlled organ building in the great expanse of the Roman Church throughout the Middle Ages. After many centuries as a "Sleeping Beauty", the organ had suddenly unleashed its full array of possibilities.

Was the magnificent, brilliantly coloured instrument of no value to the

Middle Ages and the Roman Church? Were the Renaissance and Humanism beginning to assert a perceptible influence? These questions are not illogical. In comparison with the art, music and musical instruments of the Middle Ages, it would be difficult to believe that a lack of skills and materials caused the delay in the expansion of the organ.

Regardless of the manner in which this transition occurred, there is scarcely a craft where the turn of the fifteenth century scored so deep a mark. For the first time, the tonal resources of the organ were conscientiously applied, and characteristic types of organ began to emerge.

The tonal architecture in a Werk, as previously stated, can be varied through stop selection, scaling technique, and voicing. Werks of different types may be incorporated in a larger entity. Obviously, this is a complicated matter, but, on the whole, certain primary factors are conclusive for the quality of sound:

1) The composition and scaling of the Principal ranks; the pitch of the lowest rank in the Werk; the foundation Principal; high or low mixtures and the bass-treble balance, determined by the arrangement of the "repetitions" or "breaks".

2) The number of flute stops in proportion to the Principal group; the purpose of these flutes (foundation stops, supporting stops or solo stops).

3) The use of Tierces (third-sounding stops).

4) The provision of reeds in relation to the fluework.

5) The total, the type, and the location of the Werks.

THE MOST COMMON STOP DESIGNATIONS

Denmark	*Germany*	*The Netherlands*	*England*	*France*	*Spain*	*Italy*
Principal	Prinzipal	Prestant	Open Diapason	Montre	Flautado	Tenori
Oktav	Octave	Octaaf	Principal	Prestant	Octava	Ottava
Nathorn	Nachthorn	Openfluit, Nachthoorn	Nachthorn	Flûte ouverte	Flauta aberta	Flauto aperto
Tværfløjte	Querflöte	Querpijp		Flûte traversière	Flauta traversera	Flauto traverso
	Schweitzerpfeife			Flûte allemande	Flauta octaviante	Flauto octaviante
Spidsfløjte	Spitzflöte	Spetsfluit	Spitzflöte	Flûte à fuseau		
Gemshorn	Gemshorn	Gemshoorn	Gemshorn	Flûte conique	Flauta cónica	Flauto a cuspido
						Corno di camoscio
Blokfløjte	Blockflöte	Fluit	Blockflöte			
Fladfløjte	Flachflöte	Vlakfluit				
Valdfløjte	Waldflöte	Woudfluit	Waldflöte			
Spidsgamba	Spitzgamba	Spitsgamba	Spitzgamba			
Gedakt, Dækfløjte	Gedackt	Holpijp	Gedeckt, Stopped Diapason	Bourdon	Flauta tapada, Bordón	Bordone
Quintatön	Quintatön	Quintadeen	Quintaton	Quintaton	Quintatón	Quintante
Rørfløjte	Rohrflöte	Roerfluit	Rohrflute or Chimney Flute	Flûte à cheminée	Flauta a chimenea	Flauto a camino
Spilfløjte	Spillflöte	Speelfluit				
Kobbelfløjte	Koppelflöte	Koppelfluit	Koppelflute			
Mixtur	Mixtur	Mixtuur	Mixture or Fourniture	Fourniture	Lleno, Nasardos	Ripieno, Armonia
Scharf	Scharff	Scherp	Plein Jeu	Cymbale	Claron	Acuta
Cymbel	Zimbel	Cimbel			Cimbala	

Trompet	Trompete	Trompet	Trumpet and Tuba	Trompette	Trompeta	Chiarina, Tromba
Basun	Posaune	Bazuin		Bombarde	Bombardas	Bombardo
Krumhorn	Krummhorn	Kromhoorn	Trombone	Cromorne	Cro Orlo, Violetas	
Dulcian	Dulzian	Dulziaan		Basson	Bajete, Dulciana	
Vox humana	Vox humana	Vox humana	Vox humana	Voix humaine	Voz humana	Voce umana
Regal	Regal	Regaal			Orlos, Gaitas	
Fagot	Fagott	Fagott	Fagotto, Bassoon	Basson	Bajoncillo, Fagót	Basson
Obo	Oboe	Oboe	Oboe, Hautboy	Hautbois	Oboe	Oboe
Clairon			Clarion	Clairon	Clarine	Clarino
Skalmeje	Schalmei	Schalmey	Schalmei	Chalumeaux		
Hovedværk	Hauptwerk	Hoofdwerk	Great Organ	Grand orgue		Gran Organo
Rygpositiv	Rückpositiv	Rugwerk	Choir Organ	Positif		Postivo
Brystværk	Brustwerk	Borstwerk	Echo Organ	Echo		Expressivo
Overværk	Oberwerk	Bovenwerk		Récit		
Crescendoværk	Schwellwerk	Zwelwerk	Swell Organ	Récit expressif	Cadereta	Recitativo Expressivo
	Hinterwerk					

7

The West European Organ Types

ITALY

The spirit of the Renaissance unfolded in Italy some centuries prior to its manifestations in the remainder of Europe, and with it came the greatest activity in the field of organ building. Although investigation of the archives is far from complete, there is a multitude of reports from the fifteenth century and later concerning new organs and their builders.

The Crusades had transformed Italy into the European centre of a flourishing international commerce, and so the civil economy, as well as the Church, had ample resources at its disposal. Above all, there was an intense desire to create works of art.

There was enough to do for both the Italian masters and the many foreigners who sought work and commissions in art-loving Italy. German, French, and Dutch masters were to be found there (the Spanish are seldom mentioned), but in spite of all these foreign influences and in spite of all that happened in the remainder of Europe, Italian organ building maintained its own "face", a face characterized by distinguished asceticism.

The organs could easily attain huge external dimensions, with front pipes up to 24′ length. But the total of stops was never outstanding, and only in exceptional cases was there more than one manual Werk, with pedal coupled (as previously mentioned) and the possibility of using one bass stop (Principale 16′) independently in the pedal.

We may imagine the Italian organ as a refined edition of the earlier main organ. The scaling technique and voicing were restricted to very subdued forms. In the first half of the fifteenth century, stop valves (admitting wind to a specific stop channel) began to appear, first in conformance to the spring chest system, later with sliders. Often these stop valves were restricted to the bass, so that the treble was kept as a large mixture block. In other instances, the treble had its own stop knob, and thus the rank was divided into bass and treble halves. Finally, the stop mechanisms could extend from bass to treble in the customary way.

In the early Renaissance, only one stop type was used, the Principals, arranged in ranks as they were in the organ of the Middle Ages. The octaves and fifths were arranged in consecutive order, with the exception of the low fifth ranks ($10^2/_3'$ and $5^1/_3'$) and possibly of single very high fifth or octave ranks.

The organ built for the Cathedral of Milan in 1508 (by Leonardo da Salisburgo) exemplified this type and had the following specification:

1. Tenore	Principal 8′
2. Octava	Octave 4′
3. Duodecima	Quint $2^2/_3'$
4. Quintadecima	Octave 2′
5. Decima nona	Quint $1^1/_3'$
6. Vigesima seconda	Octave 1′
7. Vigesima sesta	Quint $^2/_3'$
8. Vigesima nona	Octave $^1/_2'$

Organs of this Principal-chorus type were still being constructed at the beginning of the eighteenth century. However, the first flutes appeared in Italian specifications at the close of the fifteenth century. These were open, cylindrical stops with wide Principal scale and had a moderate intensity.

In regard to reed stops, they began to gain acceptance near the middle of the sixteenth century, usually as regal types of a rather subdued character. Nevertheless, many organs were not equipped with reeds, because the character of these stops did not harmonize with the liturgical point of view, which more or less consciously differentiated between a sacred and a secular tonal world. At some places, there even was a specific ban prescribed by the Ambrosian Ceremonial on the use of musical instruments other than the organ within the walls of the church. Wind instruments were considered to be secular, and, logically, this would also be true of the reeds of the organ.

This point of view may be traced all the way to the nineteenth century; and since the Italian organ, on the whole, has retained its ascetic character and tonal traditions in spite of developments in the remainder of Europe, this tradition was undoubtedly guided by a very definite opinion concerning what would best serve the Church and its ritual. In reality, a similar point of view also dominated the organ of the middle Ages and prolonged the tradition, but Italy was the only place where this tradition survived the Renaissance.

The vocal character of the Italian organ is frequently mentioned, and if the difference between the sacred and secular tonal world must be more specifically defined, this can be done most effectively by placing the vocal as a contrast to the instrumental.

The old Italian organ sings. The stops have been voiced with a low wind pressure (frequently 40 mm. Water Column), and in addition, the wind openings of the pipe feet are narrowed. The timbre is soft and round with a faint touch of sharpness (especially in the treble where the scales are usually narrow).

In this connection the attention must be drawn to the fact that nicks had already been employed in the fifteenth century in order to avoid inharmonics and other secondary sounds at the attack. Some written evidence has been preserved to prove the originality of these nicks and to explain their intention.

Furthermore, the old Italian organ often has an odd placement of the pipe boards (i. e. the boards supporting the pipes, not to be confused with the top boards). In all other countries these boards are placed a little below the mouths, but in Italy they are placed about 20 cms. above the mouths. This is awkward and troublesome (many of the small treble pipes must be equipped with lengthened feet), and of course this practice is restricted to open and cylindrical pipes. Undoubtedly, this peculiarity has tonal purposes: a further subdual of inharmonics and wind noise from the mouths, and a separation of the vibrations from the upper pipe openings and those at the pipe mouths.

The Principale 8′ is occasionally called *Tenore,* as a definite parallel to the tenor part in vocal polyphony, the fixed line over which the other voices are constructed. The vocal character is also met in the Italian speciality named *Fiffaro;* it is an open cylindrical 8′ flute which is tuned "in beats" with the Tenore, so that a full sound and a light vibrato are produced. In his short treatise *l'Arte organica* (1608), Costanzo Antegnati writes that this combination 'is often called "voce umana", and correctly, because of its soft song.'

Costanzo Antegnati, the fourth generation in the famous organ builder dynasty which functioned in northern Italy from the close of the fifteenth century until the middle of the seventeenth century, has given us much valuable information concerning the organs built by his family and the use of them. He designates the old Cathedral organ in Brescia, built in 1536 by his paternal uncle Gian Giacomo Antegnati, as their best instrument and gives the specification:

1. Principale tutto intiero	Principal 16′ (full manual compass)
2. Principale spezzato	Principal 16′ (a divided stop; the bass half is connected to the pedal instead of the manual keys.)
3. Ottaua	Octave 8′
4. Quintadecima	Octave 4′
5. Decima nona	Quint $2^{2}/_{3}'$
6. Vigesima seconda	Octave 2′
7. Vigesima sesta	Quint $1^{1}/_{3}'$
8. Vigesima nona	Octave 1′
9. Trigesima terza	Quint $^{2}/_{3}'$
10. Un'altra vigesima seconda (larga)	Octave 2′
11. Flauto in quinta decima	Flöte 4′
12. Flauto in ottaua	Flöte 8′
Tremolo	Tremolo

Beside the Principal ranks, it will be noted that this organ has two flute stops, one 8′ and one 4′, and an extra 2′ stop, presumably of wider scale. In another place, Antegnati mentions the *Flauto in duodecima* (Quintflöte $2^{2}/_{3}'$), and when we add the *Fiffaro* to this group, we have named the stops which constituted the Antegnati organs.

The repetitions of the high ranks will be evident from the following specification for the Antegnati organ which is still standing in S. Giuseppe, Brescia (built in 1581):

1. Principale	16′	bass		
2. Principale	16′	soprano		
3. Ottaua	8′			
4. Decima quinta	4′			
5. Decima nona	$2^{2}/_{3}'$	from c#″,	$5^{1}/_{3}'$	
6. Vigesima seconda	2′	from c#″,	4′	
7. Vigesima sesta	$1^{1}/_{3}'$	from c″,	$2^{2}/_{3}'$	
8. Vigesima nona	1′	from c′,	2′;	from c″, 4′
9. Trigesima terza	$^{2}/_{3}'$	from c′,	$1^{1}/_{3}'$;	from c″, $2^{2}/_{3}'$
10. Flauto in quintadecima	2′			
11. Flauto in duodecima	$2^{2}/_{3}'$			
12. Flauto in ottaua	4′			
13. Fiffaro (voce umana)	8′			

In considering the details pertaining to this organ, it should be noted that the manual compass, C–a‴, is unusually large (however, not by Italian standards). The organ is constructed with spring chests, and the wind pressure is 45 mm. Water Column. The tuning is 1 HT above our present pitch. In the manual stops, the pipe material is lead with a very small amount of tin and antimony. The Principale 16′ in the pedal has wooden pipes.

Besides, the spring chest is common in the Italian organs, and several of the Italian aids to registration are based on the stop action of the spring chest, such as toe levers for a plenum registration and for ranks whose stop knobs have been pulled 1/4 turn (a kind of a free combination). Such devices were useful in an organ with only one manual Werk.

The problem of reeds is not mentioned in *l'Arte organica.* Although reeds were certainly a matter of current interest, the issue apparently conflicted with the principles of the Antegnatis. There are accounts concerning the replacement of reed stops with fluework during rebuilding, and discussions referring to the additions of reed stops, but not a single example of original reed stops is known in the Antegnati organs. This family simply refused to supply reeds. The reason cannot have been hidebound conservatism, since they made many innovations in other areas. They were the first to use the Principale 16′ divided between manual and pedal, and although there was just one manual, the performance of *dialoghi* was possible because of their bass-treble division of the stops.

The pedal played a very modest role in the Italian organ. It was coupled to the manual, and the conventional compass was very small (at first, only 3 or 5 keys; somewhat later, 9 keys (F–d)). The usual manual compass was F–f‴ (often omitting F and G). The fact that F was the lowest pitch resulted in the 8′ stop being designated as a 6′; similarly, 16′ and 32′ were indicated as 12′ and 24′ respectively.

An independent pedal stop was a great rarity. The pedal was used mainly for organ point effects, and indeed it was poorly suited to any other purpose. However, Antegnati's divided Principal could, according to his instructions, be used with the 8′ Flute, thus permitting a flute solo in the bass of the manual and a Principal solo in the pedal, as well as both stops together in the treble of the manual. A duo could be performed in this way.

Costanzo Antegnati presents his instructions for registration under 12 headings. These instructions refer to the previously mentioned specification for the old Cathedral organ at Brescia, but they are universally valid in relation to this type of organ and are consistent with directions from other sources. In other words, a common tradition of registration is presented here.

(1). A *Pleno* or *Ripieno* registration, consisting of stops 1–3–4–5–6–7–8–9, is used for the prelude, the introit, the "Deo gratias", and at similar places in the service. One 16′ Principal, the flutes, and the wide 2′ stop are omitted; without these stops, the sound is "more alive, sparkling, and pleasant".

(2) A *mezzo ripieno* (half ripieno) is produced with the following stops: Principale 16′, Ottaua 8′, Vigesima nona 1′, Trigesima terza $^2/_3$′, and Flauto in ottaua 8′.

The following combinations are suggested for ensemble playing:

(3) Principale 16′, Ottaua 8′, Flauto in ottaua 8′.

(4) Principale 16′, Flauto in ottaua 8′.

(5) Ottaua 8′, Decima nona $2^2/_3$′. If the Flauto in ottaua 8′ and Ottaua 2′ are added, the result is an imitation of the Cornet.

(6) Ottaua 8′ and Flauto in ottaua 8′. Usable for coloraturas ("diminutions") and "Canzoni alla francese".

(7) The same registration with tremolo. To be used only in slow movements and never for coloraturas.

(8) Principale 16′ alone. The sound is quite "delicatissimo" and is employed during the Elevation in the High Mass.

(9) Both 16′ Principales.

(10) Flauto in ottaua 8′ alone.

(11) Flauto in ottaua 8′ and the divided Principale 16′. The peculiar function of the latter is explained above, and this registration makes possible a duet effect.

(12) Principale 16′ and Flauto in quintadecima 4′, perhaps with Ottaua 8′; a good combination for coloraturas.

Few instructions are given concerning the application of these registrations, but frequent changes of registration during the performance and in agreement with the character of the composition were emphasized as an essential effect.

We find an interesting manifestation of this principle in Girolamo Diruta's directions for registration in "Il Transilvano" II (1609). He attempts to underscore the qualities of the various church modes with corresponding tonal colours. For instance, he assigns the Ottaua 8′ with

Tremolo to the somewhat heavy Mode II, and Ottaua 8′, Quintadecima 4′, and Vigesima seconda 2′ to the gay character of Mode VII.

Voce umana (Fiffaro plus Ottaua 8′) was used in slow movements with sustained chords, and Ottaua 8′ and Decima nona 2²/₃′ in coloraturas and more animated movements. Ottaua 8′ and Flauto in quintadecima 4′, or Ottaua 8′ and Decima nona 2²/₃′ (possibly with the Quintadecima 4′ added) could be used beside the sixth Antegnati registration for "Canzoni alla francese".

As a complement to this liturgical-ascetic trend, a more secular one was also developing in the latter half of the sixteenth century among the organ builders in Italy, mostly represented by foreign masters working there. One of these was the Flemish Vincenzo Fulgentio (or Fulgenzi), who completed an organ in 1596 built on a Principale 24′; of the 26 stops, only 12 belonged to the Principal group. The remaining stops were these: *Flauto, Flauto a camino* (= Rohrflöte), *Flauto traverso, Ciamballetti* (= Cymbal), various reeds, and, of course, the cuckoo and nightingale imitations. In more moderate cases, the "secular" section was comprised of reeds only. Toward the middle of the seventeenth century, the foreign masters attained more freedom for the development of their ideas. Their large instruments had two or three manuals and several independent bass stops in the pedal. In these organs, worldly "curiosities" were represented to a degree rarely seen in other places. Beside the cuckoo and nightingale, which were almost obligatory, there were imitations of drums and animal voices, and naturally there was also a *Glockenspiel.*

However, not all churches surrendered to the foreigners. The "Ambrosian" line survived, and as late as 1908, two organs for the Cathedral of Milan were built without reed stops; this tradition was not ignored until the last rebuild in 1938. If we examine the specification of the organ completed by the brothers Serassi in 1842 (also in Milan), the basic features of the old Italian organ are easily discerned. The ripieno principle is maintained, and only string stops, gedackts and third-sounding stops have been added. The specification follows:

Manual.

1. Principal 16′	divided in bass and treble. Treble doubled.
2. Principal 8′–I	" " " " "
3. Principal 8′–II	" " " " "
4. Principal 8′–III	treble only

5. Violon 8′	divided in bass and treble
6. Flute 8′	divided in bass and treble
7. Gedacht 8′	" " " " "
8. Octave 4′–I	
9. Octave 4′–II	" " " " "
10. Octave 4′–III	treble only
11. Viola 4′	divided in bass and treble
12. Traverse flute 4′	
13. Quint $2^2/_3{}'$	
14. Octave 2′–I	
15. Octave 2′–II	
16. Flautino 2′	
17. Quartian $1^1/_3{}'$ $1^1/_3{}'$ $1'$ $1'$ $^2/_3{}'$ $^1/_2{}'$	
18. Terzian $1^3/_5{}'$ $^4/_5{}'$ $^2/_5{}'$ $^1/_3{}'$ $^1/_4{}'$ $^1/_4{}'$	
19. Mixture 4 rank	
20. Mixture 3 rank	
21. Cornet 5 rank	
22. Cornettino 4 rank	
23. Horn	not reeds
24. Vox humana	not reeds

Pedal

25. Contrabas 16′
26. Principal 16′
27. Oktav 8′
28. Principal 8′

As late as about 1960, when the Antegnati organ in S. Guiseppe, Brescia, was being restored, a seventy-year-old man, educated in the old tradition, was still at work – the organ builder Macarinelli. The old tradition had continued unbroken until then.

While the one-manual Italian organ seems rather Spartan to our concepts, we must remember that there were often two or more organs in the same church. In large churches, the archways between the choir and the aisles were adequate for containing instruments of considerable size. Here, at the liturgical centre of the church, it was customary to have two organs: one on the north side (the "gospel" side) and one on the south side (the "epistle" side). The backs of these organs bordered the aisles, and for this reason, they were also provided with front pipes and the appropriate accessories.

Since the close of the sixteenth century, the organs in the Cathedral of Milan had been arranged in this way; in 1578, the Antegnati organ (built in 1550) was moved to the gospel side. This organ was constructed on a 24′ Principale with a Ripieno of 11 ranks as well as an 8′ Flauto. In 1610, an instrument with the same appearance was completed for the epistle side. It was built by Cristoforo Valvassori and contained 9 Principal ranks, also based on a 24′ Principale, as well as an 8′ and a 4′ Flauto.

Apart from an enlargement of this organ in 1699, the two instruments were essentially unchanged until the building of the above mentioned Serassi organ in 1842 (replacing the north organ). A rebuild of the south organ was undertaken in 1854. The rebuilt instrument had two manual Werks, *Prima tastiera* and *Seconda tastiera,* but no pedal (Pedaliera). There was only a pull-down pedal. The specification was the usual ripieno type without reed stops.

The large organ, built in 1938, has a total of 169 stops, 11 transmissions, and 23 octave couplers. This very large instrument is composed of five manuals plus pedal and is erected in seven different units. The stops of the Prima tastiera occupy the two old organ cases. Altogether there are 39 reeds, many of which are high pressure stops, and, on the whole, the instrument has a distinctly orchestral character.

It is astonishing that Italy (and also the greater part of the Catholic Church in other countries) has surrendered to this organ type which is the antithesis of the old Italian, liturgical organ and the traditions of the Middle Ages. A few voices have been raised against this trend and have asserted that the Catholic Church should also have an "organ reform movement" in an effort to arrive at a more honest instrument. Should this come to pass, the old organs of Italy will certainly form the point of departure.

THE NETHERLANDS

The great events in church music toward the close of the Middle Ages were concentrated in a belt which extended from Italy through southern Germany, northern France (Burgundy), the Netherlands, and terminated in England. Even though choral technique and vocal polyphony were in the foreground at that time, instrument building (especially the building of keyboard instruments) was simultaneously undergoing an intensive development, particularly in those areas where the tendencies toward musical freedom were most widespread. Here, the organ builders apparently had "breathed the fresh air" and taken the opportunity to develop all of the new and plentiful prospects offered by their materials – prospects for which the Italian church had only little interest.

The approaching of the Renaissance and the Reformation was notably perceptible within the sacred arts and in the vicinity of the Netherlands, to a greater extent than in Italy. At all events, Dutch organ building was in the lead in the considerable development that occurred at the close of the Middle Ages and throughout most of the sixteenth century.

The spring chest, which made possible the first use and elaboration of pipe ranks as independent stops, was discovered in the Netherlands during the fourteenth century, according to Praetorius. The use of the spring chest spread over the entire Continent, until it was superseded by the slider chest, approximately one century later. Though he may be in error, Praetorius also refers to the Quintatön as a Dutch discovery. But discoveries are not the reason for speaking of the leadership of the Netherlands. Of course a strongly reciprocal effect was present through the entire "belt" (Italy-England), and it would be difficult to determine the origin of the various innovations, but it seems as if all ideas coalesced and blended in the Netherlands in order that they might be dispersed again.

In practice, this was manifested in the fact that Dutch organ builders to a great extent worked in foreign countries. Particularly from the sixteenth century, there are many references to significant Dutch instruments in France, Italy, Germany, England, and even in Denmark. It is quite typical that Herman Raphael Rodensteen (or Herman Raphaëlis), who built the organ for the cathedral of Roskilde, Denmark, was later active in Franconia and Saxony.

With several branches of the Rhine flowing through the country, the Netherlands were situated on a public highway, and frequent military and political disturbances also created a constant international contact. Within the country, various mentalities, French, North and South German, Italian, and English, were to be encountered, and thus it is not surprising that the Renaissance organ of the Netherlands, in spite of its specifically national character, came to include numerous evidences of other countries.

As early as the first half of the fifteenth century, many Dutch organs were built with two manual Werks, a *Hoofdwerk* (Hauptwerk) and a

Rugwerk (Rückpositiv). The instances in which the Rugwerk was mounted as a Rückpositiv or as a Brustwerk *(Borstwerk)* would be difficult to distinguish with certainty, but either location would have been possible. According to the style of the Middle Ages, the Hoofdwerk was a block-Werk without stop valves and was occupied exclusively by Principal ranks.

In accordance with the contract, the organ constructed in 1458 for the Oude Kerk in Delft was erected in this way: a block Hoofdwerk with 16′ Prestant in the façade, 5 ranks in the bass, and 32 ranks in the treble; in addition, a Rugwerk with 3 independent stops, Prestant 4′, Fluit 4′, and Mixtuur placed "voer an die stoel" (in front of the bench, that is, the base of the organ). This may signify that it was a Rückpositiv. However, when the manual compass is stated as two octaves, the largest pipe would have been no longer than *ca.* 70 cms., and consequently the outer dimensions of the instrument were more appropriate to a Borstwerk than a Rugwerk. "Voer an die stoel" must then be construed as "at the front in the bench", and this can be just as legitimate as "in front of the bench".

The organ in the church of Our Lady, at Zwolle, was built a few years before and was of a similar size and specification. Here it is highly probable that the Positiv was a Rugwerk. In the contract it is stated that the Prestant 4′ should be double, which indicates a treble-doubling, a standing and a hanging pipe for every note (see Fig. 60) as it is often seen in the façades from that period. Consequently, the Prestant 4′ had to be placed in the front. Since the contract does not mention the manual compass, it was presumably the normal one, F–a″.

Incredibly, the Hoofdwerks in these organs were built as blocks, when the spring chest had been known for half a century. But it is still more curious that this custom concerning the Hoofdwerk was continued until the seventeenth century in the Utrecht area, and that only a half-century earlier had the surrender to the slider chest taken place in the southern and northern parts of the country, under French and German influence respectively.

During the Renaissance, the block Hoofdwerk was something particularly Dutch, and the explanation (or the consequence) was found in their unique way of enlarging the organ: partly by the Rugwerk being specially equipped with many colourful stops, and partly (as already discussed) by the institution of an entirely new Werk called the Bovenwerk (Oberwerk), because it was placed above the Hoofdwerk. While organ builders in the neighbouring countries emancipated the single Principal

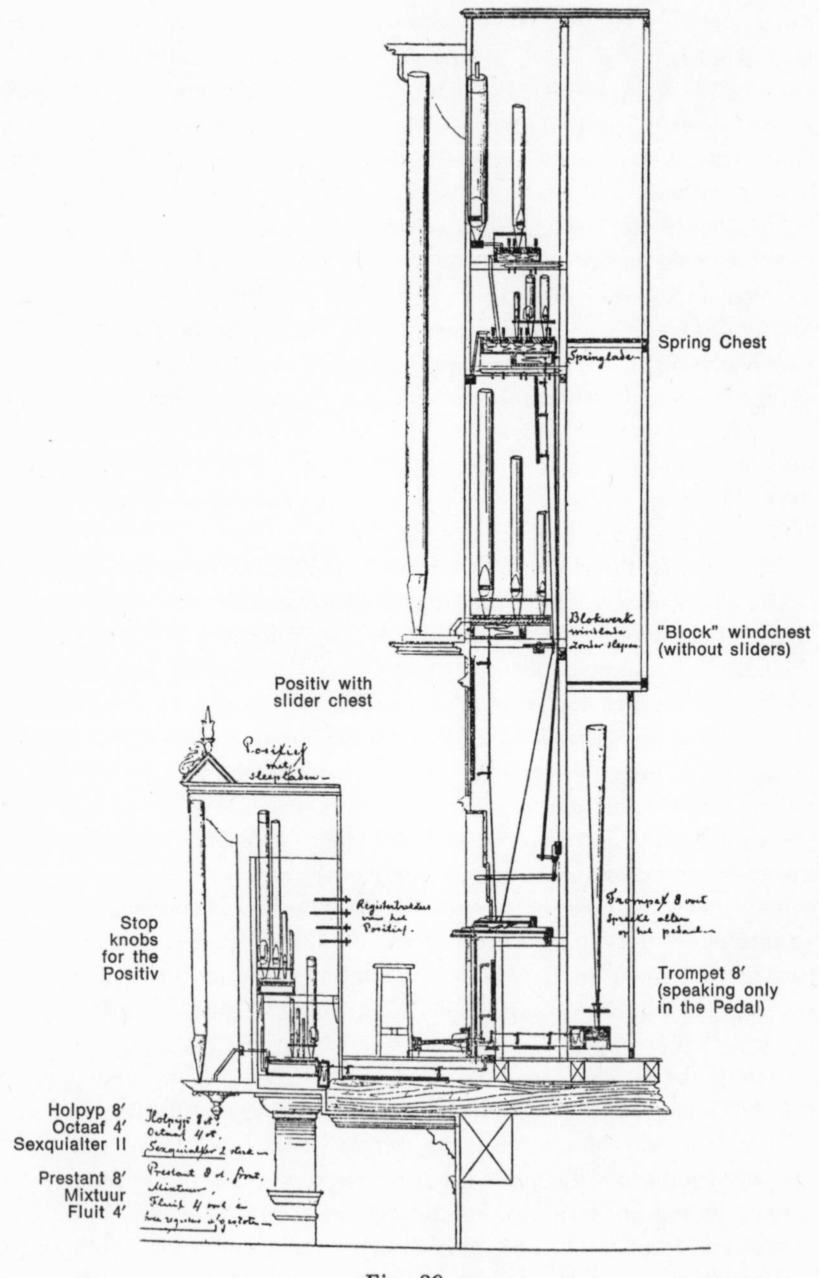
Spring Chest
Springlade
Blokwerk windlade zonder slepen
"Block" windchest (without sliders)
Positiv with slider chest
Positief met sleepladen
Registertrekkers van het Positief
Stop knobs for the Positiv
Trompet 8 voet spreekt alleen op het pedaal
Trompet 8′ (speaking only in the Pedal)
Holpyp 8′
Octaaf 4′
Sexquialter II
Prestant 8′
Mixtuur
Fluit 4′

Fig. 39.

ranks through the aid of slider chests or spring chests, and then added the flute and reed stops that they wished to use, in expanding the Hoofdwerk, the Dutch retained the Hoofdwerk as a plenum-block of Principals and placed the flute and reed stops in a supplementary and independent werk. Frequently, when an organ was to be improved, a Bovenwerk was preferred to a Rugwerk.

The extension and development from the organ of the Late Middle Ages to the Renaissance organ of the Netherlands is well illustrated by the old St. Nicolaas organ from Utrecht (Fig. 39), which has later been moved to the church of Middelburg. The oldest part of the organ, the block Werk, whose wind chest lies next above the keyboards, is believed to date from 1478 (the base is perhaps still older), and it is arranged with the Prestant 16′ in the front. The Octaaf 8′ stands farthest back on the wind chest; in front of it is the 4′ (the arrangement is incorrect in the drawing). These three stops are composed of old pipes (yet scarcely from 1478). In addition, borings are to be found in the wind chest for 16 more treble ranks and 8 bass ranks. Above the block Werk, it is possible to see the later addition, the Bovenwerk, whose wind chests have common pallets in spite of the fact that the chests are located at two levels. There are 3 plus 5 stops, and of these, the pipes have been preserved for the Roerfluit 8′, Prestant 4′, Openfluit 4′, Roerquint $2^2/_3$′, Nachthoorn 2′. The Sifflet 1′, the Tertiaan, and one reed stop are lacking. The upper intermediary compartments of the façade are made up of pipes from the Prestant 4′, and in Fig. 60, it will be seen that this stop is double, with one hanging and one standing pipe for every pitch. As appears from the drawing, the wind chests are spring chests. Until a rebuild in 1733, the Bovenwerk had its own keyboard, but at that time, it was connected to the keyboard of the Hoofdwerk.

The Rugwerk was added in 1580. Here the wind chests, which were slider chests, also lay at two levels. On the upper chest, the stops were Quintadeen 8′, Octaaf 4′, Sexquialter; on the lower chest, Prestant 8′ (in the front), Octaaf 2′, Mixtuur, Fluit 4′, Fluit 2′, and a reed stop. At the same time, an 8′ Trompet was added in the pedal. In the drawing, the Trompet appears in the base, immediately behind the keyboards.

The compass of the manuals is F–a″, but only the notes F–G–A–B♭–B are included in the lowest octave. The pedalboard has the range of C–d′ with a "short" C-octave: C–F–D–G–E–A–B♭–B. Originally, the pedal extended no farther than F, like the manuals; the expansion occurred when the Trompet 8′ was added.

In general, this small range was common Dutch practice, until north German influence led to an extension of both the bass and treble ranges, giving the manuals a compass of C–c‴, while retaining the short octave.

The Nicolaas organ has no Borstwerk. Organs with four manual Werks were great rarities during the Renaissance of the Netherlands, partly because a Rugwerk and a Borstwerk in the same organ were regarded as superfluous. The two Werks performed the same function, and the general principle was to use the Rugwerk in large organs and the Borstwerk in small ones. A combination of Hoofdwerk, Bovenwerk and Borstwerk was not unknown, but when two werks were the maximum, the Hoofdwerk and Bovenwerk were usually preferred.

Within the framework of this peculiarly Dutch pattern, numerous variants came into existence, but not as sharply differentiated types and not according to a geographical distribution. Organ builders frequently worked in foreign countries, and thus their ideas were united with local customs. But it is evident that the masters from Brabant, south of the rivers, had close contact with France and were involuntarily affected by the French mentality. And it is just as clear that the land "in between", the Overijssel, Gelderland, and Utrecht areas, must have been least influenced by foreign countries.

If we attempt to formulate some general principles, it is immediately obvious that the Brabant builders, in French style, used more reeds than the northern Dutch masters. In the Rugwerk of smaller instruments, the wider scales (and the flute character) of the reeds are often strongly represented as a contrast to the Principal character (and narrow scales) of the fluework. The Borstwerk is very rare, and the Hoofdwerk-Bovenwerk combination, with the wide scales and reeds of the Bovenwerk, is reminiscent of the French *Grand orgue*. The Pedaal was composed of single 'cantus firmus' stops; usually an 8′ reed stop and a high flue stop, but lower pitched stops could also be present.

The Groningen masters had the same predisposition as the Brabant builders for the flute character in the Rugwerk, but were somewhat more restrained with reed stops. The north German influence is evident in the Pedaal, which, in contrast to other Dutch types, has independent bass stops to supplement the cantus firmus stops. Another essential feature of the work in Groningen was the fact that the Hoofdwerk received stop valves at an early date; however, without affecting the presence of the Bovenwerk.

The Utrecht masters still insisted on the traditional block Hoofdwerk and Bovenwerk. They emphasized the Principal character in the Rugwerk, but often preferred the Borstwerk in smaller organs. The Pedaal usually had only a Trompet 8′ as an independent stop.

In Gelderland-Overijssel, there was an increasing opposition to the Bovenwerk and the block Werk, and the tendency was to combine the two Werks on a single chest with independent stops. As a result of this, the Borstwerk was frequently used, even in connection with a Rugwerk. The Pedaal was nearly always lacking in independent stops.

In general, the most distinctive feature of the sixteenth-century Dutch organ is the Bovenwerk and its concentration of wide-scaled labials and reeds with long resonators. Gradually they became a tradition in this Werk. The narrow-scaled Prestant-block of the Hoofdwerk (without reeds) and the general absence of independent bass stops in the Pedaal were also highly characteristic.

Together, these elements produce the basic character of the Netherlands Renaissance organ. A few examples of specifications will illustrate the types that have been discussed.

THE BRABANT TYPE*

Breda (1534).

Rw. Holpijp 8′
Prestant 4′
Kromhoorn 16′
Regaal 8′
Schalmei 4′

Hw. Prestant 8′
Prestant 4′
Mixtuur
Scherp

Bw. Holpijp 8′
Fluit 4′
Gemshoorn 2′
Sifflet $1^1/_3$′
Cimbel
Trompet 8′

Pd. Trompet 16′
Octaaf 8′

Bergen op Zoom (1554).

Rw. Prestant 8′
Quintadeen 8′
Roerfluit 8′
Octaaf 4′
Sifflet 1′
Mixtuur
Scherp
Schalmei 8′
Regaal 8′
Baarpijp 8′

Hw. Prestant 16′
Octaaf 8′
Mixtuur
Scherp

Bw. Prestant 8′
Holpijp 8′
Openfluit 8′
Nasard $2^2/_3$′
Gemshoorn 2′
Sifflet 1′
Cimbel
Trompet 8′
Zink 8′

Gouda (1556).

Rw. Quintadeen 8′
Principal 4′
Holpijp 2′
Cimbel
Schalmei 8′

Hw. Prestant 8′
Holpijp 8′
Octaaf 4′
Mixtuur
Scherp

Bw. Holpijp 8′
Nasard $2^2/_3$′
Nachthorn 2′
Sifflet 1′
Trompet 8′
Zink 8′

Pd. Trompet 16′
Nachthorn

* Hw. = Hoofdwerk. Rw. = Rugwerk. Bw. = Bovenwerk.

THE UTRECHT TYPE

Utrecht-Dom (1570).

Rw. Prestant 8′
Quintadeen 8′
Octaaf 4′
Superoctaaf 2′
Fluit 2′
Mixtuur
Scherp
Schalmei 8′
Touzyn 8′

Hw. Blokwerk 16′

Bw. Prestant 8′
Roerfluit 8′
Octaaf 4′
Openfluit 4′
Gemshoorn 2′
Sifflet 1′
Cimbel
Trompet 8′
Kromhoorn 8′

Pd. Trompet 8′
Touzyn 8′

Amersfoort, St. Joris (1552).

Rw. Prestant 8′
Holpijp 8′
Quintadeen 8′
Octaaf 4′
Mixtuur
Scherp
Kromhoorn 8′
Touzyn 8′

Hw. Blokwerk 16′

Bw. Prestant 8′
Roerfluit 8′
Nasard $2^{2}/_{3}'$
Gemshoorn 2′
Quint $1^{1}/_{3}'$
Sifflet 1′
Cimbel
Trompet 8′

Leiden, St. Pancras (1572).

*Bst.** Quintadeen 8′
Fluit 2′
Kromhoorn 8′
Schalmei 4′

Hw. Blokwerk 8′

Bw. Holpijp 8′
Fluit 4′
Nasard $2^{2}/_{3}'$
Gemshoorn 2′
Sifflet 1′
Trompet 8′
Zink 4′

Pd. Trompet 8′
Touzyn 8′

* Bst. = Borstwerk.

THE GRONINGEN TYPE

Groningen, St. Martini (1543).

Rw. Prestant 8′
Bordun 8′
Octaaf 4′
Fluit 4′
Nachthoorn 4′
Superoctaaf 2′
Nasard $2^{2}/_{3}'$
Fluit 2′
Sexquialter II
Mixtuur
Cimbel III
Regaal 8′
Schalmei 4′

Hw. Prestant 8′
Holpijp 8′
Quintadeen 8′
Octaaf 4′
Quint $2^{2}/_{3}'$
Superoctaaf 2′
Mixtuur IV-VI

Bw. Prestant 8′
Nachthoorn 8′
Octaaf 4′
Sexquialter II
Mixtuur IV-V
Scherp III
Trompet 8′
Vox humana 8′

Pd. Prestant 32′
Prestant 16′
Octaaf 8′
Bazuin 16′

THE GELDERLAND-OVERIJSSEL-TYPE

Nijmegen, St. Steven (1559).

Rw.	*Hw.*	*Bst.*
Prestant 8′	Prestant 16′	Quintadeen 8′
Holpijp 8′	Octaaf 8′	Superoctaaf 2′
Octaaf 4′	Octaaf 4′	Quintfluit $1^1/_3$′
Quintadeen 4′	Mixtuur	Trompet 8′
Veldfluit 2′	Scherp	
Mixtuur		
Cimbel		
Regaal 8′		

Zwolle, Broerenkerk (1556).

Hw.	*Bst.*
Quintadeen 16′	Sifflet $1^1/_3$′ or 1′
Prestant 8′	Cimbel
Holpijp 8′	Kromhoorn 8′
Octaaf 4′	Regaal 4′
Koppelfluit 4′	
Gemshoorn 2′	
Mixtuur	
Trompet 8′	

The Renaissance organ builders were numerous; there were many small workshops with a low rate of production. But instinctively we note one particular name, a noteworthy figure among those who did not produce in great quantity: the learned and widely travelled humanist, Rudolf (Huysmann) Agricola, who lived in the years 1444 - 86. In addition to his activity as a teacher of logic, he was interested in organ playing and organ building.

The organ which he built in 1479 for the St. Maarten Kerk in Groningen (incorporated as a Rugwerk in the large organ built by Andreas de Mares in 1543) confirms the fact that he was well ahead of his time. Both the Principal chorus and the flute chorus are fully developed, and a wide selection of stops is represented. Agricola's recurrent studies in Italy may well explain the fact that such a complete organ was constructed with just one manual, but on the other hand, it is evident that he had also been inspired by the organ building of other countries.

Groningen was admittedly deficient in organ builders. Far more workshops were located in the south, in Overijssel and Gelderland, and here we meet such important persons as Jacob van Bilsteyn and the Slegels. The latter family had a total of six active organ builders in five generations and produced many significant instruments both in the Netherlands and in other countries, for example, the cathedral of Osnabrück, the Liebfrauenkirche in Bremen, St. Nicolaas in Kampen, St. Stefan in Hasselt, as well as various restorations, including the Cathedral of Bremen.

The Morlet dynasty, organ builders for three generations, should also be mentioned. The organ at St. Michael in Zwolle (see specification p. 138) dates from the second generation, Jan Morlet.

Peter Jansz de Swart (1536 - 99), as well as the whole dynasty assembled round him, was rather prominent among the Utrecht masters. This company, in continual existence for six generations, was established by Master Peter (d. 1482), who built the block Werk for the previously mentioned Nicolaas organ in Utrecht and completed many other significant projects in the Utrecht area. His work was continued by his son, Geert Petersz, and by the next generation. Cornelis Geertsz, who built the organ for St. Joris, Amersfoort (see specification above), and who is believed to have built the Bovenwerk in St. Nicolaas, Utrecht. Peter Jansz de Swart was an apprentice to Cornelis Geertsz and continued the business in association with Jan Jacobsz du Lin; and their sons, Dirck Petersz and Jacob Jansz du Lin, together with the son of the latter, Jan Jacobsz du Lin (II), carried on the work until the death of Jan Jacobsz du Lin in 1632. It is no overstatement that the most characteristic art of organ building in the Netherlands has been associated with these masters; they maintained the time-honoured tradition for a very long time. Among the organs built by Peter Jansz, the specifications have already been given for the Cathedral of Utrecht and for St. Pancras, Leyden; in addition, the following restorations ought to be mentioned: Oude Kerk, Amsterdam; Our Lady, Amersfoort; St. Bavo, Haarlem; St. Maarten, Zaltbommel; and St. Vitus, Naarden.

The brilliant period concluded with Peter Jansz. The Reformation had also contributed to changing the picture, and the next generation and Jan Jacobsz du Lin II were mainly engaged for rebuilds and repairs. There were no large, new instruments in these years.

By far the largest number of builders and also most of the famous names, were living south of the rivers. This group included the van Elen family (Maastricht), the Zwits (or Sweyss) family, Daniel van der Distelen, Jan van Gennart (Antwerpen), the Mors family (Antwerpen), and above all, the three Nijhoff (or Niehoff; most of the old family names have alternate spellings) brothers who began their business in Amsterdam, but later moved to s'Hertogenbosch. Hendrik Nijhoff's son, Nicolaas Hendriksz, and his grandson, Jacob Nijhoff, carried on the craft.

Among their most outstanding instruments, particular attention should be directed to Oude Kerk, Amsterdam (1539 - 42); Oude Kerk, Delft (1545); St. Lievensmonster, Zirikzee (1548 - 49); St. Petri, Hamburg (rebuild, 1548 - 51); St. Johannis, Lüneburg (1551 - 52); St. Gertrui, Bergen op Zoom (1554 - 55); St. Jan, Gouda (1556 - 58); the Cathedral of Köln (1569 - 73) and the Cathedral of Würzburg (1616 - 18).

Some of the organ builders entirely transferred their activity to foreign countries. Flemish organ builders, as already stated, were working in Italy. They were also known in Paris, but it was exceptional for builders from the northern regions to come so far south. Herman Raphaëlis has already been discussed. Andreas de Mare confined himself to the northern and western parts of Germany and built instruments in St. Ludgeri, Norden (1567); St. Stephan, Bremen; and the Marktkirche, Hannover. Johannes Gottschalk and Gottschalk Burkert Johanson settled in Husum, and one of their instruments was the large new organ for St. Petri in Lübeck (1587 - 91). Julius Anthonius Friese constructed an organ for the Marienkirche in Danzig (1583 - 85). Gregorius Vogel (d. 1549) built organs for St. Johannis, Magdeburg; St. Martin and St. Aegidius, Brunswick; St. Nicolai and St. Katharina, Hamburg. Finally, Fabian Petersen van Sneek may be traced to Rostock. He built instruments for St. Georg, Parchim; St. Maria, Wismar, and St. Johannes, Malchin.

With these brief references, we have only sketched the energy displayed by Dutch organ builders during the Renaissance. For a qualitative evaluation of their achievement, the development of the specifications may give an impression of the monumental work created in the century prior to the Reformation of the Netherlands.

The evaluation of this development from an ecclesiastical point of view might appear in a different light. To be sure, humanism was certainly responsible for many actions at that time, and a certain liberation in a secular direction actually resulted. Many of the large organs were undeniable expressions of civic pride, because they were paid for by civic funds (at least in part), and they were the objects of civic rivalry with neighbouring towns. It is also undeniable that much of the music played on these organs was secular in origin, so secular that the actual performances on the large instruments had to take place before and after the church services. The organ and its resources had apparently stunned the unsuspecting churches. In any case, the churches were slow to understand the use of these resources.

Even before the Calvinistic Reformation (1566), the church had reacted against the unholy "organ-ostentation", and as expected the iconoclasm in the years after that included the organs. Much was spoiled, but all in all the large organs came through it. The Rugwerks suffered most; they were easily accessible and within the reach of every vandal. In addition there was the fact that the large organs, after all, were the pride of the citizens, paid for with their own money and within a period which was not too remote for them to recall.

When these affairs had calmed down and the organs had been repaired, the "concerts" before and after the church service were resumed, at the initiative of the citizens, and this slowly re-established the organ in the church and its service.

In this way, Sweelinck played the organ back to the church again, but it was hard work. Even a score of years after his death, the matter was bitterly disputed; thus it would seem that his choral variations had not been completely convincing.

These were also bad years for the organ builders. The important commissions had to be sought in foreign countries, but this very circumstance activated the contact with north Germany which later proved to be so fruitful. In foreign countries, the local traditions had to be followed, at least with regard to specifications, as is evident from the immense organ for the Petrikirche in Lübeck built by Johannes Gottschalk and Gottschalk Burkert Johanson (1587 - 91).

Hauptwerck	*Rückpositiv*	*Brustwerck*	*Pedal*
Bordun 32′	Principal 8′	Gedackt 8′	Principal 32′
Principal 16′	Quintadena 8′	Offenflöte 4′	Blockflöte 16′
Gross Octave 8′	Gedackt 8′	Quintadena 4′	Gedacktbass 16′
Gedackt 8′	Octave 4′	Sedecima 2′	Decembas 10²/₃′
Spillpipe 8′	Querpipe 4′	Sifelit 1′	Superoctav 8′
Klein Octave 4′	Blockflöte 4′	Scharff Regal	Mixtur
Klein Spillpipe 4′	Superoctave 2′	Harffen Regal	Posaune 16′
Rauschquint 2⅔′-2′	Feldpipe 2′	Geigen Regal	Dusanbass 16′
Superoctave 2′	Gemshorn 2′		Cornetbass 8′
Mixtur	Mixtur		Schalmeyenbass (4′?)
Scharffzimbel	Cimbel		
Feldtrommeten 16′	Trommeten 8′		
	Baerpipen 8′		
	Krumbhörner 8′		

At the middle of the seventeenth century, the organ regained a minor role in the Dutch church service. Another half-century had to pass, before the instrument came into general use for the accompaniment of congregational singing and for other "Protestant" functions.

This does not mean that the building of new organs had come to a standstill. Very impressive instruments were still being constructed; among them, the famous organ at St. Laurens in Alkmaar. Levinus Eekman began to work on this organ in 1639, and after his death it was completed by Jacobus Galtus van Hagenbeer (1645). Obviously, this organ was created in a period of transition. There was some evidence of new ideas, but the basic concept was rooted in the old traditions of the Netherlands. Two subsemitones (divided keys, g♯–a♭, d♯–e♭) were provided in each octave, and the keyboard of the Hoofdwerk was extended to F in the bass with the tones F, G, A, B♭, B. The specification was thus:

Hoofdwerk	*Rugwerk*	*Bovenwerk*	*Pedaal*
Prestant 16′	Prestant 8′	Borduen 16′	Prestant 8′
Prestant 8′	Quintadeen 8′	Prestant 8′	Octaaf 4′
Octaaf 4′	Octaaf 4′	Holpijp 8′	Trompet 8′
Tertiaan	Fluit 4′	Quintadeen 8′	
Mixtuer	Superoctaaf 2′	Octaaf 4′	
Scherp	Fluit 2′	Opene Fluit 4′	
Groot Scherp	Nasat $1^1/_3$′	Echo Holfluit 4,	
Trompet 8′	Quintanus $1^1/_3$′	Superoctaaf 2′	
	Sexquialter	Nasat $1^1/_3$′	
	Sufflet 1′	Gemshorn $1^1/_3$′	
	Tertie	Sexquialter	
	Mixtuur III-IV	Tertie	
	Scherp IV	Schuiflet 1′	
	Trompet 8′	Trompet 8′	
		Vox humana 4′	

New problems were now brought to the fore, and the earlier, polyphonically determined organ was not a satisfactory instrument for the performance of increasingly homophonic music. In the treble, the solo stop was not clear enough; another balance had to be created. Furthermore, a change of tonal ideal had occurred in the course of the seventeenth century, a departure from the "lieblichkeit" described by Praetorius (1618-19). The emphasis favoured a massive, weighty quality of sound.

Until this time, the third-sounding stops had been used in the Cymbal only, but now they began to appear in the non-repeating Cornets, in the Sexquialter, and in the Tertiaan. These thirds were specifically intended for strengthening the treble and for solo use, in the French manner. Reed stops made their appearance in the Hoofdwerk, and the Pedaal received independent bass stops that could provide a tonal base. An example of this trend is the organ in the Westerkerk, Amsterdam, completed in 1686.

Hoofdwerk	*Rugwerk*	*Bovenwerk*	*Pedaal*
Prestant 16′	Prestant 8′	Prestant 8′	Borduen 16′
Prestant 8′	Holpijp 8′	Fluit 8′	Prestant 8′
Quintadena 8′	Quintadena 8′	Baarpijp 8′	Octaaf 4′
Octaaf 4′	Octaaf 4′	Quintadena 8′	Quint $5^1/_3$′
Fluit 4′	Fluit 4′	Octaaf 4′	Bazuin 16′
Octaaf 2′	Octaaf 2′	Woutfluit 2′	Trompet 8′
Cornet	Siflet $1^1/_3$′	Ruyschpijp	
Mixtuur	Mixtuur	Tertiaan	
Scherp	Scherp	Quint $1^1/_3$′	
Trompet	Sexquialtera	Vox humana 8′	
	Cornet		
	Trompet 8′		

The German influence was not long in assuming a more personal character. The Lutheran circles understood the purpose of an organ far better than the Calvinists, and in Germany there was ample opportunity to witness the manner in which the art of organ building flourished as a result of this new demand. Arp Schnitger, the German master, was contracted for a comprehensive rebuild of the organ in St. Maarten, Groningen, the organ for which Agricola had laid the foundation.

It was finished in 1692, and with that a beginning was made for a significant invasion of both organs and organ builders. Schnitger himself did not manage to build many instruments in the Netherlands, but in 1721, barely two years after his death, his sons, Johann Georg and Franz Caspar, completed the work on the large new organ for the Michaëlis Kerk in Zwolle, and in 1725 followed a general rebuild and modernization of the large, previously mentioned Alkmaar organ.

To the Schnitger "school" belonged his foreman, A. A. Hinsch, and Christian Müller; the latter became the master for the great organs in Leuwarden and St. Bavo, Haarlem. Christian Vatter, who constructed the organ for Oude Kerk in Amsterdam in 1726, should also be mentioned in this connection.

The Schnitger-school organ type will later be discussed in detail. Only a few specifications will be given here for the purpose of illustrating the Schnitger organs in the Netherlands.

THE CHURCH OF ST. MARTIN, GRONINGEN

Hoofdwerk	*Rugwerk*	*Bovenwerk*	*Pedaal*
Quintadena 16′	Prestant 8′	Prestant 8′	Prestant 32′
Prestant 8′	Gedackt 8′	Holfluit 8′	Prestant 16′
Borduen 8′	Quintadena 8′	Octaaf 4′	Octaaf 8′
Octaaf 4′	Octaaf 4′	Nasat 2²/₃′	Gedackt 8′
Spelfluit 4′	Octaaf 2′	Sexquialter	Octaaf 4′
Octaaf 2′	Tertian	Mixtuur IV	Octaaf 2′
Fluit 2′	Cornet III	Trompet 16′	Nachthorn 2′
Ged.quint 2²/₃′	Mixtuur IV-VI	Vox humana 8′	Mixtuur IV
Nasat 2²/₃′	Scherp IV		Bazuin 16′
Sexquialter	Trompet 8′		Trompet 8′
Mixtuur VI	Viola di Gamba 8′		Cornet 4′
Cimbel III			Cornet 2′
Basson 16′			
Schalmey 8′			

THE CHURCH OF ST. MICHAEL, ZWOLLE

Hoofdwerk	*Rugwerk*	*Borstwerk*	*Bovenwerk*	*Pedaal*
Prestant 16′	Prestant 8′	Fluitlieflyk 8′	Prestant 8′	Subbas 16′
Quintadena 16′	Holpijp 8′	Prestant 4′	Gedackt 8′	Roerquint 10²/₃′
Octaaf 8′	Fluitdous 8′	Roerfluit 4′	Octaaf 4′	Prestant 16′
Roerfluit 8′	Octaaf 4′	Prestant 2′	Holfluit 4′	Octaaf 8′
Octaaf 4′	Fluit 4′	Flachfluit 2′	Superoctaaf 2′	Octaaf 4′
Spelfluit 4′	Quintfluit 2²/₃′	Gemshoorn 2′	Woudfluit 2′	Ruyspijp 2²/₃′
Principal 2′	Octaaf 2′	Spelfluit 2²/₃′	Prestantq. 5¹/₃′	Mixtuur VIII
Nasat 2²/₃′	Sexquialter II	Quint 1¹/₃′	Quint 2²/₃′	Fagott 32′
Ruyspijp II	Scherp IV	Sexquialter II	Siflet 1¹/₃′	Bazuin 16′
Mixtuur VI	Cimbel III	Mixtuur IV	Tertiaan II	Trompet 8′
Cimbel III	Fagott 16′	Dulciaan 8′	Scherp IV-VI	Trompet 4′
Trompet 16′	Hautbois 8′	Kromhoorn 8′	Gamba 8′ (ling.)	Cornet 2′
Trompet 8′			Trompet 4′	
Vox humana 8′				

The Alkmaar organ had the following specification after being rebuilt by Franz Caspar Schnitger (1725):

Hoofdwerk	*Rugwerk*	*Bovenwerk*	*Pedaal*
Prestant 16′	Prestant 8′	Prestant 8′	Prestant 32′ (fra F)
Prestant 8′	Quintadena 8′	Baarpijp 8′	Prestant 16′
Quint $5^1/_3$′	Octaaf 4′	Roerfluit 8′	Roerquint $10^2/_3$′
Octaaf 4′	Fluit 4′	Quintadena 8′	Octaaf 8′
Quint $2^2/_3$′	Nasat $2^2/_3$′	Octaaf 4′	Quint $5^1/_3$′
Principal 2′	Quintfluit $2^2/_3$′	Fluitdous 4′	Octaaf 4′
Flachfluit 2′	Superoctaaf 2′	Spelfluit $2^2/_3$′	Nachthoorn 2′
Tertiaan II	Waldfluit 2′	Superoctaaf 2′	Rauschpijp III
Rauschpijp II	Quintanus $1^1/_3$′	Spitsfluit 2′	Mixtuur VI-VIII
Mixtuur VI	Sexquialtera II	Sexquialtera II	Bazuin 16′
Trompet 16′	Mixtuur V-VI	Cimbel III	Trompet 8′
Gamba 8′ (ling.)	Cimbel III	Scherp IV	Trompet 4′
Trompet 4′	Fagot 8′	Trompet 8′	Cornet 2′
	Tregter Regaal 8′	Hautbois 8′	
	Vox humana 8′	Vox humana 8′	

The North German influence did not extend beyond the areas touched by the Reformed Church. This means that it did not go south of the rivers; the old tradition survived there, yet with a steadily growing inclination toward the French ideas.

This is best illustrated by the large organ for St. Jan, s'Hertogenbosch, which was built at approximately the same time as the rebuild of the Alkmaar organ. The principles are the same as in the original Alkmaar specification (p. 136), although the third-sounding stops are more typical of French custom. In some way, this is also true of the pedal specification. The keyboard of the Hoofdwerk extends to Contra-F.

HERZOGENBOSCH, ST. JAN

Hoofdwerk	*Rugwerk*	*Bovenwerk*	*Pedaal*
Principal 16′	Principal 8′	Bourdon 16′	Bourdon 8′
Octaaf 8′	Gedackt 8′	Principal 8′	Bazuin 16′
Superoctaaf 4′	Quintadena 8′	Holpijp 8′	Trompet 8′
Quint $2^2/_3$′	Octaaf 4′	Quintadena 8′	
Mixtuur VIII-XIV	Fluit 4′	Octaaf 4′	
Scherp VII-X	Octaaf 2′	Quint $2^2/_3$′	
Trompet 8′ (bass)	Quint $1^1/_3$′	Octaaf 2′	
	Mixtuur V-VIII	Sexquialter II	
	Scherp III	Cimbel III	
	Sexquialter II	Tertiaan II	
	Cornet V (treble)	Cornet IV (treble)	
	Trompet 8′	Trompet 16′	
	Dulciaan 8′	Trompet 8′	
		Vox humana 8′	

The line of demarcation which the Reformation placed in the Netherlands organ building has not been obliterated, and the primary effect of this line was the gradual erasure of the distinctively Dutch character. We see this most clearly in the pedal specifications; the northern part of the country followed the North European conventions, and the southern part followed France. In the north, there was a quick transfer to the large bass and canto solo pedal; in the south, just as in France, organ builders retained the small canto solo pedal, until Cavaillé-Coll brought forth new points of view in the nineteenth century.

Although the Dutch lost their position of leadership, and though the northern and southern districts had each entered into larger entities, it would be wrong to consider this as a decadence. A new demand arose, and a change of style occurred, but the quality remained unaffected.

FRANCE

The wind chest with stop valves was invented by the Dutch, but almost paradoxically, the Dutch retained the block wind chest for the longest period, nearly a century longer than the neighbouring countries.

In France, the new techniques for liberating single stops in the *Grand orgue* were promptly exploited, and then this Werk could reasonably be enlarged with flute and reed stops, the supplement which the Dutch preferred to install as a Bovenwerk.

Most of the French organs in the sixteenth and seventeenth centuries had only two manual Werks, *Grand orgue* and *Positif,* and a pedalboard, coupled to the Grand orgue. The pedal attained its first independent stops in the course of the sixteenth century. At that time French organ building was strongly influenced by the Netherlands to the north, but other foreign organ builders were also working in France – Germans, Italians, Spaniards and Englishmen. Several organs were built, especially for the large cathedrals, but most of these instruments have been lost. Only the façades remain – in radically altered forms.

The organ at Gisors, which is probably of Flemish origin, was built in 1580 and may serve as an example of the influence from the north:

Grand orgue	*Positif*	*Pédale*
Montre 16′	Bourdon 8′	Montre 8′
Montre 8′	Bourdon 4′	Saqueboute 8′
Bourdon 8′	Doublette 2′	
Prestant 4′	Larigot $1^1/_3$′	
Flûte 4′	Cimbale II	
Nazardquinte $2^2/_3$′	Cromorne 8′	
Doublette 2′		
Quintflûte $1^1/_3$′		
Fourniture IV		
Cymbale III		
Cornet		
Trompette 8′		
Voix humaine 8′		
Clairon 4′		

The Grand orgue is strongly characterized by the three reeds and by the tierce in the Cornet; the Positif is dominated by flutes and wide scales in general. The pedal reed, Saqueboute, extends to Contra-F and should be referred to as a 12′ stop.

The Dutch-German form of Brustwerk never achieved actual acceptance in France, but something similar is found in the so-called *Echo.* This division was designed for solo use and therefore included only the two upper octaves of the keyboard. The Echo was placed immediately behind the keyboards in the base of the Grand orgue, but it was not equipped with openings toward the nave of the church. Often it was even enclosed in a box in order to reinforce the echo effect. In the beginning, it consisted only of a 5- or 6-rank Cornet, and consequently, it was a miniature block Werk. This is true in the specification for a rebuilding of the organ in the Augustine Cloister in Paris (1586):

Grand orgue	*Positif*	*Echo*
Montre 8′	Bourdon 8′	Cornet VI
Bourdon 8′	Prestant 4′	
Prestant 4′	Flûte 4′	*Pédale*
Nazard $1^1/_3$′	Fourniture	
Flageolet 1′	Cromorne 8′	Sacqueboute
Fourniture		
Cimbale		
Trompette 8′		
Clairon 4′		

In this instance, the Echo Cornet was connected to the keyboard of the Grand orgue, but later, this Cornet was usually provided with its own manual.

Normally, the Cornet and the tierce-sounding stops that came into use at this time were incorporated in the Grand orgue. For example the St. Gervais organ in Paris, built in 1601 by Langhedul, the Brabantine, originally had the following specification:

Grand orgue	*Positif*	*Pédale*
Montre 16′	Bourdon 8′	Flûte 8′
Montre 8′	Prestant 4′	
Bourdon 8′	Doublette 2′	
Flûte ouverte 4′	Flageolet 1′	
Flûte bouchée 4′	Fourniture III	
Doublette 2′	Cymbale III	
Flageolet 1′	Cromorne 8′	
Fourniture III		
Cymbale III		
Grosse tierce $3^1/_5$′		
Nasard $2^2/_3$′		
Cornet V (3. okt.)		
Trompette 8′		
Clairon 4′		
Voix humaine 8′		

The Flûte 8′ in the pedal is identical with a wide Principal 8′, and the term Flûte is used regularly for Principals in the pedal.

Later, the Positif also acquired its Tierces, but the typical French organ did not emerge until about 1700, when Cornets, Tierces and the intense, festive reed group became the most prominent features. The organ built in 1689 by Robert Cliquot for the Cathedral in Rouen inaugurated this development:

Grand orgue	*Positif*	*Récit*	*Echo*	*Pédale*
Montre 16′	Montre 8′	Cornet III	Cornet III	Flûte 16′
Bourdon 16′	Bourdon 8′	Trompette 8′	Cymbale IV	Flûte 8′
Montre 8′	Prestant 4′		Voix humaine 8′	Flûte 4′
Bourdon 8′	Flûte 4′			Trompette 8′
Prestant 4′	Nazard 2 2/3′			Clairon 4′
Flûte 4′	Doublette 2′			
Tierce 3 1/5′	Tierce 1 3/5′			
Doublette 2′	Larigot 1 1/3′			
Quarte de Nazard 2′	Fourniture IV			
Nazard 2 2/3′	Cymbale III			
Flûte 2′	Cromorne 8′			
Tierce 1 3/5′	Voix humaine 8′			
Flageolet 1′				
Grand Cornet V				
Fourniture V				
Cymbale IV				
Trompette 8′				
Cromorne 8′				
Voix humaine 8′				
Clairon 4′				

In the following century, the art of organ building had a prosperous period in France, until the great Revolution brought it to a temporary close. It was the golden age of the autocratic monarchs, and the churches had ample means at their disposal. There was also a willingness to use these means, and above all, there was a culture which still loved a display of magnificence, but which knew how to differentiate between magnificence and ostentation.

Among the many prominent masters, the families of Cliquot, Isnard,

Thierry, Lefebvre, and Lepine must be mentioned. In addition, the clergy included many organ theorists, above all the Benedictine, Dom François Bedos de Celles. In his great work, *l'Art du facteur d'orgues,* he has given us much basic information concerning the theoretical and practical foundation for the organ building of this entire period. We understand that Dom Bedos was not only a learned theorist and observer, but that he was actively engaged in the work, with a sense of all details, from materials, tools and production methods, to scaling systems and voicing.

When reading Dom Bedos, we may get the impression that the French Baroque organ was uniform and systematized, and it is impossible to deny that both the tonal resources and their application were more simple and more regularly specified than in most of the contemporary organ types. The specifications, especially, give an appearance of standardization.

But the scales and other calculations of Dom Bedos must not be construed as "patterns" for organ builders, and in reality, it is evident that they have not been misused in this way. We may consider them as a norm, a point of reference for measuring deviations.

For study of the Baroque point of view and methods, Dom Bedos' treatise has been of extraordinarily great significance, because he has transmitted to us the theoretical basis of the craft. Otherwise, we would, of necessity, have to reconstruct it from measurements of extant instruments, where later alterations, flaws in construction, and intentional deviations could bring about numerous questions of doubt.

The French Baroque organ was composed of five manual Werks: *Grand orgue* (connected to manual II), *Positif* (manual I), *Bombarde* (manual III), *Récit* (manual IV) and *Echo* (manual V); as a sixth Werk there was the *Pédale.*

The Grand orgue (Hauptwerk) is placed in the middle of the main organ case. Its pipes are on a level with the front pipes, which, in the customary manner, constitute the foundation Principal of the Werk, the *Montre.* The pedal stops are mounted at the same level and on both sides of the Grand orgue, with the lowest-pitched Principal being mounted partially or completely in the façade.

The Positif is usually a Rückpositiv, but, in special instances, it may be mounted on the wind chest of the Grand orgue, which must then be equipped with the necessary channels for the Positif.

Likewise, the small Récit may be placed on the wind chest of the Grand orgue (but not together with the Positif); the Récit ordinarily has its own little chest centred above the Grand orgue, like a diminutive Oberwerk.

The Bombarde can almost be regarded as a part of the Grand orgue which has obtained an independent keyboard. When it was first intraduced, a single 16′ reed stop, the Bombarde, was isolated. Presumably the isolation was advantageous because this stop, with its large consumption of wind and its strong vibrations, had an adverse effect upon the other stops, a phenomenon which is not unknown in a tone groove chest when preventive measures have not been adopted. For this purely practical reason, the wind chest of the Grand orgue was rather early supplied with two grooves for each tone, and the "difficult" stops, the reeds, were placed on one groove. When it had come this far, it was simple and reasonable to connect the pallets of these grooves to a special keyboard. This also facilitated the manipulation of registrations involving the reeds, both when adding or subtracting them, or when using a single stop as a solo.

The placement of the Echo in the position of the Brustwerk, immediately above the manuals, has already been discussed.

The manual couplers were arranged in such a way that the Positif could be coupled to the manual of the Grand orgue and the Grand orgue to the keyboard of the Bombarde. Accordingly, all three manuals could be played as an ensemble from manual III, the Bombarde.

The Récit and the Echo were considered to be solo Werks and had no couplers. A pedal coupler to the Grand orgue could be found occasionally, but this was extraordinary.

As an example of this type of organ, the specification for the organ at St. Gervais, Paris, is given here. This is the "organ of the Couperins". It was built in 1601, but was later rebuilt and enlarged several times, including the restoration in 1768 by François Henri Cliquot, who gave the specification its present form:

Grand orgue

Montre 16′
Bourdon 16′
Montre 8′
Bourdon 8′
Flûte 8′
Prestant 4′
Nazard $2^{2}/_{3}$′
Doublette 2′
Quarte de Nazard 2′
Tierce $1^{3}/_{5}$′
Grand Cornet V
Plein jeu VI
I. Trompette 8′
II. Trompette 8′
Voix humaine 8′
Clairon 4′

Positif

Flûte 8′
Bourdon 8′
Prestant 4′
Nazard $2^{2}/_{3}$′
Doublette 2′
Tierce $1^{3}/_{5}$′
Plein jeu IV
Trompette 8′
Cromorne 8′
Basson-Clarinette 8′
Clairon 4′

Bombarde

Bombarde 16′

Récit

Cornet III
Hautbois 8′

Pédale

Flûte 16′
Flûte 8′
Flûte 4′
Bombarde 16′
Trompette 8′
Clairon 4′

Echo

Flûte d'écho 8′
Trompette 8′

The somewhat larger Cliquot organ, which was built in 1781 at St. Sulpice, Paris, had the following specification:

Grand orgue	*Positif*	*Bombarde*	*Récit*	*Echo*
Montre 32'	Bourdon 16'	Grand Cornet VII	Flûte de Récit 8'	Flûte 8'
Montre 16'	Montre 8'	Bombarde 16'	Cornet IV	Bourdon 8'
Bourdon 16'	Bourdon 8'	Trompette 8'	Trompette 8'	Cornet III
Montre 8'	Flûte 8'	Clairon 4'	Hautbois 8'	Trompette 8'
Bourdon 8'	Prestant 4'			Clairon 4'
Flûte 8'	Nazard $2^{2}/_{3}$'			
Grand Nazard $5^{1}/_{3}$'	Doublette 2'			
Prestant 4'	Quarte de Nazard 2'			
Grand Tierce $3^{1}/_{5}$'	Tierce $1^{3}/_{5}$'			
Nazard $2^{2}/_{3}$'	Larigot $1^{1}/_{3}$'			
Doublette 2'	Cornet V			
Quarte de Nazard 2'	Fourniture IV			
Tierce $1^{3}/_{5}$'	Cymbale V			
Grand Cornet V	Trompette 8'			
Grand Fourniture VI	Cromorne 8'			
Cymbale IV	Basson 8'			
I. Trompette 8'	Clarinette 8'			
II. Trompette 8'	Clairon 4'			
Voix humaine 8'				
I. Clairon 4'				
II. Clairon 4'				

Pédale
I. Jeu ouverte 16'
Bourdon 16'
Flûte 8'
II. Jeu ouverte 8'
Grand Nazard $5^{1}/_{3}$'
Quatre pieds (4')
I. Bombarde 16'
II. Bombarde 16'
I. Trompette 8'
II. Trompette 8'
Clairon 4'

If we now study Dom Bedos' proposed specification for a smaller organ, the same principles as in the two large instruments will be recognized:

Grand orgue	*Positif*	*Récit*	*Pédale*
Montre 8'	Bourdon 8'	Cornet V	Flûte 8'
Bourdon 8'	Prestant 4'		Trompette 8'
Prestant 4'	Nazard $2^{2}/_{3}$'		
Nazard $2^{2}/_{3}$'	Doublette 2'		
Doublette 2'	Tierce $1^{3}/_{5}$'		
Tierce $1^{3}/_{5}$'	Larigot $1^{1}/_{3}$'		
Fourniture III	Cymbale IV		
Cymbale II	Cromorne 8'		
Trompette 8'			
Voix humaine 8'			

The principles of specifications in the French Baroque organ are easily discernible. Concerning the Grand orgue, the foundation is naturally the façade Principal *(Montre)*, which may be 16′, 8′, or quite exceptionally, a 32′, depending entirely on the size of the organ. After that, the Principal group continues in the usual way up to 2′, and further to a 2′ *Fourniture* (with two octave repetitions), and the 1′ *Cymbale*, which has fifth repetition (see p. 78). Among the flute stops, a *Bourdon* 8′, is always included, and in large organs, a *Bourdon* 16′ and an open *Flûte* 8′. The wide-scaled mutations are represented by the *Nasard* $2^2/_3$′ and *Tierce* $1^3/_5$′. In larger instruments, the *Quarte de Nasard* 2′ is added; in very large organs, the *Grand Nasard* $5^1/_3$′ and *Grosse Tierce* $3^1/_5$′; and finally, the indispensable *Cornet V*.

Among the reed stops, the *Trompette* 8′ is almost certain to be present; in large instruments it is even doubled. And if the organ is medium-sized, the *Voix humaine* 8′ and *Clairon* 4′ are equally inevitable.

In the Positif, the customary practice is generally followed: the foundation Principal is an octave higher than that of the Grand orgue. The Principal ranks here also build up through the 4′ and 2′ to the mixtures. Among the mutations, the *Nasard* $2^2/_3$′ is almost a matter of course, and in the majority of cases, the *Tierce* $1^3/_5$′ and *Larigot* $1^1/_3$′ will be at hand. In larger instruments, the Positif also has its Cornet, and the *Cromorne* 8′ is just as natural in the Positif as the Trompette 8′ in the Grand orgue. In even a medium-sized organ, the Positif also has its Trompette 8′ and Clairon 4′, and possibly another reed stop.

The Bombarde manual, which originated in a separation of the Bombarde 16′ from the Grand orgue, is expanded as a Werk in larger organs; partly through a completion of the reeds with a Trompette 8′ and Clairon 4′, and partly by the addition of some flute stops (seldom Principals) or a Cornet. In the two solo Werks, Récit and Echo, the primary elements are their Cornets with the addition of single reed or flute stops.

The pedal is primarily occupied by the Trompette 8′. Next comes the Flûte 8′, which is almost a wide Principal; any further expansion usually occurs in the order of Clairon 4′, Bombarde 16′, Flûte 16′ (which can be a stopped rank), and Flûte 4′.

Beyond this, Dom Bedos suggests various mutations, for instance the following specification:

Flûte 8′ (Principal 8′)	Tierce $1^3/_5$′
Flûte 4′	I. Trompette 8′
Flûte 8′ (Holzflöte)	II. Trompette 8′
Nasard $2^2/_3$′	Cromorne 8′
Quarte de Nasard 2′	Clairon 4′

At this point, it should be noted that the pedalboard is designed to be extended with *Ravalement,* meaning that the pedal may be expanded to Contra-F, a normal Dutch-French practice that can also be applied to the Grand orgue. This extension does not always include all stops in the Werk concerned, in which case, the remaining stops begin at C in the usual way. The Ravalement partially alleviates the general lack of bass stops in the pedal.

As mentioned before, the reeds and Tierces constitute the most striking characteristics in the French organ. But there is reason to point out that, in spite of the large quantity of reed stops in the ensemble, there are relatively few variations in the elaboration of these stops. There are Trompettes at 16′, 8′ and 4′ pitches, and there are the Basson, Cromorne, Bombarde, Musette and Voix humaine (perhaps under other names), and then there are actually no more. We do not find any of the Regal variants.

In the structure of the Principal group, the mixtures represent the specifically French element. They have relatively few ranks, and these are rather low in the treble (without double ranks).

The wide-scaled mutations that are employed as single stops and in Cornets are characterized by their particular location in the specifications. For the most part, mutations appear in the low range of the eighteenth century organ. In comparison with the organs built at the close of the sixteenth century and the beginning of the seventeenth, a remarkable shift has occurred: high mutations have been replaced by those accentuating the third. Moreover, 1′ stops are rare in eighteenth century instruments.

All of the stopped flutes are rather wide in scale; a stop like the Quintatön is extremely rare. On the contrary, the half-stopped flutes are much favoured, especially the *Flûte à cheminée* (Rohrflöte) with its wide tube-scale and gay character. In order to brighten the treble, the Bourdon (Gedackt) is often made as a Rohrgedackt in the two upper octaves.

Conical pipes are limited to the treble range in stopped 4′ ranks, for the sake of greater intensity and clarity. A Spitzflöte will rarely be carried through from bass to treble.

According to our concepts, the lack of bass stops in the pedal is tantamount to a lack of foundation in the tonal structure. But there is no doubt that these stops were considered inappropriate and that the weightiness of a heavy organ pedal was contrary to the charm, lightness, and elegance which are the essence of the French Baroque. Thus the sparseness of the pedal is another earmark of this organ type.

In addition to other valuable contributions, Dom Bedos has given information about the use of the organs. Directions for registration were, on the whole, not uncommon in France, and several registrations of a much earlier date than Dom Bedos' have also been preserved. Fundamentally, all of these instructions are analogous, apart from the fact that they become more comprehensive and seem to follow the organ in its development. Consequently, the directions that we find in Dom Bedos are to be regarded as the sum of the experiences of two hundred years, the result achieved in connection with the fully developed French Baroque organ. These registrations were "read, tested, corrected, and approved" by the celebrated Parisian organists Calvière, Fouquet, Couperin, Balbâtre, and many others. Thus, a representative discussion of the French art of registration is made available.

Here are the main features:

Plein Jeu. This is composed of the entire Principal chorus (possibly including the 16′), all open 8′ stops, and all stopped ranks on the Grand orgue and Positif, coupled. (Thus, reed stops, Cornets, and wide mutations such as the Nazard and Tierce are omitted.) In the pedal, the Trompette 8′ and Clairon 4′ are used, perhaps with doubling and with the Bombarde 16′. The flue stops in the pedal are never drawn at the same time as the reeds; in certain cases, however, the flues may be used instead of the reeds, especially if a 16′ stop is included.

The Plein Jeu is used for sustained, majestic movements, or for close harmonies with syncopations and dissonant suspensions. For a lively movement, only the Positif is employed.

Grand Jeu. On the Grand orgue: Grand Cornet, Prestant 4′, Trompette 8′, Clairon 4′, possibly with doublings. On the Positif: Cornet, Prestant 4′, Trompette 8′, Clairon 4′, and perhaps the Cromorne, if the Trompettes in the Grand orgue are doubled. The Grand orgue and Positif are coupled, and the pedal is registered as in the Plein Jeu. Dom Bedos warns against the common habit of using the strong tremolo with this registration.

Duo. There are eight different registrations:

(1) Grand orgue: all foundation stops, including the 32′ if it is present; in addition, the two Nazards ($5^1/_3$′ and $2^2/_3$′), the two Tierces ($3^1/_5$′ and $1^3/_5$′), and the wide 2′ (Quarte de Nazard). This registration is called *le grand Jeu de Tierce*. On the Positif: an open 8′ stop, Bourdon 8′, Prestant 4′, Nasard $2^2/_3$′, Quarte de Nasard 2′, and Tierce $1^3/_5$′. These are termed *le Jeu de Tierce du Positif*.

The Grand orgue and Positif are not coupled. The upper part is played on the Positif and the bass part on the Grand orgue, but the bass should not go above the middle of the keyboard.

(2) The upper part can be played with the Cornet or Hautbois on the Récit, and the lower part with only the Trompette in the Positif. If there is no Cornet de Récit, the Cornet of the Grand orgue is used, or a *petit Jeu de Tierce* can be composed from Montre 8′, Bourdon 8′ and 4′, Prestant 4′, and the three wide-scaled mutations ($2^2/_3$′, 2′, and $1^3/_5$′). This registration is best suited to fast movements.

(3) The upper part is played with the Cornet de Récit and the lower part with only the Positif Trompette.

(4) The upper part, Trompette on the Récit; the lower part, *Jeu de Tierce* on the Positif.

(5) The upper part, Cromorne 8′ and Prestant 4′ on the Positif; the lower part, *le grand Jeu de Tierce* on the Grand orgue. Dom Bedos warns against playing fast passages in the bass. A trio can also be played on this registration if the two upper parts are played on the Positif and the bass on the Grand orgue.

(6) Both voices are played on the Grand orgue with Trompette 8′, Clairon 4′, and Prestant 4′.

(7) The upper part on the Positif with the two 8′ stops, Flûte 4′, Nasard $2^2/_3$′; or, better, Cromorne 8′ and Prestant 4′. For the bass, the Montre 16′, Bourdon 16′, and Clairon 4′ from the Grand orgue.

(8) For the upper part, the Cornet of the Echo; for the bass, all of the foundation stops on the Grand orgue coupled to the Positif Cromorne and Prestant 4′.

Fugue grave. On the Grand orgue: Prestant 4′, Trompette 8′ and Clairon 4′ (possibly with doublings). On the Positif: Trompette 8′, Clairon 4′, and Cromorne 8′. The Positif is coupled to the Grand orgue. The pedal is registered in the same way as the *Plein Jeu* and *Grand Jeu*. Dom Bedos advises against using the Cornet of the Grand orgue in this registration, because it deprives the reeds of their fine "sharpness" and "sweetness" in the treble, just when they have a rare opportunity of appearing in their full "brilliance and beauty". Dom Bedos also warns against the use of the strong tremulant with this registration.

A second combination is suggested for the *Fugue grave:* all foundation stops on the Grand orgue plus the Prestant 4′ and Cromorne 8′ of the Positif.

Fugue de mouvement. Usually a *Grand Jeu* or a *Grand Jeu de Tierce* is used, with manuals coupled.

Tierce en Taille. For the solo voice on the Positif, the two 8′ stops, Prestant 4′ (preferably Flûte 4′), Nasard $2^2/_3$′, Quarte de Nasard (the wide 2′), or, the Doublette 2′, and finally, the Tierce $1^3/_5$′ and Larigot $1^1/_3$′. For the accompaniment, the available 8′ stops (two or three) are drawn on the Grand orgue. In the pedal, all flue stops (16′, 8′, 4′) are employed. It is recommended that the accompaniment be raised as much as possible, preferably to the highest octave, where it will provide the best ornaments for the solo voice, as well as brilliance. In that range, the registration will act as an imitation of a Flûte traversière. The solo voice should be executed "like a song", and it should be ornamented carefully and tastefully. The organist is cautioned against the bad habit of performing long, fast scale passages and cadenzas in the solo voice.

Cromorne en Taille. The solo voice, on the Positif, is taken by the Cromorne 8′ and Prestant 4′. As before, the registration for the accompaniment is the 8′ stops from the Grand orgue. The pedal uses the flue stops again. This solo registration is most successful in the low range.

Trompette en Taille. On the Positif, the solo requires the Trompette alone or together with the Prestant 4′; the middle range is recommended. The registration for the Grand orgue and pedal is the same as before.

Quartet on four manuals (the right hand plays the two upper parts on two different manuals). First upper part on the Récit, Trompette 8′. Second upper part on the *petit Jeu de Tierce du Grand orgue.* Third part on the Positif, Cromorne 8′ and Prestant 4′; and fourth part on the three flue stops of the pedal (16′, 8′, 4′) or the *Jeu de Tierce.*

Or, first upper part on the Cornet de Récit. Second upper part on the Grand orgue, Trompette 8′ and Prestant 4′. Third part on the Positif, *Jeu de Tierce;* and fourth part on the pedal fluework.

Quartet on three manuals. The first and second upper parts are played on the Récit (Cornet); the third part on the Positif with Cromorne 8′ and Prestant 4′; and the fourth part on the pedal fluework. It is also possible to

TRIO ON THREE KEYBOARDS

Upper parts		Bass part
1. Récit: Cornet	Positif: Cromorne 8′ and Prestant 4′	Foundation stops 16′, 8′, 4′
2. Récit: Trompette 8′ or Grand orgue: Trompette 8′, Prestant 4′	Positif: Jeu de Tierce without Larigot $1^1/_3$′	"
3. Récit: Cornet	Positif: Jeu de Tierce	"
4. Récit: Trompette 8′ or Cornet	Grand orgue and Positif coupled: all 8′ stops	"
5. Grand orgue: two or three 8′ stops	Positif: Cromorne and Prestant 4′	"
6. Grand orgue: Two 8′ stops and Nasard $2^2/_3$′ + Flûte 4′ if available	Positif: Cromorne 8′ Prestant 4′	"
7. Récit: Trompette 8′	Positif: Two 8′ stops, Flute 4′, Nasard $2^2/_3$′	"
8. Grand orgue: all 8′ stops	Positif: Jeu de Tierce	"
9. Récit: Cornet, or Positif: two 8′ stops, Nasard $2^2/_3$′, Flute 4′	Grand orgue: Voix humaine 8′, Bourdon 8′, Flute 4′ (or Prestant) Mild Tremulant	"
10. Grand orgue and Positif coupled: all 8′ stops		"

play the two middle parts on the Positif, leaving only the upper part on the Récit.

Fond d'orgue. The Grand orgue and the Positif are coupled. All Principals and open and stopped flutes at 16′, 8′, 4′ pitches are drawn, as well as the complete pedal fluework. This registration is also employed without 4′ Principals.

Basse de Trompette. For the solo on the Grand orgue: Trompette 8′, Clairon 4′ (possibly with doublings) plus Prestant 4′. On the Positif: the 8′ stops, Doublette 2′ and the Larigot $1^1/_3$′. If a dialogue is to be played, the Cornet de Récit is used for the upper part, or the 8′ stops, Prestant 4′ and Cromorne 8′ on the Positif are drawn. On the Positif, a bassoon can be imitated with this registration; and on the Grand orgue, a fanfare of a trumpet or Waldhorn can be imitated.

Basse de Cromorne. The Cromorne 8′ and Prestant 4′ of the Positif are employed for the solo, and the 8′ stops of the Grand orgue are used for an accompaniment. The bassoon or *Basse de viol* may be imitated with this solo registration.

Récits de dessus (soprano solo). The two 8′ stops are used as an accompaniment, and solo registrations are suggested as follows:

1. Positif: Cromorne 8′, Prestant 4′.
2. Récit: Trompette 8′.
3. Récit: Cornet.
4. Grand orgue: Grand Cornet.
5. Positif: Jeu de Tierce.
6. Grand orgue: Trompette 8′ (I and II when available) plus Prestant 4′.
7. Positif: Trompette 8′ and Cromorne 8′. Perhaps + Prestant 4′.

Voix humaine. The Bourdon 8′ and Flûte 4′ are combined with the Voix humaine on the Grand orgue (possibly Prestant 4′ as a substitute for Flûte 4′). The accompaniment for this is executed on the 8′ stops of the Positif. The mild tremolo is used on the Grand orgue, and it is advised that the melody part be performed as a duo between bass and treble, yet without overstepping the natural limits of the human voice, which the registration imitates. For the same reason, the solo part should be played "cantabile".

Dialogue for Cornet, Cromorne and Echo. For this purpose, the Cornets of the Récit and Echo are used together with the Cromorne 8′ and Prestant 4′ of the Positif. Two 8′ stops from the Grand orgue are taken as an accompaniment.

Plein Chant (Gregorian melody). In order that the melody will be quiet and dignified, it is played on the pedal with Bombarde 16′, Trompette 8′, Clairon 4′; and the accompaniment is executed with the *Plein Jeu* registration discussed earlier. As an alternative, the melody may be played on the Grand orgue with Trompette 8′, Clairon 4′ (possibly doubled), and Prestant 4′. The accompaniment is then placed on the Positif and registered as a *Plein Jeu.* The Positif may be coupled to the Grand orgue.

Imitation of Flûte allemande (Flûte traversière). All 8′ stops from the Grand orgue and Positif are drawn, and the two Werks are coupled. Only the upper range is used.

Imitation of Flûte à bec (Blockflöte). The Grand orgue and the Positif are coupled, and the two Prestants 4′ and possibly the 4′ Flûtes are drawn.

Imitation of the Musette. If there is a Musette, it is used with a Bourdon 8′ as a solo, with an accompaniment of two 8′ stops. The tonic and dominant can be sustained on the pedal Flûte or held by lead weights on the accompaniment manual. Then a middle part can be executed on the accompaniment manual.

Imitation of the Fifre (Piccolo). On the Grand orgue, the Flûte 4′, Quarte de Nasard 2′, and Doublette 2′ are drawn; on the Positif, two 8′ stops, Prestant 4′, and Larigot $1^1/_3$′. Flute and tambourine effects may be obtained on the Grand orgue, and a drum is simulated by striking the keyboard of the Positif.

Imitation of the Flageolet. The Quarte de Nazard 2′ and the Doublette 2′ are drawn on the Grand orgue, and the accompaniment is performed on the two 8′ stops of the Positif.

Imitation of bird songs. This is done by coupling the Nazards from the Positif and Grand orgue and by playing runs, trills, and ornaments with an appropriate accompaniment.

A vocal accompaniment must be adjusted in intensity to the person or persons singing. A *Plein Jeu* is used for accompanying a large choir or congregation. Otherwise, the number of stops for the accompaniment is determined by the intensity required; perhaps nothing more than a soft Bourdon 8′ is needed.

Use of the Bombarde. The primary rule is that the Bombarde 16′ is never used alone. In the pedal, it is always accompanied by the Trompette 8′ and Clairon 4′. As a manual stop, usually provided with its own keyboard, it is combined with the Grand orgue or possibly with other stops in the Bombarde Werk. As a solo stop, it may function with the pedal reeds, as mentioned earlier. The Bombarde is coupled to the *Plein Jeu* or *Grand Jeu* of the manuals when a broader, more dignified sound must be attained for certain large chords or cadences that must be stressed, and also for organ points and finales. For slow, fugal movements, the Bombarde may be used in combination with the *Plein Jeu.*

In addition to these instructions for registration, Dom Bedos gives the following general rules. Reed stops with relatively short resonators, producing a thin, snarling sound, can attain some of the fullness that they lack by adding a Bourdon 8′ as well as an open 8′ stop and a Nasard $2^2/_3$′, if necessary. When the reed stops are of adequate length, it is best not to add the fluework. At this point, there is an interesting contrast to the older instructions, which do not require any "fullness" for the thin and snarling reeds. The tonal ideal had changed.

Dom Bedos repeatedly warns against the use of the tremolo, not because he scorns this effect, but because many of his contemporaries misused it. Some of them used it always, even for the *Plein Jeu,* so his warnings were not unjustified. However, Dom Bedos points out that if the reed stops are somewhat out of tune, the defects may be hidden be using the strong tremolo!

If the 8′ stops designated for the accompaniment and similar functions are too weak, a 4′ Flûte may be added, but never a 16′ stop. The Prestant 4′ should be avoided, because it produces a sharpness which is inappropriate for an accompaniment registration. The Tierce, the Nasard, and the Quarte de Nasard must not be included in the *Plein Jeu,* and must also be omitted from the *Grand Jeu,* as they will obscure the special character of the reed sound which is the Grand Jeu's real source of beauty.

Where the pedal fluework is indicated in the previously mentioned registrations, both the 16′, 8′, and 4′ pitches are meant; and if a 32′ is available, it is included.

So much for Dom Bedos. These registrations and instructions are an essential aid to us, not only in performances of French Baroque music, but also as a contribution to the understanding of the instruments and the tonal ideal which became the ideal of the Catholic Church in a large number of the southern countries.

SPAIN

Several of the old Spanish organs are covered by a thick layer of dust. Either they cannot be used, or they are not used. Much of Spanish organ history is still waiting for exploration in the archives. Only very few of the inhabitants of the country suspect what irreplaceable treasures are lying dormant in this way. If these organs were just allowed to rest in peace, no harm could occur, but pneumaticizing and electrification still have free rein, and much has already been lost. This is regrettable, also because we have so much to learn from Spanish organ building. The Spanish organs are something quite different from our conventional practice, and moreover, we encounter quality on a very high level here.

Concerning the exterior circumstances, we know that the Christians in northern Spain at length concentrated on the task of expelling the Moors, and these were banished at the close of the Middle Ages, just when the organ was undergoing an intensive development. We know how powerful the Spanish kingdom became later, and also that its authority, at one time, extended to both the Netherlands and Italy, not to mention the colonization after Columbus' discovery of America. We are aware that the actual power behind this authority, both then and later, was the Church, and that the same church commanded tremendous wealth. The military struggle of the Spanish Church against the Moors, its profound influence later on secular affairs, and its administrative methods, gave it an entirely different position and an entirely different physiognomy from, for example, the Italian Church.

In a curious manner, this secular aspect of the Church was reflected in the organs, seemingly splitting them in two parts – sacred and secular.

The ascetic, vocal, gentle fluework, so characteristic of the Italian organ, was the original nucleus of the Spanish instrument, too, although in a somewhat different form. But a domineering, orchestral (or secular) element, constituted by a well-developed chorus of reeds, came as a gradual addition. In basic design, this reed group was sharply contrasted with the fluework. Clearly, the two stop groups must be used independently – they were not intended for extensive collaboration. Ensembles representing a combination of the two groups would have been feasible in the later organs, but there was obviously no demand for it.

Among the oldest existing organs in Spain, the most famous one is the Emperor's organ at Toledo. It was constructed in 1549 by Juan Gaytan and was mounted over the main entrance of the church with a stone framework bordering the three flats of front pipes. The original specification is unknown, but at any rate it is known that the horizontal reeds were added in the seventeenth century. The specification, at that time, was as follows:

I. manual		*II. manual*
Flautado 16′		Flautado 16′
Violon 16′ (= Gedackt 16′)		Flautado 8′
Flautado 8′		Violin 8′ (Gedackt 8′)
Octava 4′		Flauta traversa 8′ (treble)
Trompeta magna 16′	horizontal	Octava 4′
Trompeta Real 8′	horizontal	Octava tapada 4′
Clarin de Campana 4′	horizontal	Docena y Quincena 2²/₃′, 2′
Clarin Claro 4′	horizontal	Quincena 2′
Clarin Brillante 2′ (bass)	horizontal	Nasardos V
		Nasardos VIII
Pedal I.		Lleno VIII
		Corneta VII–XIII
Contras 32′ (Contras = bass)		Trompeta magna 16′
Contras 16′ (façade)		Trompeta Real 8′
Contras 16′		Bajoncillo y Clarin 8′
Contras 8′		Violetas 8′
Contras en Octava 4′		
Pedal II.		
Contras 2′		
Contras 1′		
Bombarda 16′		
Clarines Reales 8′		
Clarines 2′		

Trompeta alta = high trumpet (4′ or 2′)
" de batalla = war trumpet
" brillante = brilliant trumpet, rich in overtones
" de campana = field trumpet
" imperial = Imperial trumpet (32′)
" magna = Great trumpet (16′)
" real = Royal trumpet
Docena = Quint 2²/₃′
Quincena = Oktav 2′
See in addition table of stop designations, p. 113–14

Here, a well-preserved Hauptwerk is connected to manual II, and a bass Werk is connected to manual I which also contains the horizontal trumpets that had been added to the front. The two pedal sections are transmissions from the bass manual, partly by octave shift, and each is connected to its own series of keys. The row of pedal keys nearest to the organ is joined to pedal I. These keys are shaped like round buttons which protrude vertically from the floor; since all of the keys are on the same level, there is no visible difference between the diatonic and the chromatic ones. The second row of keys is connected to pedal II and has the shape of ordinary chromatic pedal keys. The usual range of the pedal is C–d, a little more than an octave.

The Emperor's organ is scarcely representative of the Spanish organ. In the course of the seventeenth and eighteenth centuries, Spanish organ builders made essential progress in definitive types of placement and the construction of Werks and stops, especially the reeds. Several new cathedrals (continually larger and more pretentious) were built in these centuries. The custom of locating the choir at a central point was developed concurrently with the increasing dimensions of the church.

The main altar had its normal place in one of the arches farthest east in the nave; but instead of placing the choir in direct relation to the main altar, the first or the two first arches west of the altar remained free, and the choir then occupied the two following arches. The choir had the conventional arrangement with choir stalls on both sides, and toward the east and west it was closed with wrought-iron lattices. The organs were situated in the arches between the choir and the side aisles, in the galleries above the choir stalls. Usually there were two organs: one on the "gospel" side and one on the "epistle" side. These organs had façades and trumpets facing both the choir and the aisles.

The organ on the gospel side in Toledo Cathedral was built in the second half of the seventeenth century by José Verdalonga, and it is composed of three manual Werks: (1) a Hauptwerk facing the choir and connected to the upper manual, (2) a Werk behind it, facing the aisle and connected to the middle manual, and (3) a Werk at the bottom of the organ, partly in a swell box, connected to the lower manual. Manuals I and II have stops divided into bass and treble. The specification is:

III. manual

Flautado 16′
Flautado 8′
Violon 8′
Flauto dulce 8′ (treble)
Flauto de ecos 8′
Octava 4′
Docena $2^2/_3$′
Quincena 2′
Lleno VIII
Lyeno e Cimbala VIII
Trompeta 16′
Trompeta real 8′
Trompeta 4′
Trompeta 2′ (bass)
Trompeta imperial 32′ (treble)
Clarin coro 8′
Clarin fuerte 8′
Bajoncillo 4′
Chirima 2′ (bass)
Chirimia alta 4′ (treble)
Violeta 8′
Regalia 8' (bass)
Trompeta magna 16′ (treble)

Pedal I.

Contras 16′
Flautado 8′
Contras 4′
Contras 2′

Pedal II.

Bombardas 16′
Contras de Clarines 8′
Contras de Clarines 4′
Contras de Clarines 2′
Contras 1′
Contras $^2/_5$′

II. manual

bass	*treble*
Contrabajo 16′	Violon 16′
Flautado 8′	Flautado 8′
Octava tapada 4′	Violon 8′
Nasardo	Octava de ecos 4′
Claron	Corneta magna
Flauta 2′	Corneta tolosana
Nasardos V	Nasardos V
Trompeta de batalla 8′	Trompeta de batalla 8′
Chirimia 4′	Clarin suave 4′
Clarin 2′	Trompeta magna 16′
Orlos 8′	Trompas 8′
Tiorba 8′	Tiorba 8′
Oboe 8′	

I. manual

bass	*treble*
Flautado 8′	Flauta traversa 8′
Violon 8′	Flautado 8′
Octava 4′	Violon 8′
Flautadito 4′	Octava 4′
Docena $2^2/_3$′	Flautadito 4′
Quincena 2′	Docena e Quincena $2^2/_3$′ 2′
Quincena 2′	Quincena 2′
Quincena tapada 2′	Flautin 2′
Lleno IV	Corneta clara V
Cimbalo IV	Lleno IV
Nasardos IV	Cimbala IV
Nasardos IV–V	Corneta V–XI
Trompeta real 8′	Bajoncillo 32′
Chirimia 4′	Trompeta real 8′
Violeta 4′	Bajete 4′
	Voz 16′

Cadereta

Trompeta magna 16′	Trompeta real 8′
Clarine 8′	Bajoncillo 4′
Chirimia alta 4′	Violeta 8′
Clarinete 8′	Bajoncillo 8′

The so-called Baroque-organ on the epistle side was built in 1755–1758 by Don Pedro de Liborna Echevarria and was mounted according to the same principle as the gospel organ: a Hauptwerk toward the choir (connected to manual II in this case), a Werk toward the aisle and connected to manual III, and a Werk for manual I at the bottom of the organ built into a swell-box. The specification is this:

II. manual	*III. manual*	*I. manual*
Flautado 16′	Flautado 8′	Violon 8′
Flautado 8′	Compuestas	Tapadillo 4′
Violon 8′	Trompeta de batalla 8′ & 16′	Quincena 2′
Flauta 8′	Trompeta en octava 8′	Diezynovena $1^1/_3$
Octava 4′	Clarin 2′ & 4′	Lleno IV
Tapadillo 4′	Dulciana 8′	Cimbalo III
Nasardos IV	Orlos 8′	Corneta V–XI (treble)
Corneta VIII		Flautado de Corneta 8′
Trompeta magna 16′	*Pedal*	Trompeta real 8′
Trompeta real 8′	Contras 16′	Clarin de ecos 4′
I. Clarin 4′	Trompeta 8′	Orlos 8′
II. Clarin 4′		Tambor
III. Clarin 2′ and 4′		
Trompeta alta 2′ (bass)		
Oboe 8′ (treble)		

Instruments with four manuals also exist. The first of these was probably the epistle organ in Sevilla Cathedral, constructed between 1668 and 1673 by the Portuguese organ builder Antonio Pedro Faleiro. It was built with two Rückpositivs, one facing the choir and one toward the aisle (connected to manuals I and IV respectively), a Hauptwerk toward the choir (connected to manual II) and finally a Werk which was, in 1703, enclosed in a swell-box, one of the first known swell Werks.

In the same remarkable year (1703), another curiosity was introduced: the first "echo" Werk in organ history. It contained three reed stops: Bajón 16′, Voz 8′, and Trompeta de Ecos 8′. The "echo" was located high up under the dome of the church, about 40 metres above the floor. An ordinary mechanical action was employed to connect this Werk to the keyboard of manual IV.

Another Portuguese organ builder, Faustino Carvalho (a relative of Faleiro), brought about these innovations, and the fifth-sounding Trompetes in the Hauptwerk and pedal must also be attributed to him. The liberal use of quints in the flue stops is also noteworthy, as it clearly indicates the bass character of the pedal. The specification is:

I. manual

Flautado 8′
Flauta en octava 4′
Quincena 2′
Corneta Tolosana
Trompeta real 8′
Bajoncillo y Clarín 8′ & 4′

II. manual

Bordón 16′
Flautado 8′
Violón 8′
Octava 4′
Tapadillo 4′
Flauta chica 2′
Lleno VIII
Nasardos V
Trompeta imperial 32′ (treble)
Trompeta magna 16′
Trompeta de batalla 8′
Clarín brillante 4′
Trompeta en quinta $5^1/_3$′

III. manual

Contrabajo 16′
Flautado 8′
Violon 8′
Octava 4′
Flautadito 4′
Flautin 2′
Docena y Quincena $2^2/_3$′, 2′
Corneta clara V
Fagót 16′
Trompeta real 8′
Chirimia 8′
Orlos 8′
Clarin brillante 4′

IV. manual

Flautado de Violón 8′
Flauta tapada 8′
Octava 4′
Quincena 2′
Nasardos IV
Voz 16′ (treble)
Regalía 8′
Voz 4′ (bass)

IV. manual

Bajón 16′
Voz 8′
Trompeta de ecos 8′

Pedal

Contras profundas 32′
Contras 16′
Quinta subgravis $10^2/_3$′
Quinta gravis $10^2/_3$′
Contras 8′
Quinta $5\frac{1}{3}$′
Violón enoctava 4′
Quinta $2^2/_3$′
Violón en quincena 2′
Contras de Bombardas 32′
Contras de Fagót 16′
Contras de Clarines 8′
Contras de Clarines 4′
Trompeta en quinta $5^1/_3$′

As early as 1509, shortly after the completion of the cathedral, the first choir organ was built on the gospel side. The instrument retained its place until 1724, and at that time it had three manual Werks and a pedal built on a 32′ Principal. It was replaced by a three-manual organ of a similar size. The contract stipulated that its façade should be an exact copy of the epistle organ. Jaime Viñlagón completed this organ in 1727, and immediately after that, he started a third organ in the cathedral, the nave organ, finished in 1730.

While the purpose of the choir organs was chiefly confined to purely liturgical matters, there was a special requirement for the nave organ. Sometimes it accompanied congregational singing in those church services where such singing was permitted, and sometimes it furnished processional music when an archbishop or members of the royal family marched in or out of the church, or when an archbishop was carried to his grave.

In 1912, the two choir organs were replaced by a new double-organ, with electrical action, but the nave organ survived this and had a third Werk added. The pipes for the new Werk were assembled from the dismantled choir organs. After that, the specification was as follows:

I. manual

Tapada 8′
Octava 4′
Flauta dulce 4′
Flauta en quincena 2′
Nasardos $1^1/_3$′
Címbala IV
Clarinete 8′
Voz 8′
Regalía 4′

Pedal

Contras 16′
Contras tapadas 16′
Contras en octava 8′
Contras en quincena 4′
Violón 8′
Violón 4′
Flauta a chimenea 2′
Contras de bombarda 16′
Contras de trompeta 8′
Octava de trompetas 4′
Clarines fuertes 2′

II. manual

Flautado 16′
Violón 16′
Flautado 8′
Violón 8′
Tapada 8′
Flauta armónica 8′
Octava 4′
Flauta en octava 4′
Quincena 2′
Flautadito 2′
Lleno VI–VII
Nasardos V–VII
Címbala IV–VI
Trompeta magna 16′
Trompeta 8′
Clarines 4′

III. manual

Flautado 8′
Flauta tapada 8′
Flauta en ecos 8′
Flauta travesera
Octava 4′
Flauta travesera 4′
Flauta sevillana 4′
Flauta en quincena 2′
Docena y quincena $2^2/_3$′, 2′
Corneta magna VI–VIII
Címbala III
Voz 16′
Gaitas 8′
Trompeta 8′
Chirimía 4′

Obviously, the cathedral had great requirements for organs. There were no less than fourteen organs in the church at the close of the eighteenth century. Some of them, presumably, were positives with only one manual Werk and pedal, like the small organ in the Sacrament Chapel, which is believed to date from 1512. These stops are contained in the following specification:

Manual	*Pedal*
Flauta tapada 8′	Flauta tapada 8′
Flauta dulce 8′	Flautado 2′
Flautado en octava 4′	Fagót 16′
Flauta en quincena 2′	Regalia 4′
Címbala V	
Voz 16′	
Fagót 8′	
Trompeta 8′	
Clarin suave 4′	

A number of portatives probably were included in the total of fourteen organs. Portatives (used in medieval processions through the town) are small instruments with one or two reed stops, and such organs were still extant at the beginning of this century. They could be carried with the aid of a shoulder strap. The left hand operated the bellows, and the right hand played the keyboard.

In the study of Spanish organs, it is particularly true that isolated specifications provide a very incomplete picture of tonal proportions. If the specifications are judged on the basis of personal assumptions, the outcome is truly deceptive, because the scales and voicing are vastly different from those used in the remainder of Europe. North of the Pyrenees, the tonal atmosphere is more congenial, but Spain is something quite apart.

In the first place, the Spanish fluework usually has very narrow scaling, and a consistent scaling practice seems to prevail throughout the country. The Principals are 4–6 HT under NS, and the mixtures are considerably smaller. To this must be added the fact that the pipe mouths are also very narrow: $^{1}/_{5}$, $^{1}/_{6}$ or $^{1}/_{7}$ of the circumference in contrast to our normal $^{1}/_{4}$. Furthermore, a very low wind pressure of 45–50 mm. Water Column (ca. 2″) is employed. All this indicates a very mild and delicate voicing. The fluework, nevertheless, retains a characteristically full-bodied quality, especially because of the large mixtures.

The *Lleno,* with 4–6 ranks, is usually 4–6 HT under NS, and the mouth scale is $^{1}/_{5}$ to $^{1}/_{7}$ of the circumference, just as the lower Principals.

Occasionally, the double ranks in the Lleno are composed of conical pipes. In the Sevilla organ, from which the following examples have been taken, the Lleno has this structure:

C–B $1\frac{1}{3} - 1 - \frac{2}{3} - \frac{1}{2} - \frac{1}{3} - \frac{1}{4}$
c–b $2 - 1\frac{1}{3} - 1 - \frac{2}{3} - \frac{1}{2} - \frac{1}{3} - \frac{1}{4}$
c′–f♯′ $2\frac{2}{3} - 2 - 2 - 1\frac{1}{3} - 1 - \frac{2}{3} - \frac{1}{2} - \frac{1}{3}$
g′–b′ $2\frac{2}{3} - 2\frac{2}{3} - 2 - 2 - 1\frac{1}{3} - 1 - \frac{2}{3} - \frac{1}{2}$
c″–f‴ $2\frac{2}{3} - 2\frac{2}{3} - 2 - 2 - 1\frac{1}{3} - 1\frac{1}{3} - 1 - 1$

The *Cimbala* consists of fifths and octaves (no thirds) and strongly resembles our Quintcymbal. The three Cymbals of the Sevilla organ are arranged in this manner:

1. manual:
C–B $\frac{1}{2} - \frac{1}{3} - \frac{1}{4} - \frac{1}{6}$
c–e $\frac{2}{3} - \frac{1}{2} - \frac{1}{3} - \frac{1}{4}$
f–b $1 - \frac{2}{3} - \frac{1}{2} - \frac{1}{3}$
c′–b′ $1\frac{1}{3} - 1 - \frac{2}{3} - \frac{1}{2}$
c″–e″ $2 - 1\frac{1}{3} - 1 - \frac{2}{3}$
f″–b″ $2\frac{2}{3} - 2 - 1\frac{1}{3} - 1$
c‴–f‴ $4 - 2\frac{2}{3} - 2 - 1\frac{1}{3}$

2. manual:
C–B $1 - \frac{1}{2} - \frac{1}{3} - \frac{1}{4}$
c–f♯ $1 - \frac{2}{3} - \frac{1}{2} - \frac{1}{3} - \frac{1}{4}$
g–b $2 - 1\frac{1}{3} - 1 - \frac{2}{3} - \frac{1}{2} - \frac{1}{3}$
c′–f′ $2\frac{2}{3} - 2 - 1\frac{1}{3} - 1 - \frac{2}{3} - \frac{1}{2}$
g′–b′ $4 - 2\frac{2}{3} - 2 - 1\frac{1}{3} - 1 - \frac{2}{3}$
c″–f‴ $4 - 4 - 2\frac{2}{3} - 2 - 2 - 1\frac{1}{3}$

3. manual:
C–B $\frac{1}{2} - \frac{1}{3} - \frac{1}{4}$
c–b $1 - \frac{1}{2} - \frac{1}{3}$
c′–b′ $1 - \frac{2}{3} - \frac{1}{2}$
c″–f♯″ $2 - 1 - \frac{2}{3}$
g″–b″ $2 - 1\frac{1}{3} - 1$
c‴–f‴ $2 - 2 - 1\frac{1}{3}$

In the *Nasardos* we find the series of thirds. The pipes have a very narrow scale; the octaves are 14–15 HT under NS, the series of fifths are still narrower, and the thirds are most slender, about 18–20 HT under NS. In addition, the mouth width is only $^1/_6$ to $^1/_7$ of the circumference. The fifth ranks usually have conical pipes, of which the upper diameter is approximately one-half of the lower diameter. The cut-up is low, and the voicing is very light and delicate. The sound is rather stringy. In the Sevilla organ, the Nasardos ranks are composed in this way:

C–B	$2^2/_3 - 2 - 1^3/_5 - 1^1/_3 - 1$
c–b	$4 - 2^2/_3 - 2 - 1^3/_5 - 1^1/_3 - 1$
c′–f‴	$4 - 2^2/_3 - 2 \quad - 2 - 1^3/_5 - 1^1/_3 - 1^1/_3$

The *Corneta magna* (without repetitions) also has a third-sounding rank. Although its normal composition is somewhat reminiscent of the ordinary Cornet, the very narrow scale indicates that this mixture is not intended as a reinforcement of the treble (in spite of the notable increase in the scale, from 12–14 HT under NS to 8 HT under NS). A seventh-sounding rank is not uncommon in this stop. The Corneta magna in Sevilla is set up thus:

C–B	$4 - 4 - 2^2/_3 - 2 - 2 - 1^3/_5$
c–b	$4 - 4 - 2^2/_3 - 2 - 2 - 1^3/_5 - 1^1/_3$
c′–b′	$4 - 4 - 2^2/_3 - 2 - 2 - 1^3/_5 - 1^1/_3 - 1^1/_7$
c″–f‴	$5^1/_3 - 4 - 4 - 2^2/_3 - 2 - 2 - 1^3/_5 - 1^1/_3 - 1^1/_7$

And the Corneta magna for the Emperor's Organ in Toledo has this composition:

g–f♯′	$8 - \quad 4 - \quad 2^2/_3 - 2 - 1^3/_5 - 1^1/_3 - \quad 1 - ^2/_5$
g′–b′	$8 - \quad 4 - \quad 2^2/_3 - 2 - 1^3/_5 - 1^1/_3 - 1^1/_7 - 1 - ^2/_5 - ^1/_3$
c″–f‴	$10^2/_3 - 8 - 6^2/_5 - 5^1/_3 - 4 - 3^1/_5 - 2^2/_3 - 2 - 1^3/_5 - 1^1/_3 - 1^1/_7 - 1$

The metal pipes in Spanish organs have a very low lead content. Tin percentages of 90–98 are quite normal, although the pipes in certain organs (such as the Emperor's organ) have less tin, because the alloy contains a large amount of silver. Wood is a favoured material for flutes and stopped pipes.

The reeds can have resonators of tin alloy, brass, or wood, and the resonator forms are highly varied. The Trompetas usually have "collars" (see ill. p. 82), and double or quadruple length is frequently used in the treble, on account of the intensity.

The ordinary cylindrical resonators, comparable to the Krummhorn and Dulcian, bear such names as *Bajete, Bajón, Bajoncillo, or Clarinete.* Within this resonator group, there is a wide selection of Regal types, the latter often being grouped in the front section nearest to the keyboard. The little *Orlos* and *Voz humana* may be found there, or the characteristic Spanish stops, *Voz viejos* (Old Man's Voice) and *Voz viejas* (Old Woman's Voice). They "sit" on opposite sides of the keyboard, waiting to sing their duet. The resonator, covered by an arched lid with a centre opening, is generally conical with a wide scale. The length of these resonators seldom exceeds 12 cm.

Among the Spanish reeds, especially from the eighteenth century, we can also find completely undisguised orchestral imitations. For example, the organ in the Palaze Reale, Madrid, has an Oboe with resonators made of turned wood. These resonators are uniform in size, but they are equipped with holes that correspond to the various pitch lengths, a literal imitation of what occurs in an orchestral instrument when the keys open and close the holes. The imitation is most successful.

Lead blocks with cylindrical brass shallots, very flat and nearly semi-cylindrical, are used in most instances. The tongues are very thin, with the same width at the top and the bottom. In numerous stops, the tongue for 8′–C has a thickness of only 0.30 mm. (the maximum is 0.40). In the treble, the thickness may be reduced to 0.06 mm.

The sound is incredibly charming and free of any suggestion of heaviness. The thin reeds induce an elegance and precision of attack, and the open, horizontal location in the façade, which many of these reeds have, permits all of these qualities to achieve proper focus, especially in the case of the characteristically colourful Regals.

The Trompetas have, to some extent, an orchestral character. Their sound is bright and slender, but absolutely unforced; on the contrary, it is quite spontaneous, free and exciting.

To this must be added the acoustical resources that are connected with the location of the ordinary Spanish choir organ. The fact that the organ can speak in the direction of both the choir and the aisles permits unique acoustical effects, but we do not know anything exact about how these possibilities were used. Apparently, the tradition has been lost.

Apart from the strong emphasis on reeds, Spanish organ building has surprisingly little in common with the French style, and in comparison with the reeds, the resemblance is simply a matter of quantity, because there is a clear-cut tonal distinction between French and Spanish reeds.

For the most part, the old Spanish organ was essentially an autonomous conception, and any contact or similarity to other European organ types would be difficult to establish. In the sixteenth century, Spain probably experienced some influence from the captured Netherlands; this is suggested by the use of the name Nasardos on a mixture stop (see p. 166). At any rate, Spain, with its large, relatively high mixtures including double ranks, is much nearer to the Dutch and North European practice than to the French one. The Regals and the bass pedal tend to support this theory.

Spain and Portugal had their most important contact from the sea lanes, and therefore it is no surprise that Spanish and English organ building have some essential character traits in common. The delicate voicing of the fluework is also found in the old English organ, and the appearance of the swell-box is nearly simultaneous in Spain and England, long before it was introduced in other countries. The Spanish-English taste included a notable predilection for wooden flute stops and the use of thirds in the mixtures.

We have from that time one evidence of the direct working contact, although not between England and Spain, but between Ireland and Portugal. In about 1740 an Irishman, Eugene Nicholas Egan, built a large organ for the Cathedral in Lisbon after a competition between eight famous European organ builders, including some from Germany and the Netherlands.

About one hundred years later, A. G. Hill, the English organ builder, visited Spain for the purpose of professional study. Hill became one of the pioneers for the English organ of the nineteenth century; and although his independent methods led him to create a type of organ that had little in common with the Spanish one, the modern English organ, to a greater extent than other contemporary types, has retained one bond with the old Spanish instrument: the great preponderance of reeds.

Through Cavaillé-Coll, France also received strong Spanish influence during the same period, and it is evident that many elements in the romantic organ of the nineteenth century were prepared in eighteenth century Spanish organ building.

There is still more to be learned from the Spanish organ; there are lessons also for the present generation. If free, festive reeds could be combined with the Nordic fluework, a new union of two very valuable elements might be accomplished.

ENGLAND

The almost inevitable lack of pedal in the old English organ is probably the feature which first draws the attention of continental organists and organ builders. Both German and French-trained masters were engaged for a considerable amount of activity in England, but the first rudimentary "pull-down" pedalboards, with only one octave, came into existence at the close of the eighteenth century. It is difficult to find a logical reason for this fantastic conservatism which precluded a pedal Werk for the English organs until well into the nineteenth century.

Although the organ was just as old and as widely distributed in England as on the Continent, it was a very long time before the real development of the instrument took place. Small organs with a single manual were the rule until the middle of the sixteenth century, and the following period did not bring a development which could in any way be compared with the progress on the Continent. Vocal music was the focal point of musical activity, and the Puritans had little sympathy for organs.

It is told of the church of St. Chad's in Shrewsbury that the congregation resolved, in 1589, to sell the organ to anyone who might wish to buy it. The reason was the problem of raising money for the repair of the bells, for a decent altar chalice, and for a fence for the graveyard. In the following years, when dissension and civil war ravaged the land, there are many descriptions of the brutal destruction of church property.

The culmination of the matter was the Parliamentary resolution establishing a new church ordinance, whereby any form of music, excepting psalms, was forbidden. This resulted in the removal of the organs, the destruction of the service books, the smashing of stained glass windows, etc. Approximately twelve organs survived this madness; among them were St. Stephens at Old Radnor (from *ca.* 1500) and King's College at Cambridge (1605), the only ones of which the cases are now standing in their original places. The pipes have been discarded long ago.

The organ builders could not begin to work again until after the Restoration (1660). By that time, and for good reasons, there were scarcely any organ builders in the country. There were the Dallams, who presumably were brothers and sons of the Dallam who built the organ for King's College. There was also John Loosemore who, a few years after the Restoration, built a large organ for the Cathedral at Exeter. It was not entirely successful, but it became famous because of its 24′ Double Diapason of tin (although the attack was far from good). Large pipes were curiosities in England.

English organ building needed fresh blood at this time, and this requirement caused a Continental master to be attracted to England. Perhaps he was summoned by the king. An organ for the royal chapel at Whitehall had to be built as soon as possible, and the work was delegated to the German (Dutchman?), Bernhard Schmidt, who came to England accompanied by his two nephews, Gerard and Bernhard, who worked as his associates. This kinship supplied the nickname "Father" Smith, and the name became his trademark in England.

With the support of Charles II, Father Smith soon created a significant position for himself, and as early as the year after the delivery of the organ for Whitehall, a new instrument was finished in Westminster Abbey, the organ of Purcell and Dr. Blow.

Father Smith had been in England for only a short time when a competitor appeared. John Harris, an English organ builder who had fled to France after the violent iconoclasm in 1644, had returned to his native land, accompanied by his son, Renatus. John Harris died a few years later, but young Renatus Harris proved to be a zealous and capable competitor for Father Smith, even though he did not succeed in deposing Smith from his well-fortified position.

The culmination of the Smith-Harris struggle was the renowned "battle of organs" in the Temple Church, London, where Smith and Harris were each permitted to build an organ in the church on the condition that the instrument which proved itself to be the poorer should be removed without expense to the church. In the course of this long and complicated affair, elaborate strategy was evident on both sides (Purcell, among others, was on the side of Father Smith); but the "war" ended in a defeat for Harris and naturally a lifelong tension between the two rivals and their followers.

Two "schools", one with French emphasis and one with German-Dutch character, were consequently to be found in England in the years after the Restoration. Both schools had to conform to the specifically English conception of building; for example, the omission of the pedal. Harris favoured the reed stops to a somewhat higher degree than Father Smith, but their basic differences were related to the problems of scaling and voicing.

In accordance with the contract, Father Smith's organ for the Temple Church had the following specification:

Great organ	*Choir organ*	*Ecchos*
Prestant 8′	Gedact 8′	Wooden Gedact 8′
Holflute 8′	A Viol and Violin 8′	Wooden Gedact 4′
Principal 4′	Holflute 4′	Flute 4′
Gedact 4′	A Sadt 4′	Super Octave 2′
Quinta $2^2/_3$′	Spitzflute 2′	Cornet
Super Octave 2′	Voice Humaine 8′	Sesquialtera
Cornet II		Trumpet 8′
Sesquialtera III		
Mixture III–IV		
Trumpet 8′		

In conformance with Dutch-French custom, the manuals were extended to Contra-F. But for that matter, the manual compass is extremely varied in English organs.

The contract for Father Smith's next organ, the cathedral in Durham, has also been preserved, and according to it, the specification was this:

Great organ	*Choir organ*
Principal 8′	Gedact 8′
Principal 8′	Principal 4′
Holflute 8′	Holflute 4′
Principal 4′	Superoctave 2′
Blockflute 4′	Voice Humaine 8′
Quint $2^2/_3$′	
Superoctave 2′	
Quint $1^1/_3$″	
Cornet II	
Mixture III	
Trumpet 8′	

The presence of the two 8′ Principals in the Great organ was explained by the fact that the organ was mounted on the gallery (screen) between the choir and the nave (as at King's College, Figs. 104 and 105). Due to this circumstance, the Great organ case opened on both sides, thus requiring two sets of façade pipes. This type of situation may be the origin of the later English custom of doubling the Principals from bass to treble. Probably, there is no connection with the treble doubling found in the North European organs from the Late Gothic period.

These two organs exemplify, in broad outline, the English types of the seventeenth and eighteenth centuries. The manual Werks correspond fairly well to the continental Hauptwerk, Rückpositiv, and Brustwerk; in some instances, the latter may be conceived as an Echo Werk, in the French style. This Echo Werk received a rather early and noteworthy improvement, when the organ builders Abraham Jordan and Son discovered how to make one wall of the box, in which the Werk was enclosed, as a damper formed by adjustable louver boards. With this device, the intensity of the sound could be increased and decreased, as with ordinary swell shades.

The invention was used for the first time in 1712 in a new organ for St. Magnus Church, London. It was an enormous success in England, but more than a half-century was needed for it to cross the English Channel, in spite of Händel's enthusiastic endorsement.

As mentioned earlier, the Swell Werk came into use at the same time in Spain. And since Abraham Jordan is also known as a wine importer with connections in Portugal and among Portuguese priests, there may be an explanation to the nearly simultaneous appearance of the swell-box in these two countries.

Thirds, and mixtures with thirds came to England with Smith and Harris, but were employed in a way quite different from that used on the Continent, if we rely on Hopkins and Rimbault, whose information must come from the middle of the nineteenth century. At that time, of course, countless renovations and changes in specifications may have been made, but the uniformity manifested in the various examples indicates that the main ideas were still in existence.

The mixtures had comparatively few ranks and frequently included thirds. Such mixtures tended to be high in the bass and relatively low in the treble; at any rate, they did not go beyond $1^1/_3'$. The difficulties are compounded by the absence of a consistent plan in the composition of the ranks (including the use of the Tierce) and in the designations applied to the mixtures. For instance, *Sesquialtera* and *Cornet* carry a different connotation from the usual one on the Continent, as will appear from the examples below. First, some Harris mixtures:

1. C–c $^4/_5$–$^2/_3$–$^1/_2$
   c♯–c′ $1^3/_5$–$^4/_5$–$^2/_3$
   d′–c♯″ 2–$1^3/_5$–$^4/_5$
   d″–c‴ $2^2/_3$–2–$1^3/_5$

2. C–F 1–$^2/_3$–$^1/_2$
   F♯–f 2–$1^1/_3$–1
   f♯–f′ 4–$2^2/_3$–2
   f♯′–c‴ 8–4–$2^2/_3$

3. C–c $^1/_2$–$^1/_3$
   c♯–c′ 1–$^2/_3$
   c♯′–c″ $1^1/_3$–1
   c♯″–c‴ 2–$1^1/_3$

A Father Smith Mixture:

C–c 1–$^2/_3$–$^1/_2$
c♯–c′ $1^1/_3$–1
c♯′–c‴ $2^2/_3$–2

And two Mixtures by Green:

1. C–B 2–$1^1/_3$
   c–b′ $2^2/_3$–2
   c″–c‴ 4–$2^2/_3$

2. C–f♯ 1–$^4/_5$
   g–b′ $1^3/_5$–1
   c″–c‴ 2–$1^3/_5$

Next, some Harris variations of the Sesquialtera:

1. C–b♭ $1^1/_3$–1–$^4/_5$–$^2/_3$–$^1/_2$
   b–c‴ 4–$2^2/_3$–2–$1^3/_5$–$1^1/_3$

2. C–b 2–$1^3/_5$–$1^1/_3$–1
   c′–f♯″ 4–$2^2/_3$–2–$1^3/_5$
   g″–c‴ 8–4–$2^2/_3$–2

3. C–c $1^1/_3$–1–$^2/_3$
c♯–c′ $2^2/_3$–2–$1^1/_3$
c♯′–c″ 4–$2^2/_3$–2
c♯″–c″ 8–$5^1/_3$–4

A Father Smith Sesquialtera:

C–c′	$1^3/_5$–$1^1/_3$–1
c′–c″	2–$1^3/_5$–$1^1/_3$
c″–f″	$2^2/_3$–2–$1^3/_5$
f″–c‴	4–$2^2/_3$–2

A Sesquialtera by Green:

C–f♯	$1^3/_5$–$1^1/_3$–1
g–b′	2–$1^3/_5$–$1^1/_3$
c″–c‴	$2^2/_3$–2–$1^3/_5$

Finally, one by Snetzler:

C–g	2–$1^3/_5$–$1^1/_3$–1
g♯–g′	$2^2/_3$–2–$1^3/_5$–$1^1/_3$
g♯′–c‴	4–$2^2/_3$–2–$1^3/_5$

The eighteenth century brought no fundamental change in this type of organ. Both the nephews of Father Smith, and his foreman, Christopher Schrider, who succeeded him, and Harris' son, John, who continued the work on the other front along with John Byfield, followed rather closely in the footsteps of the old generation.

In this connection Johann Snetzler, who immigrated from Germany in 1746, ought to be mentioned because he completely adapted himself to the English style and way of building and still left his personal imprint on his organs.

The organ in St. Mary's Rotherhithe, London (a rare specimen), was built in 1765 by John Byfield, Jnr. and had the following specification:

Great	*Choir*
Open diapason 8′	Stopped diapason 8′
Stopped diapason 8′	Principal 4′
Principal 4′	Flute 4′
Nason $2^2/_3$′	Fifteenth (2′)
Fifteenth (2′)	Vox humana 8′
Sesquialtera III	
Cornet V	
Trumpet 8′	
Clarion 4′	

About 1800, the organ was enlarged by England & Russell with a swell-box and pull-down pedal (of one and a half octave, but with no pedal pipes); the specification had grown into this:

Great	*Swell*	*Choir*
Open diapason 16′	Open diapason 8′	Stopped diapason 8′
Open diapason 8′	Open diapason 4′	Principal 4′
Stopped diapason 8′	Stopped diapason 8′	Flute 4′
Principal 4′	Principal 4′	Fifteenth 2′
Twelfth $2^2/_3$′	Hautboy	Cremona 8′
Fifteenth 2′	Trumpet	
Sesquialtera III		
Trumpet		
Clarion		

A further repair and enlargement was made in 1882 by Gray & Davison, and now the specification afterwards looked like this:

Great	*Swell*	*Choir*
Open diapason 8′	Double diapason 16′	Stopped diapason 8′
Open diapason 8′	Open diapason 8′	Principal 4′
Stopped diapason 8′	Stopped diapason 8′	Flute 4′
Gamba 8′	Principal 4′	Fifteenth 2′
Principal 4′	Fifteenth 2′	Cremona 8′
Twelfth $2^2/_3$′	Oboe 8′	
Fifteenth 2′	Trumpet 8′	
Mixture II		*Pedal*
Trumpet 8′		Grand bourdon 16′

In origin as well as in development this organ displays typical English features; there is no independent pedal stop until 1882 (Subbass 16′), whereas a doubling of the Diapason 8′ in the Great occurs already in 1800.

The organ has recently been restored by Noel Mander with the following specification:

Great	*Swell*	*Choir*
Open diapason 8′	Double diapason 16′	Stopped diapason 8′
Open diapason 8′	Open diapason 8′	Principal 4′
Stopped diapason 8′	Stopped diapason 8′	Flute 4′
Principal 4′	Principal 4′	Fifteenth 2′
Twelfth 3′	Fifteenth 2′	Cremona 8′
Fifteenth 2′	Oboe 8′	
Sesquialtera III	Trumpet 8′	
Cornet V or		*Pedal*
Trumpet 8′		Grand bourdon 16′
Clairon 4′		

On the whole, there is not much information available for study from that period, but the well-known music historian, Dr. Burney, who made extensive study trips to the Continent in 1770-72, gives some clues with regard to the tonal characteristics of the old English organ in his comparison with the Continental organ types: "... I must observe, that most of the organs which I met with on the Continent, seem to be inferior to ours built by Father Smith, Byfield, or Snetzler, in everything but size. As the churches there are often immense, so are the organs; the tone is indeed somewhat softened and refined by space and distance; but when heard near, it is intolerably coarse and noisy; and though the number of stops in these large instruments is very great, they afford but little variety, being, for the most part, duplicates in unisons and octaves to each other, such as the great and small 12ths, flutes, and 15ths; hence in our organs not only the touch and tone, but the imitative stops are greatly superior to those of any other organs I have met with."

Dr. Burney's judgement of Continental organs is not entirely unbiassed, or the large organs in North Germany have made such an impression that he has forgotten the other Continental organ types. According to Praetoroius, the Netherlands longs after "Lieblichkeit", and French voicing also had the mild character that England is likely to have inherited via Father Smith and Harris.

In old English accounts, one adjective is repeatedly used, when something appreciative must be said about an organ; this is "sweet". It can be supplemented by "deep" and "melodious", and it corresponds well to the preference for soft, wooden Gedackts and other wooden flutes, which is evidenced by the specifications and partially preserved instruments. In this connection, the double Principals, the Swell Werk, and the small Mixtures can also be mentioned.

A decisive change occurred in English organ building toward the middle of the nineteenth century. On the basis of hearsay, it is known that Mendelssohn's association with the Victorian Court was considered to be the direct or indirect stimulus for this action. At any rate, he had to explain that he could not play Bach nor his own compositions on most of the English organs, and for a very good reason – they had no pedal Werk.

William Hill was probably the first organ builder to take up the challenge, and his organ for St. Luke's, Manchester (1840), had the following specification:

Great organ	*Choir organ*	*Swell organ*
Double Open Diapason 16′	Open Diapason 8′	Double Open Diapason 8′
Open Diapason 8′	Stopped Diapason 8′	Open Diapason 8′
Stopped Diapason 8′	Clarabella 8′	Stopped Diapason 8′
Principal 4′	Dulciana 8′	Principal 4′
Twelfth $2^2/_3$′	Principal 4′	Doublette II 2′
Fifteenth 2′	Wald-Flute 4′	Cornopean 8′
Octave Fifteenth 1′	Oboe-Flute 4′	Cremona 8′
Sesquialtera III	Fifteenth 2′	
Mixture II	Piccolo 2′	*Pedal organ*
Posaune 8′	Cremona 8′	Open Diapason 16′
		Bourdon 16′
		Trombone 16′

Still, the pedal had pipes only for the lowest octave; the rest had to be transmitted from the manual. But other innovations appeared. Three years before, he had built his first high-pressure reeds, and during the next year a large organ of 52 stops was finished for George Street Chapel, Liverpool, and here the Pedal had six stops, namely:

Open Diapason 16′
Bourdon 16′
Principal 8′
Fifteenth 4′
Sesquialtera V
Trombone 16′

After that it seems as if all resources were concentrated on creating not only a Pedal Werk, but an organ type corresponding to the authority and power of the Empire: and at the Great Exhibition in 1851 the accomplishments not only of the English but also of the Continental masters could be seen and heard. For example, both Cavaillé-Coll and Walcker were represented, but the German, Edmund Schulze, found a better acceptance on the English market because his voicing in many respects complied with English taste.

The most remarkable instrument at the Exhibition was an organ of 70 stops built by the thirty-year-old Henry Willis. However, this organ was a continuation of William Hill's efforts and a beginning of the Victorian Romantic organ type which is still respected in England and can be found in a great number of church and concert organs.

The development of pneumatic and electric systems was also making progress with Willis, and the high-pressure reeds were refined to a very high quality. But in spite of this development toward an orchestral character, the unequal temperament was still applied in 1867 in St. George's Hall, Liverpool.

The organs from the Hill firm and those from the Willis dynasty are clearly different. Hill was influenced by classical traditions of scales and voicing, and Willis was influenced by his own time; but there is not much difference to be seen from the specifications. Hill's organ for Trinity College, Cambridge (ca. 1860), had the following stop list:

Great organ

Double Open Diapason 16′
Open Diapason 8′
Open Diapason 8′
Salicional 8′
Gamba 8′
Stopped Diapason 8′
Quint $5^{1}/_{3}$′
Principal 4′
Wald Flute 4′
Nason 4′
Twelfth $2^{2}/_{3}$′
Fifteenth 2′
Full Mixture III
Sharp Mixture II
Trumpet 8′
Clairon 4′

Choir organ

Double Dulciana 16′
Dulciana 8′
Open Diapason 8′
Claribel 8′
Viola da Gamba 8′
Stopped Diapason 8′
Stopped Flute 4′
Principal 4′
Flautino 2′
Cremona 8′

Swell organ

Double Diapason 16′
Open Diapason 8′
Salicional 8′
Cone Gamba 8′
Stopped Diapason 8′
Suabe Flute 4′
Principal 4′
Fifteenth 2′
Mixture III
Double Trumpet 16′
Trumpet 8′
Cornopean 8′
Oboe 8′
Clarion 4′

Solo organ

Harmonic Flute 8′
Harmonic Flute 4′
Vox angelica 8′
Lieblich Flute 4′
Piccolo 2′
Tuba mirabilis 8′
Vox humana 8′
Orchestral Oboe 8′

Pedal organ

Sub-bourdon 32′
Open Diapason 16′
Open Diapason 16′
Violon 16′
Bourdon 16′
Principal 8′
Bass Flute 8′
Fifteenth 4′
Mixture III
Trombone 16′
Clarion 8′

In this organ the range of the pedal was C–f (30 keys). The word "double" in connection with a stop name does not means that the stop in question has two ranks. As may be seen from the specification, it concerns the pipe length, since it can only be used in reference to 16′ stops.

The nearly contemporary Willis organ in St Paul's Cathedral, London, had these stops:

Great organ

Double Diapason 16′
Open Diapason 8′
Open Diapason 8′
Claribel Flute 8′
Quint $5^1/_3$′
Principal 4′
Flute harmonique 4′
Twelfth $2^2/_3$′
Fifteenth 2′
Fourniture III
Mixture III
Trombone 16′
Tromba 8′
Clairon 4′

Choir organ

Bourdon 16′
Stopped Diapason 8′
Dulciana 8′
Violoncelle 8′
Lieblich Gedact 8′
Claribel Flute 8′
Flute harmonique 4′
Principal 4′
Flageolet 2′
Corno di Basetto 8′
Cor anglais 8′

Pedal organ

Double Diapason 32′
Open Diapason 16′
Open Diapason 16′
Violon 16′
Octave 8′
Violoncello 8′
Mixture III
Contra Posaune 32′
Bombardon 16′
Clarion 8′

Solo organ

Harmonic Flute 8′
Concert Flute 4′
Corno di Basetto 8′
Oboe 8′
Tuba major 8′
Clarion 4′

Swell organ

Contra-Gamba 16′
Open Diapason 8′
Lieblich Gedact 8′
Salicional 8′
Vox angelica 8′
Principal 4′
Fifteenth 2′
Echo Cornet III
Contra Posaune 16′
Cornopean 8′
Hautboy 8′
Clarion 4′

According to tradition, Willis characterized his organ with these words, "Nothing in the world can be compared with it." Nevertheless he later improved his instrument by adding an altar organ with these stops: Contra-Gamba 16′, Gamba 8′, Vox angelica 8′, and Vox humana 8′. Besides, a "Tuba organ" was built, of which the Tubas 16′, 8′, and 4′ were located high up in the dome of the church, and the Tuba Major 8′ and Clairon 4′ immediately above one of the organ cases. At the same time, the pedal was enlarged with Violon 16′, Bourdon 16′, Open Diapason 16′, Octave 8′, and Ophecleide 16′.

The initiative of Mendelssohn did not result in any "Bach-organ". Regardless of personal opinions about the Willis tonal proportions, his type of instrument must be acknowledged as both sensible and reasonable, as long as it is used in a cathedral. The classification of the manual Werks into Great, Choir, Swell and Solo, and the construction of Principal groups, flute groups, string groups and reed groups in the individual Werks are logically formed and based on good traditions.

In evaluating the outcome of nineteenth-century endeavours, it must certainly be admitted that English organ building, especially that of the Willis dynasty, had the courage and the requisite skills to exploit them to the fullest. The accomplishments are admirable, and when the organ builders of our own time (including the English builders) have decided to break with this trend, the reason is not only a new tonal ideal but the need for an organ with a more universal capacity in regard to organ literature – including the Romantic music, which has proved to be of living interest to the younger generation.

SOUTH GERMANY

A geographical and cultural boundary between North and South Germany has always existed, but the Reformation created a sharper line and lengthened it westward along the Rhine. In relation to the organ, Europe thereafter was split into a Protestant north and a Catholic south. The stylistically unified north included Holland, North Germany and Scandinavia; a larger and more heterogeneous south was comprised of France, South Germany, the Netherlands south of the rivers, Austria, Silesia, and on the periphery, Italy and Spain.

The professional contact between South German organ builders and Italy set an explicit stamp on their style of building, primarily at the beginning of the seventeenth century, but the specifications also furnish evidence of influence from the other side, particularly from the Netherlands, and traces of highly individualistic methods.

As in Italy, the majority of the fluework belonged to the Principal group, but mutations were coupled in two or more ranks, partly in repeating mixtures and partly in non-repeating instrumental imitations. Flutes and reeds were rarities. In contrast to the Italian organ, the pedal had more independent stops, often including a Trompete or Posaune, and, like the Dutch instruments, there were normally two manual Werks, Hauptwerk and Rückpositiv.

This is the organ type that we encounter in Arnold Schlick's *Spiegel der Orgelmacher und Organisten* (Mirror for the organ builders and organists). This little treatise, which was saved for posterity by pure coincidence, was published in 1511, and its ten chapters contain all sorts of information about the stops of the organ, pipe materials, tuning, voicing, and about its placement and technical arrangement.

Arnold Schlick was a blind court organist in the Palatinate, and in addition, he was active in various capacities at the University of Heidelberg. Thus he lived at a centre of learning, with numerous contacts in all directions, especially because of his many professional journeys.

In describing stops, he first mentions *Principals* and *Oktaves* with long, i. e. narrow, scales. He writes that the super-octave appears only in large organs, which means that the free ranks were seldom higher than 4′ pitch. The Principal ranks were simply collected into a block as in the Netherlands, however, with the difference that the lowest ranks could act as free stops.

Next, he discusses the conical pipes of the *Gemshorn* family, commonly used at the 4′ and 2′ pitches, and the *Zimbel,* which must not be so low that the individual ranks are distinguishable, but high and incisive.

Then the *Hintersatz* and the large Mixtur are discussed with regard to the size, which must be calculated according to the size of the church and the organ. However, Schlick believes that there should be 16–18 ranks in the treble, even in small organs.

His last group is the instrumental imitations, and the *Rauschpfeife* is the first referred to. There is no clarification of this term; it may be either the 2-rank *Rauschquint* ($2^2/_3$′–2′) or the South German *Rauschwerck,* a reed stop and a mixture. The next stop, the *Hölzern Gelächter* (see p. 81), is another typical instrumental imitation. The same is true of the *Zink,* whose tonal character, according to Schlick, comes very close to that of the original wind instrument. It may be constructed as a reed or as a Sesquialtera ($2^2/_3$′–$1^3/_5$′). The *Schwegel,* a Principal with a narrow mouth, was undoubtedly intended to imitate the instrument of the same name, but Schlick was obviously not satisfied with the result. However, the organ-Schwegel came to play a significant role, but his happened in a different manner.

The importance of the pedal as a canto solo Werk was strongly emphasized by Schlick; he advised that the organ bench must be high enough for the feet to "float" over the pedal board. Lifting the legs made the fast passages too difficult. The specifications from that period show that the pedal also functioned as a bass Werk, and this is clearly stated by Schlick.

Schlick evaded the details of the Regals, because he refused to "poach on the preserves" of the organ builders by disclosing their secrets; nor do Trompetes and Posaunes get any commentary beyond a remark that the ensemble between a trompete and a good, high mixture "pleased him very much". Curiously enough, stopped pipes are not mentioned at all.

Schlick was opposed to the low mutations and especially the low thirds, which he had probably heard in France. "With them, pleasant chords are impossible," he said, "because no matter how the keys are touched, they always produce dissonances and a frightful sound." In general, fifths and thirds must be held to a modest intensity; otherwise, the sound would be opaque. Large pipes were to be avoided in the mixtures, because they made the sound rough and coarse.

Schlick also disapproved of the octave shift in the stops transmitted to the pedal (these stops speak an octave lower than the corresponding manual stops), because this treatment of a melody stop made it too low. The pedal, as a bass Werk, obviously did not interest him.

For the Rückpositiv, he recommends the following stops: a Principal of wood or tin (if tin is used, the voicing must be "woody" that is, mild and singing); a *Gemshörnlein* (probably a 2′); a *Zimbelchen;* and finally, a *Hintersätzlein.* Nothing more is said about specifications.

Nevertheless, the "mirror" gives an adequate impression of Schlick's tonal ideal. The "Gothic" sound appealed to his taste, the slender, light and fresh sound, built up of light Principals, high mutations and a few reed stops.

The two Münster organs in Freiburg and Überlingen, built by Jerg Ebert from Ravensburg in 1545 and 1548 respectively, represent the Schlick organ:

FREIBURG

Hauptwerk	*Rückpositiv*	*Pedal*
Prinzipal	ain lieblichs fleutlin	Prinzipal ainer Octav tiefer dann das manual
Octaven	Zimbolin	
dreifach zimblen	ain hörnlin	ain gewaltiger Hindersatz
Hindersatz	ain mixturlin	Trommeten
faberthon		ain verdeckt Hörnlein
verdeckte Fleuten	Vogelgesang	
	Hörtrummen	

ÜBERLINGEN

Hauptwerk	*Rückpositiv*	*Pedal*
Prinzipal	Octav	Posaune
zugedeckt Flauten	Mixtur	Subbas 16′ (1596)
Octav	Zimbl	
Quinte	Hörnlein	
Faberthon		
Zimbl		
Mixtur		
Hörnlein		

In southern Germany, as in France, the Benedictines were the primary exponents of the art of organ building, and it was not unusual for monks to be concerned with organ building, both in theory and in practice. South Germany also had its Dom Bedos, the erudite P. Christophorus Vogt (1648–1721), who lived in Ottobeuren. Beside his administrative duties as assistant prior and later as prior of the monastery, he managed to live an amazingly active life as church and cloister architect, as practising organ builder, and as a consultant and leader in various new organ installations. In many instances, his organs were incorporated in the rebuilding or erection of churches where he functioned as an architect. Unfortunately, he left nothing of importance in writing, and accounts of his instruments are very sparse. It would have been interesting to know the details of this synthesis of theology, architecture and music.

One of his instruments, in Holzen Cloister, is well enough preserved to furnish some idea of his style of building. The organ was completed in 1705 in connection with an extensive rebuilding of the church, which he was also directing. Although the church was heavily damaged by a stroke of lightning in 1775, and though further changes came with a major restoration in 1794, the type of organ and the general plan are well preserved. The specification is this:

Hauptwerk	*Positiv*	*Pedal*
Principal 8′	Waldflöte 8′	Subbas 16′
Salicional 8′	Chorflöte 8′	Octavbass 8′
Viola 8′	Bordun 8′	Rauschquinte 4′ 2²/₃′
Flötten 8′	Flauto occlusa 4′	Cornet III (originally VII)
Octave 4′	Sufflöte 4′	
Quinte 2²/₃′	Flageolet 1′ ¹/₂′	
Octave 2′	Cymbale II–III	
Cimbale II		
Mixtur III		
Vox humana 8′		

In the Hauptwerk, the Principal 8′ is wide and flutelike; it stands in the part of the façade facing the nave. The Salicional 8′, which is also rather wide, is in the front facing the nuns' cloister. The Viola 8′ is a wooden string stop, and the Flött 8′ is likewise wooden, but is stopped. The Cimbale II consists of a complete 2′ and 1¹/₃′, and the Mixtur has the ranks 1′, ²/₃′, ¹/₂′ with octave repetition; originally there were five ranks. The Vox Humana stands on a special wind chest above the keyboard. In the Positiv, the Waldflöte 8′ has open wooden pipes with wide scale, and the Chorflöte 8′ also has wooden pipes, but a rather narrow scale; the sound is almost like a Principal. The Bordun 8′ and the Flauto Occlusa 4′ have stopped wooden pipes. The Flageolet has octave repetitions at c′ and c″, and the Cymbale has the ranks 2′, 1¹/₃′, and 1′, with repetition at d″.

The numerous 8′ character stops and the many wooden stops are a special South German-Austrian feature. Even in this relatively small organ there are two string stops, and one of them is wooden. The warm, "sweet" sound was favoured, and the Schlick sound-ideal no longer existed. The Positiv is certainly no Rückpositiv, but something like a Brustwerk, or more correctly, a French Echo Werk, because the wind chest is placed in the base of the organ behind the keyboards, almost on floor level for the sake of the long 8′ pipes. Nothing at all has been done to assist the instrument in speaking freely and freshly. The pedal is placed behind the Positiv.

There was a natural limit to what Christophorus Vogt could accomplish with regard to organs, though he had able assistance from his foreman, Jörg Hofer, who also worked independently now and then. Most organs were, here as in other places, built by professional organ builders. One of the great names was the family of Egedacher, which had many artistic generations and branches working in Bayern-Württemberg from the beginning of the seventeenth century to approximately the close of the eighteenth century.

The culmination of the Egedacher activity came at the beginning of the eighteenth century, primarily in the work on the Salzburg Cathedral organ. Joseph Christoph Egedacher, the court organ builder at Salzburg, and his son, Johann Christoph, began the work in 1703. About two years later, the organ was completed, and its specification was:

I. manual	*II. manual*	*Pedal*
Prästant 8′	Viola 8′	Infrabass 32′
Holzprincipal 8′	Salicional 8′	Principal 16′
Coppel 8′ (Gedackt)	Octav 4′	Principal 8′
Quintatön 8′	Rohrflöte 4′	Octave 4′
Octave 4′	Quinte $2^2/_3$′	Holz-octave 4′
Nachthorn 4′	Waldflöte 2′	Mixtur VIII
Flöte 4′		
Superoctave 2′		
Quinte $1^1/_3$′		
Sesquialtera IV		
Mixtur VI		
Cymbel		

This was the last instrument by Joseph Christoph. Soon after its completion, he had to retire from professional life, and his death occurred in 1706, at the time when his son was finishing an important enlargement of the organ. The enlargement consisted chiefly of adding a third manual with "rare" stops, especially reeds. Young Egedacher's model was the famous organ at St. Maria Maggiore in Trento, Italy.

The turn of the generation brought an immediate change in style. But even though Johann Christoph borrowed his inspirations from Italy, much that he saw and heard there had its origin in north-eastern Germany, because the Trento organ was built by Eugen Casparini, son to the organ builder Adam Caspari from Sorau in Niederlausitz.

As appears from the specification below, the reeds particularly, together with the so-called Rauschwerk (reeds and mixtures), came to characterize the enlargement. Flutes, Flageolet and Piffero are also mentioned in the description of "rare" stops. The specification was as follows:

I. manual	*II. manual*	*III. manual*	*Pedal*
Prästant 8′	Viola 8′	Principal 8′	Infrabass 32′
Holzprincipal 8′	Salicional 8′	Flauten 4′	Principal 16′
Coppel 8′	Octave 4′	Piffaro 4′	Subbas 16′
Quintatön 8′	Rohrflöte 4′	Flet duss 4′	Principal 8′
Octave 4′	Quinte $2^2/_3$′	Flageolett 2′	Octave 4′
Nachthorn 4′	Waldflöte 2′	Swegl 2′	Holz-octave 4′
Flöte 4′	Harpa 16′	Cornetti II	Mixtur VIII
Superoctave 2′	Rauschwerck XIII	Fagott 8′ (Disk.)	Rauschwerck X
Quinte $1^1/_3$′		Trombone 8′ (Disk.)	Bombardon 16′
Sesquialtera IV		Posaun 8′ (Disk.)	Sordunen 8′
Mixtur VI		Scarpa 4′	
Cymbel		Schalmei-Obona 4′	

With this instrument, Egedacher's type of organ was clearly defined. Among those instruments which were entirely his own, the specifications given here will be confined to the two cloister organs in Salem:

LIEBFRAUEN ORGAN (1716)

Hauptwerk	*Positiv*	*Pedal*
Prästant 8′	Coppel 8′	Infrabass 32′
Holz-Principal 8′	Salicional 8′	Bourdon 16′ (Prp.)
Viola 8′	Principal 4′	Principal 8′
Quintatön 8′	Rohrflöte 4′	Jula $5^1/_3$′
Octave 4′	Quintflet $2^2/_3$′	Quint $2^2/_3$′
Nachthorn 4′	Flachalet 2	Superoctave 2′
Spitzflet 4′	Starkes Rauschwerck VIII	Mixtur VI
Quinte $2^2/_3$′	Trompone od. Harpfen 8′	Bombardon 16′
Superoctave 2′		
Rauschquinte $2^2/_3$′ 2′		
Mixtur VI		
Cymbel IV		
Fagott 8′ (Bass)		
Flauten 8′ (Disk.)		

DREIFALTIGKEITS ORGAN (1720)

Hauptwerk	*Rückpositiv*	*Pedal*
Subbas 16′	Coppel 8′	Infrabass 32′
Prästant 8′	Principal 4′	Bourdon 16′ (Prp.)
Salicional 8′	Rohrflet 4′	Subbas 16′
Gamppa 8′	Quintflet $2^2/_3$′	Principal 8′
Viola 8′	Bauernflet 2′	Jula $5^1/_3$′
Octave 4′	Superoctave 2′	Octave 4′
Spitzflet 4′	Mixtur VI	Quinte $2^2/_3$′
Quinte $2^2/_3$′	Flachalet (Disk.)	Mixtur VI
Waldflet 2′	Fagott 8′ (Bass)	Bombardon 16′
Superoctave 2′	Vox humana 8′	Fagott 8′
Mixtur IV		
Cymbel IV		
Cornet IV		

When Johann Christoph Egedacher visited Trento in order to become acquainted with Casparini's style of building, he did not meet the master. A few years before, Casparini had gone back to his native Germany to end his life and his work there. But there are many reasons to believe that there had been personal contact, a half-century earlier, between Casparini and the Egedachers. When Casparini, at the age of twenty, left his father's workshop as a journeyman organ builder in order to go to Italy, he worked for about three years with various masters in Bavaria (Bayern), and there he could scarcely have missed the large Egedacher family.

After several years of travel in Italy, Casparini established himself in Padua, and as his first larger work he accomplished the rebuilding and enlargement of the organ in St. Maria Maggiore in Trento, the organ that Johann Christoph Egedacher visited on his organ-pilgrimage. It was an impressive instrument of 42 stops, and although many concessions were made in favour of the usual Italian practice, he was still able to adapt his own ideas to the whole situation.

The organ had two manual Werks and an independent pedal with a ripieno of seven stops. In the Hauptwerk *(Organo grande)* the ripieno was constructed of twelve stops, and in addition, this Werk contained the common fluework, *Voce umana,* three flute stops, two *Cornetti* (Cornetto piccolo II and Cornetto grande III), a *Piffaro* (overblowing Traversflöte), and various reed stops. The Positiv *(Organo minore)* had five stops: *Flauto stoppo, Flauto aperto,* and three ripieno stops. Besides, there was a little extra wind chest with a Fagott, which was intended as a solo stop.

Casparini worked in Italy for half a century, and many large assignments were entrusted to him; he was an experienced man, when, in 1697, he finally returned to his own country.

At that moment, a new organ was needed for the church of St. Peter and Paul (in Görlitz) which had been rebuilt after a fire. The municipal government did not hesitate in choosing the distinguished old master in preference to the three others who had already made their offers. This organ, built in the years 1697–1703, was the last of Casparini's large instruments. It was a perfect assignment; he had an opportunity to demonstrate his ideals and his skill, and the organ was a worthy conclusion to his professional life. There were three manual Werks, Hauptwerk, Oberwerk and Brustwerk; and a pedal Werk with anything but Italian dimensions:

Hauptwerk	*Oberwerk*	*Brustwerk*	*Pedal*
Prinzipal 16′	Quintaden 16′	Gedackt 8′	Gross Principal 32′
Prinzipal 8′	Prinzipal 8′	Prinzipal 4′	Octave 16′
Vox humana 8′ (lab.)	Ondamaris 8′	Octave 2′	Quintaden 16′
Viola di Gamba 8′	Octave 4′	Plockflöte 2′	Bordun 16′
Rohrquinte 5 1/3′	Gedeckte Fleut 4′	Nasat 1 1/3′	Quintaden 8′
Superoctave 4′	Spitzflöt 2 2/3′	Sedecima 1′	Tubalflöt 8′
Salicet 4′	Sedecima 2′	Scharf-Mixtur II	Gemshorn 8′
Offene Flöte 4′	Glöcklein-Thon 2′	Hautbois 8′	Gross Quinte 5 1/3′
Gedacktpommer 4′	Super-Sedecima 1 1/3′		Tubalflöt 4′
Decima nona 2 2/3′	Cornette 5 1/3′ 4′ 3 1/5′		Jubal 4′
Plockflöt 2′	Scharf II		Super-Octave 4′
Zink 2 2/3′ 1 3/5′	Cymbel II		Bauernflöte 1 1/3′ 1′
Rauschpfeife II			Helle Cymbel 1 1/3′ 1′
Mixtur III			Scharf II
Bombart 16′			Mixtur XII
			Mixtur V
			Posaune 16′
			Fagotti 16′
			Krumhorn 8′
			Tromba 8′
			Jungfernregal 4′

If we attempt to form an idea of the sound on the basis of this specification and the available information, the immense pedal Werk undoubtedly attracts the attention. Beside the Principal group, which is built up with large mixtures, five of the organ's seven reeds are placed here, and in contrast to this, the manual Werks have small mixtures, a 16′ Bombart (Trompete), and a weak Schalmei 8′ (Oboe).

This apparent lack of proportion is a bit of a puzzle, but a part of the explanation is found in the absence of any pedal couplers. Moreover, there was no intention that all of the pedal stops should be used simultaneously. Many of them were solo stops, and the use of such stops was largely governed by their location.

The manual Werks were located in the usual way: at the bottom, the Brustwerk; above it, the Hauptwerk; and at the top, the Oberwerk. The pedal was divided into five sections: at the bottom, one section which flanked the Brustwerk; above it, the largest section, which correspondingly flanked the Hauptwerk; a third section, behind the Hauptwerk; a fourth section, above it and behind the Oberwerk; and finally a fifth section, which was distributed on both sides of the Oberwerk.

The seeming doubling of several pedal stops was necessitated by this distribution, which also simplified pedal registration since the different sections became operative or inoperative by the aid of valves.

The pedal stops were separated as follows:

Flanking the Brustwerk:	Tromba 8′ (in the façade)
	Jubal 4′
	Cymbel 1$^1/_3$′–1′
Flanking the Hauptwerk:	Gross Prizipalbass 32′ (façade)
	Octavbass 16′
	Gemshorn 8′
	Gross Quinte 5$^1/_3$′
	Posaune 16′
Behind the Hauptwerk:	Bordun 16′
	Quintaden 8′
	Fagott 16′
Flanking the Oberwerk:	Tubalflöte 4′
	Mixtur V
	Mixtur XII (circular flats in the façade)
	Bauernflöte 1$^1/_3$′–1′

	Scharf II
	Jungfernregal 4′
Behind the Oberwerk:	Quintaden 16′
	Tubalflöte 8′
	Superoctave 4′
	Krummhorn 8′

The Hauptwerk, with wide scaling and a 16′ foundation, had a broad, majestic sound underscored by the Bombart 16′. The Oberwerk had narrower scales and a brighter sound "as if the clearest cymbal bells were mingling with the deep tones". The Brustwerk was fresh and "delicate".

On the whole, the sound had more warmth and more fundamental than the citizens of Görlitz were obviously accustomed to; they complained that the organ was lacking in adequate "Penetranz" and "durchschneidendes Wesen" (bite and penetrating character), especially when the church was filled. Casparini replied that he could easily make the organ twice as loud by laying some bricks on the bellows (that is, increase the wind pressure!), but then the "argentine" (silvery) sound would disappear, and the brilliance would become coarse.

Casparini sought the delicate brilliance as well as "Gravität" ("body"). Some changes in the specification during the course of the work will demonstrate his methods for underscoring the latter. The Rohrflötenquint $5^1/_3$′ was originally intended as a $2^2/_3$′; the Bombart 16′ was similarly planned as a Trombet 8′; the Salicet 4′ was specified as a 1′; and the same is true of the Plochflöt 2′.

The pedal was changed in the opposite direction. Here, the Scharff II was added, and the large Mixtur in the round façade flats was increased to 12 ranks.

To obtain a complete picture of this type of organ, the innumerable toys (Spielereien) must not be ignored. In reality, these toys were invented centuries ago (possibly they are older than the organ itself), but it is astonishing to see that they crossed the threshold of the church and even were tolerated in the High Church Italian organ. Very little is known about the time and place for their use, but Casparini certainly would not have lavished so much time and effort on them, if some childish souls (including his own, perhaps) had not derived some happiness and pleasure from them.

In the Görlitz organ, ordinary imitations of cuckoos and nightingales were merely the beginning. There were "*cymbelsterne*" and "suns" rotating on the front with an accompaniment of tinkling bells; there were drum imitations (produced by dissonant pipes), kettledrums, etc. Casparini's mania for amusement must be credited with the idea of mounting the large façade mixture in 17 circular flats composed of radiating pipes. These flats inspired the name of "Sun Organ". In a statement of the various extra items, we can find: "*Alle Engel klingend gemacht*" – the fifteen cherubs had been furnished with real trumpets!

Everyone is entitled to a private opinion about this kind of thing. But when a widely known and seriously working master of organ building, near the age of 80, uses a part of his last years for such "trifles", his dignity has at all events not gone to his head; and so there is every reason to construe these "trifles" as healthy nature and humour rather than childishness.

Eugen Casparini succeeded in building an organ for the castle church in his native town, Sorau, before he died, in 1706. His son, Adam Horatio, and his grandson continued his work and the traditions within the area of Silesia (Schlesien), where Casparini's style of building gradually formed a school.

Later, by a somewhat remarkable detour to the west, his influence reached far beyond his own locality. Andreas Silbermann, a young Saxon who left home in great haste to avoid military conscription, was employed by Casparini and worked with him in the years when the Görlitz organ was under construction.

This was a good start for a young, inquisitive organ builder, but the prospects for the future with the old Casparini were perhaps not too promising. At any rate, Silbermann left Görlitz as soon as the organ was completed and continued his travels. He visited many famous organs and came as far as Alsace, before he settled down, and in Strassburg, he began, on a small scale, as an independent organ builder.

About this time, his brother Gottfried, who was five years younger, also had to leave home. Gottfried was rather temperamental and seemingly incapable of holding any work; at length, he had to go to jail for some wild pranks, but he escaped, and after some rambling, he also landed in Strassburg, where his brother promised to take him as an apprentice, when he had served an apprenticeship as a joiner.

Gottfried settled down there, and while he was learning the joiner's trade, Andreas Silbermann went to Paris in order to become acquainted with French organ building. In the years 1704–06, he worked with Thierry.

After his homecoming, Andreas made serious efforts to develop his business, and Gottfried proved to be a good partner for him. The date on which Gottfried became a journeyman is unknown, but in 1709 he was referred to as a master after the completion of the organ for St. Peter's in Strassburg, with the following specification:

Hauptwerk	*Rückpositiv*	*Pedal*
Bordun 16′	Coppel 8′	Subbas 16′
Principal 8′	Principal 4′	Octavbass 8′
Coppel 8′	Nazard $2^{2}/_{3}'$	Prestant 4′
Octave 4′	Octave 2′	Mixtur IV
Quinte $2^{2}/_{3}'$	Terz $1^{3}/_{5}'$	Trompetenbass 8′
Superoctave 2′	Mixtur III	
Mixtur III		
Cymbel III		
Cornet V		
Terz $1^{3}/_{5}'$		

Soon afterward, Gottfried left Strassburg (the reason is unknown). With two journeymen and an apprentice, he returned to Saxony, and during the years 1709–10, he built his first instrument in his birthplace, Frauenstein. The organ was very well received. Mentzer, organist of Freiberg Cathedral, was among those who served as inspectors, and this probably accounts for the fact that Silbermann, in the same year, signed a contract with the Freiberg City Council for a large new Cathedral organ having three manuals – his most famous instrument. Hereafter, his career in Saxony was assured.

In the same period, Andreas Silbermann finished work on the organ for Maursmünster (Marmoutier), one of his most important instruments:

Hauptwerk	*Rückpositiv*	*Brustwerk*	*Pedal*
Bordun 16′	Bordun 8′	Rohrflöte 8′	Flötbass 16′
Principal 8′	Principal 4′	Octave 4′	Octavbass 8′
Bordun 8′	Flöte 4′	Quinte $2^2/_3$′	Flöte 4′
Octave 4′	Quinte $2^2/_3$′	Octave 2′	Posaune 16′
Quinte $2^2/_3$′	Octave 2′	Terz $1^3/_5$′	Trompete 8′
Octave 2′	Terz $1^3/_5$′		
Terz $1^3/_5$′	Mixtur III		
Cornet V	Krummhorn 8′		
Mixtur III			
Zimbel III			
Trompete 8′			
Vox humana 8′			
Clairon 4′			

The Mixtur stops of the Hauptwerk and the Rückpositiv were identical in composition and had the following ranks:

C–B	$1^1/_3 - 1 - {}^2/_3$
c–b	$2 - 1^1/_3 - 1$
c′–b′	$4 - 2^2/_3 - 2$
c″–c‴	$8 - 4 - 2^2/_3$

The Hauptwerk Zimbel had these ranks:

C–B	${}^1/_2 - {}^1/_3 - {}^1/_4$
c–b	$1 - {}^2/_3 - {}^1/_2$
c′–b′	$2 - 1^1/_3 - 1$
c″–g″	$2^2/_3 - 2 - 1^1/_3$
g♯″–c‴	$4 - 2^2/_3 - 2$

French influence is easily discernible in this specification: the internal structure of the Werks; the use of the mutations (especially thirds and cornets); the small mixtures without double ranks; and the little Brustwerk-Récit with just two stop knobs – one for 8′, 4′, and $2^2/_3$′, and another for 2′ and $1^3/_5$′. The reeds conform to the French style, and the Bourdons are constructed as Rohrflötes in the treble.

Strangely enough, some years went by after Andreas Silbermann's trip to France before he really started to do extensive work with reed stops. The organ for St. Peter's in Strassburg (already mentioned) is typical of these years. Aside from the Terz and Cornet, the plan of the fluework is not particularly French. Casparini's authority is still perceptible.

With regard to specifications, the organs of Andreas Silbermann have come to a stabilization by the Maursmünster organ; and his most famous instrument, the enlargement, or more accurately the rebuilding, of the large Gothic organ in Strassburg Münster, reveals the same tendencies on a larger scale:

Hauptwerk	*Rückpositiv*	*Brustwerk*	*Pedal*
Bourdon 16′	Principal 8′	Gedackt 8′	Principal 16′
Principal 8′	Gedackt 8′	Principal 4′	Subbas 16′
Gedackt 8′	Octave 4′	Nazard 2²/₃′	Principal 8′
Octave 4′	Flöte 4′	Octave 2′	Octave 4′
Nazard 2²/₃′	Nazard 2²/₃′	Terz 1³/₅′	Posaune 16′
Octave 2′	Octave 2′	Mixtur III	Trompete 8′
Terz 1³/₅′	Terz 1³/₅′	Trompete 8′	Clairon 4′
Cornet V	Quinte 1¹/₃′	Vox humana 8′	
Mixtur IV	Mixtur III		
Zimbel III	Zimbel III		
Trompete 8′	Krummhorn 8′		
Vox humana 8′			

Unfortunately, this instrument was later "remodelled" beyond all recognition. Andreas Silbermann's final large instrument, however, is intact in the Benedictine Cloister at Ebersmünster. The organ was built in 1730, and its specification and mixture composition adhere to the same lines as those at Maurmünster. On the other hand, the very wide Principal scales indicate a trend toward a fuller, softer, rounder sound. The organ is disposed in this way:

Hauptwerk	*Rückpositiv*	*Brustwerk*	*Pedal*
Bordun 16′	Gedackt 8′	Gedackt 8′	Subbas 16′
Principal 8′	Principal 4′	Principal 4′	Octave 8′
Gedackt 8′	Nazard 2 2/3′	Cornet III	Posaune 16′
Octave 4′	Octave 2′	Trompete 8′	Trompete 8′
Nazard 2 2/3′	Terz 1 3/5′		Clairon 4′
Octave 2′	Mixtur III		
Waldflöte 2′	Krummhorn 8′		
Terz 1 3/5′			
Cornet V			
Mixtur III			
Zimbel III			
Trompete 8′			
Vox humana 8′			
Clairon 4′			

The undeniable uniformity in the specifications by Andreas Silbermann makes it possible to formulate a basic outline which covers, with amazing accuracy, the majority of cases and is generally in agreement with French practice. First, the Hauptwerk has seven stops: Bourdon 8′, Prestant 4′, Nazard 2 2/3′, Doublette 2′, Cornet V, Fourniture III or IV, and Cymbale II or III. As the eighth stop, a Tierce 1 3/5′ may be added; a ninth stop, Montre 8′; a tenth, Bourdon 16′; an eleventh, Voix humaine 8′; a twelfth, Trompette 8′; and a thirteenth, Clairon 4′.

The Rückpositiv has a corresponding group of four stops as its foundation: Bourdon 8′, Prestant 4′ (or Flöte 4′), Nazard 2 2/3′, and Doublette 2′. Additional stops appear in this order: Fourniture III, Tierce 1 3/5′, Cromhorne or Trompete 8′, Voix humaine 8′, Montre 8′, Larigot 1/3′, Cymbale III.

The small Brustwerk is usually restricted to a Solo-Cornet, but in larger instruments there may be a reed and one or two small flue stops.

This succession is typical of the pedal stops: Subbass 16′, Octavbass 8′, Trompette 8′, Posaune 16′, Prestant 4′, Clairon 4′, Principal 16′, Fourniture IV.

Andreas Silbermann and his son, Johann Andreas, were not eager to build large organs. In their estimation, anything in excess of 40 stops was meaningless, and only in one instance, St. Blasien, did they use a total of 47 stops.

After the death of Andreas Silbermann, in 1734, the firm was continued for two generations; first by his son, Johann Andreas, and afterwards by Johann's son Josias Andreas. These changes of generation did not bring about progressive ideas, but the family traditions were conserved and practised, diligently and reverently.

Gottfried Silbermann adopted a different course. This is unmistakable in the specification for his first large organ, the previously mentioned instrument for the Cathedral in Freiberg, which was begun in 1710:

Hauptwerk	*Oberwerk*	*Brustwerk*	*Pedal*
Bordun 16′	Quintatön 16′	Gedackt 8′	Untersatz 32′
Principal 8′	Principal 8′	Principal 4′	Principal 16′
Viola di Gamba 8′	Gedackt 8′	Rohrflöte 4′	Subbas 16′
Rohrflöte 8′	Octave 4′	Nazard $2\frac{2}{3}'$	Octavbass 8′
Octave 4′	Splitzflöte 4′	Octave 2′	Octavbass 4′
Quinte $2\frac{2}{3}'$	Octave 2′	Terz $1\frac{3}{5}'$	Mixtur VI
Octave 2′	Flageolet 1′	Quinte $1\frac{1}{3}'$	Posaune 16′
Terz $1\frac{3}{5}'$	Echo-Cornet V	Sifflöte 1′	Trompete 8′
Cornet V	Mixtur III	Mixtur III	Clairon 4′
Mixtur IV	Cymbel II		
Cymbel III	Krummhorn 8′		
Trompete 8′	Vox humana 8′		

Points of similarity to the Strassburg organs are still visible, particularly in the stop lists for the Hauptwerk and the Brustwerk, of which the latter was preferred instead of a projected Rückpositiv. However, the most striking innovation is the presence of an Oberwerk, which may be a reflection of North German influence. While the Dutch Oberwerk was comprised of wide-scaled stops designed to supplement the narrow-scaled stops of the Hauptwerk, Gottfried Silbermann, like Casparini, used almost the opposite arrangement. Large, pompous scales were given to the Hauptwerk; much narrower scales and a weaker voicing, a "penetrant" sound, were found in the Oberwerk. The effect was enhanced by basing the Brustwerk on a 4′ Principal.

The composition of the Mixtures is given below:

Mixtur-Hauptwerk:

C–B	$2 - 1\frac{1}{3} - 1 - \frac{2}{3}$
c–b	$2\frac{2}{3} - 2 - 1\frac{1}{3} - 1$
c′–b′	$4 - 2\frac{2}{3} - 2 - 1\frac{1}{3}$
c″–C‴	$5\frac{1}{3} - 4 - 2\frac{2}{3} - 2$

Zimbeln-Hauptwerk:

C–B $1^1/_3 - 1 - {}^2/_3$

Mixtur-Oberwerk:

c–b $2 - 1^1/_3 - 1$
c′–b′ $2 - 1^1/_3 - 1$
c″–c‴ $4 - 2^2/_3 - 2 - 1^1/_3$

Zimbeln-Oberwerk:

C–B $1 - {}^2/_3$
c–b $1^1/_3 - 1$
c′–b′ $2 - 1^1/_3$
c″–c‴ $2^2/_3 - 2$

Mixtur-Brustwerk:

C–B $1 - {}^2/_3 - {}^1/_2$
c–b $2 - 1^1/_3 - 1$
c′–b′ $2^2/_3 - 2 - 1^1/_3$
c″–c‴ $4 - 2^2/_3 - 2$

The mixtures follow a very simple pattern with almost exclusive use of the fifth repetition at the c's. The Brustwerk Mixtur constitutes the only exception; it has octave repetition at c, and from that point, it runs like the Mixtur of the Oberwerk and the Zimbeln of the Hauptwerk. The non-repeating pedal Mixtur (Pleinche) has the following ranks at C: $2^2/_3 - 2 - 1^1/_3 - 1 - {}^2/_3 - {}^1/_2$.

In scaling technique, the Silbermann brothers built on the fixed-variable scales. Beyond the basic scale of 1:2, the preferred scale in northern Europe and France, they made considerable use of the ratio 3:5. This scale was well-known in Italy, and it would be easy to surmise that Casparini brought a knowledge of this scale to the north. Andreas Silbermann used this ratio, especially in his first organs. Later, he shifted, by degrees, to the customary French practice. Gottfried Silbermann favoured the basic scale of 3:5 for the wide-scaled stops (fifth and third mutations) and the stopped pipes.

In the subsequent development of Gottfried Silbermann's organs, there is a conspicuous systematization of both specifications and scales. This is clear from a comparison of the specifications for the following instruments which encompass a period of 23 years.

St. Jacobi Freiburg - 1718	*Forchheim 1724*	*St. Georgien Rötha - 1718*	*Grosshart-mannsdorf - 1741*	*Langhenners-dorf - 1721*
Hauptwerk	*Hauptwerk*	*Hauptwerk*	*Hauptwerk*	*Hauptwerk*
		Bordun 16′		Bordun 16′
Principal 8′	Principal 8′	Principal 8′	Principal 8′	Principal 8′
Quintatön 8′	Quintatön 8′		Quintatön 8′	Quintatön 8′
Rohrflöte 8′	Rohrflöte 8′	Rohrflöte 8′	Rohrflöte 8′	Rohrflöte 8′
Octave 4′	Octave 4′	Octave 4′	Octave 4′	Octave 4′
Spitzflöte 4′	Spitzflöte 4′	Spitzflöte 4′	Spitzflöte 4′	Spitzflöte 4′
Quinte $2^2/_3$′	Quinte $2^2/_3$′	Quinte $2^2/_3$′	Quinte $2^2/_3$′	Quinte $2^2/_3$′
Octave 2′	Octave 2′	Octave 2′	Octave 2′	Octave 2′
	Cornet III	Cornet III	Cornet III	Cornet III
Mixtur III	Mixtur IV	Mixtur III	Mixtur IV	Mixtur III
Cymbel II		Cymbel II		
Oberwerk	*Oberwerk*	*Oberwerk*	*Oberwerk*	*Oberwerk*
Gedackt 8′	Gedackt 8′	Gedackt 8′	Gedackt 8′	Gedackt 8′
		Quintatön 8′		
Principal 4′		Principal 4′		
Rohrflöte 4′	Rohrflöte 4′	Rohrflöte 4′	Rohrflöte 4′	Rohrflöte 4′
Nazard $2^2/_3$′	Nazard $2^2/_3$′	Nazard $2^2/_3$′	Nazard $2^2/_3$′	Nazard $2^2/_3$′
Octave 2′	Octave 2′	Octave 2′	Octave 2′	Octave 2′
			Gemshorn 2′	Waldflöte 2′
Terz $1^3/_5$′	Terz $1^3/_5$′	Terz $1^3/_5$′	Terz $1^3/_5$′	
	Quinte $1^1/_3$′	Quinte $1^1/_3$′	Quinte $1^1/_3$′	Quinte $1^1/_3$′
Sifflöte 1′	Sifflöte 1′	Sifflöte 1′	Sifflöte 1′	Sifflöte 1′
Cymbel II	Cymbel II	Mixtur III	Cymbel II	Cymbel II
Pedal	***Pedal***	***Pedal***	***Pedal***	***Pedal***
Subbas 16′	Principal 16′	Principal 16′	Subbas 16′	Subbas 16′
Trompete 8′	Octave 8′	Trompete 8′	Octave 8′	Trompete 8′
Posaune 16′	Posaune 16′	Posaune 16′	Posaune 16′	Posaune 16′

The organ for the church of Ss. Peter and Paul (1723 - 25) in Reichenbach represents the most pronounced deviation from the normal plan:

Hauptwerk	*Oberwerk*	*Pedal*
Bordun 16′	Principal 8′	Principal 16′
Principal 8′	Quintadena 8′	Octave 8′
Viola di Gamba 8′	Grobgedackt 8′	Posaune 16′
Rohrflöte 8′	Rohrflöte 4′	Trompete 8′
Octave 4′	Nazard $2^2/_3$′	
Quinte $2^2/_3$′	Octave 2′	
Octave 2′	Quinte $1^1/_3$′	
Terz $1^3/_5$′	Sifflöte 1′	
Flageolet 1′	Sesquialtera II	
Cornet III	Mixtur III	
Mixtur III	Vox humana 8′	

The regular specification is also the foundation of some large organs. The organ for St. Johannis in Zittau, built in 1741, has this arrangement:

Hauptwerk	*Oberwerk*	*Brustwerk*	*Pedal*
Principal 16′	Quintatön 16′	Gedackt 8′	Untersatz 32′
Principal 8′	Principal 8′	Principal 4′	Principal 16′
Viola di Gamba 8′	Gedackt 8′	Rohrflöte 4′	Octave 8′
Rohrflöte 8′	Octave 4′	Nazard $2^2/_3$′	Octave 4′
Octave 4′	Rohrflöte 4′	Octave 2′	Mixtur VI
Spitzflöte 4′	Nazard $2^2/_3$′	Gemshorn 2′	Posaune 16′
Quinte $2^2/_3$′	Octave 2′	Quinte $1^1/_3$′	Trompete 8′
Octave 2′	Sesquialtera	Sifflöte	Clairon 4′
Terz $1^3/_5$′	Mixtur IV	Mixtur III	
Cornet V	Vox humana 8′	Schalmey 8′	
Mixtur VI			
Cymbel III			
Fagott 16′			
Trompete 8′			

His last instrument, built in 1754 for the Catholic Court Chapel in Dresden, is of a similar construction and size (46 stops). Gottfried Silbermann died in this organ late one evening in August 1753, while he was working on the voicing. He was 71 years old and died unmarried and childless. His foreman, Zacharias Hildebrand, assumed his duties and completed the Dresden organ.

From his first large instrument, the Cathedral organ of Freiburg (1710), to his last one, Gottfried Silbermann maintained his principles of design with almost stereotyped precision. A greater consistency in the use of single mutations was characteristic of his later work. His mixture compositions follow very definite and very simple patterns. Like the Freiburg mixtures, repetitions occur only at the c's, and fifth repetition is used almost without exception. The variety in mixture types is actually made by the abridgement of a certain basic plan.

	I	II	III	IV	V
C–B	2	– 1⅓	– 1	– ⅔	– ½
c–b	4	– 2⅔	– 2	– 1⅓	– 1
c′–b′	2⅔	– 2	– 1⅓	– 1	– ⅔
c″–c‴	5⅓	– 4	– 2⅔	– 2	– 1⅓

By taking rows I, II, III, IV, the result is the low four-rank Mixtur; with rows II, III, IV, V, the high four-rank Mixtur. Rows III, IV, V create a three-rank Cymbel; rows III and IV, a low two-rank Cymbel; and IV and V, a high two-rank Cymbel. The names Mixtur and Cymbel are frequently applied to the same ensemble. In such cases, the scaling determines the choice of the name.

On the whole, the simplification is very prominent in the organs of Gottfried Silbermann. Many tonal effects are completely ignored; for example, the wide, open flutes, the overblowing flutes, and the string stops (his Viola di Gamba was a fairly wide, conical stop, nearly a Spitzflöte). The pedal is a close parallel to the Spartan lines of the French pedal, although Silbermann's voicing of the bass lends more emphasis to that Werk. While he does not comply with the French custom of providing an abundance of reeds, his selection of stops is strongly reminiscent of the French one.

With regard to the rather sparse pedal, it is necessary to remember that there was always a pedal coupler to the Hauptwerk in the Silbermann organs. The usual method of installing a coupler was to equip the Hauptwerk wind chest with an extra series of pallets, placed in a special wind chamber and connected with the pedalboard. By admitting or restricting the wind supply for this chamber, the pedalboard was coupled or uncoupled from the stops of the Hauptwerk, a method which was much older than Silbermann.

Gottfried Silbermann soon abandoned the Rückpositiv; obviously the Werk principle was losing ground. Only when three manual Werks were projected was one of them a 4′ Brustwerk with a Positiv-type specification.

However, in later instruments, he also has a Principal 8′ in the Brustwerk, when the space is available. The Hauptwerk and Oberwerk are regularly based on an 8′ Principal. This formula was natural and valid for him, although he may decide upon a Principal 16′ for a large Hauptwerk instead of, or in addition to, the customary Bourdon 16′.

The brighter character of the Oberwerk and Brustwerk is usually underscored by higher mixtures and mutations, but the essential character of the Werks is determined by means of scaling and voicing. The Hauptwerk has *grosse und gravitätische* (large and full-bodied) scales, the Oberwerk has *scharfe und penetrante* (bright and penetrating) scales, and the Brustwerk has *delicate* scales and, of course, a corresponding voicing.

Even in the structure of the instrument, it is seen that the Werk principle is no longer considered. The manual Werks are certainly still mounted somewhat according to tradition: the Brustwerk lowest, the Hauptwerk above that, the Oberwerk uppermost; but if there is a lack of vertical space, the Brustwerk is apt to be arranged as a Hinterwerk behind the Hauptwerk. The individual organ cases for the single Werks have disappeared; all of the pipes stand side by side in the same large case which, moreover, has become essentially deeper, because the large pedal ranks are placed behind the manual Werks, as done by Casparini at Görlitz.

The kinship between Gottfried Silbermann's organs and the Görlitz organ is very obvious. On the other hand, there is only a minimal amount of influence from the North-German style of building. Silbermann knew the North-German organs, but probably they were the antithesis of his tonal ideal and his tendencies toward standardization. He had his principles. By no means conservative, Silbermann's building indicates that he was well in advance of his contemporaries. We know that he accomplished a specialization in the assignment of work, something entirely new at that time; the full impact of this was not sensed until recently.

According to the contemporary judgement of his type of sound, northern Germany was not altogether remote. Shortly after Gottfried Silbermann's death, Adlung wrote the following: "in his organs, real connoisseurs of organs find nothing to be blamed, except (1) the far too uniform specifications, which might be due to an extreme caution that prevented him from employing any stops offering the slightest risk of failure; (2) the greatly exaggerated tempering (the mean-tone tuning which he would not give up); (3) the far too weak mixtures and cymbels which cause his instruments, especially in large churches, to have inadequate "bite" and penetrating quality: three things that he could easily have changed. Conversely, his admirers recognize the excellent quality of the workmanship and materials, the durability and neatness, the simplicity in the construction, and the remarkably fine and rich voicing. Finally, the exceptionally easy and comfortable key action."

Johann Sebastian Bach simply said, "He built good organs;" but we know that Bach could well imagine something beyond what Silbermann provided in the organ, and his feeling is shared by many people today. We can no longer share the tremendous enthusiasm of the 1930s for these organs, because we have seen too many of the resources that Silbermann neglected. In the light of contemporary judgement, he prefigured the coming decadence in the very areas where he was in advance of his time.

Registration instructions pertaining to the Silbermann organs have been preserved. On the back of the contract concerning the organ for Fraureuth (1742), Pastor M. Heinrich Rothe wrote out a "Summary of How the Stops should Be Drawn". The specification for the organ is this:

Hauptwerk	*Oberwerk*	*Pedal*
Principal 8′	Gedackt 8′	Subbas 16′
Quintatön 8′	Rohrflöte 4′	Posaune 16′
Rohrflöte 8′	Nazard $2^{2}/_{3}'$	
Octave 4′	Octave 2′	
Spitzflöte 4′	Quinte $1^{1}/_{3}'$	
Quinte $2^{2}/_{3}'$	Sifflöte 1	
Octave 2′	Sesquialtera II	
Terz $1^{3}/_{5}'$	Cymbel II	
Cornet III		
Mixtur IV		

1 *Cornet Ensemble.* Solo, Hauptwerk: Principal 8′, Rohrflöte 8′, Octave 4′, Spitzflöte 4′, Cornet III.
Accompaniment, Oberwerk: Gedackt 8′, Rohrflöte 4′.
Pedal: Subbass 16′.

2 *Glockenspiel,* "Steele"-play. Solo, Oberwerk: Gedackt 8′, Nassat $2^{2}/_{3}'$, Tertia $1^{3}/_{5}'$, Sifflöte 1′.
Accompaniment, Hauptwerk: Rohrflöte 8′, Spitzflöte 4′.
Pedal: Subbass 16′.

3 *Nazard Ensemble.* Solo, Oberwerk: Gedackt 8′, Rohrflöte 4′, Nassat $2^{2}/_{3}'$.
Accompaniment, Hauptwerk: Rohrflöte 8′, Spitzflöte 4′.
Pedal: Subbass 16′.

4 *Sifflöte Ensemble.* Solo, Oberwerk: Gedackt 8′, Rohrflöte 4′, Sifflöte 1′.
Accompaniment, Hauptwerk: Rohrflöte 8′, Spitzflöte 4′.
Pedal: Subbass 16′.

5 *For use with the Tremulant.* One of the 8′ stops: Principal 8′, Rohrflöte 8′, Quintaden 8′, Gedackt 8′.
Pedal: Subbass 16′.

6 *For Playing a Two-Part Composition with the Tertia.* Hauptwerk: Principal 8′, Rohrflöte 8′, Octave 4′, Quinta $2^2/_3$′, Octave 2′, Tertia $1^3/_5$′, possibly with the Mixtur.
Oberwerk: Gedackt 8′, Rohrflöte 4′, Nassat $2^2/_3$′, Octave 2′, Quinta $1^1/_3$′, Sifflöte 1′.
Pedal: Subbass 16′.

7 *Brilliant and Clear Registration.* Hauptwerk: Principal 8′, Octave 4′, Octave 2′.
Oberwerk: Gedackt 8′, Rohrflöte 4′, Octave 2′, Sifflöte 1′.
Pedal: Subbass 16′, Posaunenbass 16′.

Recorded registrations are also available for the organ in Grosshartmannsdorf (spec. p. 199). They are essentially the same as those given before, but one additional bit of information has been appended: *"Pure" Pleno.* Hauptwerk: Principal 8′, Rohrflöte 8′, Octave 4′, Quinta $2^2/_3$′, Octave 2′, Mixtur IV. Oberwerk: Gedackt 8′, Rohrflöte 4′, Octave 2′, Sifflöte 1′, Cymbel II. Pedal: Subbass 16′, Octavbass 8′, Posaunenbass 16′.

Here, as in French registrations, the flute stops are considered as a part of the pleno registration, nor are they banned from other registrations involving Principals. Nevertheless, pure Principal chorus registrations can also be found: Principal 8′, Octave 4′, possibly plus Quint $2^2/_3$′, and further, the Octave 2′ (note that the Quint $2^2/_3$′ is drawn before the Octave 2′).

South German contact with the French school was not confined to Andreas Silbermann. Young Karl Riepp (b. 1710) was trained by Jerg Hofer, the closest associate of P. Christophorus Vogt, but the death of Hofer (1731) forced Riepp to apply in several other places, and the first of these was Strassburg. However, he was rejected by Andreas Silbermann and instead had to spend a year with Merckel, a Strassburg master whose work was not up to much. Riepp then tried his luck in France where he worked for a few years with different masters, mostly Parisians. In 1735, he attained citizenship in Burgundy and began an independent business with his brother Ruppert Riepp. Some years later, the brothers moved to the city of Dijon which was their home for twenty years.

During his very first years in France, Riepp made contact with the leading masters of organ building, later including Dom Bedos who assisted him in various instances. In the specifications for his French instruments, there is actually nothing to reveal his German origin or education. This is the stop-list for the organ which was built in 1741 - 44 at St. Chapelle du Roi in Dijon:

Grand orgue	*Positif*	*Récit*	*Pédale*
Montre 16′	Bourdon 8′	Cornet V	Flûte 8′
Bourdon 16′	Prestant 4′	Trompette 8′	Bombarde 16′
Montre 8′	Flûte 4′		Trompette 8′
Bourdon 8′	Nazard $2^2/_3$′		Clairon 4′
Prestant 4′	Doublette 2′		
Gr. Nazard $5^1/_3$′	Tierce $1^3/_5$′		
Gr. Tierce $3^1/_5$′	Larigot $1^1/_3$′		
Nazard $2^2/_3$′	Fourniture III		
Doublette 2′	Cymbale II		
Quarte de Nazard 2′	Cromorne 8′		
Tierce $1^3/_5$′	Voix humaine 8′		
Cornet V			
Fourniture IV			
Cymbale IV			
Trompette 8′			
Voix humaine 8′			
Clairon 4′			

At the time that the Riepp brothers established themselves in Dijon, the corner-stone was being laid for the new diocesan church in Ottobeuren, the town next to the birthplace, Eldern. But not until twenty years later had the building progressed to the point of time for thinking about an organ and furnishings. Karl Riepp was seriously interested, and in spite of his long exile, he had not forgotten his own country, and he had certainly not been forgotten. By degrees, the attention of the authorities was centred on him, and finally he received one of his largest assignments here. This was only the beginning of his work in that region. In the time which followed, Germany, rather than France, was the centre of his activity. This was quite natural after the successful result in Ottobeuren. He built two organs there: a small instrument with two manuals and pedal on the gospel side, the so-called "Heiliggeist" organ (organ of the Holy Spirit), and a larger one with four manuals and pedal on the epistle side, the "Dreifaltigkeit" organ (organ of Trinity). Both organs were finished for the "Thousand Years' Festival" in 1766, and they have been kept almost unchanged up to the present. This is the specification of the Heiliggeist organ:

Hauptwerk	*Positiv*	*Pedal*
Copel 16′ (Gedackt)	Flauta 8′	Principal 16′
Principal 8′	Copel 8′	Copel 16′
Flauta 8′	Prestant 4′	Flauta 8′
Gamba 8′	Flet 4′	Flet 4′
Salicet 8′	Quint $2^2/_3$′	Quint $2^2/_3$′
Copel 8′	Doublet 2′	Fagott 8′
Octave 4′	Mixtur IV	
Flet 4′	Cornet III	
Doublet 2′	Schalmey 8′	
Mixtur IV		
Cimbal III		
Cromorne 8′		

DREIFALTIGKEITS-ORGAN

Grand orgue	*Positif*	*Récit*	*Pédale*
Copel 16′	Principal 16′ (treble)	Cornet V	Principal 16′
Principal 8′			Copel 16′
Flauta 8′	Flauta 8′	*Echo*	Octave 8′
Gamba 8′	Copel 8′		Gamba 8′
Salicet 8′	Octave 4′	Copel 8′	Quint $5^1/_3$′
Copel 8′	Flet 4′	Flet 4′	Flet 4′
Prestant 4′	Gamba 4′	Larigot $2^2/_3$′–2′	Mixtur III
Flet 4′	Nasard $2^2/_3$′	Terz $1^3/_5$′–1′	Bombarde 16′
Terz $3^1/_5$′	Quarte de Nas. 2′	Hoboi 8′	Trompete 8′
Quinte $2^2/_3$′	Terz $1^3/_5$′		Trompete 4′
Terz $1^3/_5$′	Quinte $1^1/_3$′		
Waldflet 2′	Fourniture V–VI		
Cornet V	Trompete 8′		
Mixtur IV	Cromorne 8′		
Cimbal IV–VI	Vox humana 8′		
Trompete 8′	Clairon 4′		
Clairon 4′			

During the period that these organs were under construction, Karl Riepp went to Strassburg for several consultations with Johann Andreas Silbermann. Judging from Silbermann's memoranda, Riepp was effusive in his praise of the Silbermann instruments. Silbermann was not unaware that Riepp was a born flatterer, but he gave him permission to observe his work; Riepp undoubtedly profited from the experience.

The organs in Ottobeuren are not true French types. Contrary to French practice, Riepp has used string stops. "They cannot be eliminated in Germany," writes Riepp himself; furthermore, open flutes have been included, and there is a 16′ treble Principal in the Positif. The pedal ensemble is also more extensive than the average French pedal, and the Tierce emphasis is somewhat modified.

The mixtures have definitely more to do with South Germany than with France. Double ranks are employed, and there is a greater variation in construction and repetition schemes. The Cimbal IV - VI in the Grand orgue of the Dreifaltigkeit organ has the following structure:

C–B $1 - 2/3 - 2/3 - 1/2$
c–e $1\,1/3 - 1 - 2/3 - 2/3 - 1/2$
f–b $1\,1/3 - 1 - 1 - 2/3 - 1/2$
c′–e′ $2\,2/3 - 2 - 1\,1/3 - 1 - 1$
f′–b′ $2\,2/3 - 2 - 1\,1/3 - 1\,1/3 - 1$
c″–e″ $5\,1/3 - 4 - 2\,2/3 - 2 - 1\,1/3 - 1\,1/3$
f″–c‴ $5\,1/3 - 4 - 2\,2/3 - 2\,2/3 - 2 - 2$

The corresponding mixture has fifth repetition, just the opposite of Dom Bedos' principles.

C–e $2\,2/3 - 2 - 1\,1/3 - 1$
f–e′ $4 - 2\,2/3 - 2 - 1\,1/3$
f′–e″ $5\,1/3 - 4 - 2\,2/3 - 2$
f″–c‴ $8 - 5\,1/3 - 4 - 2\,2/3$

The Cimbal III in the Heiliggeist organ is in better agreement with Dom Bedos:

C–B $2/3 - 1/2 - 1/3$
c–b $1 - 2/3 - 1/2$
c′–e′ $1\,1/3 - 1 - 2/3$
f′–b′ $2 - 1\,1/3 - 1$
c″–e″ $2\,2/3 - 2 - 1\,1/3$
f″–c‴ $4 - 2\,2/3 - 2$

The Fourniture V - VI in the Positif has fifth repetition and even a slight divergence from the usual forms of repetitions. By giving alternate repetitions to alternate ranks, in several instances, he creates an amusing system of rank doublings, and the treble, consequently, is not so deep.

C–E	$1 - \frac{2}{3} - \frac{2}{3} - \frac{1}{2} - \frac{1}{3}$
F–B	$1\frac{1}{3} - 1 - \frac{2}{3} - \frac{2}{3} - \frac{1}{2}$
c–e	$2 - 1\frac{1}{3} - 1 - \frac{2}{3} - \frac{1}{2}$
f–b	$2 - 1\frac{1}{3} - 1\frac{1}{3} - 1 - \frac{2}{3}$
c′–f♯′	$2\frac{2}{3} - 2 - 1\frac{1}{3} - 1\frac{1}{3} - 1$
g′–c″	$2\frac{2}{3} - 2 - 2 - 1\frac{1}{3} - 1\frac{1}{3} - 1$
c♯″–e″	$4 - 2\frac{2}{3} - 2 - 2 - 1\frac{1}{3} - 1\frac{1}{3}$
f″–g″	$4 - 2\frac{2}{3} - 2\frac{2}{3} - 2 - 2 - 1\frac{1}{3}$
g♯″–c‴	$4 - 4 - 2\frac{2}{3} - 2\frac{2}{3} - 2 - 2$

The Mixtur IV in the Rückpositiv in the Heiliggeist organ has both fifth and octave repetition, but the double ranks are arranged so that all ranks do not repeat simultaneously.

C–E	$1\frac{1}{3} - 1 - \frac{2}{3} - \frac{1}{2}$
F–B	$1\frac{1}{3} - 1 - 1 - \frac{2}{3}$
c–e	$2 - 1\frac{1}{3} - 1 - \frac{2}{3}$
f–b	$2 - 1\frac{1}{3} - 1 - 1$
c′–e″	$4 - 2\frac{2}{3} - 2 - 1\frac{1}{3}$
f″–c‴	$4 - 4 - 2\frac{2}{3} - 2$

The Hauptwerk Mixtur in the same organ has this composition:

C–B	$1\frac{1}{3} - 1 - \frac{2}{3} - \frac{1}{2}$
c–b	$2\frac{2}{3} - 2 - 1\frac{1}{3} - 1$
c′–b′	$4 - 2\frac{2}{3} - 2 - 1\frac{1}{3}$
c″–c‴	$5\frac{1}{3} - 4 - 2\frac{2}{3} - 2$

Consequently, the possibilities of variation are fully exploited.

Riepp's technique in regard to scales is like that of Dom Bedos: a basic scale of 1:2 plus the additive constant, however, a somewhat varying "constant", especially in the 8′ stops. The scales are generally narrower than those used by Dom Bedos.

Immediately after the completion of the Ottobeuren organs, Karl Riepp embarked upon another large assignment. In the Cistercian Monastery at

Salem a rebuilding of one of the Egedacher organs was desired in connection with a rebuilding of the monastery choir. However, Riepp's work was not limited to a single instrument, the Liebfrauen organ, for when it was finished, he was asked to continue immediately with the large Dreifaltigkeit organ in the same church, and after that came the Tabernackel organ.

These instruments were prepared with infinite care, and no inconvenience was avoided on the part of the monastery in order to arrive at the best possible result. The organ documents show that many of the leading figures of that time were consulted: Dom Bedos, Cl. Balbâtre (the famous Parisian organist), the masters of organ building H. Cliquot, J. A. Silbermann, Joseph Gabler, and several others.

The Liebfrauen organ was built in 1766 - 68, and the specification was:

Hauptwerk	*Positiv*	*Pedal*
Copel 16′	Salicet 8′	Principal 16′
Principal 8′	Copel 8′	Subbas 16′
Gamba 8′	Principal 4′	Octave 8′
Copel 8′	Gamba 4′	Violon 8′
Octavej 4′	Nazard $2^{2}/_{3}$′	Flet 4′
Terz $3^{1}/_{5}$′	Superoctave 2′	Mixtur IV
Nazard $2^{2}/_{3}$′	Terz $1^{3}/_{5}$′	Bombarde 16′
Octave 2′	Larigot $1^{1}/_{3}$′	Trompete 8′
Terz $1^{3}/_{5}$′	Mixtur V	Clairon 4′
Cornet V	Trompete 8′	
Mixtur IV	Cromorne 8′	
Cimbal IV	Clairon 4′	
Trompete 8′		
Vox humana 8′		
Clairon 4′		

The specification of the Dreifaltigkeit organ (1769 - 1773):

Hauptwerk	*Positiv*	*Echo*	*Pedal*
Bourdon 32′	Salicet 8′	Flaut 8′	Principal 32′
Principal 16′	Copel 8′	Gamba 8′	Principal 16′
Bourdon 16′	Copel 8′	Copel 8′	Bourdon 16′
Principal 8′	Principal 4′	Flet 4′	Flet 8′
Gamba 8′	Flet 4′	Cornet III	Gamba 8′
Flet 8′	Superoctave 2′	Serpent 8′	Quinte $5^1/_3$′
Copel 8′	Larigot $1^1/_3$′		Flet 4′
Octave 4′	Cornet V		Mixtur IV
Flet 4′	Mixtur IV		Bombarde 16′
Superoctav 2′	Cimbal III		Trompete 8′
Mixtur VI	Trompete 8′		Clairon 4′
Cimbal V	Vox humana 8′		
Cornet V	Clairon 4′		
Bombarde 16′			
Trompete 8′			
Clairon 4′			

Finally, the Tabernackel organ was rebuilt in 1766 - 1768. The organ is divided into two sections with Hauptwerk and Récit on one side and the Positiv on the other. Each of the two sections has its own console. The mechanical action would have become too complicated if all three Werks had been played from the same place; but the pedal Werk is connected to both consoles. The specification is:

Hauptwerk	*Récit*	*Pedal*	*Positiv*
Bourdon 16′	Copel 8′	Bourdon 16′	Flet 8′
Flet 8′	Cornet IV	Flet 8′	Copel 8′
Gamba 8′	Chalumeaux 8′	Gamba 8′	Octave 4′
Copel 8′		Flet 4′	Gamba 4′
Octave 4′		Bombart 16′	Flet 4′
Flet 4′		Trompete 8′	Superoctave 2′
Superoctave 2′			Mixtur V
Mixtur VI			Cornet III
Cornet V			Trompete 8′
Trompete 8′			Cromorne 8′
Vox humana 8′			Clairon 4′

From the Heiliggeist organ in Ottobeuren to this organ, the trend constantly proceeds away from the French and in a direction of the more gentle side of the South German style. In the Hauptwerk of the Tabernackel organ, a Principal was originally planned, but later it was omitted in favour of an 8′ flute, and it is quite remarkable that this organ has neither a fifth nor a third as single mutations, although such stops were specified in the first proposal. The big, "rauschende" (pealing) effect was also omitted from consideration.

Karl Riepp has left detailed instructions for registration at both Ottobeuren and Salem, but only those from Salem have been preserved. They are divided into four sections, of which the first two refer to the Liebfrauen organ and the Dreifaltigkeit organ, and the fourth to the Tabernackel organ (the third one will be discussed later). Part of the instructions may be difficult to interpret; Karl Riepp makes liberal use of abbreviations, and his expressions and spellings are a droll mixture of French and South German. For this reason, the original text will here and there be added.

First he gives some stop combinations without further elaboration concerning their use:

1 Hw. Principal 8′, Copel 8′.
2 Hw. Bourdon 16′, Principal 8′, Copel 8′. Ped. Principal 16′.
3 For Chorales. Hw. Bourdon 16′, Principal 8′, Copel 8′, Octave 4′, Nazard $2^2/_3$′, Octave 2′.
4 Alternate Chorale Registration. Hw. Bourdon 16′, Principal 8′, Copel 8′, Octave 4′, Octave 2′, Mixtur, Cymbel.
5 "Tierce-playing". Hw. Bourdon 16′, Principal 8′, Copel 8′, Octave 4′, Octave 2′, Nazard $2^2/_3$′, Terz $1^3/_5$′.
6 For a fugue. Hw. Octave 4′, Cornet V, Trompet 8′, Clairon 4′. Ped. Bombarde 16′, Trompete 8′, Clairon 4′.
7 Solo. Flet 4′, Copel 8′–Serpent 8′ (Echo?). (Text: "Solo flut traver on the Pos. Copel 8′, Principal 4′, Nazard $2^2/_3$′.
8 Solo on the Hw. Vox humana 8′, Copel 8′, Octave 4′. Accompaniment on the Pos. Copel 8′, Principal 4′, Nazard $2^2/_3$′.
9 Solo on the Hw. Gamba 8′, Octave 8′, Octave 4′. Accomp. on the Echo. Flet 8′, Copel 8′.
10 *Tierce en taille.* Pos. Copel 8′, Principal 4′, Nazard $2^2/_3$′, Superoctave 2′, Terz $1^3/_5$′, Larigot $1^1/_3$′.
11 Pos. Copel 8′, Principal 4′, Gamba 4′.
12 Echo. Serpent 8′, Flet 4′.
13 Pos. Principal 4′, Cromorne 8′. Hw. Principal 8′, Copel 8′.

14 "Basse de Trompette". Hw. Trompete 8′, Clairon 4′, Octave 4′. Pos. Copel 8′, Superoctave 2′, Larigot $1^1/_3$′.

15 Solo on the Pos. Copel 8′, Principal 4′, Nazard $2^2/_3$′, Superoctave 2′, Terz $1^3/_5$′, Larigot $1^1/_3$′. Accomp. Hw. Principal 8′, Copel 8′.

16 Hw. Bourdon 16′, Principal 8′, Bourdon 8′, Octave 4′, Nazard $2^2/_3$′, Octave 2′, Terz $1^3/_5$′. Pos. Principal 4′, Trompete 8′, Clairon 4′.

In the second section, he calls attention to the "ordinary fondamenter" of the organ: Principal 8′, Copel 8′, Octave 4′ and Superoctave 2′. The main foundations are the Copel 16′ and Copel 8′ in the Hauptwerk, the Salicet and Copel in the Positiv, and the Principal 16′ and Subbass 16′ in the pedal.

A chorale registration comes next: Hw. Bourdon 16′, Principal 8′, Copel 8′, Flet 4′, Octave 2′, Mixtur and Cymbel. Ped. Principal 16′, Flet 8′ and Copel 8′. When "Corale extras" are desired, the Bombarde 16′ and Trompete 8′ of the pedal and the reeds of the Positiv may be added.

The next registration is called "Tierce spille", which corresponds to the French *Jeu de Tierce*. A running bass is played on the Hauptwerk with the following stops: Bourdon 16′, Principal 8′, Copel 8′, Octave 4′, Terz $3^1/_5$′, Nazard $2^2/_3$′, Octave 2′, Terz $1^3/_5$′ and Larigot $1^1/_3$′. For the interludes, the Cornet is used on the Echo, and in a duo with it, the Positiv may be used for the bass passagework.

The next registration must be expressed in Riepp's own words: "Wan der prelat sich anklait kan man ein Fug schlagen mit Bombarde trompette et Clairon im pedali / in dem manuale trompett et Clairon Cornet octave / im positife principall trompette clairon." (While the prelate is putting on his vestments you can beat a fugue with Bombarde, trompette, etc.) He concludes this section with the words: "*Wass mörers ist, ist in der malzeith einem guthen koch*" (More important is a good cook for the meal).

The comparison does not occur quite accidentally, because Karl Riepp knew very well how to appreciate the pleasures of the table. Beside his activity as an organ builder, he was a wine-grower on a large scale and a wine merchant. He asserted that this business was more lucrative than organ building. He also made a good business in this respect with the monasteries in Ottobeuren and Salem.

In the third section, both the wine merchant and the organ builder appear. The form is facetious, but the registrations can well be taken in all seriousness.

The individual stops are presented in this way: Principal 16′ – a roast;

Bourdon 16′ – the bread in the soup; Principal 8′ – rice in the soup; Gedackt 8′ – roast beef; Octave 4′ – the wine; Flet 4′ – a first course; Quinte – Sauerkraut; Octave 2′ – salt; Mixtur and Cymbel – various spices; Cornet – caper sauce; Vox humana – ox tongue (!); Bombarde – wild boar ham; the Récit-Cornet – pheasant; Larigot – weak custard; Salicional – sugar bread; Echo-Cornet – coffee; Gamba 4′ – Rosolio (a liqueur), etc. The pedal is Burgundy wine; the Positiv, a sweet for women. The Quinte and Terz are nothing in themselves, but with the corresponding foundation, they are a sweet for men.

Next we learn what must be played on different occasions. First, an ordinary meal which ought to be consumed *gravitätisch,* because large bites should be eaten slowly; otherwise, they may lodge crosswise in the throat. Naturally it is a chorale registration (like no. 4). If a more solid meal is needed, reed stops must be drawn. If the organist can play the Bombarde as a solo in the pedal with this registration, it is a meal for a general or a great prelate and the convention.

For an organist's dinner, he suggests a fugue registration (like no. 6), and the organ builder gets *Jeu de Tierce.* For the appetite of women, he serves a Cornet solo on the Echo, accompanied by Principal 8′ and Copel 8′ on the Hauptwerk. An officer gets a Trompete solo on the Rückpositiv. A German gourmet is placated with Hauptwerk Gamba 8′, Copel 8′, Prestant 4′; Positiv Salicet 8′, Copel 8′, Gamba 4′; pedal Subbass 16′, Flet 8′, Flet 4′.

A Flet 8′ and Copel 8′ on the Hauptwerk, and Salicet 8′ and Copel 8′ on the Positiv, and an 8′ Flet in the pedal can be suitable nourishment for old men; but children and students must have a Vox humana duo in one of two ways: Hauptwerk, Vox humana 8′, Copel 8′, Prestant 4′, Nazard $2^{2}/_{3}$′; Positiv, Salicet 8′, Copel 8′, Nazard $2^{2}/_{3}$′, Flet 4′, or secondly, Copel 8′, Prestant 4′, Gamba 4′ on the Positiv; Flet 8′ in the pedal.

The true delicacy for "organ enthusiasts" is "Basse de Cromorne". Positiv: Cromorne 8′, Prestant 4′; Hauptwerk: Bourdon 16′, Montre 8′, Prestant 4′; pedal: Flet 8′. The solo is played in the bass of the Positiv.

A quartet will be most suitable for erudite organists and musicians. The menu runs like this: Hauptwerk: Bourdon 16′, Principal 8′, Copel 8′, Prestant 4′; Positiv: Copel 8′, Prestant 4′, Cromorne 8′; Récit: Cornet V; Pedal: Subbass 16′, Flet 8′, Gamba 8′.

And for those who take no interest at all in organ playing, something ought to be served on the Echo. That will suit them best.

The other recipes in this "cookery-book" correspond, just as several of the above mentioned registrations, approximately to Dom Bedos' instructions, published hardly ten years later.

Riepp ends this third section with a note that these "banquets also can be used in Lent and, moreover, by severe and narrow-hearted people, because the organ makers are merely wind-chefs."

The directions for registration which refer to the Tabernackel organ differ from the foregoing only to the extent demanded by the more Germanized stop-list. First, three basic registrations, here entirely without Principals, are introduced: (1) Flet 8′, Copel 8′; (2) Bourdon 16′, Flet 8′, Copel 8′; (3) Bourdon 16′, Flet 8′, Copel 8′, Flet 4′. For these registrations the pedal stops can be used in the following order: Flet 8′, Subbass 16′, Flet 4′, Gamba 8′, according to need.

The chorale registrations are consequently composed of Bourdon 16′, Flet 8′, Copel 8′, Octave 4′, Superoctave 2′, Mixtur; and in the pedal: Trompete 8′ or Subbass 16′ and Flet 8′, possibly also Flet 4′. When two flutes are used, the Trompete must be omitted. If the Cornet is included on the manual, the Bombarde 16′, and Trompete 8′ can be included in the pedal.

For a *Grand jeu,* he indicates Octave 4′, Cornet V and Trompete 8′ on the Hauptwerk, and Bombarde 16′, Trompete 8′, Flet 4′ in the pedal.

The Cornet on the Récit can be accompanied by Copel 8′ and Octave 4′ on the Hauptwerk; if this Cornet must function in a duo, the Trompete 8′ and Octave 4′ on the Hauptwerk are a proper foil.

For a trio, Vox humana 8′, Copel 8′, Flet 4′ are suggested as bass voices, the Récit Cornet as a treble voice, and the Flet 8′ and 4′ in the pedal.

The Vox humana 8′ can be used alone or together with the Copel 8′ and Flet 4′. If the registration is to be stronger, the Octave 4′ may be included.

"Basse de Trompette" (Trompete 8′ and Octave 4′ on the Hauptwerk) is used as a counterpart to the Récit-Cornet. "*Disses ist die melange Regullare aber ein organist kan hundert lay wäxlungen machen nach seinem Caprise oder goux,*" Riepp concludes. (This is the ordinary combination, but an organist can make a hundred kinds of variations according to his own caprices and taste.)

Among his associates, there were many skilful organ builders who continued as independent masters after his death, with a growing inclination toward the South German style of building. The most significant of them was Johann Nepomuk Holzhey who was entrusted with the work on the new organ for the Cloister in Neresheim (near Ulm) in 1792. Because of the Napoleonic Wars, the organ was not completed until 1798, and the specification reveals a great deal concerning the new period which was about to come, and a development away from French ideas. The reeds were almost the only thing left. The specification is:

I. Manual	*II. Manual*	*III. Manual*	*Pedal*
Bordun 32′	Principal 8′	Nachthorn 8′	Principal 16′
Principal 16′	Feldflöte 8′	Dulciano 8′	Subbas 16′
Octave 8′	Gamba 8′	Fugara 4′	Flaute 8′
Piffaro 8′	Salicional 8′	Spitzflöte 4′	Violonbas 8′
Violoncel 8′	Unda maris 8′	Flöte 2′	Flöte 4′
Quintatön 8′	Bordun 8′	Hörnle III	Bombard 16′
Coppel 8′	Flauta travers 4′	Vox humana 8′	Trompete 8′
Octave 4′	Hohlflöte 4′		Clairon 4′
Gedacktflöte 4′	Flageolet 2′		
Quinte $2^2/_3$′	Nazard III		
Octave 2′	Sexquialter V		
Cornet VI	Sonnet II		
Mixtur VI	Duce clarinet 8′		
Cimbel VI	Hoboi 8′		
Trompete 8′			
Krummhorn 8′			
Clairon 4′			

Development in South Germany would have taken an entirely different turn, if Joseph Gabler, in his time, had been chosen to build the organs for the monastery church in Ottobeuren. He was a strong candidate, and for good reasons; a few years earlier (in 1750), he had completed the largest work of his life, the organ for the monastery church in Weingarten. At that time, this organ was, as later, one of the most famous organs in Europe because of its absolutely fantastic structure and elaboration, not only of the front, but also with regard to the tonal aspect.

The South German tonal ideal, extending from the utmost "sweetness" to the enormous mixture "roar" is represented here; but any further classification of the organ is difficult. The detail work is so sumptuous that the organ must almost be considered as unique. This is immediately evident from the specification:

I. Manual – Hauptwerk.

Praestant 16′
Principal 8′
Rohrflöte 8′
Piffaro 8′ V–VII — C–B **8 – 4 – 4 – 2 – 2**
c–b 8 – 4 – 4 – 4 – 2 – 2 – 2
c′–c‴ 8 – 8 – 8 – 8 – 4 – 4 – 4

Octave 4′
Superoctave 2′ — C–b′ 2′ – 1′
c″–c‴ 2′ – 2′

Hohlflöte 2′
Sesquialter XI–VIII — C–B $2 - 1^1/_3 - 1 - 1 - {}^2/_3 - {}^2/_3 - {}^1/_2 - {}^1/_2 - {}^2/_5$
c–b $4 - 2^2/_3 - 2 - 2 - 1^1/_3 - 1^1/_3 - 1 - {}^4/_5 - {}^4/_5$
c′–b′ $5^1/_3 - 4 - 2^2/_3 - 2 - 2 - 1^1/_3 - 1^1/_3 - 1^1/_3 - 1^1/_3$
c″–c‴ $5^1/_3 - 4 - 2^2/_3 - 2^2/_3 - 2 - 2 - 1^1/_3 - {}^1/_3$

Mixtur X–XI — C–B $2 - 1^1/_3 - 1 - {}^2/_3 - {}^1/_2 - {}^1/_2 - {}^1/_3 - {}^1/_3 - {}^1/_4 - {}^1/_4$
c–b $4 - 2^2/_3 - 2 - 1^1/_3 - 1 - 1 - {}^2/_3 - {}^2/_3 - {}^1/_2 - {}^1/_2$
c′–b′ $4 - 4 - 2^2/_3 - 2 - 2 - 1^1/_3 - {}^1/_3 - 1 - 1$
c″–c‴ $8 - 8 - 5^1/_3 - 4 - 4 - 2^2/_3 - 2^2/_3 - 2 - 2$

Cymbel XII — C–B $1 - 1 - {}^2/_3 - {}^2/_3 - {}^1/_2 - {}^1/_2 - {}^1/_3 - {}^1/_3 - {}^1/_4 - {}^1/_4 - {}^1/_4 - {}^1/_4$
c–b $1 - 1 - 1 - 1 - {}^2/_3 - {}^2/_3 - {}^2/_3 - {}^2/_3 - {}^1/_2 - {}^1/_2 - {}^1/_2 - {}^1/_2$
c′–b′ $2 - 2 - 2 - 2 - 1^1/_3 - 1^1/_3 - 1^1/_3 - 1^1/_3 - 1 - 1 - 1 - 1$
c″–c‴ $4 - 4 - 4 - 4 - 2^2/_3 - 2^2/_3 - 2^2/_3 - 2^2/_3 - 2 - 2 - 2 - 2$

Trompete 8′

II. Manual – Oberwerk.

Bordun 16′ I–III — C–B Holzgedackt, c–b′ Holzgedackt + Viola,
c″–c‴ Spitzflöte + Viola + Viola

Principal 8′
Violoncello 8′ I-III — C–c ♯′ I; d′-b′ II; c″–c‴ III.
Koppel 8′ (Gedackt)
Salicional 8′
Hohlflöte 8′ (Holzflöte)
Unda maris 8′

Mixtur IX–XII — C–B $4 - 2^2/_3 - 2 - 1^3/_5 - 1^1/_3 - 1 - {}^4/_5 - {}^2/_3 - {}^1/_2$
c–b $4 - 2^2/_3 - 2 - 1^3/_5 - 1^1/_3 - 1 - 1 - {}^4/_5 - {}^2/_3 - {}^2/_3 - {}^1/_2 - {}^1/_2$
c′–b′ $5^1/_3 - 4 - 3^1/_5 - 2^2/_3 - 2 - 2 - 1^3/_5 - 1^3/_5 - 1^1/_3 - 1^1/_3 - 1 - 1$
c″–c‴ $8 - 6^2/_5 - 5^1/_3 - 5^1/_3 - 4 - 4 - 3^1/_5 - 3^1/_5 - 2^2/_3 - 2^2/_3 - 2 - 2$

Kronpositiv – II. Manual.

Octave douce I C–b 4′; c′–c‴ 8′
Viola douce II C–b′ – 4′ – 2′; c″–c‴ – 4′ – 4′
Nasat 2′
Cymbel II C–b′ – 2′ – 1′; c″–c‴ – 2′ – 2′

III. Manual – Echowerk.

Bordun 16′
Principal 8′
Quintatön 8′
Flöte 8′
Viola dolce 8′
Octave 4′
Hohlflöte 4′
Piffaro dolce II — C–b Quintatön 4′; c′–c‴ Quintatön 8′ + Viola 8′
Superoctave 2′
Mixtur V–VI — C–B $2 - 1^{1}/_{3} - 1 - {}^{2}/_{3} - {}^{1}/_{2}$
c–b $2 - 1^{1}/_{3} - 1 - {}^{2}/_{3} - {}^{1}/_{2} - {}^{1}/_{2}$
c′–b′ $4 - 2^{2}/_{3} - 2 - 1^{1}/_{3} - 1 - 1$
c″–c‴ $8 - 5^{1}/_{3} - 4 - 2^{2}/_{3} - 2 - 2$

Kornett VI–V — C–B $1 - {}^{2}/_{3} - {}^{1}/_{2} - {}^{1}/_{3} - {}^{1}/_{4} - {}^{1}/_{4}$
c–b $2 - 1^{1}/_{3} - 1 - 1 - {}^{2}/_{3} - {}^{1}/_{2} - {}^{1}/_{2}$
c′–c‴ $4 - 2^{2}/_{3} - 2 - 2 - 1^{3}/_{5}$

Oboe 8′

IV. Manual. – Epistel-Positiv.

Principal doux 8′
Flute douce 8′
Quintatön 8′
Violoncelle 8′
Rohrflöte 4′
Querflöte 4′
Flauto traverso II Rohrflöte 4′ + Offenflöte 4′
Piffaro VI–V — C–D♯ $4 - 2 - 1 - 1 - {}^{1}/_{2} - {}^{1}/_{2}$
E–c $4 - 2 - 1 - {}^{1}/_{2} - {}^{1}/_{2}$
c♯–b $4 - 2 - 1 - {}^{1}/_{2}$
c′–b′ $8 - 4 - 2 - 1$
c″–c‴ $8 - 4 - 4 - 2 - 2$

Flageolet 2′		
Kornett XI–VIII	C–B	$2 - 1\frac{1}{3} - 1 - \frac{2}{3} - \frac{2}{3} - \frac{1}{2} - \frac{1}{2} - \frac{1}{3} - \frac{1}{3} - \frac{1}{4} - \frac{1}{4}$
	c–b	$2 - 1\frac{1}{3} - 1 - 1 - \frac{2}{3} - \frac{2}{3} - \frac{1}{2} - \frac{1}{2} - \frac{1}{3} - \frac{1}{3}$
	c′–b′	$4 - 2\frac{2}{3} - 2 - 1\frac{1}{3} - 1 - 1 - \frac{4}{5} - \frac{4}{5}$
	c″–c‴	$4 - 4 - 2\frac{2}{3} - 2\frac{2}{3} - 2 - 2 - 1\frac{3}{5} - 1\frac{3}{5}$
Vox humana 8′		
Oboe 4′		
Carillon (Glocken)	f–c‴	

Hauptpedal. (C–g).

Kontrabass 32′ + 16′		
Subbas 32′		
Octavbass 16′		
Violonbass 16′ – II		
Mixturbass V–VI	C–B	$8 - 5\frac{1}{3} - 4 - 2\frac{2}{3} - 2$
	c–g	$8 - 5\frac{1}{3} - 4 - 4 - 2 - 2$
Bombarde 32′		
Posaune 16′		
La Force		
Carillon C–g		

Pedal-Positiv. (Evangelien-Rückpositiv). (C–g).

Quintatönbass 16′		
Superoctavbass 8′		
Flûte douce 8′		
Violoncello 8′		
Hohlflöte 4′		
Sesquialter VII–VI	C–E	$4 - 2 - 1\frac{1}{3} - 1 - 1 - \frac{2}{3} - \frac{2}{3} - \frac{1}{2} - \frac{1}{2} - \frac{2}{5} - \frac{2}{5}$
	F♯–g	$4 - 2 - 1\frac{1}{3} - 1 - 1 - \frac{2}{3} - \frac{2}{3} - \frac{1}{2} - \frac{1}{2} - \frac{2}{5}$
Kornettbass XI–X	C–E	$2\frac{2}{3} - 1\frac{3}{5} - 1\frac{1}{3} - \frac{4}{5} - \frac{2}{5} - \frac{2}{5} - \frac{2}{5}$
	F♯–g	$2\frac{2}{3} - 1\frac{3}{5} - 1\frac{1}{3} - \frac{4}{5} - \frac{2}{5} - \frac{2}{5}$
Trompete 8′		
Fagott 8′		

Extensive comment is not required by such a specification. The double rank principle is used to excess here, though it had gone out of use (apart from the mixtures) in most places in Europe at this time and was employed in the eastern districts only. As a compensation, all of the scales are very narrow; from this point of view, Gabler's technique may be considered as the construction of timbres from ensembles of ranks. He does not rely on the usual variations in scaling.

In designing his choruses, he employs ranks at the same pitch or at the distance of an octave. He does not use fifth or third mutations; they appear only in the mixtures and are not presented as individual stops. Gabler's use of the third in the mixtures is noteworthy; he does not conform to the well-known western methods, but often places a very high third rank in the mixtures, sometimes also a very low one. For example, the Mixtur on manual II had the third $6^2/_5'$, a 32′ combination tone. On the contrary, he can well specify a Sesquialtera without a third in the treble and a Cornet without a third in the bass. The Piffero stop here has become a pure octave mixture.

The reed stops, according to the usual South German style, are only sparsely represented, and from the beginning, they were probably not especially good, as they were all (except the Vox humana) rather quickly replaced or rebuilt.

The tremendous mixture "roar" is the most characteristic quality of this organ; it is a "*Rauschen*" of dimensions that we Scandinavians have difficulty in imagining and perhaps difficulty in appreciating. But it is a facet of the South German tonal ideal, seen under a magnifying glass.

NORTHERN EUROPE

Clarity and freshness accompanied by a constant augmentation of tonal resources prevail in the North European organ. Here we find all possibilities gradually taken into use, combined with intuitive logic in a conclusive and constructive, richly varied entity; this organ type is rarely characterized by omissions, but generally by varied emphasis on the different components.

Two eventful epochs set their decisive impact on the development of organ building, the Reformation and the Thirty Years' War. The Reformation created an entirely new requirement for the organ, when the chorale, sung in the vernacular by the congregation, was introduced as an essential part of the church service. The organ was used for both the accompaniment of this chorale and for interludes. This stimulated an immense development of the instrument, in quantity and quality.

The Gothic, Pre-Reformation organ, which usually had only one manual Werk and pull-down pedal (possibly with the transmission of some manual stops to the pedal), acquired more Werks. The Rückpositiv and Brustwerk were added at an early date, and later the Oberwerk. Above all, the pedal was enlarged with independent stops, including bass and canto solo voices. A kind of richly developed and very colourful organ existed about the turn of the sixteenth century, but then came the Thirty Years' War (1618–48) and destroyed organ building for almost two generations.

For the greater part of North Germany, it took a long time after the close of the war before anyone could think about organs again, and a still longer period elapsed before the work made satisfactory progress. Traditions had been lost, money was scarce, and bunglers and third-rate copyists flourished in a completely uncontrolled way.

Only in those places not directly touched by the devastations of the war, especially Sweden and Denmark, did the work go on at approximately its customary pace. It is certainly not too much to say that the court of Christian IV (Denmark) was the musical centre of northern Europe in that period; and many fine traditions survived and flourished there.

In 1681, Andreas Werckmeister published his *Orgelprobe* with detailed instructions about the proper testing and conceivable weaknesses of an organ. His intention was to stop the bunglers, so that gradually, the honest and efficient masters could take the leadership.

The following period brought, if possible, a richer organ and organ playing than those of the Reformation. This period has been called the "Golden Age of Organ Building", and not without reason, for the North European Baroque organ was really a great achievement with regard to the virtuoso utilization of the tonal devices pertaining to the organ.

There was a pleasant interchange of ideas between organ builders, organists and composers; but there is one more essential link in this connection – the congregation, which participated actively in the church service. The organ was needed.

Before the Second World War, the oldest tonal testimony concerning North European organ building was still to be found in Lübeck. Until the Marienkirche was bombed in 1942, pipe material from the middle of the fifteenth century constituted a part of the organ in the Totentanz Chapel, and the Hauptwerk was that of the organ built in 1477. The nearly unchanged gigantic front of the larger organ on the west wall had the original 32′ façade Principal (from 1516, Fig. 44). But all of this, and the furnishings of the church, were totally consumed by incendiary bombs.

The Jacobikirche fortunately escaped the havoc; the last Gothic organ in Lübeck was spared.

Today the specification is:

Hauptwerk	*Rückpositiv*	*Brustwerk*	*Pedal*
(15th century)	Gedackt 8′	(1636)	Subbas 16′
Principal 16′	(1636)	Gedackt 8′	Principal 8′
Octave 8′	Quintatön 8′	Quintatön 4′	Spillpfeife 8′
Spillpfeife 8′	Principal 4′	Waldflöte 2′	Flöte 4′
Octave 4′	Holflöte 4′	Cimbel II	Posaune 16′
Rohrflöte 4′	Octave 2′	Regal 8′	
Octave 2′	Scharff	Schalmei 4′	
Mixtur IV	Krummhorn 8′		
Trommet 8′	Trechterregal 8′		

The Totentanz organ also had three manual Werks:

Hauptwerk	*Rückpositiv*	*Brustwerk*	*Pedal*
Quintatön 16′	Principal 8′	Gedackt 8′	Principal 16′
Principal 8′	Rohrflöte 8′	Quintatön 4′	Subass 16′
Spitzflöte 8′	Quintatön 8′	Nachthorn 2′	Octave 8′
Octave 4′	Octave 4′	Quinte 1$^{1}/_{3}$′	Gedackt 8′
Nasat 2$^{2}/_{3}$′	Rohrflöte 4′	Nachthorn 1′	Octave 4′
Rauschquinte II	Flöte 1$^{1}/_{3}$′	Mixtur IV	Quintatön 4′
Mixtur VI–X	Sesquialtera II	Krummhorn 8′	Octave 2′
Trompete 8′	Mixtur VI–VIII	Schalmei 4′	Nachthorn 1′
	Dulzian 16′		Mixtur IV
	Trichterregal 8′		Zimbel II
			Posaune 16′
			Dulzian 16′
			Trompete 8′
			Schalmei 4′
			Cornett 2′

Both organs tell the same story: the Hauptwerk and a transmission pedal were built first, and the Rückpositiv, Brustwerk and Pedal were added later. The Hauptwerk of the Totentanz organ was constructed in 1475–77 by Johannes Stephani. In 1557–58, the Rückpositiv was added by Jacob Scherer, Hamburg. The Brustwerk, built by Henning Kröger, Wismar, did not appear until 1621–22, and at the same time the pedal was extended with independent stops. After many later changes, Karl Kemper, Lübeck, reconstructed the organ in 1937.

The Late Gothic organ is also represented by the old Petri organ at Malmö Museum, Sweden. In its restored form, the Hauptwerk probably has lost a part of its original structure (from *ca.* 1500), and the pedal stops, which were added in the base in 1759, are certainly not "Gothic". But the nucleus up to the mixtures is remarkably well preserved. The new Rückpositiv, contemporary with the reconstruction of the main organ, is a reproduction of a specification for a Rückpositiv, built in 1579 and vanished years ago. The specification of the organ to-day is the same as stated in Hülpher's Organ MS (1773):

Hovedværk	*Rygpositiv*	*Pedal*
Borduna 16′ (ca. 1500)	(1941)	Dulcian 16′ (1579)
Principal 8′ (ca. 1500)	Gedackt 8′	Trumpet 8′ (1941)
Gedackt 8′ (ca. 1500)	Principal 4′	Cornettin 2′ (1941)
Oktava 4′ (1941)	Blockflöjt 4′	
Spetsflöjt 4′ (1500?)	Oktava 2′	
Zimbelquinte $2^{2}/_{3}'$	Quinta $1^{1}/_{3}'$	
(ca. 1500)	Sesquialtera II	
Rohrquinte $2^{2}/_{3}'$ (ca. 1500)	Regal 8′	
Oktava 2′ (ca. 1500)		
Mixtur IV (1941)		
Scharf IV (1941)		
Trumpet 8′ (1941)		

By 1941, the original Octava 4′, Mixtur, Scharf and Trumpet of the Hauptwerk had disappeared, but the number of ranks in the mixtures could be established from the holes in the top boards. The Principal 8′ (the façade pipes) has the treble doubling which is common in Gothic organs. It begins at f♯, and both ranks have the same width scale.

Pedal transmissions are not present in the Malmö organ, but the pedal keyboard is connected to a row of valves in the wind chest of the Hauptwerk, as described on p. 201 in relation to the Silbermann organs. Obviously this arrangement did not suffice for the organ playing of the Reformation, and the three reed stops given to the pedal in 1579 must have been considerable gain. A lack of space in the base of the instrument was the reason why no more pedal stops were incorporated. About ten years later, the Rückpositiv was added by master Hans Brebus, Copenhagen, as a natural consequence of the development made by Lutheran church music.

The story repeats itself in other organs. Even the big Marien organ in Lübeck, which was planned as a giant organ from the beginning, received its additions. The first more detailed information about this organ is to be found in the *Syntagma musicum*, or nearly one hundred years after Bartold Hering had built the organ, and at that time various changes had already been made. Considerable repair was accomplished in 1560–61, and the same year brought the addition of the Positiv, whose Renaissance front (see Fig. 44) was later used for the screen organ in the choir. Jacob Scherer was in charge of the work. The specification left by Praetorius will be exactly reproduced here:

Oben in der Orgel sind 7 Stimmen.

1. Principal und Ventile
2. Grossoctava
3. Kleinoctava
4. Ruschquint
5. Scharff Zimbel
6. Superoctava
7. Mixtur

In der Brust 5 Stimmen.

1. Regal
2. Zinck oder Cornett
3. Krumbhorn
4. Baarpfeife
5. Gedackt

Im Pedal 14 Stimmen.

1. Gross Principal Unter Bass
2. Duppelt Unter Bass
   Ventile zu allen Röhren
   Bässen oben in der Orgel/
   als Dulcian B. Schalmeyen B.
   und Cornett B.
3. Unter Bass
   Ventile zu allen Pfeifen und
   Bässen im Stuel
4. Mixtur Bass im Stuel
5. Trommeten Bass
6. Bassunen Bass
7. Schalmeyen Bass
8. Feldpfeifen Bass im Stuel
9. Klein Octaven Bass
   Ventile zum Bassunen und Trommeten B. im Stuele
10. Dulcian Bass
11. Cornett B.
12. Gross Octaven Bass im Stuel
13. Dezehm Bass im Stuel
14. Quintadehnen Bass im Stuel

Im Rückpositiff 20 Stimmen.

1. Gemshörner
2. Blockpfeiff 4 fuss
3. Principal
4. Zimbel
5. Mixtur
6. Superoctava
7. Principale
8. Feldpfeife
9. Octava
10. Borduna
11. Offenflöit von 8 fuss
12. Gedact von 8 fuss
13. Dulcian oder Fagott 8 fs.
14. Querpfeife 4
15. Offenflöit 4
16. Octava 4
17. Superoctav
18. Mixtur
19. Dulcian oder Fagott 16
20. Trommeten

The exact interpretation of such information is difficult if not impossible, but at all events, the specification indicates that the Hauptwerk was a true Principal Werk according to the style of the Middle Ages or the Netherlands. However, it was no block Werk. The Brustwerk was remarkably small and almost like a Regal, and the Rückpositiv and a part of the pedal are the realization of the highest desires of the Reformation and the Renaissance.

Apart from the little Jacobi organ and the Malmö organ, only a very few instruments have been preserved in a condition approximately the original one. Otherwise, there are only fragments here and there, more or less accidental remnants that have escaped the rebuildings of later periods, generally for economic reasons. Reverence for historical objects was an unknown concept in such a period of progress.

Without Michael Praetorius's *Syntagma musicum,* we would have been poorly informed, but this treatise can compensate for many organs. It provides reliable descriptions of the stops and the technical organization of the organ and describes a series of old and new organs (almost all of which have been destroyed). Moreover, the "fragrance" of the time and the instruments is clearly projected by the text. In every line, we observe the zest and the appreciative wondering that characterize this whole period of expansion, and we understand that the organs have also voiced thanks and a *Te Deum* for the revelation of this wealth of ideas.

"Und gleich wie die heilige Schrift im Bapsthumb so lange zeit verborgen / und nur einen gemeinen Larven gleich geblieben; Also auch die musica und derselben Instrumenta und Opera fast immer in einem schlechten und bald nichtigen Stande beruht hat. Biss dass sie / wie jetzt gedacht / und durch Gottes gnädigen väterlichen Willen erhoben / und gleich aus einer schwarzen verdunkelten Wolcken wieder herfür kommen und erhellet / und bey dieser unser zeit von Tag zu Tage also hoch gestiegen und verbessert ist / dass es numehr fast nicht wol höher wird kommen können" (During the long era of the Papacy, Holy Writ has been concealed as in the figure of a common larva. Music and her instruments and works were similarly kept in a wretched and almost non-existent state – until they, as we now think, by the gracious and fatherly will of God were raised and returned to light from the dark, menacing clouds. And in our lifetime they have made such advances and improvements that any further progress is almost impossible).

Praetorius was no "arm-chair organ builder". In his position as Kapellmeister at the court of Braunschweig, he arranged that one of the leading contemporary masters of organ building, Esaias Compenius, was appointed "Royal Organ and Instrument Maker as well as Organist". A creative partnership was established between the two men. One of the results was the section in the *Syntagma musicum* called *De organographia,* and the chamber organ for Duke Heinrich Julius was another. This organ, now standing in the Frederiksborg Castle Church in Denmark, was presented to Christian IV by his sister, the Duke's widow.

Neither in the specification, the scales, nor the voicing has this organ anything to do with the usual style of building of the period. The instrument is a curiosity, perhaps an experiment, but at any rate, a unique proof of the degree of advancement in both tonal technique and craftmanship.

Compenius' other instruments offer further evidence of his predilection for the "*frembder, sanffter, subtiler*" (strange, soft and subtle) sound of the wooden pipes, but here, he and Praetorius had to make an entire organ with wooden pipes. Certainly some sport was also involved, because a decrease in the size of the wooden pipes makes them increasingly difficult to handle, and the extremely small pipes used in mixtures are not, with even the most perfect workmanship, comparable to those made of metal. This purely practical matter, allied with the fact that a chamber organ and not a church organ was in question, had certain consequences for the specification:

Upper Manual	*Lower Manual*	***Pedal***
Principal 8′	Quintadehna 8′	Grosser Gedacktflöiten Bass 16′
Gedacktflöte 8′	Klein Gedacktflöte 4′	Gembshorn B. 8′
Klein Principal 4′	Principal-Diskant 4′	Quintadehna B. 8′
Gemshorn oder klein Violn 4′	Blockpfeifen-Diskant 4′	Querflöiten B. 4′
Blockpfeifen 4′	Super Gemshörnlein 2′	Nachthorn B. 2′
Nachthorn 4′	Nasatt $1^1/_3$′	Bawrflöiten Bässlein 1′
Gedackt Quint $2^2/_3$′	Klein repetiert Zimbel I	Sordunen B. 16′
Supergedacktflöitlin 2′	Krumbhorn 8′	Dolzian B. 8′
Rankett 16′	Geigend Regal 4′	Jungfrawen Regal Bass 4′

The Klein repetiert Zimbel has the following structure: C–A, $^1/_6$′; B♭ –c, $^1/_4$′; f–a, $^1/_3$′; b♭–d♯′, $^1/_2$′, e′–a′, $^2/_3$; b♭–d♯″, 1′; e″–c‴, $1^1/_3$′.

Only three and one-half of the organ's twenty-seven stops belong to the Principal group: the Principals 8′ and 4′ of the upper manual, the treble

Principal of the lower manual and the Zimbel. In the remaining fluework, ten ranks are stopped; four of these are Quintatöns. The total of the decidedly flutelike stops comes to twelve and one-half, and five of these are completely stopped; Gedacktflöte 8′, Gedackt Quint $2^2/_3$′, and Supergedacktflöitlin 2′ of the upper manual; Klein Gedacktflöte 4′ of the lower manual, and Grosser Gedacktflöiten Bass 16′ of the pedal. The Bawrflöiten Bässlein 1′ in the pedal is half-stopped like a Rohrflöte, and the Querflöiten B. 4′ is a narrow, open, overblowing flute. The remaining stops are open, conical flutes of rather wide scale: Gemshorn 4′, Blockpfeifen 4′ on the upper manual, Blockpfeifen Diskant 4′, Super Gemshörnlein 2′, Nasat $1^1/_3$′ on the lower manual, and Gemshorn B. 8′ on the pedal.

It is worthy of note that all of the stopped flutes (also the little 1′ Rohrflöte on the pedal) are shaped as Spitzgedackts, obviously with the purpose of obtaining a brighter sound. Even the Gedackt 16′ of the pedal is a Spitzgedackt.

For organ problems in general, this organ may have little significance, but as study material it has a great interest; every detail still has its original form in spite of the restoration in 1891. The original bellows of the organ are still in use, and no electrical blower is employed. The wind pressure is not completely steady; it varies between 55 and 65 mm. Water Column, according to the positions of the bellows.

If we try to describe the sound, we involuntarily return to the expressions of Praetorius, "frembder, sanffter, subtiler". By "frembder", he almost means "ethereal", but a direct translation is also justified, as there is something "foreign" and "strange" about this organ. Its tonal structure is far from normal. For example, there are no Principals for a pleno, and the flute ranks do not fulfill this assignment. The organ case has a very subduing effect on the sound, and the relative intensity between the front pipes and the enclosed pipes is not completely natural. The reed stops especially are too assertive, when the door panels are open. It can be debated whether Compenius on the whole aimed at a tutti effect in the usual sense. It was indeed a chamber organ, designed for an essentially smaller room with acoustics of an entirely different nature from those in the castle church where it now stands. But there can be no doubt that the intention was to develop a series of characteristic stops having quite extraordinary qualities, and that this facet of organ building was most attractive to Compenius.

His church organs display the same tendency, as shown for example in the specification for the Bückeburg organ, his last work. He just managed to complete it, before he went to Denmark (1615) for installing the "Wooden Organ". He died in Frederiksborg and was buried there – no one knows where.

The Bückeburg specification is:

Hauptwerk

Gross Principal 16′
Gross Quintadehn 16′
Gross Octava 8′
Gemshorn 8′
Gedackte Blockpfeife 8′
Viol de Gamba 8′
Querpfeife 4′
Octava 4′
Klein Gedact Blockpfeiff 4′
Gemshorn Quinta $2^{2}/_{3}$′
Klein Flachflöit 2′
Mixtur VIII–XIV

Rückpositiv

Principal 8′
Gross Nachthorn 8′
Gedacktflöite 8′
Nasatt Pfeife 4**
Klein Rohrflöit 4′
Klein Octava 2′
Klein Gedackt 2′
Suiflöit 1′
Klingend Zimbel III
Rankett 16′
Krumbhorn 8′

Brustwerk

Rohrflöiten 8′
Nachthorn 4′
Offenflöit 4′*
Klein Gemshorn 2′
Holquintlein $1^{1}/_{3}$′
Zimbel II
Regal 8′
Geigend Regal 4′

Pedal I

Sub-Principalbass 32′
Gross Rohrflöit B. 16′
Gross Gemshorn B. 16′
Holpfeifen B. 8′
Gross Nachthorn B. 8′
Querflöiten B. 8′
Octaven B. 4′
Klein Gemshorn B. 4′
Trommeten B. 8′
Posaun oder Bombard B. 16′

Pedal II

Hornbässlein 2′
Bawrpfeifflein 1′
Zimbel Bass III
Sordunenbass 16′
Dolcianbass 8′
Cornet Bass 2′

Also in this large organ, Compenius took a remarkably small interest in the Principal group; character voices of 8′ and 4′ pitch are predominant. Only the Hauptwerk has a fairly complete Principal chorus in support of its large mixture. Compenius did not emphasize mutations and mixtures,

* Wooden Principal with ivory covering, like the pipes of the Frederiksborg organ.
** Common Wooden Principal.

and with regard to the reeds, he again preferred the character stops. On this point he concurs with his contemporaries.

Was a new organ type about to emerge? Compenius was a man who had difficulty in coming to terms with habits and traditions. The Frederiksborg organ tells us about many fresh, new thoughts and gives many ingenious solutions to difficult problems, both technical and tonal. But Compenius seems to have been lost in his excellent details, and he did not possess, to the same degree as his contemporaries, a sense of organization for these details.

The organ built by Heinrich Compenius (relative of E. C.) in 1604 for the Magdeburg Cathedral has a better plan:

Hauptwerk	*Brustwerk*	*Rückpositiv*	*Pedal*
Principal 16′	Flachflöte 4′	Principal 8′	Untersatz 32′
Quintadehn 16′	Principal 2′	Quintadehn 8′	Quintadehn 16′
Grosse Octava 8′	Mixtur VI	Octave 4′	Principal 16′
Grob Gedackt 8′	Zimbel II	Rohrflöte 4′	Gedacktbass 16′
Grosse Quinte 5¹/₃′	Grob Regal 8′	Schwiegel 4′	Gemshorn 8′
Klein Octava 4′	Singend Regal 4′	Gemshorn 4′	Octava 8′
Nachthorn 4′		Quinta 2²/₃′	Nachthorn 4′
Klein Gedackt 4′		Gedackt Quinta 2²/₃′	Bawrflöit 1′
Klein Quint 2²/₃′		Suiflöit 2′	Zimbel III
Nasatt 2²/₃′		Klein Gedackt 2′	Posaune 16′
Mixtur XII–XV		Mixtur III	Klein Posaune 8′
Zimbel III		Zimbel II	Schalmey 4′
		Dulcian 16′	Singend Cornett 2′
		Trommeten 8′	

The rather curious specification of the Brustwerk must be considered with the knowledge that this Werk is played from the keyboard of the Hauptwerk.

Furthermore, the specifications from that time show that the use of reed stops in the manual Werks was still a controversial subject. Samuel Scheidt's organ in Halle (St. Moritz Kirche) was built in 1624 by Heinrich Compenius. This instrument probably represented a collaboration between the two men and had the following specification:

Hauptwerk	*Rückpositiv*	*Pedal*
Quintadena 16′	Gedackt 8′	Offenflöte 16′
Principal 8′	Quintadena 8′	Octave 8′
Gedackt 8′	Principal 4′	Octave 4′
Octave 4′	Gedacktflöte 4′	Spitzflöte 1′
Gedacktflöte 4′	Octave 2′	Posaune 16′
Nasat $2^2/_3$′	Gemshorn 2′	Cornett 2′
Octave 2′	Sifflöte $1^1/_3$′	
Mixtur III	Spitzflöte 1′	
Trompete 8′	Mixtur III	
	Krummhorn 8′	
	Schalmei 4′	

A suggestion by Scheidt for the specification, that was certainly never realized, indicates a desire for more reeds in the Hauptwerk. The style is completely French, since there are both Trompete 8′, Trompete 4′, and Vox humana 8′, and in addition a treble Sesquialtera V in the fluework. The pedal had just three stops: Gedackt 8′, Gedackt 4′ and Trompete 8′. The Rückpositiv was strangely restricted to a Principal chorus and a Krummhorn 8′.

The organ by Gottfried Frietzsche in the Castle Church at Sondershausen, was built contemporaneously with the Bückeburg organ. Frietzsche comes rather near to the tonal ideal of Esaias Compenius, but the specification is more logical.

Hauptwerk	*Brustwerk*	*Rückpositiv*	*Pedal*
Quintadehn 16′	Gemshorn 4′	Grob Gedackt 8′	Principal 16′
Schön Principal 8′	Octave 2′	Principal 4′	Subbas 16′
Hölzern Principal 8′	Blockflöit 2′	Klein Gedackt 4′	Rohrflöte 16′
Quintadehn 8′	Quintadetz $1^1/_3$′	Querflöit 4′	Zimbel
Scharff Octave 4′	Schwiegelpfeiff 1′	Octavlin 2′	Posaune 16′
Nachthorn 4′	Geigen Regal 4′	Quintlein $1^1/_3$′	Trommet 8′
Quinta $2^2/_3$′		Zimbeln	Singend Cornet 2′
Nasatt lieblich $2^2/_3$′		Bäer-Pfeife 8′	
Mixtur VI			
Zimbel II			
Dolcian oder Ranckett 16′			

When the Brustwerk, as in the Magdeburg organ, is planned as a supplement to the Hauptwerk, the Principal group is completely represented with 8′, 4′, $2^2/_3$′, 2′, Mixtures and Zimbel. Furthermore, the flutes have a similar, complete structure ending in the 1⅓′ and 1′ of the Brustwerk. With Frietzsche, it is interesting to note the common doubling of the 8′ Principal with a Holz-Principal whch is described as *sehr eng und leblich,* i. e. with a mild string character like the Frederiksborg Principals. On the other hand, the Nachthorn 8′ is specified as a wide, open stop with a sonorous, flute-like character, not a "quinty" Gedackt of the type used by Compenius. The reed stops are arranged with 16′ and 8′ Trompetes in the pedal and otherwise "Schnarrwerk" (reeds voiced on a low wind pressure).

The structural composition of the Principal and the flute ranks, and the relation between these groups, is, generally, one of the most essential ideas in the development about 1600. There has already been some discussion of the Dutch method of constructing the Hauptwerk, solely with Principal ranks (partly as a block Werk) and assembling the flutes and the wider ranks and the reeds in the Oberwerk. This custom was brought to Germany by Dutch masters, but the Oberwerk was adopted only as a fourth Werk and without noticeably changing the character of the other Werks.

Particularly the Scherer family (the "Hamburgers" as Praetorius called them) took up the new idea. Applications of the Oberwerk may be found in various places, one of them being the well-known Jacobi organ in Hamburg. It was erected in 1535, but Hans Scherer the Elder rebuilt the organ twice (1588 - 90 and 1605 - 06). According to Praetorius, the specification after the second rebuild was:

Hauptwerk	*Rückpositiv*	*Oberwerk*	*Brustwerk*	*Pedal*
Principal 16′	Principal 8′	Principal 8′	Spitzflöte 4′	Principal 32′
Quintadehn 16′	Gedackt 8′	Holpipe 8′	Quintflöte 2²/₃′	Principal 16′
Octava 8′	Quintadehn 8′	Flöite 4′	Waltflöit 2′	Gross Bass 16′
Holpipe 8′	Octava 4′	Querflöte 4′	Krumbhorn 8′	Mixtur 10²/₃′
Querpipe 8′	Holflöit 4′	Nasatt 2²/₃′		Octava 4′
Holflöit 4′	Blockflöit 4′	Gembshorn 2′		Spillpipe 4′
Russpipe II	Gemshorn 2′	Kleinflöt 2′		Gembshorn 2′
Mixtur	Ziflöit 1′	Klingende Zimbel III		Spitzquinte 1¹/₃′
Scharp	Kling. Zimbel	Trompette 8′		Mixtur
	Mixtur	Regal 8′		Zimbel
	Scharp	Zincke 8′		Bassaune 16′
	Baarpfeife 8′			Krumbhorn 16′
	Regal 8′			Trommete 8′
	Krumbhorn 8′			Cornett 2′
	Schalmeyen 4′			

The Dutch prototype is easily discernible in this and similar specifications. The Principal ranks of the Hauptwerk have not yet been entirely emancipated from the block Werk principle; only the Principals 16′ and 8′ are independent stops; the Russpipe II (Rauschquint) and the large Mixtur and Scherp (Cymbal) continue this group, the Mixtur often having 12 - 15 ranks. Reed stops do not appear. In the Rückpositiv, only the 8′ and 4′ of the Principals are "free" stops. The Oberwerk has an 8′ Principal, and the remainder comprises flutes and wide-scaled labials (flues) and reeds in the best Dutch style.

When Scherer does not employ an Oberwerk, the Hauptwerk has changed appearance. St. Maria in Bernau (1572 - 73) may serve as an example:

Hauptwerk	*Rückpositiv*	*Pedal*
Principal 16′	Principal 8′	Principal 16′
Octave 8′	Rohrflöte 8′	Bauernflöte 1′
Gedackt 8′	Octave 4′	Posaune 16′
Quintadena 8′	Spillflöte 4′	
Quint $5^1/_3$′	Rohrquinte $2^2/_3$′	
Octave 4′	Octave 2′	
Rohrflöte 4′	Nachthorn 2′	
Quintadena 4′	Sifflöte $1^1/_3$′	
Nasat $2^2/_3$′	Zimbel III	
Octave 2′	Trompete 8′	
Blockflöte 2′	Singend Regal 4′	
Sifflöte $1^1/_3$′		
Mixtur XII	*Brustwerk*	
Scharff III	Bärpfeife 8′*	

In order to get the correct impression of what the Scherers considered to be the essentials, two specifications of smaller instruments will be given here. They can then be compared with the Jacobi organ. First, the Martini Kirche in Kassel (1610, Hans Scherer the Younger):

* Connected to the Hauptwerk manual.

Hauptwerk	*Rückpositiv*	*Oberwerk*	*Pedal*
Principal 16′	Principal 8′	Principal 8′	Principal 32′
Quintadehn 16′	Gedackt 8′	Holpfeife 8′	Octave 16′
Octave 8′	Quintadehn 8′	Gemsshorn 4′	Untersatz 16′
Holpfeife 8′	Octava 4′	Waldflöite 2′	Gedackt 8′
Flöiten 4′	Querpfeife 4′	Nasatt 1¹/₃′	Rauschpfeife 4′ 2²/₃′
Rausch-Pfeife II	Mixtur	Zimbel	Posaunen 16′
Mixtur	Scharff	Trommette 8′	Trommeten 8′
Scharff	Krumbhorn 8′	Zincken 8′	Cornet 2′
	Messing-Regal 8′		

Next, the Brüderkirche in Kassel:

Hauptwerk	*Rückpositiv*	*Pedal*
Principal 8′	Grobgedackt 8′	Offenes Principal 16′
Octave 4′	Principal 4′	Untersatz 16′
Kleingedackt 4′	Querpfeife 4′	Octave 8′
Nasat 2²/₃′	Flötgen 4′ (evt. 2′)	Posaune 16′
Octave 2′	Waldflöite 2′ (evt. 1′)	Dulcian 16′
Mixtur	Octavlin 2′	Trommeten 8′
Scharff	Mixtur	Cornett 2′
Zimbel	Klein Regal 4′	
Trommete 8′		
Zinche 8′		

The Hauptwerk in the Martini organ is almost a copy of the one in the Jacobi organ; one "luxury" stop, the Querpfeife, has been removed. The Rückpositiv has lost the top of the flute ranks and a couple of reed stops, but the Principal group is intact. In the Oberwerk, the structure of a flute chorus is maintained with a considerable reduction in stops. The Brustwerk is completely absent. The solo flues of the pedal have also disappeared, but the bass stops are retained in full strength.

Even in the essentially smaller Brüder organ, the bass pedal is well developed, but the treble stops are only represented by the Cornet 2′. Here, the Oberwerk has been omitted, but its reeds and Zimbel have migrated to the Hauptwerk, which, for that matter, has an ordinary composition of the Principal ranks with 8′ foundation. The Rückpositiv is now a 4′ Werk, and in regard to reeds, the space permits only a 4′ Regal.

The Scherers exploited every conceivable type of width scale, but the narrow scales did not decrease to the point of becoming string stops. On the contrary, curiosities like overblowing Spitzgedackts could appear, as well as the common overblowing Traversflöte, and on the whole, the stop types are copiously represented and richly varied.

Scandinavia. During the Renaissance and Baroque, the art of organ building in Scandinavia was closely allied with North Germany and the Netherlands, because almost all of its practitioners were masters whom the kings summoned from the south. The majority came from the Hamburg-Lübeck area and from the Netherlands, with which Denmark had natural intercourse through the duchies of Schleswig-Holstein and the sea lanes.

The Dutchman, Herman Raphaëlis Rodensteen, who built the organ in Roskilde Cathedral, Denmark, has already been mentioned. His successor, Hans Brebus, also came from the Netherlands. Brebus was active in Denmark until about 1615, but for the larger projects, Christian IV had already procured, shortly after 1600, another organ builder of greater importance, Nicolaus Maas of Stralsund, Mecklenburg Province, Germany.

In the *Syntagma musicum,* a specification is found for the large instrument that he built in 1594 for the Mariakirche in Stralsund. This organ, without question, explains why he, a citizen of Copenhagen, was awarded a contract as early as 1604 for a similar but smaller instrument for the Nicolaikirche in Flensborg. According to the contract, the specification was this:

Hovedværk	*Rygpositiv*	*Brystværk*	*Pedal*
Principal 16′	Principal 8′	Gedackt 8′	Untersatz 16′
Quintatön 16′	Gedackt 8′	Waldfleut 2′ (4′?)	Pompenbass 8′
Octave 8′	Blockflöte 8′	Sifflöt 2′	Gedacktbass 8′
Dultzen 8′	Octave 4′	Regal 2′ (8′ ell. 4′?)	Octavbass 4′
Gedackt 8′	Querflöte 4′		Gemshornbass 4′
Octave 4′	Kappeldous 4′		Quintatönbass 4′
Hohlflöte 4′	Superoctave 2′		Bauernflötenbass 2′
Gemshorn 4′	Zimbel III		Zimbelbass III
Superoctave 2′	Diskant-Zincke 8′		Posaunenbass 16′
Mixtur X	Geigenregal 4′		Trompetenbass 8′
Zimbel III			Schalmeienbass 4′
Trompete 8′			Cornetbass 2′

If this specification is compared with the Scherer instruments, the reader's attention is immediately captured by the contrasting Hauptwerks. Maas utilizes the fully developed Hauptwerk with Principal ranks 16′, 8′, 4′, 2′ as single stops accompanied by the large, concluding Mixtur and

Scharf or Zimbel. Furthermore, a good flute chorus is a part of the Hauptwerk design; this is also true of Scherer's instruments when the organ in question has no Oberwerk. In addition to the Principal and flute choruses, Maas has a Trompete. The greater number of organ builders in the Baltic region are tardy in adopting the Oberwerk, but in compensation, they soon reject the. block Werk conception of the Hauptwerk and begin to enlarge this Werk with flutes and reeds.

In the pedal, Scherer places his emphasis on the bass stops; Maas has a comparatively large number of treble stops. The 16′ range is very thin and often limited to transmissions from the Hauptwerk.

In the Rückpositiv and Brustwerk, there are no appreciable differences between the two organ builders, but Maas's relatively light pedal, in contrast to the imposing Hauptwerk, causes the entire character of the sound to be lighter and thinner than the sound created by Scherer. This "Gothic" balance is a salient characteristic of the northern countries, and is preserved in the instruments for several generations.

The "Gothic" sound is also exemplified in the long series of significant instruments built for Christian IV by Johann Lorentz, who was employed as Maas' foreman and succeeded him (Maas died in 1615).

Lorentz' first assignment was to finish the organ that Maas had begun for the new Frederiksborg Castle Church. For the most part, this organ served as a model for the organ that Lorentz was contracted to build, in 1619, for the Church of the Holy Trinity in Kristiansstad, Scandia (Swedish land after 1645). The Kristiansstad organ was not completed until about ten years later. The specification is preserved in records of a later date, and according to the oldest of these (from 1674) was the following:

Hovedværk	*Rygpositiv*	*Pedal*
Principal 16′	Principal 8′	Untersatz 16′
Octaua 8′	Gedact 8′	Octaua 8′
Quintadehna 8′	Octaua 4′	Gedact 8′
Spillflöit 8′	Kleingedact 4′	Quintadehna 8′
Octaua 4′	Superoctaua 2′	Octaua 4′
Spillflöit 4′	Scharff III	Basun 16′
Querflöit 4′	Trompet 8′	Dulcian 8′
Superoctaua 2′	Cornet 4′	Skalmeie 4′
Gemshorn 2′ (evt. $1^1/_3$′)		
Mixtur VI		
Zimmel III		
Dulcian 8′		

Again the light pedal Werk is characteristic, and with the exception of the Basun 16′, Skalmeie 4′, and perhaps the Untersatz 16′, all of the pedal stops were probably transmissions from the Hauptwerk. The pedal was not construed as a bass Werk.

There is a scarcity of details pertaining to the Lorentz organs, but the majority had some resemblance to the one above, that is, Hauptwerk, Rückpositiv and a light pedal which usually conformed to the Gothic style of duplexing from the Hauptwerk.

This is equally true for the other Lorentz organs: St. Olai in Elsinore (1625); Sorø Monastery Church (1628), where the Gothic main organ was rebuilt with the addition of a Rückpositiv; the Maria Church in Elsinore (1634), which may have had a Brustwerk; Kronborg Castle Church (1636); and Nakskov Church (1648). (All of these churches are located on the Danish island of Sjælland, except Nakskov Church, which is located on the island of Lolland.) At Nakskov, his last instrument, the pedal specification is a close parallel to the one at Kristiansstad, that is, Untersatz 16′, Principal 8′, Grobgedackt 8', Oktav 4′, Scharff, Basun 16′, Trompet 8′, Skalmeie 4′.

Unfortunately, there is no authentic information about his most important instrument, the organ for the Nicolai Church in Copenhagen. The only copy of the specification is contained in a memorandum by Andreas Reuter, who alludes to the condition of the organ just prior to the church fire in 1795:

Hovedværk	*Rygpositiv*	*Brystværk*	*Pedal*
Bordun 16′	Quintatön 8′	Gedackt 8′	Principal 16′
Principal 8′	Gedackt 8′	Octave 4′	Untersatz 16′
Gedakt 8′	Principal 4′	Rohrflöte 4′	Gedakt 8′
Spitzflöte 8′	Flauto 4′	Superoctav 2′	Octave 8′
Octave 4′	Quinte 2²/₃′	Quintflöte 1¹/₃′	Quintatön 8′
Spitzflöte 4′	Octave 2′	Zimbel II	Octave 4′
Querflöte 4′	Gemshorn 2′	Regal 8′	Rauschquinte 2²/₃′
Superoctave 2′	Querflöte 2′	Geigenregal 4′	Mixtur VI
Nasat 1¹/₃′	Tertia 1³/₅′		Posaune 16′
Terzian II	Scharff III		Trompete 8′
Mixtur VI	Krummhorn 8′		Schalmey 4′
Trompete 8′	Knopfregal 4′		Cornet 2′
Vox humana 8′			

The full bass of the impressive pedal may rely chiefly on transmissions from the Hauptwerk, but there is a strong probability that Lorentz, in this instance, actually built an independent pedal Werk. The financial records at the Petri Church, Copenhagen, indicate that he built free-standing bass towers for the pedal ranks; and in the Nicolai Church, Copenhagen, Lorentz was practically forced to use this procedure to provide the requisite space.

The Terzian is the one feature in the Hauptwerk which is not typical of Lorentz; it probably replaced a Cymbel or a Scharff. But it is perfectly rational for the Hauptwerk to have a Bordun 16′ without a Principal 16′. Thus the Hauptwerk is based on an 8′, and this corresponds to the Rückpositiv based on a 4′. These facts can be stated with some degree of certainty, because the foundation Principals are seldom altered at a later date – they are the façade pipes.

In the Rückpositiv and the Brustwerk, only the Tertia 1³/₅′ does not agree with Lorentz's type of specification. Presumably Lorentz had a Quint 1¹/₃′ or a 1′ stop here.

Present-day knowledge of his scaling technique is confined to the study of the façade pipes in Kristiansstad and Elsinore (the Rückpositiv of the Maria Church). The Principal scales are extremely narrow, and this is a means of underlining the slender or "Gothic" quality of sound.

This tonal ideal did not go out of fashion until the period after the Thirty Years' War, the Middle Baroque. Indicative of that trend, the contract between Trinity Church (Copenhagen) and the Hamburg organ builder, Hans Christoph Frietzsch (son of Gottfried Frietzsche), includes a specific condition that the Trinity organ must be a mate to the Lorentz organ in the Nicolai Church, except that "wide scaling" must be employed. The latter provision is made still more definite by specifying that F in the Trinity organ must have the same width as C in the Nicolai organ; the announced purpose was to make the organ tone seem "deeper and more impressive". From the specification, it is evident that the same idea motivated the use of various other devices as well.

Hovedværk	*Rygpositiv*	*Brystværk*	*Pedal*
Principal 16′	Principal 8′	Grobflöit 8′	Principal 16′
Borduen 16′	Gedakt 8′	Octaua 4′	Untersatz 16′
Quintadena 16′	Quintadena 8′	Quintadena 4′	Octaua 8′
Octaua 8′	Octaua 4′	Querpfeiff 4′	Octaua 4′
Hohlflöit 8′	Blockflöit 4′	Zimbel II	Nachthorn 4′
Octaua 4′	Super Octaua 2′	Regal 8′	Superoctaua 2′
Nasat 2²/₃′	Siefflöit 1¹/₃′		Feldpfeiff 2′
Super Octaua 2′	Sedetz 1′		Mixtur VI
Rauschpfeiff II	Sexquialter II		Bosaun 16′
Mixtur VIII	Scharff VI		Trombet 8′
Zimbel III	Trombet 8′		Dulcian 8′
Trombet 16′	Krumbhorn 8′		Schalmei 4′

The "deep and impressive" feature is strongly emphasized by the four 16′ stops of the Hauptwerk. The Trombet 16′ is preferred to a Trombet 8′ in order to stress the 16′ character of the Hauptwerk which is clearly contrasted with the 8′ and 4′ foundations of the Rückpositiv and Brustwerk respectively. In the Rückpositiv, Lorentz uses a characteristic innovation, a third-sounding stop, the Sesquialtera.

Hans Heinrich Cahmann, who came to Sweden during the reign of Karl XI, was responsible for the introduction of the "Hamburg line". The large new organ for the Cathedral in Uppsala was Cahmann's most outstanding instrument. He completed it in 1698, the year before his death.

Judging by the specification, this instrument was unrivalled in Scandinavia. However, it was completely destroyed by a fire in 1702. The specification was the following:

Huvudverk	*Ryggpositiv*	*Bröstverk*	*Pedal*
Principal 16′	Quintadena 16′	Gedackt 8′	Principal 32′
Borduna 16′	Principal 8′	Principal 4′	Principal 16′
Octava 8′	Quintadena 8′	Gedackt 4′	Untersatz 16′
Gedackt 8′	Spetsflöit 8′	Octava 2′	Octava 8′
Salicional 8′	Octava 4′	Gemshorn 2′	Gedackt 8′
Quinta $5^1/_3$′	Quinta $2^2/_3$′	Waldflöit 1′	Quinta $5^1/_3$′
Octava 4′	Octava 2′	Sesquialtera II	Octava 4′
Rörflöit 4′	Decima 2′	Scharff III	Octava 2′
Nasat $2^2/_3$′	Mixtur IV	Dulcian 8′	Rauschpfeife II
Octava 2′	Cymbel II	Skalmeia 4′	Mixtur IV
Mixtur IV	Trumpet 8′		Basun 32′
Scharff III			Basun 16′
Trumpet 16′			Trumpet 8′
Trumpet 8′			Skalmeja 4′
			Cornet 2′

With this organ, Cahmann raised Swedish organ building to a high level, but his professional life in Sweden was very brief. His son, Johan Niclas Cahmann, became the most influential organ builder in Sweden.

Among his remaining instruments, the most interesting one is undoubtedly the organ in Löfsta Bruk (1728), which has the following specification:

Huvudverk	*Ryggpositiv*	*Pedal*
Quintadena 16′	Gedackt 8′	Subbas 16′
Principal 8′	Quintadena 8′	Principal 8′
Rörflöit 8′	Principal 4′	Gedackt 8′
Quintadena 8′	Flöit 4′	Quint $5^1/_3$′
Octava 4′	Quinta $2^2/_3$′	Octava 4′
Spetsflöit 4′	Octava 2′	Rauschquint II
Quinta $2^2/_3$′	Mixtur IV	Mixtur IV
Octava 2′	Vox humana 8′	Bassun 16′
Mixtur V		Trumpet 8′
Trumpet 8′		Trumpet 4′

The composition of the mixtures is notable, because they contain thirds. The Mixtur for the Hauptwerk has the following ranks:

C–b	$1^1/_3 - 1 - {}^4/_5 - {}^2/_3 - {}^1/_2$
c′–c″	$2^2/_3 - 2 - 1^3/_5 - 1^1/_3 - 1$
c♯″–c‴	$5^1/_3 - 4 - 3^1/_5 - 2^2/_3 - 2$

At C, the Mixtur of the Rückpositiv is comprised of $1^1/_3$–1–$^4/_5$–$^2/_3$ ranks, and it repeats at f♯ and f♯″. The Pedal Mixtur has the same ranks, making no use of repetition. The Rauschquint has the usual composition, $2^2/_3$–2.

Apparently the North European interest in Tierces originated in the Netherlands during the first half of the seventeenth century, at the same time that organs were finally being tolerated for the accompaniment of congregational singing. The Tierces contributed the desired reinforcement of the soprano line, but surely their sonority would have been equally welcome.

While Buxtehude was serving as organist, the large organ in the west gallery of Lübeck's Marienkirche was modernized by various additions and some rebuilding, a process which resulted in a specification that fully complied with current demands. The specification was this:

Hauptwerk	*Stuhlpositiv*	*Brustwerk*	*Pedal*
Principal 16′	Bordun 16′	Principal 8′	Principal 32′
Quintadena 8′	Principal 8′	Gedackt 8′	Octave 16′
Octave 8′	Rohrflöte 8′	Octave 4′	Subbas 16′
Spitzflöte 8′	Quintatön 8′	Rohrflöte 4′	Octave 8′
Octave 4′	Octave 4′	Nachthorn 2′	Gedackt 8′
Rohrflöte 4′	Blockflöte 4′	Schweitserpfeife 2′	Octave 4′
Nasat $2^2/_3$′	Spillflöte 2′	Sifflöte $1^1/_3$′	Nachthorn 2′
Rauschpfeife II	Sesquialtera II	Sesquialtera II	Bauernflöte 1′
Mixtur X–XV	Mixtur V	Mixtur VI–VIII	Mixtur VI
Scharff IV	Scharff IV–V	Zimbel III	Posaune 32′
Trompete 16′	Dulcian 16′	Krummhorn 8′	Posaune 16′
Trompete 8′	Trichterregal 8′	Regal 8′	Dulcian 16′
Zinck 8′	Bärpfeife 8′		Trompete 8′
	Vox humana 8′		Krummhorn 8′
			Cornett 2′

The ultimate development of the Baroque organ in Northern Europe occurred in the Hamburg-Lübeck area, not in the Netherlands. Hans Christoph Frietzsch has been discussed, and his brother-in-law, Fr. Stellwagen of Lübeck, is also deserving of mention. But in recent years, discussions of Baroque organ building have been so centred on one personality, perhaps unjustly, that we are inclined to identify this entire period with his name – Arp Schnitger (1648–1719).

A number of preceding specifications indicate that the fundamental lines were established long before Schnitger reached maturity. But Schnitger and his school began their work with a fresh, youthful vitality in the years subsequent to the difficult decades after the Thirty Years' War; the organ builders found that their opportunities were rapidly increasing.

One additional factor has contributed to Schnitger's prominence: many of his instruments are still in use.

Possibly the best understanding of his ideas will be gained by comparing the specification for his rebuild of the Jacobi organ in Hamburg (1688) with the Scherer specification p. 230. Schnitger's specification was:

Hauptwerk	*Rückpositiv*	*Brustwerk*	*Oberwerk*
Principal 16′	Principal 8′	Principal 8′	Principal 8′
Quintadena 16′	Quintadena 8′	Octave 4′	Holzflöte 8′
Octave 8′	Gedackt 8′	Hohlflöte 4′	Rohrflöte 8′
Spitzflöte 8′	Octave 4′	Waldflöte 2′	Octave 4′
Gedackt 8′	Flöte 4′	Sesquialtera II	Rohrflöte 4′
Octave 4′	Querflöte 4′	Scharff V	Spitzflöte 4′
Rohrflöte 4′	Blockflöte 2′	Dulcian 8′	Nasat $2\frac{2}{3}'$
Superoctav 2′	Sifflet $1\frac{1}{3}'$	Trichter Regal 8′	Octave 2′
Blockflöte 2′	Sesquialtera II		Gemshorn 2′
Rauschpfeife II	Scharff VI–VIII	*Pedal*	Mixtur IV–VI
Mixtur VI	Dulcian 16′		Zimbel
Trompete 16′	Bärpfeife 8′	Gross Principal 32′	Trompete 8′
	Schalmey 4′	Principal 16′	Krummhorn 8′
		Subbas 16′	Trompete 4′
		Octave 8′	
		Octave 4′	
		Nachthorn 2′	
		Rauschpfeife II	
		Mixtur VI	
		Posaune 32′	
		Posaune 16′	
		Dulcian 16′	
		Trompete 8′	
		Trompete 4′	
		Cornett 2′	

The Oberwerk Mixtur has these ranks at C: 1–$\frac{2}{3}$–$\frac{1}{2}$–$\frac{1}{3}$; and at c‴, 4–$2\frac{2}{3}$–2–2–1–$\frac{1}{3}$. The Zimbel is planned in this manner: C, $\frac{1}{6}$–$\frac{1}{8}$–$\frac{1}{10}$; c‴, 2–$1\frac{3}{5}$–$1\frac{1}{3}$. At C, the Rückpositiv Scharff has: $1\frac{1}{3}$–$\frac{2}{3}$–$\frac{1}{2}$–$\frac{1}{3}$–$\frac{1}{4}$; and at c‴, 4–4–$2\frac{2}{3}$–$2\frac{2}{3}$–$1\frac{1}{3}$–$1\frac{1}{3}$.

In Schnitger's rebuild of the organ, the Brustwerk was converted into an independent Werk including an 8′ Principal (although the latter is simply a wooden treble Principal). Schnitger is consistent in using some type of Principal chorus in each of the four manual Werks; each is terminated with a large Mixtur, suitable in pitch to the character of the Werk.

The reeds have a definite importance as pleno stops. Although the Oberwerk is present, the Hauptwerk is crowned with a reed stop related to the Principal group. Schnitger's reeds tend to accentuate the fundamental in order to supply the "deep and impressive" sound.

The pedal has become entirely independent and no longer borrows its stops from the Hauptwerk.

Within his forty years of professional activity as a masterbuilder, Schnitger succeeded in building nearly 150 organs, and many of them were large, four manual instruments. His reputation was unchallenged. Contracts were offered to him in England, France, Spain, and even Russia, but the greater share of his instruments are found in north-western Germany (Friesland) and the northern provinces of the Netherlands, where they are also tonally at home.

In view of the construction methods, the means of transportation and travel conditions, these 150 organs constitute an impressive achievement. The best explanation for this is Schnitger's remarkable ability to organize his production. He employed fifty men, and such a business required a system representing a radical departure from earlier methods.

Hitherto organ builders had found it necessary to travel from one church to another with crew and tools, building the whole organ "on location" with materials procured by the church. This method had been losing favour for some time. Nevertheless, production to the Schnitger dimensions was something new, and the instruments bore unmistakable evidence of the system. In many instances, his organs were built in the workshop. Schnitger was compelled to devise certain standardized patterns or procedures, but they were somewhat different from the types used, for example, by Silbermann. Careful scrutiny is necessary to discover the patterns, because the diversified combinations of models actually yielded the variants demanded by the individual cases; they did not lead to stagnation in the work. The Schnitger organs are solid handwork executed with first-class materials. Few profound reflections or speculations are implied; instead, they represent an extraordinarily sound intuition which is far more valuable. It provides the natural freshness and spontaneity that we find irresistible. This is not "fussy" work – it is something that they "got quickly off their hands".

The variants in Schnitger's type of specification must be illustrated here with some examples. First, Vincent Lübeck's instrument at St. Nicolai, Hamburg, which was finished the year before the Jacobi organ:

Hauptwerk	*Rückpositiv*	*Brustwerk*	*Oberwerk*
		Blockflöte 8′	
Principal 16′	Bordun 16′	Principal 4′	Principal 8′
Quintadena 16′	Principal 8′	Rohrflöte 4′	Quintadena 8′
Rohrflöte 16′	Quintadena 8′	Nasat 2²/₃′	Hohlflöte 8′
Octave 8′	Gedackt 8′	Waldflöte 2′	Rohrflöte 8′
Spitzflöte 8′	Octave 4′	Quinte 1¹/₃′	Octave 4′
Salicional 8′	Blockflöte 4′	Mixtur IV–VI	Spillflöte 4′
Quinte 5¹/₃′	Querflöte 2′	Dulcian 8′	Nasat 2²/₃′
Octave 4′	Sifflöte 1¹/₃′	Bärpfeife 8′	Nachthorn 2′
Octave 2′	Sesquialtera II		Mixtur VI
Flachflöte 2′	Mixtur VII–IX	*Pedal*	Zimbel III
Rauschpfeife II	Dulcian 16′		Trompete 8′
Mixtur IX–X	Trichterregal 8′	Principal 32′	Vox humana 8′
Scharff III	Schalmei 4′	Octave 16′	Trompete 4′
Trompete 16′		Octave 8′	
		Quinte 5¹/₃′	
		Octave 4′	
		Nachthorn 2′	
		Rauschpfeife III	
		Mixtur X	
		Posaune 32′	
		Posaune 16′	
		Dulcian 16′	
		Trompete 8′	
		Krummhorn 8′	
		Trompete 4′	
		Cornett 2′	

Next, some smaller instruments: first, two organs with three manuals and pedal: Altenbruch and Lüdingworth.

Hauptwerk	*Rückpositiv*	*Brustwerk*	*Pedal*
Quintatön 16′	Principal 8′	Gedackt 8′	Untersatz 16′
Gedackt 8′	Quintatön 8′	Flöte 4′	Principal 8′
Octave 4′	Gedackt 8′	Octave 2′	Gedackt 8′
Waldflöte 2′	Octave 4′	Quinte 1$^1/_3$′	Octave 4′
Mixtur V	Flöte 4′	Scharff III	Mixtur IV
Cimbel III	Quinte 2$^2/_3$′	Knopfregal 8′	Posaune 16′
Vox humana 8′	Octave 2′		Trompete 8′
Trompete 8′	Blockflöte 2′		Cornett 2′
	Sesquialtera II		
	Mixtur IV		
	Dulcian 16′		
	Krumhorn 8′		

Hauptwerk	*Rückpositiv*	*Brustwerk*	*Pedal*
Quintatön 16′	Gedackt 8′	Hohlflöte 8′	Gedackt 16′
Principal 8′	Principal 4′	Flöte 4′	Principal 8′
Rohrflöte 8′	Spillflöte 4′	Octave 2′	Octave 4′
Octave 4′	Waldflöte 2′	Mixtur IV	Nachthorn 2′
Rohrflöte 4′	Octave 2′	Regal 8′	Rauschquinte II
Nasat 2$^2/_3$′	Sifflöte 1$^1/_3$′		Mixtur V–VI
Octave 2′	Sesquialtera II		Posaune 16′
Rauschpfeife II	Terzian II		Trompete 8′
Mixtur VI	Mixtur IV–VI		Cornet 2′
Cimbel III	Vox humana 8′		
Trompete 8′			

And two organs with two manuals and pedal; first, Steinkirchen:

Hauptwerk	*Oberwerk*	*Pedal*
Quintatön 16′	Gedackt 8′	Principal 16′
Principal 8′	Rohrflöte 4′	Octave 8′
Rohrflöte 8′	Octave 2′	Octave 4′
Octave 4′	Spitzflöte 2′	Quinte 5$^1/_3$′
Nasat 2$^2/_3$′	Quinte 2$^2/_3$′	Octave 2′
Octave 2′	Terzian II	Rauschpfeife II
Gemshorn 2′	Scharff III–V	Posaune 16′
Sesquialtera II	Krummhorn 8′	Trompete 8′
Mixtur IV–VI		Cornet 2′
Cimbel III		
Trompete 8′		

Then Neuenfelde, where Schnitger lived and was buried:

Hauptwerk	*Rückpositiv*	*Pedal*
Quintatön 16′	Gedackt 8′	Principal 16′
Principal 8′	Quintatön 8′	Octave 8′
Rohrflöte 8′	Principal 4′	Octave 4′
Octave 4′	Blockflöte 4′	Flöte 4′
Spitzflöte 4′	Quintflöte $2^2/_3$′	Nachthorn 2′
Nasat $2^2/_3$′	Octave 2′	Rauschpfeife II
Octave 2	Sifflöte $1^1/_3$′	Mixtur V
Spitzflöte 2′	Sesquialtera II	Posaune 16′
Rauschpfeife II	Terzian II	Trompete 8′
Mixtur V–VI	Scharff IV–V	Cornett 2′
Cimbel III	Krummhorn 8′	
Trompete 8′		
Vox humana 8′		

It seems strange that Schnitger's successors, his two sons and closest associates, left Hamburg and went their separate ways after his death in 1719. As mentioned on p. 137, the sons and three of his trusted crew went to the Netherlands where they succeeded in making reputations as independent masters; a number of large and important instruments may be credited to them. Near the end of his life, Arp Schnitger himself went to the Netherlands; his organ type had had its day in the Hamburg area. New ideas and a new era were on the way.

Schnitger's final instrument was intended for the Hauptkirche in Hamburg; this organ was finished by one of his associates, Lambert Daniel Carstens. Carstens and his brother-in-law, Johann Dietrich Busch, had previously operated a business in Itzehoe. In 1721, the Danish king licensed Carstens as an organ builder in the duchies of Schleswig-Holstein. This soon led to closer contact with Denmark. Carstens' first large organ in Copenhagen, the Garrison Church, was completed in 1725; and at about this time, he took up residence in the capital.

In the following years Carstens produced a long series of sizeable instruments in Denmark: first, the Cathedral of Århus, later, the Cathedral of Viborg. He was at the height of his activity immediately after the Copenhagen fire in 1728, when he provided new organs for most of the principal churches: Petri Church, Trinity Church, the Church of the Holy Spirit, Holmens Church, Christiansborg Castle Church, and finally the

Church of Our Lady, the last and largest one of his instruments. According to the contract, the specification was:

Hovedværk	*Rygpositiv*	*Brystværk*	*Pedal*
Principal 16′	Principal 8′	Principal 8′	Principal 16′
Bordun 16′	Gedakt 8′	Weitpfeif 8′	Subbas 16′
Oktav 8′	Oktav 4′	Salicional 8′	Rørquint $10^2/_3$′
Spidsfløjte 8′	Fløjte 4′	Oktav 4′	Oktav 8′
Oktav 4′	Nasat $2^2/_3$′	Fløjtedus 4′	Gedakt 8′
Spidsfløjte 4′	Oktav 2	Oktav 2′	Oktav 4′
Quint $2^2/_3$′	Gemshorn 2′	Siffløjte $1^1/_3$′	Rauschpfeife II
Rauschpfeife II	Siffløjte $1^1/_3$′	Decimant 1′	Nachthorn 2′
Mixtur VI	Scharff IV–VI	Sesquialtera II	Mixtur VIII
Cimbel III	Dulcian 16′	Scharff IV	Basun 32′
Trompet 16′	Krumhorn 8′	Dulcian 8′	Basun 16′
Trompet 8′		Vox humana 8′	Dulcian 16′
			Trompet 8′
			Trompet 4′
			Cornett 2′

To ascertain the general tendencies in North Germany during the post-Schnitger period, it is natural to ask what Johann Sebastian Bach desired in an organ. Schnitger was 37 years old when Bach was born, and Bach was 34 when Schnitger died. Thus they belonged to different generations. In his boyhood, Bach had known Georg Böhm's organ in St. Johannis, Lüneburg, Schnitger's Katharina organ in Hamburg, and the organs in the Marienkirche at Lübeck. But fate unaccountably prevented him from being fortunate enough to hold a position in a church with a large organ or to have a new organ built for one of his churches. Furthermore, there is no trace of his intimate collaboration on a large instrument with one of the great organ builders of the time; this would seem to be a reasonable expectation, because he was frequently invited to serve as a consultant and examiner of organs. Unfortunately, our information concerning this aspect of his profession is inadequate for drawing a complete picture, but the evidence at hand indicates no marked deviation from the Baroque tonal ideal.

In the course of his year as organist in Mühlhausen, Bach made detailed suggestions for the rebuilding of the organ in the Blasiuskirche, and these suggestions furnish the most specific information relative to his tonal concept. At least, they provide some guidance.

For the beginning, two technical improvements were recommended: an enlargement of the bellows, and an overhaul of the wind chests to correct all deficiencies of the wind supply. This was a cardinal point in Bach's estimation. Ph. E. Bach says that his father began the examination of an organ by pulling all of the stops to determine whether its "lungs" were functioning properly. From several delivery records, there is evidence that Bach was quite exacting in this matter. He was opposed to extremely low wind pressures; the minimum was 60 mm. Water Column.

In these respects, Bach considered only a few organs to be satisfactory. The weaknesses may be partially attributed to the musical forms of earlier periods which did not place such exacting demands on the instruments. Bach had actually presented a new requirement: a greatly augmented quantity of wind and its proper apportionment so that each pipe received a fair share. Finally, the large variations in the wind consumption must not induce wind jerks.

Bach's first point concerning the specification at Mühlhausen suggested the addition of a stopped Untersatz 32′ "which gives dignity to the entire Werk". After that, the Posaune 16′ (pedal) was to have new and longer resonators, and the reeds and shallots were to be altered to make the Posaune "produce a sound with more pomposity." In the Hauptwerk, the plan was to exchange the Trompete 8′ with a Fagott 16′, because the latter "is serviceable for all sorts of new inventions and has a very delicate sound."

His intention was to replace the Gemshorn on the Hauptwerk with a Viola di Gamba that would sound well with the Salicional 4′ on the Rückpositiv. The Principal-Quint $2^2/_3{}'$ would be exchanged for a Nasat $2^2/_3{}'$, a more agreeable stop in ensembles.

Nothing was to be changed in the Rückpositiv, but a new Brustwerk was projected as an addition; it should be equipped with a coupler to the Hauptwerk. The final specification was this:

Hauptwerk	*Rückpositiv*	*Brustwerk*	*Pedal*
Quintatön 16′	Gedackt 8′	Stillgedackt 8′	Untersatz 32′
Principal 8′	Quintatön 8′	Flöte 4′	Principal 16′
Viola di Gamba 8′	Principal 4′	Principal 2′	Subbas 16′
Octave 4′	Salicional 4′	Terz $1^3/_5$′	Octave 8′
Gedacktflöte 4′	Octave 2′	Quinte $1^1/_3$′	Octave 4′
Nasat $2^2/_3$′	Spitzflöte 2′	Mixtur III	Rohrflöte 1′
Octave 2′	Quintflöte $1^1/_3$′	Schalmey 8′	Mixtur IV
Sesquialtera II	Sesquialtera II		Posaune 16′
Mixtur IV	Cymbel III		Trompete 8′
Cymbel II			Cornett 2′
Fagott 16′			

For the most part, the style of the middle Baroque characterizes this specification, but the few changes that Bach recommended are significant indications of his personal desires. Emphasis is placed on a full-bodied sound (by no means a recent development), and the sense of "delicacy" is also noticeable. The Tierces are rather aggressive, and the mixtures have a small number of ranks. The Brustwerk coupler and Bach's attention to the wind supply show that he wanted the possibility of combining all Werks in a large *tutti*. In this organ, we only miss an evidence of his well-known predilection for reeds.

If these things are compared with advances in other localities, it is clear that the actual innovations were to be found with persons other than Bach. He did not advocate dissolution of the Baroque Werk character or the surrender of the Werk principle. These new trends, both typical of Gottfried Silbermann, were foreign to his needs and ideas. Bach required the complete organ, and this was what he attempted to create in Mühlhausen, although his funds were much too limited. He never attained his goal. Current events moved in a direction contrary to his – they were moving backwards.

In fact, nothing less than a full-scale liquidation of the Baroque organ was in progress. Even the repeating mixture, almost a foregone conclusion, began to waver. Mattheson (1739) preferred the Italian custom. Near the beginning of the nineteenth century, Deimling went to the extreme of permitting only octave ranks in the mixtures, and Zang would have no mixtures at all.

Sorge's campaign in the 1770's against the old scaling methods and against the unequal temperament is also an essential feature in the events. In 1740, Sorge and Tartini had discovered combination tones, and this was the small beginning of scientific research in acoustical phenomena which exercised a considerable influence on the events of the following century.

After Bach, the function of the organ was drastically changed. Homophonic music required sounds with qualities and dimensions different from those produced by Baroque organs; changes in the instruments consequently had to come.

They came quickly. Georg Joseph Vogler, one of the most dynamic prophets of this movement, appeared on the stage in the last half of the eighteenth century. The fact that he, a conductor, music theorist, and opera composer, took the initiative indicates the background for his ideas. They signified a complete break with all of the hallowed traditions; orchestral principles were the basis for the new design of the organ. Vogler was supported by recent discoveries in acoustical research, and he referred to a harmonic and a physical acoustics, that is, the theories related to the newly discovered combination tones. And then he worked with the anatomical acoustics, recognizing the human ear as a link in the system.

In regard to organ aesthetics, he asserted that this question must be put to each pipe: "What do you accomplish alone, and what do you mean to the ensemble?" Excellent principles.

To produce a light-weight and comfortable action, he insisted on simplicity in its design. For this reason, Vogler preferred a chromatic pipe arrangement on the wind chests. He had no interest in façade pipes or any type of casework involving pipes.

His description of the "simplification" system is very elaborate and specious in its pseudo-scientific manner. In relation to traditional methods, he believed that his system would produce a greater effect with fewer pipes; a more detailed account here would lead much too far, and the practical results are more interesting and more instructive.

His ideal organ would have five manuals: the first for Principals and mutations with wide scale; the second for Principals and mutations with narrow scale. The third manual Werk would consist exclusively of a full reed group; the fourth manual would have nothing but string stops; and the fifth would have only flutes – a purely orchestral arrangement.

For some of his reed stops, he used free reeds (like those in the reed organ or harmonium). Probably he was the first in Germany to use the swell box. He extended the range of the manuals downward to F; in the pedal, the treble went up to g′. On both the manuals and the pedal, he employed a division into bass and treble halves.

Not until the beginning of the nineteenth century were his ideas adopted in some new instruments; for example, in St. Peter's Pfarrkirche in Munich. The specification there was the following:

I. manual	*II. manual*	*III. manual*
Principal 16′	Principal 16′	Posaune 16′
Principal 8′	Gross Nasat $10^2/_3$′	Contrafagotto 16′
Nasat $5^1/_3$′	Principal 4′	Krummhorn 8′
Terz $3^1/_5$′	Terz $3^1/_5$′	Trompet 4′
Principal 2′	Carillon $2^2/_3$′ $1^3/_5$′	
Quint $1^1/_3$′	Principal 1′	

IV. manual	*V. manual*	*Pedal*
Theorbe 16′	Flauto 8′	Fundamentalbass 32′
Viola di Gamba 8′	Gemhorn 4′	Principal 16′
		Violonbass 16′
		Gross Nasat $10^2/_3$′
		Principal 8′
		Violoncello 8′
		Flautone 8′
		Klein Nasat $5^1/_3$′
		Flûte a bec 4′
		Bombarde 32′
		Serpent 16′
		Bassethorn 8′
		Clarinet 4′

Mutations are present, but they, with very few exceptions, were clearly intended to operate downward: they form difference tones. It is conceivable that the newly discovered combination tones might inspire a theorist – this was an ingenious and inexpensive method of fabricating "dignity". But it is surprising that the results were not more distressing to Vogler himself. Was he unable to hear? Or was he so spellbound by his own ideas that the facts were completely overshadowed?

Others could hear, and he was not very successful, especially with other organ builders. He was given the opportunity to build, or supervise, only a few new organs. However, he was frequently awarded contracts for redesigning old organs.

After this foreign, erudite, widely-travelled, charming musician had given one of his sensational concerts (in that respect, he was a public success), anyone present was easily convinced when he made an offer to improve an organ. With the application of his new system he needed just a few days and a small amount of money.

In Copenhagen, he managed to redesign at least two organs: the Botzen organ in Our Saviour's Church and the Carstens organ in the Reformed Church, where the young composer Weyse was the organist.

A study of the organ in the Reformed Church (finished 1799), is particularly revealing. Vogler removed the mixtures. An 8′ Gedackt in the Hauptwerk was shifted on the wind chest so that it formed a Quint $10^2/_3$′ in the treble. In a similar way, a Terz $6^2/_5$′, Quint $5^1/_3$′, and Terz $3^1/_5$′ were conjured up from other stops to obtain both 32′ and 16′ pitches for the Hauptwerk. Furthermore, the Quintatön 16′ was changed to a Bourdon 16′, and a new Clarinet 4′ was installed instead of the Mixtur. The Brustwerk was enclosed in a swell box, and it received a Vox Angelica with free reeds, a 16′ treble Gamba, etc.

This change of specification seems ridiculous, especially to those who are acquainted with the small, intimate space in the Reformed Church; and we can well understand that Weyse personally moved the majority of mutations back into place again, when Vogler had gone. The church authorities were somewhat hesitant about Vogler's payment.

There was undoubtedly a great deal of the charlatan in Vogler; but his knowledge and intuition cannot be denied. The nature of the force compelling him toward caricature can be debated, but we must concede that he was unswerving in his conviction. This conviction forecast the basic character of the impending events – with the emphasis that only a caricature can provide.

THE NINETEENTH CENTURY

Any description of organ building during the late eighteenth century, a transitional period where old and new were wrestling and blending, would be a very complicated undertaking. But close attention is merited by one large instrument, the organ completed in 1768 for the Michaëliskirche in Hamburg. It was the work of Johann Gottfried Hildebrand (son of the Silbermann apprentice Zacharias Hildebrand). The expenses for the organ were defrayed and paid in advance by Johann v. Mattheson, Legation councillor and organ theorist; consequently the instrument reflected his ideas. The specification for the organ was:

Hauptwerk	*Oberwerk*	*Brustwerk*	*Pedal*
Principal 16′	Bordun 16′	Rohrflöte 16′	Principal 32′
Quintatön 16′	Principal 8′*	Principal 8′*	Subbass 32′
Octave 8′*	Unda maris 8′	Flötetraversiere 8′	Principal 16′
Gemshorn 8′	Spitzflöte 8′	Kleingedackt 8′	Subbass 16′
Viola di Gamba 8′	Quintatön 8′	Rohrflöte 8′	Rohrquinte $10^2/_3$′
Gedackt 8′	Octave 4′	Octave 4′	Octave 8′
Octave 4′	Spitzflöte 4′	Rohrflöte 4′	Quinte $5^1/_3$′
Gemshorn 4′	Quinte $2^2/_3$′	Nasat $2^2/_3$′	Octave 4′
Quinte $5^1/_3$′	Octave 2′	Octave 2′	Mixtur X
Quinte $2^2/_3$′	Rauschpfeife II	Terz $1^3/_5$′	Posaune 32′
Octave 2′	Echo-Cornett III	Quinte $1^1/_3$′	Posaune 16′
Sesquialtera II	Cymbel V	Sifflet 1′	Fagott 16′
Cornett V	Trompete 8′	Rauschpfeife II-III	Trompete 8′
Mixtur VIII	Vox humana 8′	Cymbel V	Clairon 4′
Scharff V		Chalumeaux 8′	
Trompete 16′			
Trompete 8′			

* with treble doubling.

The Casparini-Silbermann style, in a very pretentious manner, had invaded Hamburg itself. Mattheson's emphatic contribution to the controversy (Schnitger, North Germany, vs. Casparini-Silbermann, South Germany) cost him 44,000 German marks. In examining the specifications for the single Werks and especially for the pedal, we can still discern traces of the good old Hamburg customs, but on the whole, this instrument shows a decisive break with the Werk organ of the Middle and Late Baroque. This is also evident in the façade (Fig. 78); the gigantic German organ of the nineteenth century is not too remote. Unfortunately, this magnificent, extremely interesting organ was consumed by the fire that destroyed the church in 1906.

By looking at the specification for Marcussen and Reuter's organ in Christiansborg Castle Church, Copenhagen 1827, it is not difficult to trace the continued development of the new trends; the ideas of both Vogler and Zang are perceptible.

Hovedværk	*Overværk*	*Positiv*	*Pedal*
Quintatön 16′	Bordun 16′	Viola di Gamba 8′	Untersatz 32′
Principal 8′	Principal 8′	Gedackt 8′	Principal 16′
Quintatön 8′	Rørfløjte 8′	Fugara 4′	Subbas 16′
Quint $5^1/_3$′	Oktav 4′	Fløjte 4′	Quint $10^2/_3$′
Oktav 4′	Rørfløjte 4′	Valdfløjte 2′	Oktav 8′
Spidsfløjte 4′	Quint $2^2/_3$′	Cornet V	Quintatön 8′
Superoktav 2′	Superoktav 2′	Fagot 8′	Superoktav 4′
Siffløjte 1′	Terz $1^3/_5$′		Nathorn 2′
Sesquialtera II	Dolcian 8′		Basun 16′
Rauschfløjte 2′ $1^1/_3$′			Fagot 16′
Trompet 8′			Trompet 8′

There are no repeating mixtures in this organ, but the mutations do not go lower than the "Gravitätsquint" $5^1/_3$′ ("Pompous Fifth"). The Hauptwerk Principals have wide scaling; the Oberwerk Principals narrow scaling. In the Positiv, the Principals have yielded in favour of the strings, although the latter might be considered as narrow Principals. This Werk has a swell box. The series of pipes are mounted chromatically on the wind chests. There is no pipework façade, only a lattice (grill). In spite of certain reminiscences of Vogler, the traditional methods are predominant. The Casparini-Silbermann style has been modernized, and this example reveals a great deal about the ambitions of two young, progressive organ builders at the beginning of the nineteenth century.

In the publications of the period, one expression is repeatedly encountered: "the completion of the organ." The phrase is an accurate description of the nineteenth century philosophy of organ building. Today such an expression may provoke some indulgent smiles because the "technically" worst of the Baroque organs have been destroyed and forgotten. We have experienced the aftermath of the nineteenth century and the ensuing return of the Baroque organ under a romantic spotlight. But if we imagine the conditions existing about 100–150 years ago, we may comprehend the desire for something more complete than the Baroque organs, and in all fairness, the nineteenth century did produce some changes in organ building which are indispensable today.

From a technical point of view, Baroque organs were not extremely well-constructed, even though many of them have been undeniably tenacious of life. Often the mechanical action was heavy and noisy. The wind chests were unduly sensitive to heat and dampness; jammed sliders, ciphers, and "runs" were nothing unusual. Insufficient and unsteady wind was almost a rule, and the workmanship was often rough and inexact, especially when judged with the eyes of a joiner used to machine precision. Many features were far from perfection, but science was on the brink of discoveries leading to new and far more "certain", "accurate" measurements for scaling, voicing, and tuning.

In 1833, Töpfer published a treatise relating to the mysteries of organ building. The new theory in his treatise was based on mathematical and physical deductions, with numerous tables for scaling, calculations for borings and wind chambers, pallets, and bellows, mechanical action, etc. Töpfer produced a number of similar studies, and in 1855 he finally published the *Lehrbuch der Orgelbaukunst,* inspired by Dom Bedos' *l'Art du facteur d'orgues* and actually to be regarded as a completion of this work, including additions and revisions.

Appreciable advances in craftsmanship had been made in the beginning of the nineteenth century; then came the arrival of machine tools. The German organ builder, Eberhard Friedrich Walcker, relates how he, in 1850, had a planing machine installed to smooth the sheets of tin required for tin pipes. His own words constitute a succinct explanation of the situation. He writes that manufacture is facilitated and "brought to the peak of perfection, because the tin sheets are prepared according to mathematically calculated thicknesses, not at random or by touch. The chief value of a stop made in this way is clearly demonstrated in the uniformity of the timbre. Uniformity of timbre is not only conditioned by the controlled thickness of the material in a single pipe, but also by the control of the progressive decline in the thickness of material, from the largest to the smallest pipe in a rank."

Perfection was synonymous with precision. The imperfections of the old, bulging church arches were repaired with fine, smooth cement plaster. And similarly, the organ would be elevated to mathematical unimpeachability. This was the ultimate.

Above all, the tuning must be exact, and considerable experimentation was devoted to the new types of tuning slides and tuning slots. A first-class pipe was equipped with two tuning slots: one for approximate regulation and one for exact regulation. An evaluation of reeds was based, typically, on their ability to stay in tune. This was tantamount to saying that only the stops with long, tuned resonators could meet the high standards. For that reason the Regals were regarded as inferior stops; their thin, snarling tone was also out of favour.

The speech of the fluework had to be completely precise and devoid of subsidiary noises. For that reason, nicking, roller beards, front beards, side beards, and other voicing techniques were employed to a continuously increasing extent.

But equal significance should be attached to another aspect of the matter. To the same extent as people lost the sense for timbres, a demand for dynamic variation arose. The ideal was moving in the direction of the gigantic organ which could be manoeuvred, with practically no effort on the part of the performer, from the weakest *pianissimo* to a sonorous, impressive *tutti*.

Several practical problems had to be solved in this connection. First, the bellows required some enlargement and improvement if they were to provide the necessary quantities of wind, and this wind had to be properly distributed. The problem was old, but the requirements were gradually increasing. Secondly, the retention of a light, comfortable key action was desired, in spite of additional and larger pallets, higher wind pressures, and frequently very large distances. Thirdly, the stop action had to be flexible enough to permit the degree of manipulation associated with crescendo and diminuendo.

The first solution to the action problems came from an Englishman, Charles Spackmann Barker, who invented the "Barker lever" in 1830. It is illustrated in Fig. 34 (at the left) and discussed on p. 102.

Usually the larger manual Werks were equipped with the Barker lever, whereas the smaller Werks retained direct mechanical action. The lever was installed in such a way that the small Werks, when coupled to the large Werk, were assisted by the lever belonging to the latter. Thus the coupling of several manuals was achieved without a heavier action.

The so-called "free" combinations for registration also appeared near the middle of the nineteenth century. In the same era, there were other inventions that facilitated registration, such as collectives (i. e. combination pistons) and the general crescendo pedal, "*welches letzteres eine ganz gewaltige Wirkung macht*" (the latter producing a quite enormous effect), according to Walcker.

In these years Walcker was converted to the use of cone wind chests. The advantages in this type of wind chest were in close relation to the demands of the period: each pipe had its own pallet, and none could steal wind from another; there were no difficulties with sliders, etc. The stop pallets were unbelievably easy to manipulate. And our present-day objections to the stop channels had no effect whatever on the organ types of the nineteenth century.

With all these contrivances and inventions, the prospects were really unlimited; the number of gadgets was determined by the financial resources, and money was plentiful in France, England and Germany.

The inevitable result was mammoth organs and mammoth factories, and it was assumed that the sublime heights were within reach. The asthmatic Baroque organ was nothing in comparison to this extravagance; the Baroque was forgotten in the ecstasy of progress. There was no purpose for it.

The profile of this movement was defined by men like Eberhard Friedrich Walcker, Friedrich Ladegast, and Wilhelm Sauer in Germany and Aristide Cavaillé-Coll in Paris. These men, who also had rather close contact with each other, did not stop with the building of the giant organ; they organized a mass production of giant organs. The German firms made considerable exports to Russia and America beside large contracts in their own country, and Cavaillé-Coll's instruments also travelled to the most distant parts of the globe.

In his early years, Walcker had some contact with Vogler and studied his theories, but he surpassed Vogler in his comprehension of practical matters. This is immediately apparent in Walcker's first large instrument, completed in 1833 for the St. Paulikirche in Frankfurt a.M.:

I. manual	*II. manual*	*III. manual*	*Pedal I*
Untersatz 32′	Gedackt 16′	Quintatön 16′	Bassus major 32′
Gr. Praestant 16′	Praestant 8′	Praestant 8′	Principalbass 16′
Viola di Gamba 16′	Salicional 8′	Harmonica 8′	Contre-Bass 16′
Flauto major 16′	Dolce 8′	Dolcissimo 8′	Octavbass 16′
Gross Octav 8′	Gr. Gedackt 8′	Bifra 8′	Violonbass 16′
Viola di Gamba 8′	Quintatön 8′	Hohlflöte 8′	Quint $10^2/_3$′
Gemshorn 8′	Quintflöte $5^1/_3$′	Lieblich Gedackt 8′	Octave 8′
Offene Flöte 8′	Octave 4′	Spitzflöte 4′	Violoncel 8′
Quint $5^1/_3$′	Flöt travers 4′	Flute d'amour 4′	Terz $6^2/_5$′
Octave 4′	Rohrflöte 4′	Nasard $2^2/_3$′	Quint $5^1/_3$′
Hohlflöte 4′	Gemshorn $2^2/_3$′	Flautino 2′	Octave 4′
Gemshorn 4′	Octave 2′	Clarinette 8′	Flöte 4′
Fugara 4′	Mixtur V	Physharmonica 8′	Posaune 16′
Terz $3^1/_5$′	Posaune 8′		Trompete 8′
Quinte $2^2/_3$′	Vox humana 8′		Clarine 4′
Klein Octave 2′			Krummhorn 2′
Waldflöte 2′			
Terz (treble) $1^3/_5$′			*Pedal II*
Superoctav 1′			
Cornet V			Gedackt 16′
Mixtur V			Praestant 8′
Scharff IV			Gedackt 8′
Fagott 16′			Gedackt 4′
Trompete 8′			Waldflöte 2′
			Fagott 16′

An elaborate commentary is unnecessary. The Casparini-Silbermann line is repeated with a Vogler-type stress on the 32′ of the Hauptwerk. Nearly the same principles are evidenced in all Walcker's organs from that period: the large, heavy Hauptwerk and two or three other manual Werks, diminishing in intensity and weight; and a fluty bass pedal, which, for the sake of registration, was separated into primary (strong) and secondary (weak) groups (however, there is only one pedalboard).

The Ladegast and Sauer organs were similar in construction, but the sound was brighter. On the whole, the Vogler bass mutations disappeared from general use with the Walcker instruments.

In France, the tendency of the nineteenth century was basically the same, but there was a different point of departure, namely the old French traditions, reinforced by the spiritual inheritance of Cavaillé-Coll. Representative of the third generation in a French-Spanish family of organ builders, raised and educated in both countries, Cavaillé-Coll had extraordinary qualifications for reforming and rejuvenating the French art of organ building.

In 1833, at the age of 22, he made his first professional visit to Paris. While in the city, he incidentally learned of a competition concerning a new organ for St. Denis. Just a few days remained before the final submission date, but he succeeded in delivering so persuasive a project that he and his father were awarded the contract.

Eight years elapsed before delivery and dedication of the organ; the time was lengthened by repair work going on in the church. This was not an impediment; a great deal of experimentation was necessary before his new ideas could be incorporated in an instrument. A variety of technical problems was encountered. The organ was large, and the action was far too heavy when the manuals were coupled. This was a matter of primary importance

But good luck often comes from bad! Barker, who failed to market his invention, the Barker lever, in England, was currently attempting to sell it in France, and his lever was nothing less than an absolute condition for the ensuing development. Barker and Cavaillé-Coll became partners, and at St. Denis, the Barker lever had its first practical test. The specification of the organ was this:

Grand orgue

Montre 32′
Montre 16′
Bourdon 16′
Montre 8′
Flûte harmonique 8′
Viole de gambe 8′
Bourdon 8′
Prestant 4′
Flûte oct. 4′
Quinte $2^2/_3'$
Doublette 2′
Gr. Fourniture IV
Gr. Cymbale IV
Fourniture IV
Cymbale IV
I. Trompette 8′
II. Trompette 8′
Basson 8′
Clairon harm. 4′
Cornet à pavillon 8′

Positif

Bourdon 16′
Salicional 8′
Flûte harmonique 8′
Bourdon 8′
Prestant 4′
Flûte oct. 4′
Flûte 4′
Nazard $2^2/_3'$
Doublette 2′
Octavin 2′
Tierce $1^3/_5'$
Fourniture IV
Cymbale IV
Trompette harm. 8′
Hautbois 8′
Cromorne 8′ + 4′
Clairon 4′

Bombardes

Bourdon 16′
Bourdon 8′
Flûte 8′
Prestant 4′
Nazard $2^2/_3'$
Doublette 2′
Grand Cornet VII
Bombarde 16′
I. Trompette 8′
II. Trompette 8′
I. Clairon 4′
II. Clairon 4′

Récit expressif

Flûte harmonique 8′
Bourdon 8′
Flûte octaviante 4′
Quinte $2^2/_3'$
Octavin 2′
Trompette harm. 8′
Voix humaine 8′
Clairon harm. 4′

Pédales

Flûte ouverte 32′
Flûte ouverte 16′
Flûte ouverte 8′
Flûte ouverte 4′
Gr. Nazard $5^1/_3'$
Bombarde 16′
Basse-contre 16′
Basson 8′
I. Trompette 8′
II. Trompette 8′
I. Clairon 4′
II. Clairon 4′

The traditions associated with the old French organ are easily recognizable in this specification, but the changes are also visible. For the most part, the plan is reminiscent of Dom Bedos' unexecuted proposal for a large 32′ organ: the distribution and characteristics of the manual Werks, the structure of the Principal ranks (for example, the division of the Fourniture and Cymbale of the Hauptwerk into distinct low and high sections with four ranks each), the reed group with the 8′ and 4′ Trompettes doubled, and the expansion of the Bombarde Werk with more fluework. In the pedal, the French traditions are upheld: only Principals and reeds are specified, although there is a decisive bass emphasis.

In spite of all similarities, the organ is intrinsically different from the old French organ. The scales are considerably wider, the wind pressure and the voicing are much stronger, and the character of the sound is more massive. These observations are valid in the case of the Principal ranks (the mixtures and mutations are still comparatively weak) and particularly in reference to the overblowing flutes, reeds and strings. The overblowing flutes were expected to contribute to the intensity of the whole ensemble, and the overtones of the string stops were forced in order to make their tone resemble, as much as possible, the orchestral string tone. The Gedackts had a very wide scaling (a thick sound) for strengthening the foundation tone of the organ. In keeping with his progressive ideas, Cavaillé-Coll made early use of the Danish (Reuter) tuning slot. He employed it to a far greater extent than Reuter himself.

Reuter's invention, or discovery, called for placing the tuning slot a little below the upper edge of the pipe. He observed that this resulted in better speech from the large pipes in the 16′ and 8′ range, but the concomitant effect was a sound that was definitely more massive and rounded, both qualities being well-suited to the tonal ideal of the period.

Reuter confined his use of the tuning slot to the larger pipes (up to 1′ length), but Cavaillé-Coll gave tuning slots to even the smallest mixture pipes. There is good reason to assume that Cavaillé-Coll's procedure was motivated by a tonal concept rather than the technicalities of tuning. Of course large amounts of nicking and related voicing techniques were utilized.

The first solution to the problem of manipulation was implied by the arrangement used in his large organs. For technical reasons pertaining to the wind supply, it was necessary to lay out the ranks belonging to the large manual Werks on two wind chests, and this scheme functioned simultaneously as a means of registration. The lower-pitched stops, *Jeux de Fonds,* were assembled on one chest and the remainder of the ensemble, *Jeux de Combinaison,* on the other. With the assistance of valves that controlled the admission of wind to each chest, these groups of stops became operable or inoperable.

For the Notre Dame organ in Paris, the arrangement is the following:

I. Man. Grand choeur
Jeux de Fond

Principal 8′
Bourdon 8′
Prestant 4′
Quinte $2^2/_3$′
Doublette 2′
Tierce $1^3/_5$′
Larigot $1^1/_3$′
Septieme $1^1/_7$′
Piccolo 1′

Jeux de Comb.

Tuba magna 16′
Trompette 8′
Clairon 4′

II. Man. Grand Orgue
Jeux de Fond

Violonbasse 16′
Bourdon 16′
Montre 8′
Flûte harm. 8′
Viole de Gambe 8′
Bourdon 8′
Prestant 4′

Jeux de Comb.

Octave 4′
Doublette 2′
Fourniture V
Cymbale V
Basson 16′
Basson-Hautbois 8′
Clairon 4′

III. Man. Bombardes
Jeux de Fond

Principal 16′
Sousbasse 16′
Principal 8′
Flûte harm. 8′
Gr. Quinte $5^1/_3$′
Octave 4′

Jeux de Comb.

Gr. Tierce $3^1/_5$′
Quinte $2^2/_3$′
Septieme $2^2/_7$′
Doublette 2′
Cornet V
Bombarde 16′
Trompette 8′
Clairon 4′

IV. Man. Positif
Jeux de Fond

Montre 16′
Bourdon 16′
Flûte harm. 8′
Salicional 8′
Bourdon 8′
Unda maris 8′
Prestant 4′

Jeux de Comb.

Flûte douce 4′
Doublette 2′
Piccolo 1′
Plein jeu III–VI
Clarinette 16′
Cromorne 8′
Clarinette 4′

V. Man. Récit expressif
Jeux de Fond

Quintaton 16′
Viole de Gambe 8′
Voix celeste 8′
Quintaton 8′
Dulciana 4′
Basson-Hautbois 8′
Voix humaine 8′
Clarinette 8′

Jeux de Comb.

Flûte harm. 8′
Flûte oct. 4′
Quinte $2^2/_3$′
Octavin 2′
Cornet III–V
Bombarde 16′
Trompette 8′
Clairon 4′

Pedales
Jeux de Fond

Principal Basse 32′
Contre Basse 16′
Sous Basse 16′
Grosse Quinte $10^2/_3$′
Flûte 8′
Violoncelle 8′
Grosse Tierce $6^2/_5$′
Octave 4′

Jeux de Comb.

Quinte $5^1/_3$′
Septieme 4–$^4/_9$′
Contre-Bombarde 32′
Bombarde 16′
Basson 16′
Trompette 8′
Basson 8′
Clairon 4′

Gradually, Cavaillé-Coll abandoned Dom Bedos' formula for mixture composition. A few examples from his later years are given here to indicate the direction in which he moved.

Fourniture V Grand orgue:

C–e	$2 - 1\frac{1}{3} - 1 - \frac{2}{3} - \frac{1}{2}$
f–f′	$4 - 2\frac{2}{3} - 2 - 1\frac{1}{3} - 1$
f♯′–f″	$8 - 5\frac{1}{3} - 4 - 2\frac{2}{3} - 2$
f♯″–g‴	$16 - 10\frac{2}{3} - 8 - 5\frac{1}{3} - 4$

and the related *Cymbale:*

C–B	$\frac{2}{3} - \frac{1}{2} - \frac{1}{3} - \frac{1}{4}$
c–e	$1 - \frac{2}{3} - \frac{1}{2} - \frac{1}{3}$
f–b	$1\frac{1}{3} - 1 - \frac{2}{3} - \frac{1}{2}$
c′–e′	$2 - 1\frac{1}{3} - 1 - \frac{2}{3}$
f′–b′	$2\frac{2}{3} - 2 - 1\frac{1}{3} - 1$
c″–e″	$4 - 2\frac{2}{3} - 2 - 1\frac{1}{3}$
f″–g‴	$5\frac{1}{3} - 4 - 2\frac{2}{3} - 2$

Another example of a *Fourniture:*

C–e	$2 - 1\frac{1}{3} - 1 - \frac{1}{2}$
f–b	$2 - 1\frac{1}{3} - 1 - \frac{2}{3}$
c′–e′	$2 - 2 - 1\frac{1}{3} - 1$
f′–b′	$2\frac{2}{3} - 2 - 2 - 1\frac{1}{3}$
c″–g‴	$4 - 2\frac{2}{3} - 2 - 2$

Finally, a *Plein-Jeu V:*

C–e	$2\frac{2}{3} - 2 - 1\frac{1}{3} - 1 - \frac{2}{3}$
f–b	$4 - 2\frac{2}{3} - 2 - 1\frac{1}{3} - 1$
c′–f♯′	$4 - 2\frac{2}{3} - 2 - 1\frac{1}{3} - 1\frac{1}{3}$
g′–b′	$4 - 2\frac{2}{3} - 2 - 2 - 1\frac{1}{3}$
c″–f♯″	$8 - 4 - 2\frac{2}{3} - 2\frac{2}{3} - 2$
g″–g‴	$8 - 4 - 4 - 2\frac{2}{3} - 2$

The interior of a large Cavaillé-Coll organ is an impressive sight. The craftsmanship and materials are absolutely first-class, but the immense dimensions catch the eye. Beside a profusion of large pipes, there is a huge, complicated action occupying a prodigious amount of space.

Cavaillé-Coll believed that a pipe must have ample space around it if it is to function independently of its neighbours; the collaboration between the pipes was a secondary consideration. He expressed his opinion in these words: it should be possible to walk around each pipe. To the mechanical parts of the action he had a similar attitude. The cathedrals were spacious, and an instrument with the height, width and volume of a five-story house was not unique. A substantial amount of space was needed for the large feeder and reservoir bellows, as well as the Barker levers and the apparatus for the pneumatic action. Convenient staircases and bridges were obligatory so that the organ builder could gain admittance to any part of the action and the pipes. Perhaps no one realized how much of the sound was being devoured by this paraphernalia – there was certainly something to feed on!

Now to the manipulation. Primary attention should be given to the evolution of the old French Récit into a large *Récit expressif,* a crescendo Werk with swell shades and powerful dynamic effects. The valves for the various Werks of the instrument and the couplers between the Werks were controlled by a row of levers above the pedalboard. The succession of these levers was prescribed by a specific system. This is the arrangement, from left to right, at Notre Dame (Paris):

1 *Effets d'orage* (thunder). This lever can bring about a simultaneous depression of the twelve lowest keys on the pedalboard.
2 *Tirasse Grand Choeur:* Manual I to Pedal Coupler.
3 *Tirasse Grand Orgue:* Manual II to Pedal Coupler.
4 *Anches Pédales:* Toe lever for the pedal reeds.
5 Toe lever for *Jeux de Fond,* Grand Choeur.
6 " " " " " " Grand Orgue.
7 " " " " " " Bombardes.
8 " " " " " " Positif.
9 " " " " " " Récit.
10 Toe lever for *Jeux de Combinaison,* Grand Choeur.
11 " " " " " " Grand Orgue.
12 " " " " " " Bombardes.
13 " " " " " " Positif.
14 " " " " " " Récit.
15 Tutti.
16 Coupler. Manual I – I
17 " " II – I
18 " " III – I
19 " " IV – I
20 " " V – I

21 Tremolo.
22 Swell Pedal.

Accordingly, all of the manual Werks can be coupled to manual I, and to facilitate free use of these possibilities, the Grand Choeur Werk (manual I) can also be coupled or uncoupled from its own keyboard. Thus it may be withdrawn in cases where the coupling of two or more of the other Werks is desired. The general principle is that previously prepared groups of stops can be manipulated by levers which free the hands for playing.

The French crescendo is constructed in terraces, by gradually adding groups of stops and covering the transitions with the crescendo Werk, which is potent enough to affect the *tutti*. The General Crescendo does not appear in Cavaillé-Coll's organs: on the other hand, the larger organs usually have pneumatic action and one free combination. In his small organs with mechanical action, toe levers are frequently available for the mixtures and reeds, with the obvious purpose of procuring greater freedom for the hands.

The Cavaillé-Coll organ clearly relies upon a limited palette of colours – never the strong ones. Quintatöns and conical or cylindrical-conical stops appear as true exceptions, nor is there much implementation of single mutations. The main varieties in the fluework are: Principals, overblowing flutes, string stops, and wide Gedackts. The latter, adhering to the old French style, may be shaped like a Rohrflöte in the treble. In spite of their impressive number, the reeds are not greatly diversified. Trompettes are found at the 32′, 16′, 8′, and 4′ pitches. Then come the Hautbois, Clarinette, Basson, Cromorne, Voix humaine – and this is the end of the list. The names, of course, can be somewhat varied.

In the twenty-stop organ at the Church of Jesus, Copenhagen 1890, the majority of these variants are represented, even several times.

I. Man. Grand Orgue	*II. Man. Récit expressif*	*Pédales*
Bourdon 16′	Flûte traversière 8′	Sousbasse 16′
Montre 8′	Viole de Gambe 8′	Flûte 8′
Salicional 8′	Voix celeste 8′	Bourdon 8′
Flûte harm. 8′	Flûte octaviante 4′	Bombarde 16′
Bourdon 8′	Octavin 2′	
Flûte douce 4′	Trompette harm. 8′	
Prestant 4′	Basson-Hautbois 8′	
Plein-jeu IV	Clairon 4′	

This small instrument also proves that the goal was the maximum extension of a large dynamic range: the enormous *tutti,* the crescendo leading to it, and the decrescendo in the opposite direction.

The cathedral is the condition for the success of this instrument. Large masses of sound require space, and the long, rolling echo of the cathedral conveys the enormity of the room and the organ to the listeners. This echo also endows the piano and pianissimo effects with the remoteness and mystery which are equally important aspects of the Romantic sound ideals.

The Cavaillé-Coll organ is the Romantic-Symphonic cathedral organ. In reality, this organ is very limited and specialized; its resources, with reference to the complete organ literature, are not over-comprehensive. But it symbolizes an epoch, and a superb achievement, which produced instruments and music embodying an entirely new concept of the organ and its inherent possibilities. In the midst of a decadent industrialization period, Cavaillé-Coll retained an artistic level of organ building.

A tremendous amount of inspiration was generated by this activity in France. There was a noticeable impact in Sweden. The large firms of Åkermann & Lund and Zetterquist completely adopted the style, and a long series of distinguished instruments from that period are still in existence. In Denmark, the introduction of French ideas was largely due to Daniel Köhne. The organ for the Holmens Church was presumably the beginning, and later came those for the cathedral of Viborg and Sakskøbing Church; these still exist.

However, these French-inspired instruments were no slavish copies, least in regard to the specifications. The smaller organs often had a directly impoverished character, simply because their sole task was to accompany the hymn-singing and to furnish modest preludes and interludes. The tonal resources were confined to a strong Hauptwerk and bass pedal for leading the singing and a few weak stops acting as a "prelude"-Werk.

Immediately before the serious inroads made by pneumatic action and industrialization, the tonal standards were so low that it is not surprising to find, in the following period, that technical conveniences had completely diverted all attention from the sound. The reawakening, whose effects we have experienced, came after the First World War.

8

The Organ Façade

The architecture of the tonal world is no new concept, but the last 35 years of organ building seem to have developed our understanding of this idea. On gradually discovering the rich resources of the organ, we have reached a comprehension of the intimate coherence between aural and visual architecture, and we have seen that these two elements, in a highly concentrated fashion, can be combined and synthesized in the organ.

The organ, in particular, provides instructive illustrations of tonal proportions; here, pitches and timbres seem to lead a more self-determined life; they are not reduced to being mere details and inferior components of music. The tonal character of the instrument may be regarded as an autonomous construction consisting of structure and proportions just like visual architecture. However, the essential and most interesting facet in organ building and organ history is the collaboration between music, architecture and the composition of the instruments.

Deep in the subconscious lies a feeling that the timbres should provide the music with a credible expression, an underscoring of the musical statement. We know that this can be accomplished most effectively, and know that it is certainly indispensable; but usually we do not remember that visual architecture, too, may contribute to a collaboration with music and timbre.

And yet, when reading about architecture, we repeatedly encounter expressions such as time, rhythm, line effect, intervals, proportions, tension and relaxation, colour and colour combinations – all concepts that are familiar to the musician in his own field.

In looking at organs, the pitches in the chromatic series of pipes immediately present an architectural design. From antiquity, this chromatic series, as previously stated, has been determined on the basis of such reliable ratios as 1:2, 1:3, and 2:3, in the case of pipe lengths. The diameters of the octaves (for the Principals) have a ratio which varies slightly in the vicinity of the Golden Section. Overtones, or timbre constituents, are attained by dividing the pipe lengths of the fundamental by 2, 3, 4,

5, etc., and through this process we derive the pitches already present in the scale.

Nothing could be more propitious for visual architecture; these, without exception, are the well-established numbers and proportions which characterize the most distinguished architecture throughout the world, from Solomon's Temple to the Danish country church.

Man's conception of harmony has always been closely associated with simple numerical relationships, but there is something curious in the fact that precisely the same numbers are valid for both the eye and for the ear. The distance between music and architecture is not overwhelming.

Speaking pipes in natural dimensions are the implicit central element in the "musical" organ façade, and the arrangement of the Werks, as well as their individual construction, should enhance this effect. The external appearance is also governed by purely technical matters such as the wind chests and the action, if these matters are handled in a natural manner. Other considerations of a similar importance are the decorative elements and the available room and space.

A brief survey of historical organ types will best illustrate the problems.

Chromatic, or more accurately, diatonic pipe arrangement was employed in many old organs (positives, portatives, and larger instruments), when the pipes were either small enough, or the keys large enough, to permit a direct mechanical connection from the key to the pipe pallet without the use of lateral displacement (roller boards).

Fig. 40 shows a rank of pipes in standard scale (NS) consisting of the 32′, 16′, 8′, 4′, 2′, 1′, and $^1/_2$′ octaves, the range encompassed by the front pipes. If we imagine ranks of pipes with another width scale, the diameters will be relocated by a certain number of half-steps throughout the rank, without the pipe lengths being changed. Of course the pipes must be somewhat longer if the diameters are smaller, but the amount is negligible and has no practical role in this context.

Portions of this rank of pipes, connected to the keyboard as 32′, 16′, 8′, 4′, or the 2′ foundation Principal, have served for centuries as the actual understructure of the organ front.

At the moment when the organs became so large that their key-to-pallet connections had to be transferred sideways by means of rollers, the organ builders gained a free hand with respect to the succession of the ranks. They began to "improvise" with designs made from ranks of pipes, that is, to create various groupings on the basis of decorative and practical values.

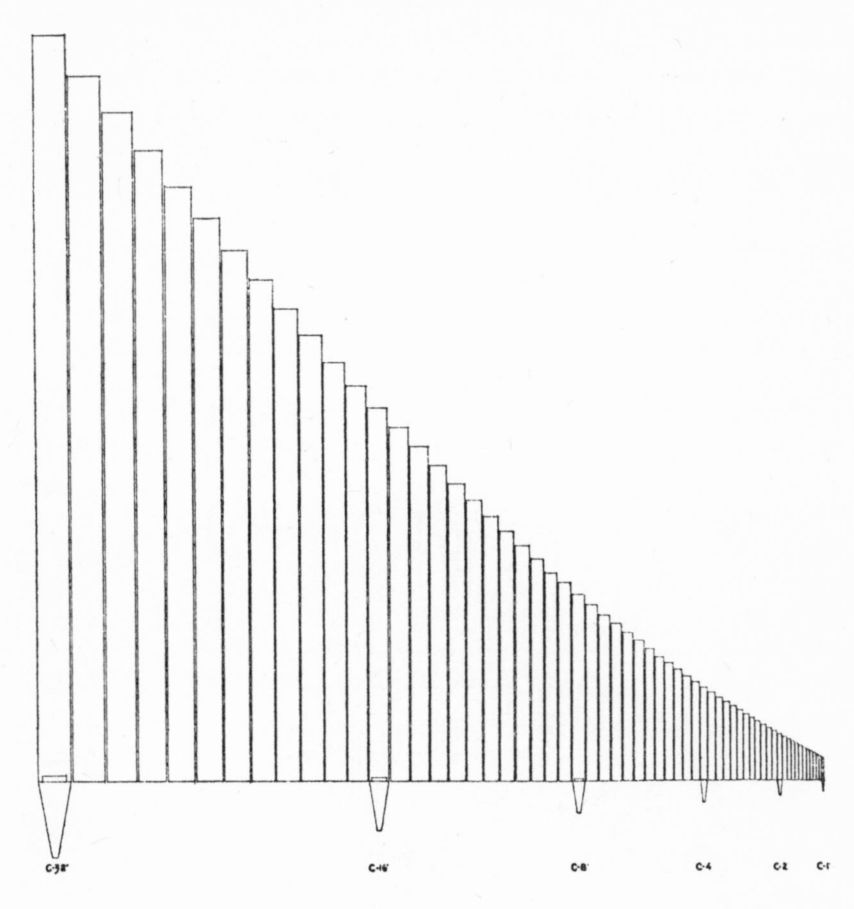

Fig. 40.

Symmetry was naturally the primary objective, but oddly enough, a full-scale exercise of this principle was not immediately attempted. According to our meagre supply of information, it appears that the first step was to erect only the C-octave as a symmetrical rank of pipes in the outer wings, while the continuation of the rank was installed "scalewise", in Praetorius' own words, between these two large groups of pipes.

Praetorius' description of the Halberstadt organ (1361) notes this principle, and it is reiterated in some remaining portions of organs from Gotland (Swedish island), presumably the oldest organ components in

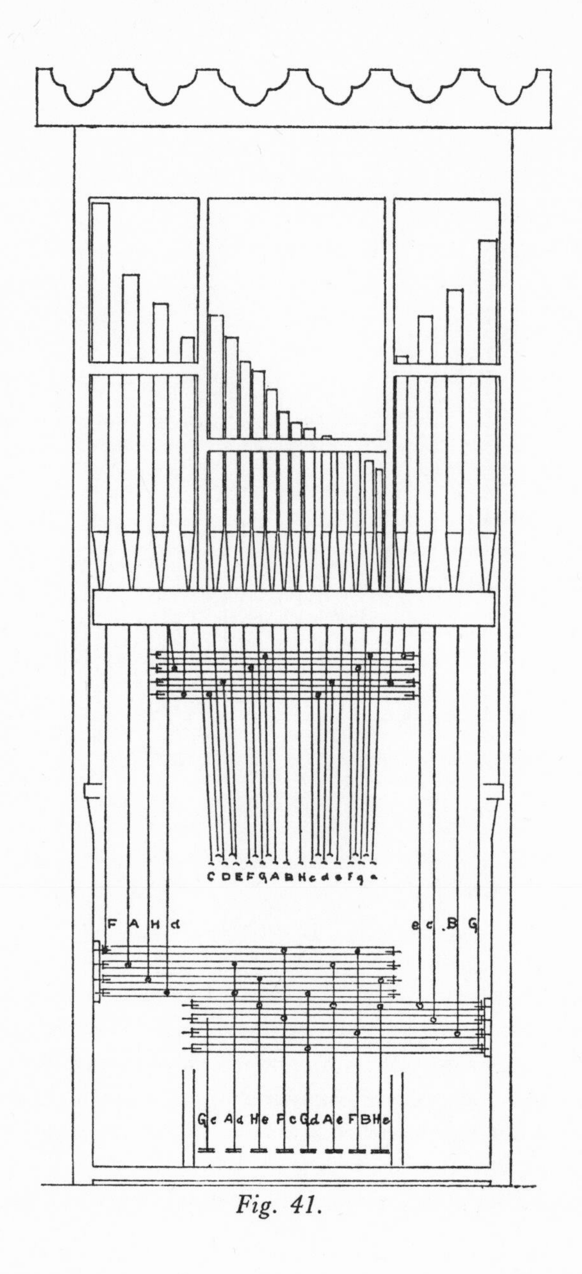

Fig. 41.

existence. Five organs from the close of the fourteenth century and the beginning of the fifteenth are represented in this group: Sundre, Norrlanda, Anga, Etelhem, and Hejnum (now in the Nordiska Museet, Stockholm). These are relatively small instruments with 4′ Principals in the façade; the other ranks, up to seven, adhere to the usual mixture-block formula.

The Norrlanda instrument is in the best condition. Most of the wind chest, the keyboards, and parts of the mechanical action still exist. These factors, in combination with pitch designations for the manual keys, make it possible to establish the exact order of the pipes.

Fig. 41 is a copy of a sketch showing the mechanical action and a reconstruction of the pipe arrangement. From this sketch, the two symmetrical side compartments appear to be connected with the pedalboard. The middle compartment is arranged scalewise but not chromatically, due to the systematic separation of the half-steps. The white keys are directly connected with the pallets located above them, while the eight black keys, in octave pairs, are coupled to the same roller, the same pallet, and the same pipe. (A peculiar key situated above the black keys functions as an "Evakuant"; it emits the wind in the event of ciphers.)

The whole arrangement contributes evidence relating to the significance of half-steps and explains why complete symmetry was not adopted immediately. For that event the mechanical action would have been more complicated because the white keys would also have required rollers.

The connection between the outer flats and the pedalboard brings to mind still older organs where an eventual extension of the bass, made at a later date, was joined to the pedalboard. Initially these bass pipes were called *Bordun*.

The pedal section shows that every key is attached to two pallets, but unfortunately specific pitches are not indicated as they were for the manual keys. However, the system can be re-established with some degree of certainty; combining pairs of tones, as indicated by the action, is only practicable with the series F, G, A, B♭, B, c, d, e. The largest pipe, at the left, could not possibly be a C (as concluded by Hennerberg and Wester), because a C pipe is too long to stand in this flat or even in the organ case; besides, if the series begins with C, the combination of pairs is futile. On the other hand, if the series begins with F, this pipe length is satisfactory in the façade, and the pitches are linked in fourths and fifths as indicated in the sketch.

So much for the lowest rank. The construction of the Hintersatz is more difficult to determine. There are several conceivable methods. The wind chest shows four ranks on each pedal note (however, six on B), and the system of pairing reveals that the normal construction in octaves and fifths could not have been applied to the single pallets; only octave ranks would have been feasible. Again, B is an exception. On the manual, there are five to six ranks for every key, and the arrangement was presumably normal, with octave and fifth ranks.

The tiny Sion organ in Switzerland (*ca.* 1400; Fig. 42) represents the next step in the development. Here, the pipe flat in the middle has also acquired a symmetrical division. The rank is divided into a "C side" and a "C# side", meaning that the pipes standing on one side produce alternate pitches in the chromatic series, and the pipes on the other side provide the intervening pitches in the series. (In the picture, the pipes have been drawn incorrectly; they should not have equal lengths on the C and C# sides). The wind chest, visible below the pipes, is also divided into two halves. It is easy to see that the slender base, the "chair", and the two corbels under the outer wings of the pipes follow the contours of the mechanical action, just as the upper part of the organ case conforms to the profile of the pipes. The folding doors, which can envelop the pipe flats, are an integral part of the form. These folding doors were important for two reasons: (1) the organs, as well as the altars, had to be covered during Lent; and (2) dampness, dirt, and church rats were a greater problem in those days.

The front pipes (casework) were always the largest single ranks in the instrument: the foundation Principal. Other ranks were hidden behind the front pipes, following the same sequence and standing parallel to them. Thus the outward appearance of these early organs was carefully adapted to the instrument itself. Although the same principle was retained for years afterward, the decorative aspect steadily assumed a larger role, in both the skeletal design and in the ornaments which first supplemented the structural form and later dominated and veiled it.

At the point where every key-pallet connection was given its own roller (each movement was transferred laterally after the initial key depression), complete freedom in the grouping of pipes was achieved. Regardless of the pipe sequence, the inconvenience was the same.

The use of a clear-cut C and C# division, with either the bass or the treble in the middle, is rather exceptional. The five-sectional division put in an early appearance and has enjoyed the widest acceptance throughout all subsequent periods. The large pipes are arranged in three main flats and the treble pipes in two intermediary flats, as, for example, in the St. Petri organ at Malmö Museum (Fig. 43). In this instance, only the pipe layout for the centre flat is self-symmetrical; the pipes in the other flats are symmetrical in relation to the central axis of the organ.

The large organ of the Marienkirche in Lübeck (Fig. 44) had a similar arrangement in the main case, with the exception of the self-symmetrical intermediary flats. In the Kiedrich façade (Fig. 45), the outer flats also have internal symmetry.

In each of these three organs, the centre flat is the tallest. This is the natural outcome of placing the organ directly under the middle of an arch.

In the Totentanz organ (Fig. 46), the middle section is lowered to make way for the light coming from the rear; for this reason, the largest pipes were placed in the outer flats. Here, as in many other instances, the organ not only complies with external, predetermined conditions but co-operates with them, often in the form of contrasting lines.

It is characteristic of many Late Gothic organs to have the largest pipes located at the extremes of the side flats. The pipe contour at the top of these flats then runs contrary to the lines of the arch, while the high centre flat produces a complementary movement in relation to the outer flats. In the main section of the Totentanz organ, this complementary effect was relinquished, because the effect was fully provided by the slender, pointed-arch opening at the rear (a window at the original location of the organ). The objective was to avoid covering the window.

The small organ of the Jacobikirche in Lübeck (Fig. 47) shows a similar condition in the main section. A considerably weaker effect is created by its posterior brick niche with pointed arch (an earlier window?), and for this reason, the counter-movement in the organ front is modified by the internal symmetry of each pipe flat.

The main section of the Garding organ (Schleswig-Holstein, near the Danish border) is closely related to the preceding instrument, but the outward and upward movement is further curtailed by interchanging the two sets of outer flats; in other words, the largest flats are pulled in toward the central treble compartment, and the next largest flats are on the outside.

A seven-sectional division was usually preferred in larger organ fronts when the façade pipes belonged to a 16′ Principal.

The Hauptwerks in the large organs at Sorø Monastery Church and the

Jacobikirche of Lübeck (Fig. 49) illustrate this type of case design. Again the largest pipes are arranged in three primary flats, in the middle and in the outer wings. The rank is continued in two flats adjacent to the outside flats, and finally, the treble pipes stand in the four flats closest to the centre flat. These four flats are arranged in vertical pairs; the pipes in the lower sections are inverted, and their feet extend up toward the pipes in the upper sections, but otherwise they are exactly like them. The lower flat is like a reflection of the upper one, and we might easily conclude that this was a decorative whim, partially executed with non-speaking pipes. At that time, mirror effects were in vogue, and mirroring did require twice as many treble pipes as were actually necessary.

The explanation lies in the doubling of the treble pipes that was common practice in the Late Gothic organs and, in a much later period, in Dutch organs. This practice is also traceable in the Petri organ at Malmö; the doubled treble pipes stand abreast in the extremely broad intermediary flats, and contrary to a previous opinion, there are no mute pipes.

The ultimate in complementary and contrasting line, reinforced through pipe groupings and ornaments, is attained in the pipe compartments for the organs at Sorø and the Jacobikirche, Lübeck. Perhaps this is demonstrated best in the Jacobi organ (the large one), which has retained the Late Gothic style of termination for the upper ends of the pipe flats. The Sorø organ lost this ornamental "crown" in 1628 when the Rückpositiv was added.

The sevenfold division of the large organ façades naturally implied variable resources, but apparently they were not exploited in the Scandinavian countries.

In the Annenkirche (Fuggerkapelle) in Augsburg, there is an interesting example of a round window, behind the organ, that has regulated the entire structure (Fig. 50). The upper contour of the organ case complies perfectly with the shape of the window, and the horizontal diameter of the window has even determined the height of the side compartments. There is a strong counter-movement to the curvature of the case, but the form of the wings and the corbels causes a slight relaxation. The Rückpositiv, with its unusually regular and simple lines, also contributes to the stabilization.

A ninefold division of the pipe compartments is found at Rheims (Fig. 51). The available drawing does not reveal whether the treble compartments were involved in a double arrangement, but this seems probable.

Almost all of the pipe compartments in the previously discussed fronts are actually "flat"; only at Sorø and Kiedrich do the centre flats project like "towers". The basic outline of these towers is a half-hexagon, the most common shape for Late Gothic towers in northern Europe, with the exception of the Netherlands.

By periodic expansions of the keyboard compass, the number of pipes in the front Principal had to be augmented. To provide space for the increased number of pipes without increasing the width of the façade, the latter had to be reshaped by means of towers. But there was seldom any need for this in North Germany and Scandinavia.

On the whole, a simple, lucid construction is the distinguishing feature of the oldest façades, and a detail of this simplicity is the use of one length for the feet of the front pipes. As a result, the pipe mouths form a consistent, horizontal line, from which the natural pitch lengths rise to an animated but absolutely "honest" upper contour.

Light, graceful ornamentation accompanied this animated pipe contour in complete harmony, and the organ case showed a fair degree of compliance to the pipe contour. Since most of the flats had rectangular frames, one purpose of the ornaments was to fill out the vacant spaces above the pipes; otherwise the closed back of the organ case caused these spaces to resemble black holes. In some instances, the ornaments did not extend all the way down to the pipes; a narrow opening, a small expression of architectural honesty, was allowed to remain so that the pipe contour was unobstructed, a condition which seldom was respected when the original front pipes were replaced by new ones.

Today the ornaments of the pipe flats frequently are called "shades" or "blinds". Both expressions are misleading, as they connote something that hangs, whereas the design is characterized by an upward movement. Often it is a luxuriant vine climbing up from the lowest corner; a series of light, miniature pointed arches; or some other motif which actively shares in the ascending movement that portrays the Gothic spirit.

Carved ornamentation was not the sole embellishment. Painted decorations in vermilion, green, ochre and golden tones covered pilasters and other surfaces (see the Malmö Petri organ), and the pipes were not forgotten. What a temptation it must have been to paint a face around the mouth of a pipe and then let the ornaments twist and turn in an ascending stream: the pipes could also be pinched into artistic shapes as in the Schemda façade (Figs. 58 and 59). For the shutters, routine ornamentation did not suffice, and the artists who executed these assignments were by no means second-rate craftsmen. The Augsburg façade, for example, was painted by Hans Holbein the Younger.

All of these fronts had one salient point in common; the relatively narrow base and the corbels supporting the pipework that often exceeded the breadth of the base. Sometimes the wingspread of the organ was augmented by shutters. All this imparted a feeling that the instrument floated lightly and effortlessly in space, like its own light, brilliant sound.

Irrespective of the constructivism and logic exemplified in the entire conception, the impression of artful pedantry is totally absent. On the contrary, the artlessness of every detail seems so spontaneous that even well-informed persons are inclined to forget both logic and construction. The ornamentation and the painting are partly responsible, but anyone who fails to see more in the Late Gothic organs has but a minimal knowledge of their excellent composition.

The Italian organ façades from the same period have an identical simplicity in their undisguised pipe arrangement with one rank. One Werk was also the rule in these organs, but the external equipment soon reached enormous dimensions. Parts of a few Gothic fronts can still be found (for example, St. Petronio, Bologna, Fig. 52), but the Renaissance is predominant in representation (as in the Siena and Tirano façades, Figs. 54 and 55). Buoyancy and weightlessness are hardly characteristic of these cases. They are firmly anchored in the solid stone wall of the church and provided with every worldly splendour that the well-nourished citizens of the Renaissance were able to muster. Perhaps this display was a compensation for the lack of tonal brilliance in the organ, but the one poor rank in the front seems to be overwhelmed and engulfed by a sumptuousness whose form, extent and meaning are entirely inappropriate to the instrument. The organ and its casework are excellent when considered individually, but the internal unity is absent.

In the fifteenth and sixteenth centuries, technical progress in the Netherlands was well ahead of other European countries. Many Dutch organs were built with two manual Werks: Hoofdwerk and Rugwerk or Hoofdwerk and Borstwerk; and towers were used to a great extent, especially in smaller organs (Figs. 57, 63, and 65). Very little is known concerning fifteenth century organ cases. By the sixteenth century, most of the original Rückpositivs had been replaced by larger and better versions, and the main organs followed the same general trend.

The form is mildly reminiscent of the Strassburg Münster organ (Fig.

56), presumably the last of the Late Gothic organs with its original Rückpositiv. Both the Hauptwerk and the Rückpositiv date from the close of the fifteenth century. The shutters on the main organ, however, are a product of the rebuilding done by Silbermann in the eighteenth century; the original folding shutters were removed on this occasion. See p. 195 for a discussion of the instrument.

The allocation of the instrument as Hauptwerk, Pedal, Rückpositiv and Brustwerk is clearly apparent in the front. In the Hauptwerk and Rückpositiv, the middle section consists of the largest pipes standing in an ordinary C and C# arrangement in three compartments; together they form a tower with the usual outline, the half-hexagon. The neighbouring compartments of treble pipes are self-symmetrical, and in addition, those of the Rückpositiv "turn the corner" and produce two pointed towers shaped like a right angle.

Generally speaking, the few remnants of organs from that period have been rebuilt beyond recognition. The old organ from St. Nicolaas, Utrecht, (Figs. 60) is a good illustration for this point. With the addition of the Oberwerk above the existing block Werk (see p. 127), the intermediary compartments of the façade had to be lengthened with "mirror" compartments to conceal the new Werk, and this probably also caused the middle compartment to be converted into a protruding one. The central tower, in any event, is not original.

Intermediate compartments in two, three, or more tiers were, on the whole, a natural consequence of the Oberwerk. On some occasions, the compartments with long pipes, from the middle range, had to be arranged in two tiers. It was general practice to erect the large pipes in two flat, outer compartments, the following pipes in double-tiered towers, and the smallest in intermediate compartments with sufficient tiers to fill out the height. The possibilities were infinite and inconsistent; the Oberwerk had destroyed the logical form. The Oberwerk had to be hidden, because it did not always have Principal stops with pipes suitable for the façade; this Werk was merely a supplement to the Principal chorus of the block Werk. A spacious organ case where the vertical space could be utilized for the entire breadth of the case, was both practical and necessary if block Werk as well as Oberwerk were used – the latter in two levels as at Utrecht. The animated upper contour, so familiar in the northern Late Gothic style, and the structural function of the Werk were relinquished in the location of the façade pipes. Instead, the dominant role was assumed by practical and decorative values. The mirror flats for the treble doubling were useful when intermediate flats with small pipes had to be lengthened, but when this procedure was inadequate, flats with dummy pipes were the only solution.

In the decorative sense, the abundance of small pipes had a variety of conceivable uses, including the typically delicate, graceful effect of these pipes and their arrangement in the compartments. In spite of all decorative purposes, one basic concept was retained: natural pipe dimensions; this ensured a degree of regularity in the planning. Beside the mirror flats, another common treatment is deserving of mention; the organ in St. Bavo, Haarlem is an example (Fig. 69). The separations between the tiers are marked by narrow, slanting ornamental bands. Nothing more is required, because alternate positions (right and left) are assigned to the large and small pipes in the flats.

Towers were seldom designed for these large main façades; covering the entire front had eliminated any surplus of pipes. Owing to the expense involved, the largest pipes were rarely used in towers. Instead, medium-sized pipes were employed, and it is obvious that decoration – not a lack of space – was the paramount inducement for such towers. On the other hand, towers are found in small organs and in Rückpositivs, and no country has surpassed the lively, intensely varied façade designs and pipe groupings achieved in the Netherlands during the century prior to the Reformation; even the side walls of the organ case often had pipe flats (see the Alkmaar choir organ, Fig. 63).

Pipe flats on the side walls were generally used in Rückpositivs and similar Werks which projected from a gallery railing or a wall. This type of design circumvented the problem of an awkward effect easily created in such a location when a Werk has the normal rectangular outline. Furthermore, this natural outline was often veiled by gradually advancing the pipe flats at the middle of the front, as in the case of the Rückpositiv in the Cathedral of Roskilde (Fig. 64). This Rückpositiv is the work of a Dutch master from the middle of the sixteenth century, and even though its present form is somewhat "Baroqued", the original graduated basic plan has been retained.

A more conventional form is presented by the Rückpositiv of the Nicolaas organ at Utrecht (Fig. 60); it is built as late as 1580, but the form is also known from older instruments. Two slightly curved side wall flats connect the balustrade with the front, which consists of three angular towers with no intervening straight-line compartments. The inner walls of the outer towers are used for the treble pipes, which are doubled and mounted in mirror flats to fill out the vertical space.

After all, none of these forms is greatly deviating from the rectangular outline of the wind chest; but this compliance is lacking in the façades of Jutfaas (Fig. 65) and Monnikendam, both from the first half of the sixteenth century. Five towers project from a base that is almost semi-circular. The central tower and the two outer ones are semi-circular; between them are two angular-shaped towers; and the five towers are separated by four straight compartments of pipes. As a result, the organ-related structure is ignored in favour of decorative ideas, not only in the basic form but also in the towering top ornament that completely diverts all attention from the pipe flats.

The variety of pipe groupings and the casual construction in the sixteenth century Dutch organs causes some difficulties in the definition of the prevailing custom, but nevertheless, certain general traits may be designated: (1) the relatively flat, almost rectangular main façades with shutters and many small-pipe compartments, and (2) the very malleable Rückpositivs and small organs, whose wealth of towers and side-wall flats represent a degree of contrast to the main façades, but which simutaneously imitate their methods at one point, the use of small-pipe flats. Although not required or necessitated by the instrument, it was the Dutch custom to arrange these flats in sufficient tiers to absorb the height. This can be motivated by the existence of some Rückpositivs with wind chests at two levels; and it has been debated whether this is the reason for treble doubling and mirror flats being used considerably longer in the Netherlands, or whether the reverse is the case. Mirror flats are even seen in organs from the middle of the seventeenth century, and the main features of the characteristically Dutch fronts are retained until the North German influence begins at the close of the seventeenth century.

The details, of course, were affected by stylistic trends, and this aspect of the design was connected with the public position held by the large organs (see p. 134). City architects worked on the façades, and naturally this led to the incorporation of customs derived from architecture and furniture making. The city architects, however, were assigned to the large organs only; the small organs, and occasionally the Rückpositivs of the large organs, were designed by the organ builders. For example, in looking at Hendrik de Kayser's organ front in the Nieuwe Kerk, Amsterdam (1655,

Fig. 66), the traditional structure is still traceable, but the form and the general concept are clearly secular in their derivation. The front pipes have been subjected to some artificial treatment in order to mount them in prettified shapes and to make them fill out the given framework. This façade is dominated by its distinguished architecture, proportions, ornaments, etc., but the vivid tonal picture which the pipes could provide is extremely distorted.

From a stylistical point of view, the large organ by Jacob van Kampen in the St. Laurentius Kerk, Alkmaar (1645, Fig. 67), has some resemblance to the Amsterdam organ, but it is much more natural, both in the total structure and in the pipe grouping. The exaggerated space behind the colossal façade is of course disproportionate, but the same is true of many large Dutch organs from that period. The enormous rooms required certain dimensions in the organ façades, particularly in the height, and these gigantic façades voraciously swallowed all of the large pipes, leaving only the small pipes to the wind chests behind them. When we see the original specification for the Alkmaar organ (p. 136), for instance, it is not difficult to imagine that there was ample space for the Hauptwerk and Oberwerk of an organ behind a façade that is sixteen metres in height (figured from the floor of the loft). The same may be said of the Herzogenbosch organ (Fig. 68).

The specifically Dutch organ was terminated with instruments and façades of this type. The North German style of building won acceptance in the Netherlands when the Reformed Church finally began to use the organ in church services. Through the development of Dutch ideas and the addition of some original thoughts, North Germany had already assumed the position of leadership. This entire evolution was also reflected in the construction of the organ front.

At the beginning of the sixteenth century, a serious interest was concentrated on Rückpositivs, and toward the middle of the same century, these Werks were added to many organs. A few Gothic positivs were undoubtedly in existence, but unfortunately they have disappeared. More Renaissance positivs are known: the large organ for the Marienkirche, Lübeck, the Totentanz organ, and St Petri, Malmö, for example. There are still more Baroque or seventeenth-century positivs: the two Jacobi organs in Lübeck, those at Garding and Sorø among others, all built in front of Gothic main organs. Concurrently with the Rückpositivs, Brustwerks were added in the unoccupied space below the Hauptwerk wind chest. The Oberwerk, as the fourth Werk in large organs (see p. 230), was adopted at a later date by the North German builders.

The creation of a large, independent pedal Werk, which became the bass foundation and canto solo Werk of the organ, was a specifically North German achievement. The large pipes necessary for this purpose could not be accommodated on the same chest with the Hauptwerk ranks. For this reason, the organ builders mounted the pedal ranks in special "houses" on both sides of the main organ, either coupled to it or in complete isolation on the gallery railing.

The fully developed organ with four manual Werks and independent pedal had been accomplished and simultaneously a very logical and constructive division of the façade, of which the individual sections were occupied by their respective foundation Principals.

For the purpose of design, the clear distribution of the Werks and the interplay of different Principal groups were the finest conceivable building material. Certain relationships existed between the façade Principals of the various Werks. The largest organs might have 32′ Principal in the pedal towers, a 16′ in the flats belonging to the Hauptwerk, an 8′ Principal in the Rückpositiv and possibly in the Oberwerk, and a 4′ Principal in the Brustwerk. A smaller instrument could have a 16′ in the pedal, an 8′ in the Hauptwerk, and a 4′ in the Rückpositiv; feasible additions would be an 8′ or 4′ in the Oberwerk and a 2′ in the Brustwerk. In other instances, there was only a Hauptwerk-Rückpositiv-Pedal, or a Hauptwerk-Brustwerk-Pedal. Occasionally the pedal Werk was small enough to be combined, in Gothic style, with the Hauptwerk. A single Werk was also possible.

The space in the front did not always accommodate an entire rank, from bass to treble. Sometimes vertical restrictions made it necessary for the low-pitched, long pipes to be placed inside the organ case or even to be replaced by stopped pipes; in other situations, a part of the treble had to be omitted from the façade when the latter was not broad enough. Due to this problem, the façade pipes of a 32′ Principal are rarely extended below F; in several instances, the keyboard compass was no greater, but even with the normal keyboard compass, the organ builders usually preferred to place these pipes inside the case, because the casework location created innumerable practical and architectural problems.

This is not a violation of principles, and admittedly the octave ratio is only one of several workable ratios. But it is important that the pipes incorporated in the façade make a consecutive series. In other words, if some pipes are to be omitted, they must be the extreme section of the bass or the treble, possibly from both ends but not from the middle. The earlier organ builders seldom violated this principle.

The interaction between towers and straight compartments had become an essential feature in the design. Towers were a necessity after the enlargement of the keyboard compass (a similar increase is noted in pipe scaling), but their decorative assets were not disregarded by Baroque masters. While the Nordic tower shapes were less diversified than those used by the Dutch, they had more of the composure inherent in the functionally disciplined form. This is not synonymous with a lack of vitality; the shape of the tower could be round, polygonal or pointed, and the straight compartments emphasized the plane from which the towers projected. The form of the towers was further underscored by the massive profiles bordering them above and below, simultaneously contributing a strong horizontal effect and an impression of breadth, enhanced by the thicker pilasters between the pipe flats and by the sections of the pedal Werk at the sides. The light, ascending quality was disappearing; designs were more powerful, heavy and obvious, but not more vital – this was only a reflection of a more "realistic" form of life.

In keeping with these new forms, the front pipes customarily had feet with unequal lengths, thus causing the lines of the mouths to play a role in the appearance. This practice may also be found in the Gothic period, especially in the Netherlands, but it was not prevalent in the north until the Renaissance. (Today, feet with unequal lengths can appear in various Gothic organs, but this is usually attributable to a later replacement of the original pipes.) The small pipes always had the longest feet, and accordingly the lines of the mouths climbed toward the treble. Proportional lengths for pipe feet and pipe bodies are unknown, practically speaking, among other reasons because it is impossible to apply this principle to a whole rank; the large pipes would have preposterously long feet; and with the smallest pipes the feet would shrink so much that the pipes would be unusable in any façade.

There was a double purpose for the variable pipe feet: firstly, to bring the upper contour of the pipes under control, a mitigation of the violent movements in the natural pipe contour; and secondly, to insure, as a matter of practical interest, that the organ case would not be too low at the points where the flats with the small pipes were standing. This was partially achieved by regulating the mouth lines; the small irregularities which appeared at the top were concealed by permitting the ornaments to extend a short way down over the pipes. These ornaments hid just the tip ends of the pipes, and so neither the function nor the natural pipe dimensions were distorted. Nevertheless, it was a departure from the immanent structure of the organ components and prefigured the later practice of letting decorative considerations govern the composition.

For years afterward, North European organ fronts were constructed from five components: Hauptwerk, Rückpositiv, Oberwerk, Brustwerk and Pedal. This form was the dominating one until the close of the eighteenth century, or as long as the Werk principle was in general usage.

In a single instrument, each of these components might be treated independently; the permissible variations were limitless. The pictures (Figs. 69–77) furnish a mere suggestion.

The pedal towers on both sides were, of course, the sections which were least varied. Beyond the separation into two towers, no other division was customary. The usual basic design for towers was semi-circular, polygonal or flat. In some instances they formed an arc of a three-quarter circle. Conversely, pointed (angular) towers were almost unknown in the pedal. A symmetrical pipe arrangement was favoured for the compartment; in straight compartments, asymmetry was also practicable, with the largest pipes on the outside or the inside. The pedal flats were seldom large enough to accommodate all of the pipes in the foundation Principal, and the surplus pipes were stationed behind the façade.

In the greater number of organs, preference is given to the fivefold division of the façade sections of the Hauptwerk, Oberwerk, and Rückpositiv, and the largest pipes are usually mounted in a central tower outlined like an arc or a polygon. The continuation of the rank takes place in two side towers, whose basic plan is either the same as the central tower or an angular outline. The spaces between the three towers are allocated to the treble which stands in two straight compartments, with either a self-symmetrical pipe layout or a reduction in the size of the pipes leading to the central tower or to the side towers. Sometimes the treble compartments are in two tiers if, for practical reasons, a greater height is desired in the organ case. In the Nordic façades, the upper compartments almost always have dummy pipes, because the treble pipes could easily be accommodated in the lower compartments, and treble doubling was a phenomenon exclusively associated with the Gothic style and the Netherlands.

When the Hauptwerk and the Rückpositiv are contemporary with each other in origin, the same pipe arrangement, or approximately the same, may be expected in the two Werks. Since there is generally an octave between the foundation Principals of the two Werks, the Rückpositiv acts as a diminished edition of the Hauptwerk, corresponding closely to the tonal difference between the two Werks.

With the addition of an Oberwerk to the Hauptwerk, as in St. Bavo, Haarlem (Fig. 69), the main façades were most sumptuous, but also less functional. The design in functional cases is such that two Werks cannot without further consideration be mounted one above each other. For sheer practicality, a horizontal division between the Hauptwerk and Oberwerk sections is desirable, and a degree of artifice is quite necessary. In the Hauptwerk section, every possible means must be utilized to "stretch" the intermediary flats in an effort to absorb the vertical distance leading to the bass pipes of the Oberwerk. Particular difficulty turns up if the Hauptwerk is based on a 16′ Principal and the Oberwerk on an 8′ Principal. This increases the problems relating to both the height and the breadth, and the only defensible solution is to omit the lowest half-octave of the Principal 16′ from the front.

The large pipes could be placed in two outer towers, thus lowering the central tower, when a window or similar object made this expedient. But apart from this, variants in Baroque pipe arrangements were largely concerned with the intermediary flats, or the addition of treble flats outside the outer towers. The distribution of the bass pipes into three towers served as a consistent organizational principle for the single Werks, at least when the "functional" North European Renaissance or Baroque organ is concerned.

In broad façades, the straight intermediary compartments were frequently supplied with more animation; this could be accomplished by a separation in the middle, or by underscoring this separation with a three-sectional intermediate compartment and giving its centre portion the shape of a small, angular tower. A division into tiers might also be compulsory. In cases where the pedal towers were connected with the middle section of the organ, a number of small, straight compartments were required between the outer towers of the Hauptwerk and those of the pedal.

The designs for the Rückpositiv were also elaborate and changeable. In the Netherlands style, the outside towers were often joined to the gallery railing by straight or curved compartments, or the straight intermediary compartments were replaced by angular towers. If a Rückpositiv with a strong forward projection was desired, the side towers would be turned outward in anticipation, so to speak, of the connection to the gallery railing.

The Brustwerk was seldom of great significance in the façade. With rare exceptions, it stood behind two straight compartments of dummy pipes which were fitted to hatches that swung open on hinges. Occasionally the dummy pipes in these hatches have mouths on both the front side and the back; it was clearly intended that the Brustwerk could be played with open hatches when a freer sound was desired.

The reason for the lack of speaking pipes in the Brustwerk portion of the façade was that this Werk, in the traditional arrangement, was accessible only from the front. The stop action for the Hauptwerk followed the sides of the Brustwerk, and the trackers for the Hauptwerk were behind it. Consequently, the hatches in the façade were necessary as an entrance when the Brustwerk needed tuning or repairs. Under normal circumstances, speaking pipes could not be used in such hatches; at any rate, it would be inconvenient.

During the eighteenth century, both the Brustwerk and the Rückpositiv fell into disrepute, especially the Rückpositiv. This attitude inaugurated the "liquidation" of the functional organ case. When the organ had only two Werks, Hauptwerk and Oberwerk, the construction could still be done with common sense. But when the time came that the Rückpositiv, and perhaps more, had to be concealed in the main organ case behind the other Werks, on one side, or wherever possible, the first and decisive step had been taken toward making the façade into a "blind".

The disappearance of the Rückpositiv indicates, in another way, something of substantial importance pertaining to the evolution of the instrument.

The weightless, floating quality embodied in organs of the Gothic period had, oddly enough, not been lost in the greater breadth, the pedal towers and other heavy details of the Baroque. The Rückpositiv produced an elongated oval impression, and the decorations (the top pieces, the side wings, and the hanging ornaments) underscored this effect, by tapering the contour as a whole at the top and the bottom. The outline of the organ resembled a rhombus standing on end; this eliminated any possibility that such a form could rest on the ground – it had to float.

In looking at the Michaëlis organ in Hamburg (Fig. 78), the Casparini organ in Görlitz, or the organs by Gottfried Silbermann, we find an altogether different conception in agreement with the tonal ideas represented by these masters. The Rückpositiv has vanished, the base of the main organ occupies the full width of the front, and the separation of Werks in the façade gradually withdraws in favour of practical and decorative influences.

A similar pattern is evident in Swedish organs from the latter half of the eighteenth century. In the Cathedral of Växiö (Fig. 79), the separation into Werks can still be detected. The front displays an 8′ Hauptwerk with treble in the middle and a pedal Werk arranged on both sides. Above this is a 4′ Oberwerk, a "crown Werk". The functional elements are well organized, but the whole organ is firmly and solidly rooted in the ground with no chance for escape.

More refinement is exercised at Karlskrona (Fig. 80), but the demarcation of the Werks has been obliterated. The sculptures on the sides are appropriate, and there is some logic in having the towers diminish in size as they ascend. The entire construction rises into the air like a Tower of Babel, seemingly to extraordinary heights, because the steadily diminishing towers reinforce the perspective. But the "Tower of Babel" soon began to crumble. It happened at the very moment when perfection – "the sky" – seemed to be within arm's reach.

In regard to construction, casework problems have always been less complex in France than in the north because the organs were less pretentious. The French probably used Rückpositivs as early as the Dutch, but they had no Oberwerk. Due to their size and location, the subsequent addition of the small Werks (Récit, Echo and Bombarde) had no effect on the façade (see p. 141–5). The pedal flue stops were few in number and rarely large enough to prohibit their inclusion in the Hauptwerk façade section, as in most of the organs of the sixteenth century.

In other words, the constructional material in the façades was simply the Hauptwerk (with a few pedal ranks) and the Rückpositiv. This situation prevailed until the middle of the nineteenth century when the large bass pedal Werk was introduced in French organ building. By that time, the addition of a pedal Werk was of no structural importance, because the façade had degenerated to a "curtain".

The basic design in French organ cases traditionally has been very simple, and the modifications are related mostly to the shape, the size and the equipment.

Throughout most of the sixteenth century, straight compartments were predominant. Later, towers came into fashion (semi-circular towers enjoyed the greatest popularity), and these round towers and straight compartments were used during the entire eighteenth century. Of course, exceptions to this statement exist, but they are relatively isolated.

The drawing of the Rheims Cathedral organ (Fig. 51) made ca. 1583 by the organist, Jacques Cellier, gives a very good idea of a representative type from the beginning of the sixteenth century (1532). It is a large instrument with a 32′ front Principal, and a great many traits are reminiscent of contemporary Nordic types: the horizontal lines of the pipe mouths, the freedom of the upper pipe contour, the compartments built up from the same horizontal line, etc. But the narrow, slender compartments and the fact that each is self-symmetrical is indicative of the French style. Identical ones are found in the organs at Tours and Mans, where the main façades are also nine-sectional. However, the rebuildings done at Rheims, Tours and Mans in the years of the Renaissance have radically altered the original character.

At Amiens (Fig. 81), the largest pipes are placed in fairly narrow flats, whereas the intermediary flats have an unusual width; this width may, however, be attributed to a later rebuild. Succeeding periods have also left their stamps on this case in another way – the ornaments; and here we find a unique instance of a decrease in the lengths of the pipe feet which is proportional with the decrease of the pipe lengths.

Many sixteenth century façades were "modernized" when the Rückpositivs were added. In Denmark, the Sorø organ is a good illustration, because the addition of its Rückpositiv (1628) accompanied the loss of the case shutters; and instead of the Gothic finials, the Royal coat-of-arms and some Baroque top pieces were mounted on the main organ.

By the middle of the sixteenth century, a great number of French organs already reflected the growing prominence of Renaissance designs. Usually the changes were far-reaching in nature.

The Gothic nucleus in the Chartres façade (Fig. 82), for example, is completely invisible. After observing the great breadth of this organ, as well as its profusion of pipe compartments in eloquent shapes, round towers, polygonal towers, pointed towers, straight compartments, and slanting compartments in typical Dutch abundance, we might imagine that the inspiration came from a more northern or Dutch conception. This is not the case. There was a Hauptwerk and a pedal with *ravalement,* extending to 16′ F, and a Rückpositiv with an 8′ Principal. The generous width of the façade is necessitated by the restriction in depth. It is altogether natural and desirable that every available means be employed to vary and decorate such a large surface. Nor is it unreasonable for the decorative element to dominate when the instrument itself fails to provide adequate material for architectural purposes.

There are other examples of this among French Renaissance organs. The organ case at La Ferté Bernard (Fig. 83) is almost as non-functional as the Jutfaas front, and its design was possibly determined by the somewhat older Gothic loft upon which it is built. St. Bertrand de Comminges has an angular-shaped organ which is built into a corner of the church; external circumstances have again played a large role. These instruments, however, are exceptional.

Like the organ at Moret (Fig. 84), the customary Renaissance type has a uniform, smooth pipe arrangement whose rectangular contour is clearly outlined, although it is broken by a taller, central flat, or in later designs, by two or three round towers.

With the coming of the eighteenth century, this heavy quadrangular form was dissolved, towers became increasingly popular, and the straight intermediary flats were no longer terminated with heavy profiles at the top, but with slender ornaments whose elegant, undulating lines joined the round towers.

These lines, however, are not determined by the natural pipe lengths. A rear view of an instrument, in a drawing by Dom Bedos, shows that the front pipes had a certain "excess length", meaning that they were a little longer than required by the corresponding pitch lengths. A perforation in the back of the surplus piece made it inoperative.

This was a decisive retreat from the natural "tonal architecture" of the organ and a move toward conversion of the organ façade into a decorative screen, which architects and sculptors could mould freely and without reference to genuine organ precepts.

Nevertheless, many of these façades embody so much good tradition and so much of the honest organ conceptions that they do not seem dreadfully false, in spite of the distorted pipe dimensions (Figs. 85 and 86).

The main trend, however, was easily discernible, and it was apparent in still another way. From Dom Bedos' drawing and countless eighteenth-century organs, it can be seen that a chromatic pipe arrangement was normal in the Rückpositiv (with the exception of the lowest octave), although the fronts had a symmetrical pipe arrangement and an entirely different pipe grouping. The chromatic layout was most convenient for the action.

Dom Bedos went so far as to publish a sketch for an absolute "curtain" façade having no pipes (Fig. 87). It is not surprising that Dom Bedos was influenced by contemporary trends, and this is particularly true when we remember the scarcity of real organ material for the French façades. But yet it is strange to see how the designs by degrees were scamped; the creative imagination seemingly was limited to round towers and straight compartments; these motifs were used repeatedly, to the point of being tedious. In the St. Cecile Cathedral at Albi there is a series of no less than nine round towers and eight straight compartments in the main organ, and five round towers and six more compartments in the Rückpositiv. These patterns are synonymous with the disappearance of the true organ façade in France.

The St. Sulpice façade, 1784 (Fig. 88), demonstrates another facet of the evolution. The Neo-Classicism now governed the designs, and these designs, no matter how successful as architecture, contribute nothing to the organ. The casework pipes are seemingly of equal length (no one knows what happens behind the massive cornice above), and this makes them flagrantly "unmusical" to the observer. If they are speaking pipes, after all, the sculptures in front of their mouths are, from the voicer's point of view, very badly placed. A worse arrangement of organ pipes would be difficult to contrive. It would have been more honest to use no pipes in this façade – it is merely a "curtain".

Although Spanish organs surpass the French in possessing a far richer groundwork for the creation of a functional façade, the structural concept has not been allowed to dominate the appearance. A natural connection between the interior and the exterior may be studied in examples from the fifteenth century and the beginning of the sixteenth; for example, the small organ in Salamanca (Fig. 90) and the organ in Zaragoza (Fig. 91). In many of the later and larger organs, with two or three manuals, there are also examples of the largest rank standing in the lowest and largest façade compartments, but these compartments are supplemented with countless others which are totally unrelated to the position of the Werks standing behind them; this is even true of the façades with speaking pipes. Neither the level nor the pitch series has any connection with the placement or arrangement of the wind chests. To illustrate, the three-sectional pipe grouping at the top of the Tarragona organ (Fig. 92) is not in alignment with an Oberwerk; it is simply a decoration. Of course the speaking pipes in the façade can be more or less dominating, and these pipes can be more or less "honest", that is, more or less distorted by ornaments or by excessive lengths, which are found rather early in Spanish organs. Moreover, compartments of dummy pipes were very common, not only small compartments as in the Nordic style, but sometimes even the largest flats having the most sizeable pipes. Such large, dummy compartments are usually recognized from the abnormal pipe diameters (see Fig. 96, Granada).

The horizontal reeds are definitely the most functional element in the façade. Their measurements are not fallacious, and the arrangement is suitable for the sound and for simple, practical matters as tuning, dust, etc. But not even these pipes have a close, natural union with their wind chest. Each pipe has a wind tube, frequently long and crooked. Like the façade fluework, the sequence of pitches is quite independent of the pipe sequence on the wind chests.

Very few consistent principles can be formulated in relation to façade construction. With further study of the seventeenth and eighteenth centuries, it is unmistakably clear that these façades do not lack components from the instrument; but their development has been conditioned by altogether different and extraneous matters. Ornaments were undoubtedly of primary importance, and the sculptor worked with extreme freedom, not only with the ornaments but also with pipes and pipe compartments.

The general tendency has many points of similarity to the main course of events in France. In the Late Gothic era, Spanish organ builders maintained a functional casework design; then came the Renaissance with heavy, rectangular forms, resulting in pipe flats whose sole obligation was to cover an empty space; and finally, the ornaments and designs of the Baroque shattered the stiff rectangles, without introducing more honest organ structures in their place.

The organs in Salamanca (1380, Fig. 90), the Zaragoza Cathedral (1473, Fig. 91), Perpignan (1504, Fig. 89), which was Spanish territory at that time, and Toledo (1755, Figs. 98 and 99) describe this trend more effectively than many words.

Though the "Emperor" organ at Toledo (Fig. 93) is an exception, it is noteworthy as a very early example of a "curtain" façade. The five stone arches over the south door of the cathedral are filled in with front pipes belonging to the Flautado 16′ and Flautado 8′. Overlengths were used to a great extent in order to suit the pipes to the arches. In the nineteenth century, an organ case was often planned on the basis of external conditions, but this instance occurred in the middle of the sixteenth century.

The horizontal trumpets, added during the late seventeenth century, are not really successful in this setting. They speak more convincingly from an environment of gilded ornaments, and the majority of them are placed in just such surroundings. Ornaments and gold played a spectacular role especially in the eighteenth century. Thus in the case of the large organ for Toledo Cathedral finished in 1797, the organ itself cost 54,000 reales; the wood carving, 46,000 reales; and the gilding for the woodwork and carving, 36,000 reales.

Although this organ had two façades, toward the nave and the aisle respectively, these figures confirm the importance of the organ front and the relative values placed on each phase of the work. Numerous other examples could be cited, including many where the woodwork was gilded from top to bottom.

The South German Baroque and Rocco façades are more graceful and elegant than the Spanish façades, and the pipes' flats are given greater prominence in relation to the ornaments. Dummy pipes are used less, but here again the composition is largely controlled by outside factors.

The famous organs in Weingarten and Ottobeuren will serve as illustrations (Figs. 100 and 101). Obviously the basic design for the Weingarten organ is affected by the building and the six windows which literally are framed and encircled by the organ. The two Rückpositivs are definitely the most functional elements because two Werks are located there: on the epistle side, the fourth manual Werk of the organ; and on the gospel side, the small pedal stops: the canto solo pedal (see specification p. 217). Both façades have incorporated a little more than the two lowest octaves of the 8′ Principal from each Werk, and the pipe dimensions have not been disfigured by overlength or comparable procedures. In two large façade sections behind the Rückpositiv, three tiers are allocated to the remaining Werks: at the bottom, an Echo Werk, in the middle, the Hauptwerk; and at the top, the Oberwerk. With the assistance of wind trunk connections, four Oberwerk ranks have been mounted centrally at the very top as a so-called "crown Werk". The large pedal ranks are installed in the two main organ cases, and the 32′ pedal Principal furnishes the large façade pipes, though not in a continuous sequence – this is clearly indicated by the lengths. Consequently this façade possesses a certain amount of functional organization; and in spite of the very diffuse arrangement, the motivically unrelated outer sections of the main façade, and the isolation of the connecting "bridge sections" from the wind chests, there are only eight non-speaking pipes in the façade.

The intimate relation of sanctuary and organ in the South German Rococo period is unsurpassed. Beyond the colour and material, there is no actual distinction between the stucco ornaments of the building and the wooden ornaments of the organ. Ornaments are sprayed over any structure – a structure which is necessary, of course, but has no further interest for the *joie de vivre* that is so characteristic of the southern temperament. This wealth of ornamentation has been called *erstarrte Musik* (frozen music), and the conception is both accurate and legitimate.

A description of these ornaments and their stylistic development (the very area where the Spanish and South German façades are so well-endowed) is outside the scope of this work, but ornaments can also be considered as functional material. With the exception of the "Age of Reason and Accuracy", the organ has never been without ornaments; they were either carved in the wood or painted on the case or the pipes.

Some of the wooden ornaments, as mentioned before, had a truly practical role, because they occupied certain vacant spaces in the façade. But ornaments were usually occasioned by an entirely different set of circumstances. A "rational" explanation is impossible; this would be as futile as an attempt to explain the textless *melismas,* the jubilant coloraturas appended to the generally "objective" Gregorian songs. Augustinus described the *jubilus* in this way: "Unto whom should we shout with joy except to God whose nature cannot be expressed. For if you have no words for it, and yet you cannot be silent, what else remains but shouting with joy, so that your heart rejoices and your immense jubilation is not severed and measured in syllables."

After some study of the organ and its resources, we must conclude that the ratio for blending "logic" and *melismas* is simply a matter of temperament. To completely omit all ornaments is just as non-functional as to permit their domination of all constructions.

The strictly practical, "logical" arrangement of the organ case (the distribution into Werks, the placement of the Werks, the action, the ranks of pipes and their dimensions) is not a particularly complex matter. Although these considerations provide a good foundation with many fine possibilities, the combination of these resources must be handled with discretion, in regard to the instrument and to the casework.

For good results, the divisions and the proportions are of the utmost importance, and it would be interesting to know how the early organ builders treated this aspect of the matter. There is an appalling scarcity of information; the few drawings which have been preserved are little more than casual sketches lacking correct proportions and measurements, and there is nothing of significance in writing.

We are obliged to study the results, but the method of production is still open to conjecture. At first glance, the consistent use of strong, natural principles is apparent. It is impossible to determine with certainty which things are due to hereditary habits or personal, instinctive understanding, and which things are due to experience and preliminary calculation. It is equally difficult to say who should have credit for the outcome: the church architects, the sculptors, or the organ builders. No specific answer can be supplied, and besides, it is more important to find out why the good instruments are good.

The organ in the Haderslev Cathedral, Denmark, will serve as a valuable illustration. After being restored to its original form, it is probably one of the most effective examples of good proportions.

In the plan (Fig. 73), the Lichtmass (i. e., the measurements for the available space as defined by the roof-walls-floor at the west wall of the church) of the auditorium is determined by three squares whose sides are designated by L. The points of support for the arches are located on the horizontal bisector of the upper square. The organ is inscribed in the centre square, and if the horizontal bisector of this square is drawn, it defines the underside of the Hauptwerk pipe compartment; and this compartment is also inscribed in a square, whose sides are one-half the length ($^1/_2$ L) of the sides in the square circumscribing the whole instrument. In other words, it has the width of $^1/_2$ Lichtmass of the church. If this measurement is divided in half ($= {}^1/_4$ L), the height for the intermediary flats of the Hauptwerk is obtained, and by taking one-third of half the Lichtmass ($= {}^1/_6$ L), the width of the pedal towers is derived.

In looking at the two galleries, the organ gallery above and the choir gallery below, we see that they are enclosed in a square of which the upper side follows the top edge of the organ gallery, the lower side rests on the floor line, and the vertical sides define the width of the galleries. Besides, the lower edge of the choir gallery is on a line which horizontally bisects the lowest square of the auditorium; and the top of the railing for this gallery subdivides the upper half of this square. Thus the old ratios of 1 : 2,

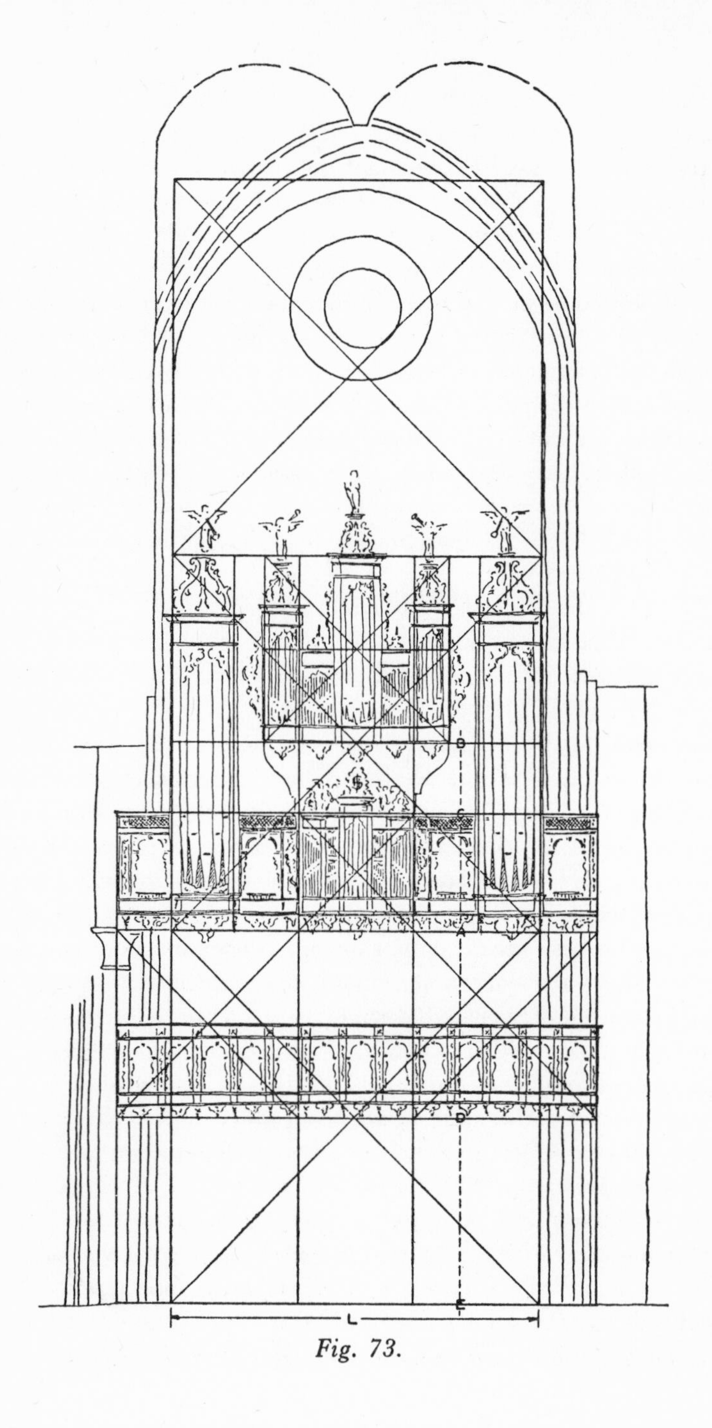

Fig. 73.

1 : 3, and 2 : 3, based on the Lichtmass of the room, have been used extensively.

As for the width of the galleries: how is this width related to the church space and to the organ? Or, what is the relation of the upper edge of the organ gallery railing to the floor line?

The sectio aurea, the Golden Section, comes into action here. If the height of the base for the main organ, AB ($= \frac{1}{2}$ L), is reduced in proportion to the Golden Section, the balustrade height, AC, is the result; that is, the relation of AB to AC is the same as AC to BC.

However, the distance of $\frac{1}{2}$ L recurs between the two lower edges of the galleries; thus we can say that the relation of AD to AC is the same as AD to DC – still the Golden Section. Since the length DE is also $\frac{1}{2}$ L, the ratio of DE to DC is likewise comparable to the Golden Section, and therefore the ratio of DC to EC must be the same.

The following equations have been derived:

$$\frac{BC}{AC} = \frac{AC}{AD} = \frac{AD}{DC} = \frac{DC}{EC}$$

If the width EC is assigned to the galleries, two results are obtained: (1) the galleries, as stated before, are enclosed in a square, and (2) the sides in the rectangle, formed within the square by the galleries, have the ratio of the Golden Section.

This is one aspect of the matter. In the middle of the organ gallery railing, the Rückpositiv is situated in a square whose sides correspond to the height of the railing. Owing to this, the width (and also the height) of the pipe sections for the Hauptwerk and Rückpositiv have the ratio of the Golden Section. Moreover, the distance between the outer towers of the Hauptwerk is the same as the width of the Rückpositiv, so that its width has the same proportion to the total width of the Hauptwerk.

The organization of the Rückpositiv resembles the plan of the Hauptwerk: the distance between the outer towers is related to the total width as in the Golden Section.

If this distance is reduced while maintaining the same proportions, the width for the central tower in the Hauptwerk is attained; if one further reduction is made, the result is the width of the central tower in the Rückpositiv.

From the width of the galleries to the width of the central tower in the

Rückpositiv, the internal divisions are such that the graduated widths form a geometric progression of seven steps having the ratio of the Golden Section.

As a parallel to this, the graduations in height, calculated from the horizontal bisector of the auditorium, are arranged in five steps with the same dimensions. Countless geometrical curiosities are waiting to be discovered. Squares and rectangles having the Golden Section overlap and supplement each other in the most delightful puzzle. This is evident when the two verticals in the Rückpositiv square are extended to the floor line. These two extended lines are intersected by the lower edge of the choir gallery, thereby producing two "golden" rectangles one above the other. On either side of the Rückpositiv square, there are twin rectangles, and the rectangles which outline the base of the Hauptwerk and the middle section of the pipework are congruent with them. The longest side in each of these rectangles is $^1/_2$ L, and thus the two squares located under each of the pedal towers also have side lengths of $^1/_2$ L.

Closer study of the diagram is amusing, because it fully explains why these very simple numbers and relationships have, for centuries, been symbols for the harmony of the universe and why they have been used as reliable guides when a harmonious and beautiful result was desired.

There is no necessity for mentioning further examples because the techniques will be the same, and the method of application, in most instances, will be inferior. The organ in Tønder Church, Denmark, adheres to a similar plan and has approximately the same dimensions as the Haderslev organ, but the deviations from the "plan" are more pronounced, and the relations to the room could not be executed so ideally as at Haderslev.

It is not unusual to find Werks, or parts of Werks, whose outer contours are defined by a square, or whose internal divisions are based on the Golden Section, as in the Haderslev Hauptwerk and Rückpositiv. But all types of deviations from this specific pattern are common; nor was everything computed with mathematical precision at Haderslev.

The relationship of the organ to the room and surroundings is rarely determined by a single method. In the first place, all rooms are not equally well-proportioned or well-suited for an entirely consistent structure; in the second place, the early organ builders were never pedantic in the application of their good principles. The art of proportion had already fallen into a state of decline by the Baroque period. In organ building there were many practical things to be considered, and the internal relations had to be modified at some points. For example, the exact width of a pipe compartment cannot be stated in advance; this is especially difficult when large pipes must be mounted, because the width varies greatly in accordance with the total number of pipes. One pipe more or less can be a decisive factor, and if the pipe compartment has to be self-symmetrical, two pipes must be added or subtracted at the same time. However, the tower design is a great advantage here, because the alteration of the width can be executed to some extent by means of this projection. In compartments with small pipes, the solution is considerably easier since the empty spaces between the pipes permit a certain degree of control.

At any rate, balance can be achieved. There is no lack of examples, and it is certainly not difficult to distinguish these instances from those where matters have been treated more freely.

The Haderslev organ can also illustrate one or two of these points. Figure 72 B shows the appearance of the organ after a rebuilding at the close of the eighteenth century and during the restoration of the church in 1844. The mutilated pedal towers were changed to 8′ height and moved back into the loft. In addition, they were pulled in closer to the centre, and the railing in front was pieced together with the available remnants, which made it impossible for the width of the organ loft to correspond with that of the choir loft. The broad outer panels are the end pieces of the railing which ought to stand in the longitudinal direction of the church.

Moreover, the galleries were supplied with new rafters, in 1780, and this caused them to be raised by approximately one-half of a metre. The heavy wooden construction below the choir gallery, and the arcades are products of the nineteenth century. On the same occasion, the railing from the demolished choir screen was also moved to the choir gallery where its height and width measurements fitted perfectly.

Thus the two galleries were placed a little too high and had unequal widths; and the pedal towers did not have the proper placement. That was enough for totally disrupting the entire appearance.

And yet this would be considered a beautiful organ if there had been no opportunity for comparing it with the correct installation.

One objection will undoubtedly be raised against these ideas concerning proportions: the effect of perspective. The façade of the Rückpositiv indeed stands in front of the pedal towers, and the façade of the Hauptwerk is still farther back. If we walk down through the nave toward the organ, the

Rückpositiv and the pedal towers will seem higher and higher in relation to the main organ.

In view of this, does the geometrical composition have any significance? What is the purpose of having the instrument look well in a horizontal projection if it is never seen from this direction?

The proportions maintain their effectiveness, because the Hauptwerk is clearly seen to be standing behind the Rückpositiv and the pedal towers. The effect of perspective is notable, for example, in the cornices of the pedal towers, and the eye automatically makes the necessary correction in height.

Of course, the horizontal distances (between Rückpositiv-pedal towers and Rückpositiv-main organ) are presumed to have a reasonable relation when viewed from the nave of the church (the longitudinal direction). But if the proportions are well-conceived in both vertical and horizontal projection, they will also be good in perspective, even though the latter changes constantly in accordance with the position of the observer. These are ancient principles.

9

The Location of the Organ

The function of the organ has been of primary importance in determining its location in the church, but space conditions and other practical matters concerning the installation have played important roles, too.

During the Middle Ages, and even today in many countries, the liturgical functions of the organ determined its natural location to be within or in the vicinity of the choir. The organ was usually mounted on the north wall above the choir stalls, as this was advantageous for windows and light. There might also be two organs, one on the north wall and one on the south wall.

Even in large churches, the organs mounted at these places had to be relatively small; usually they had the shape of a flat "Swallow's nest" built very close to the wall in order not to dominate. When the organs became larger, this location had to be abandoned, and then the organ was moved out into the church.

The arms of the transept offered many possibilities for organ installation, and the distance to the choir was not too great for the organ to perform its liturgical functions excellently. One of the oldest descriptions concerning such an installation dates from the year 1114. It deals with Canterbury Cathedral where an organ was erected in the northern part of the transept ("above the arch") with a positive placed on the floor below. The main organ and the positive had not yet coalesced.

Especially the Netherlands and France make use of the transept (from the fifteenth to the seventeenth centuries). Within the arms of the transept the location could be the east or west wall, often close to the nave (see Fig. 62, St. Bavo, Haarlem), or it could be the end walls, generally the northern one. Particularly in France, this position was preferred in the sixteenth and seventeenth centuries (for example, Rheims, Fig. 51, and Rodez or Tours and Le Mans, where the organs stand in the south transept).

In England, the organs at that time were smaller – small enough to be placed on the rood-screen which separated the choir and the nave (for instance, King's College, Figs. 104 and 105). This location may be something of a surprise to the Continent (excepting France), but as the purpose of the screen was to separate the choir and the nave, the reinforcement of this separation by an organ was not considered extraordinary. From an acoustical point of view, this position was perfect, and of course there was a double front, toward the choir and the nave respectively.

The older choir organs were not always demolished and removed when a rood-screen organ was built. From Durham, for instance, there are records of three organs, the largest of which was mounted on the screen. This distinguished instrument with wooden pipes and rich ornaments was opened and used only on festival days. The second one was placed on the north side of the choir and was played when the four Fathers of the Church were read (Augustine, Ambrose, Gregory and Hieronymous). Obviously this organ was the oldest instrument and rather loud – it was called the Cryer! The third organ stood opposite to the Cryer and was used at ordinary church services. Each organ therefore had its duties in the sacred ceremonies "to the better celebrating thereof".

In Spain, the necessity of two choir organs gradually became the custom, and for quite similar reasons. Here the cathedrals were so large that even instruments of considerable dimensions could obtain adequate space in the arch between the choir and the aisles. However, it must be noted in addition to this that the choirs in the Spanish churches are located nearer to the middle of the church than in the churches of the northern countries. The organs are constructed with a depth corresponding to the thickness of the walls. Thus the fronts, toward both the nave and the aisles, are approximately on a level with the surface of the walls; only the horizontal trumpets project.

In other countries, the size of the organ is generally the reason for mounting it on the side walls or on the west wall of the nave; for liturgical duties, the large churches probably also had a choir organ.

As early as the fifteenth century, several nave organs were in existence. The Cathedral of Roskilde, for example, had one on the south wall, where the organ is still placed. Some other extant examples are the organs in Chartres (Fig. 121), Strassburg Münster (Fig. 56), and La Ferté Bernard (Fig. 83), all dating from the sixteenth century. Among the west wall organs, the large Marien organ in Lübeck (Fig. 44) must be mentioned first and foremost. On the whole, Germany and the Netherlands have been ahead of other countries with this location, because their organs were larger and required the acoustically ideal position provided by the west wall of the nave. France also has examples of west wall organs, for instance, Amiens (Fig. 122).

In several churches, the large west windows characteristic of the Gothic cathedrals have hindered the placing of an organ at this ideal location (although in the Marienkirche, Lübeck, no attention was paid to this). But with the Reformation in the Lutheran countries, the organ was literally driven toward the west, partly because the large instruments could only be accommodated there, and partly because a great deal of the church service (the congregational singing, for example) included the contribution of the layman in the church.

The Lutheran churches could also have choir organs, and some of these were new churches built according to the church service of the Reformation. A clear and natural tendency to unite the altar and the pulpit at a central position in the room is characteristic of these churches (Luther was personally interested in these efforts). If possible, the organ has also been included in this combination. It is then mounted above the altar, and the pulpit may be placed between the altar and the organ, if the vertical space is sufficient.

Probably, the first attempt in that direction was made in the castle church in Schmalkalden (1590), and among the Scandinavian examples, the Christianschurch in Copenhagen (Fig. 120) and Kongsberg Church in Norway can be mentioned. Around such a liturgical centre the congregation was gathered as close as possible with the aid of as many balconies as possible. In other words, the congregation had moved into the choir, and there was no longer a layman's section.

However, these churches constitute exceptions, and the west wall of the nave has proved to be the established location for the organ in the northern and western parts of Europe – with the exception of England. The English liturgy still requires the organ to be located near the altar; but this creates great difficulties because of the decided 8′ organ type which is still preferred. A location to the west in smaller churches has been eagerly debated, because the insignificant length of such churches could not impair the connection between the altar and the organ. The instrument would have more space available, but simultaneously, problems with occasional west windows would arise.

The systems of electrical action, which appeared at the turn of the century, resulted in complete freedom for organ location. Now it was possible (and it was tempting in the large churches) to divide the organ into as many sections as desired and to place these sections anywhere in the church. It was even possible to mount a section above the vaults of the church and to conduct the sound through a long channel, making the tonal effect "celestially remote". Finally, the organist could be placed anywhere, except at a place where he could hear his own organ and organ playing precisely – the distance prevented it. The use of these organs is extremely limited, and there is no reason to dwell on these instruments. The boundless freedom in this area has certainly not created results worth mentioning, but it has given us a means for a better understanding of the fact that compliance with the laws of natural proportions is a useful yoke.

10

The Organ Reform Movement

The period between the two World Wars is now sufficiently far away for us to begin to survey what actually occurred. Within these twenty years all of the fundamental principles from the preceding century and a half were revalued.

Even now an organ builder cannot entirely dissociate himself from these circumstances in order to consider them objectively because he is still involved in the affair. There was no break in development during the Second World War or after it. In Denmark especially, organ building continued along the established lines, almost independent of external events.

An organ builder who has been active in the movement will naturally view the issues through prejudiced eyes, and besides, he will be inclined to regard the subject from inside. On the other hand, a subjective survey may be useful to those who are unfamiliar with this area. And this survey will be attempted here.

The Scherer-Schnitger organ at St. Jacobi, Hamburg, was rediscovered by Harms and Hans Henny Jahnn at the beginning of the 1920s; but the significant fact is that these prophets did not speak to deaf ears. Albert Schweitzer had done that for a number of years, even though his ideas, in general, were much the same. To Harms and Jahnn an entire generation listened with open ears and was able to experience the tonal realm represented by the Jacobi organ. Generation after generation had used this organ without noticing anything unusual about it; it was generally considered to be an unimportant, antiquated, yet not worthless instrument; but now people began to listen in a completely different way, and a wealth of tonal resources was thrown open to contemplation, suggesting an entirely new trend.

With the increasing appreciation of polyphony in classical organ literature, the interest in Baroque organ types was quite natural. An acquaintance with this tonal realm was an essential condition for a complete understanding of this music.

This hypothesis proved to be accurate: the bright and clear sound transmitted polyphonic clarity most successfully, and the timbres were more individualistic, more characteristic of the organ, and more varied, largely because of mutations and Schnarrwerk (low-pressure reeds). This voicing technique could be used profitably in new organs as well as old ones.

Very cautiously, organ builders began to supplement the customary specifications with some few mutations – a Quint $2^2/_3'$, a 2′ and a Tierce $1^3/_5'$, possibly coupled in a Cornet. But the higher mutations ($1^1/_3'$ and 1′) were too risky; they would "scream". The lower mutations were accepted, especially when made with a wide Nachthorn scale, a narrow mouth and very soft voicing. This made them blend and subordinate to the rest of the Romantic ensemble.

As the organ builders became more courageous they started to experiment with the higher mutations and the repeating mixtures; they also learned more about appropriate placement of these innovations in the specifications. But the entire conception of sound was still anchored in the Romantic organ, and aside from the very wide scales, which were usually applied in single mutations, the standard scales were still used.

The problem of scaling was the next point for consideration, and the scaling of the Principals was given particular attention. Development inclined to smaller diameters and lower cut-ups, and this general principle came as a reaction (with the usual exaggeration) against the high wind pressure and high cut-ups of the Romantic organ.

Little by little the width scales were improved, and a great step forward was made when it was discovered that the Reuter tuning slot distorted the sound, making it flat and ugly. It was reformed altogether.

An improved style was gradually adopted in the specifications; the concept of tonal structure became a matter of increasing interest. The organ builders realized that the stops had to be judged mainly according to their ensemble capabilities. They discovered the value of basing the various manual Werks on Principal ranks, an octave apart; and finally they learned how to combine these Werks into a larger entity.

The great advance came when the technique of voicing was also revised. The improvements of specification and scaling could not be exploited while organ building was bound to the Romantic ideas of voicing, that is, so long as the sound was being spoiled by extremely weak voicing. To avoid an assertive sound, organ builders had reduced the tonal intensity by a sharp curtailment in the wind supply at the pipe foot – without any regard to the timbre. The understanding of what a pipe was created for had to be revived.

One thing was left. The machine-like exactness of the voicing ideal inherited from the nineteenth century resulted in the use of many artifices (nicks, beards, etc.) to obtain the perfect attack and tone. Now it was clear that this smoothly polished voicing actually robbed the pipes of some of their most valuable qualities; the "imperfections" of many old pipes (chiffing and odd sounds at the attack) indeed provided the "spices" of the lively and vibrant timbre.

Of course, this did not imply that the pipes should speak at random. On the contrary, here was a tonal material which needed rejuvenation. Seemingly the single tone and the equalizing of the rank had to be made somewhat "imperfect" in order to improve the ensemble. This did not simplify the task for the voicer; he had to develop an exquisite sense of timbres; and people who did not know better often accused him of poor workmanship.

When Grundtvig's Church, Copenhagen, was built all of the bricks were chosen with special care so that the colour would be as uniform as possible. All of the bricks used for the masonry of the interior were machine-polished and laid with the utmost accuracy.

But when the son of the same architect began building the Bethlehem Church, Copenhagen, the bricks used were as motley as the clay in the tile-works could make them; hand-cut bricks were used, and they were left unpolished.

Today anyone can judge which masonry is most vivid, and which kind of voicing is most satisfactory. There are still a good many organs from the 1920's and 30's for comparison.

An artificial patina was mentioned in connection with the new trends. But the concept of tonal patina must also be considered in relation to voicing technique. For good reasons, some years had to pass before this phenomenon was observed.

A tonal refinement occurs during the aging of an organ, but what really happens to the pipes has not yet been explained. This change can even be traced when the pipes are only ten years old, and the voicer can confirm that old pipes are easier to work with than new ones. As an experiment, pipes have been made of metal sheets from old pipes, but the result was not the same. Without doubt, a certain individual adjustment must occur between the vibrations of the air in the pipe and the resulting vibrations of the pipe wall; and we know that this adjustment, among other things, is perceptible in a shifting of the tonal balance in favour of the fundamental.

The good voicer knows how to take this change into consideration while he is working: because of this coming maturation, the sound in a new organ must have some "overbalance" in the upper partials and the highest inharmonics.

This factor must be taken into particular consideration when the tonal character of old organs and the tonal ideal of the old masters are judged or discussed. The old organ builders would probably fail to recognize their own instruments if they had an opportunity to hear them now; and if we want to form a concept of their tonal ideal, we must reconstruct it with the use of imagination and the scales.

With the gradual advances made in the work with tonal technique, it was recognized that the wind chests as well as the action had an important tonal function. The tonal qualities of the tone-groove chest, in comparison with those of the stop-channel chest, have already been mentioned. Furthermore, the reasons for avoiding stop-channel chests and electric and pneumatic action have been discussed.

In time, organ builders have realized that the sound and its development were adversely affected when the organ case was made too deep (in the longitudinal direction of the room). They also discovered the advantage of enclosing each Werk of the organ (the manual Werks as well as the Pedal) in a wooden "house" fitting closely around the Werk in question and opening only at the front (the side facing the room). This unified the sound and gave it direction.

On the basis of these conclusions, the location of two or more Werks behind each other must be objectionable (or impossible), although this had often been done before. Every Werk must be a part of the façade, and thus it was necessary to work with the height and the breadth always, with the least possible depth for the "houses". These centralized and well-planned structures also proved to be favourable for the installation of mechanical action.

For practical reasons the organ structure started right at the gallery floor with the Rückpositiv; in this way unduly high constructions were avoided, and this position also proved to be excellent for the acoustics. In the main organ the largest of the manual Werks (the Hauptwerk) was accomodated, and below this there might be space for a Brustwerk; finally an Oberwerk (or "crown" Werk) could be mounted above the Hauptwerk if the vertical space was sufficient. The pedal Werk, with its long pipes, had a natural place on both sides of the manual Werks if the width of the room permitted this; in a smaller organ it might be combined with the Hauptwerk to restrict the breadth of the instrument.

This expansion of the organ into a flat arrangement behind the front had one more advantage: the tonal characters of the Werks were underscored by the acoustical effects conditioned by their location. The bright sound of the Rückpositiv was free and near; the broader sound of the Hauptwerk was situated higher in the room; the lighter sound of the Oberwerk was more remote; and the delicate and slender tones of the Brustwerk were close to choir and soloists.

While the details relating to specifications and Werk-placement were being co-ordinated and shaped, the demand for an organ façade asserted itself as an integral part of this complex. If there was a central idea in the instrument and its mounting, this idea naturally and inevitably had to assume a visual character.

This was closely allied with the contemporary trend toward functionalism, and of course all decorations were discarded in the beginning; only pipes and pipe groupings were used in the façade. The idea of such fronts made exclusively of pipes was older than functionalism, but the unique feature was that natural pipe dimensions and Werk-structure again determined forms and sections.

The Werk-cases arrived later, and at first they caused some confusion in the principles. Of course, they might be hidden behind a rank of tall front pipes; but the arrangement was impractical, and injurious to the sound, because the houses had to be reduced in height or the front pipes to be lifted into a higher position than the other pipes of the Werk in question – and moreover, it was a functional fraud. The organ cases did influence the sound; and thus the only honest solution was to let them enter the picture. And this is what happened.

The specification, the scales, the Werk-structure, and the fronts had certain fundamental resemblances to the North European Baroque organ; and of course some persons construed the development as a rather sterile attempt at a stylistic copy, as a partial revival of the Baroque organ.

This attitude is concurrent with a fairly violent reaction against several "modern" phenomena: the exaggerated emphasis on foundation sound during the Romantic period, the string stops, the swell-boxes, pneumatic and electric action, excessive aids for registration, etc.

The older generation did not conceive of this sudden and radical revaluation, and the younger generation sometimes proceeded too categorically (this is characteristic in a period of change), but the ground had to be cleared in preparation for the new ideas, and some things had to be excluded for the time.

Those who have followed the developments will certainly concede that the way of working was thoroughly honest. Stylistic copy was not used as a short-cut, apart from the decorative equipment of a few organ façades. On the contrary, the fear of a stylistic copy pervaded the entire period, and perhaps it is demonstrated most clearly in the organ façades. This fear, which is easily explained with a background of the Neo-Gothic and similar phenomena of the nineteenth century, accounts for a great number of the initially stiff, but honestly creative efforts and the superficial pseudo-modern creations which were also on the scene.

Structural honesty was frequently exaggerated, because the beauty of expedience had gradually become a dogma. This led to the habit of making an exhibition of the construction. There were experiments, for example, with placing the small pipes in front of the larger ones; or the tuning slots might be placed quite shamelessly on the front side of the pipes; or the whole instrument was suspended in the middle of the room with no house except a glass-box.

For the same reason, the swell-boxes were debated. Moulding the sound of the pipes in this way was not honest. They were created with a definite and unalterable tonal intensity, and they ought to remain like this. The crescendi and diminuendi should be produced by connecting and disconnecting the stops. Moreover, the swell-boxes could not, for good reasons, have front pipes as required by the new principles.

The asymmetrical, chromatic rank of pipes was, of course, attractive to those who revolted against the old-fashioned symmetry; but the symmetrical C and C♯ arrangement proved to be the better for both the tuning and the sound, and a further distribution into groups with small pipes and large pipes was still more profitable. The organ builders also realized that, in the majority of cases, a location of the large pipes foremost in the Werk provided a better balance and blend. Thus many concessions, large and small, had to be made to the Baroque masters, as the problems were gradually examined.

Those having personal contact with the work and the problems certainly had few speculations concerning stylistic imitations. The steady stream of new information was so convincing that there was seldom any occasion for hesitating. Piece by piece the Romantic organ was dismantled, because the new methods were preferable.

Why have we then arrived at a type which is so close to the North European Baroque organ? The answer must be that such a similarity is unavoidable when we want to work in a natural way with all of the resources inherent in the organ; the majority of these resources were already represented in the Baroque organ of northern Europe, united into a completely logical and structural entity.

Besides, the new organs contain much more than the North European Baroque; and if the ingredients must be definitely located, influences from France, Spain, South Germany and Italy can be detected. The entire organ history of Europe has been our inspiration.

And there was good use for all of this information. Especially in Scandinavia the varied assignments require anything pertaining to good tonal technique. There are cathedrals, modern concert halls, and a considerable number of medium-sized and small churches; in brief, all spatial dimensions and all types of acoustics, ranging from the long, flattering echo of the cathedral to the completely revealing "dead" room.

History, first and foremost, has taught us that every assignment can be and ought to be solved in a completely individual manner. The organ has an adaptability to widely varied purposes, and the architecture, specification, scales, voicing, and technique can, in every single instance, be united into a new artistic synthesis.

Gradually the condition for creating this synthesis in new organs was realized: a radical change in the methods of production, a change which might appear to be a retreat because it would represent a break with the usual present-day efforts toward specialization and rationalization.

The nineteenth-century tendencies toward accuracy led to specialization. This happened with the best intentions because it was assumed that the ultimate in quality could be attained with the aid of specialists; and besides, specialization was supposed to promote production. During the nineteenth century, the following practice was standardized: first, a specification was drawn up by a musician who would later supervise the voicing. Generally musicians cared very little about the scales because the natural scientists and the organ theorists had established good and tested models. Thus the tonal result was determined only by the specification and the skill of the voicer. The engineer from the organ factory was responsible for designing the instrument and calculating the height and width required for the covering front; and when this had been done, the architect could begin work on the design for the indispensable "screen".

With sufficient space, the collaboration could be performed amicably and quickly in that way – *if* this can be referred to as collaboration; the various specialists really had very little to do with one another. The musician was precluded from computing how much space the organ would occupy or how it should be erected because these matters were outside his expert-knowledge. The organ engineer who had to arrange the specified stops calculated the spatial dimensions without regard to the relations between the church and the instrument because this was outside his expert-knowledge. The voicer did not interfere with technical matters nor with the arrangement, because this was outside his expert-knowledge, and the architect was helpless against all these specialists because their work was outside his expert-knowledge. An impartial discussion between the parties concerned was difficult because the points of contact were few and small; and specialists who do not understand each other are not inclined to moderate the demands within their own fields.

This was the situation when matters were worst, and countless organs remain as testimony to an absence of method and clashes of authority. They stand like monuments of victory sometimes for one expert and sometimes for another.

These organs have given us an emphatic lesson in what must *not* be done. They have taught us the impossibility of creating an organ by adding specialists who have nothing to do with each other; and they have vigorously underscored this experience from organ history: a central idea must be the basis of an organ, and the details must be valued from their ability to coalesce.

The organ master builder, therefore, must have a knowledge and comprehension of everything pertaining to the organ. He must be able to draw up the specification, prepare the scales, determine the arrangement and layout of the Werks as well as the basic structure of the front, and he must have enough knowledge of architecture to be able to collaborate with the architect. Preferably, he must be able to draw the front himself. He should be able to voice his instrument, and beyond everything else, he must have a thorough understanding of craftsmanship, materials and construction, and, as a matter of course, he must also look after the financial details. These are the minimum demands.

From the architect a very thorough knowledge of the technical and tonal design of the organ is demanded. A thorough preparation is required for competence in this field, and thus, organ assignments should be given to the architects who have made this an area of specialization. It would save a good deal of time and insure good results.

But what is the task of the organist, the musician? The situation has been changed by the recent recognition of the mutual connection between the specification and the individual scale calculations of the stops, as well as by many practical considerations for the erection of the instrument. Besides, it is a very common misunderstanding that musical talent is a requisite for anyone who deals with the tonal problems of the organ. Music without timbre can certainly not be imagined, but music and timbre are two different things, and timbres appear in conjunction with phenomena other than music. A person may be quite musical without having a well-developed sense of timbres, and conversely, he may have a well-developed sense of timbres (and the ability to produce them on musical instruments) without being musical, with everything that this implies of rhythmical sense and sensitivity to intervals and their combination.

There are very skilful organ builders who may almost be described as unmusical, but they nevertheless understand how to voice an organ. Correspondingly, there are capable organists who have very little information or none at all concerning scale calculation, space acoustics, and the numerous practical items which require consideration when an organ must be planned. These things are certainly the concern of the organ builders, but even here, it would be desirable for the "specialists" to have more in common.

When the specification is being prepared, it is the natural duty of the musician to present the demands of organ literature to the organ builder, but his primary responsibility lies in the future, in the use of the organ. He must play it, gain experiences from it, draw inspiration from its resources, compose music for it and thereby inspire organ-building to further advances. The organ builder must be a diligent listener because the "style" of an instrument is not revealed until it is actually in use. Much time is required; such development will often extend throughout several generations.

So much for the principles that we have come to respect. The details are demonstrated best in a survey of some actual examples.

First, a smaller organ with three manuals and pedal, the organ in Jægersborg Church (near Copenhagen), Figures 107 and 108. The Werk-structure is quite evident from the façade: the Rygpositiv on the balustrade; above it, the small, open Brystværk; in a central position at the top, the Hovedværk; and on both sides of this, the Pedal, represented by the two outer towers. The front pipes of the Rygpositiv are a Principal 4′, and those of the Hovedværk an 8′ Principal, of which the C and C# have been transferred to the pedal towers since the height of the room was inadequate. The basic outline of the pedal towers comprises five sides of a regular octagon (in order that the largest possible number of pipes for the Pedal Oktav 8′ can be mounted in the front). The Brystværk, based on a Principal 2′, is entirely open with the small stops and the tiny Ranket 16′ at the front, to supply the maximum tonal contrast to the other manual Werks. There are doors in this case (as shown in Fig. 108) so that this Werk can be closed and used as an Echo Werk. The house of the Brystværk is just 2′ high. This explains why the twelve largest pipes of the

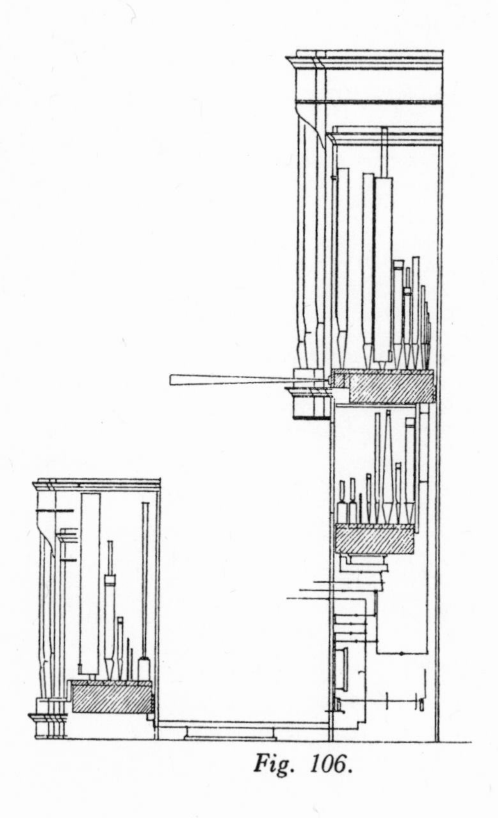

Fig. 106.

Gedakt 8′ are mounted above on the wind chest of the Hovedværk. Figure 106 shows a cross-sectional view through the organ, the three manual Werks and the console; the Trompet 8′ of the Hovedværk is mounted in Spanish style, *en chamade,* at the front edge of the wind chest and with direct connection to its grooves. For this reason, the sequence of pitches is the same as in the façade fluework (and the other stops of the Hovedværk). The ten largest Trompet pipes have been mounted vertically in the central tower of the Hovedværk, to save space and to keep these bass pipes from being too predominant.

All of the façade pipes are made of copper and decorated with ornaments in genuine gilt. The copper is untreated and has been left in its dark brown, somewhat enflamed hue. The woodwork, which is also a natural finish, has been done in Danish oak.

The bellows are located immediately behind the organ, in order to restrict the depth of the organ case to a minimum. The specification of the Jægersborg organ is:

Hovedværk	*Rygpositiv*	*Brystværk*	*Pedal*
Principal 8′	Trægedakt 8′	Gedakt 8′	Subbas 16′
Rørfløjte 8′	Principal 4′	Spidsgedakt 4′	Oktav 8′
Oktav 4′	Rørfløjte 4′	Principal 2′	Gedakt 8′
Dækfløjte 4′	Quintatön 2′	Quint $1^1/_3$′	Fagot 16′
Rørquint $2^2/_3$′	Scharf II	Cymbel I	Regal 4′
Oktav 2′	Krumhorn 8′	Ranket 16′	
Mixtur IV			
Trompet 8′			

Many people classify this organ as a seventeenth-century instrument when they try to determine its age from a photo of the façade. Invariably the profiles and ornaments are responsible for this error since neither the pipe groupings, the shape of the towers, nor the materials has a relationship to any historical period. The organ was built in 1944, and, as explained in the preceding account, the construction was carried out along strictly functional lines and with all possible simplicity. An experiment was made in using ornaments inspired by the views mentioned previously (p. 290).

In the specification, the tonal characters of the different Werks are greatly varied, with the ensemble in mind, of course. The character of the Hovedværk is emphasized by the free-sounding Trompet 8′, which also gives this Werk a dominating reed sound. As a contrast to this, we have the 4′–type Rygpositiv with the bright Scharf II and the slender, narrow–scaled Krumhorn 8′. Perhaps the Quintatön 2′ should be mentioned because it is one of our few innovations among the organs stops. (Jægersborg, however, is not the first instance of its use.) The Quintatön 2′ goes all the way up to d#‴ as a stopped rank.

The Brystværk is retained as a light flute Werk with a Principal 2′ as the only Principal stop. The Quint $1^{1}/_{3}$′ has stopped pipes in the bass and Gemshorn scale in the treble, and the Cymbel I also has a wide, flute-like scale. In addition, there is the richly coloured, entirely free-sounding Ranket 16′, which gives a curious "Gravität" to the whole Werk, and, at the same time, is usable as a solo stop. Some discussion may arise as to whether the doors which can be closed in front of the Brystværk are a natural device for the organ, since echo and swell-boxes first appeared in conjunction with the beginning decadence. But it is a fact that closing these doors creates particularly fine echo effects and a very suitable regulation of the intensity when the Brystværk must be used for accompanying soloists. Pedantic ideas carry no great weight in opposition to these advantages. The doors, in this instance, must be controlled with both hands, and so the worst abuse, the crescendo effect, is avoided.

With due consideration to the relatively small church, all of the scales are very narrow, and the voicing is mild. This treatment gives the fluework a somewhat Spanish character, and the two free-sounding reeds contribute to the enhancement of this effect. At Jægersborg, however, an absolute ensemble of fluework and reeds has been the objective. Unfortunately the Pedal had to be limited to the five stops listed.

In the Gustav Church, the Swedish church in Copenhagen (Fig. 109), the available space did not permit all of the Werks to be present in the façade. The Hovedværk had to be erected under a fairly small, low arch; there were no problems with the pipe arrangement since the arch permitted only the ordinary C and C# arrangement, with the largest pipes in the middle. The arch governed both the fronts of the Hovedværk and Rygpositiv and the organ houses, which comply with the pipe contour. The side doors were chiefly decorative, but they can be closed.

The Pedal was necessarily concealed behind the Hovedværk, and this location was also the only feasible position for the third manual Werk, which, under the given conditions, could be installed most successfully as a Crescendo Werk.

The woodwork for the case is done in natural Danish oak, but the front pipes are tin. Here ornaments have been used again, in an outline almost like a trellis following the sections of the pipes. The scales and voicing are of a type similar to those in the Jægersborg organ because the church, in this instance too, is smaller in size. However, the reeds have been placed inside the organ house in the customary way.

The specification of the Gustav Church organ is:

Hovedværk	*Rygpositiv*	*Crescendoværk*	*Pedal*
Principal 8′	Trægedakt 8′	Gedakt 8′	Subbas 16′
Rørfløjte 8′	Principal 4′	Quintatön 8′	Oktav 8′
Oktav 4′	Rørfløjte 4′	Principal 4′	Gedakt 8′
Dækfløjte 4′	Quintatön 2′	Blokfløjte 4′	Oktav 4′
Quint $2^2/_3$′	Nasat $1^1/_3$′	Gemshorn 2′	Fagot 16′
Oktav 2′	Scharf II	Sivfløjte 1′	Cornet 2′
Mixtur V	Vox humana 8′	Sesquialtera II	
Trompet 8′		Cymbel III	
		Dulcian 16′	
		Krumhorn 8′	

The small choir organ in the Grundtvig Church, Copenhagen, has been mounted in the large side gallery at the eastern end of the north aisle. The height was especially favourable although the organ had to give way in the middle to the large window at the rear; the breadth permitted both the Hovedværk and Pedal to be housed in the main organ. These two Werks were combined on the same wind chest by assigning the alternate grooves in the bass to the Hovedværk and the intervening ones to the Pedal. For example, the grooves of C of the Hovedværk and C of the Pedal are adjacent to each other, etc., thereby making it practicable to arrange transmissions of Hovedværk stops to the Pedal (which was actually done in the case of two stops).

The façade pipes are composed of the two lowest octaves of the Hovedværk Principal 8′ and the Rygpositiv Principal 4′. No more pipes could be accomodated because all of the pipe compartments are flat. With the omission of the small treble pipes, it is possible to give the pipe feet lengths which are directly proportional to the length of the pipe body itself, as was done on this occasion. This increases the movement of the upper contour of the pipe compartments, because the long pipes are longer and the short ones shorter than in common practice, where the shortest pipes have the longest feet, or all of the pipe feet are of equal length. One of the disadvantages resulting from proportional pipe feet is that the height of the organ house is too restricted at the small pipe compartments and too excessive where the large pipes are standing (Fig. 110, the façade).

The specification for the choir organ of the Grundtvig Church is:

Hovedværk	*Rygpositiv*	*Pedal*	
Principal 8′	Trægedakt 8′	Subbas 16′	
Nathorn 8′	Principal 4′	Nathorn 8′	trm.
Oktav 4′	Rørfløjte 4′	Oktav 4′	trm.
Quint 2²/₃′	Quintatön 2′	Fagot 16′	
Oktav 2′	Scharf II		
Mixtur IV	Krumhorn 8′		

In the cathedral of Haderslev, Denmark (Fig. 72 A), a choir gallery from an earlier period is located under the organ gallery. When a new organ was planned in connection with the restoration of the church, a fairly large swell-box was placed behind a lattice at the rear of the choir gallery, and this Werk could be played from the large console (manual III) in the loft above and from an independent console in the choir gallery.

The organ proper, with an 8′ Hovedværk, 4′ Rygpositiv, 2′ Brystværk, and 16′ Pedal (as well as the usual Sunday choir) then had an ideal location in the organ loft, and the choir gallery was used only for concerts with instrumentalists and a big choir. Of course, very few churches have the height for such an arrangement, but if the organ loft is wide enough, the width can also be utilized.

In the monastery church of Sorø, Denmark (Fig. 48 A), there is so much space on both sides of the organ and behind it (one reason being the narrow base of the main organ) that a choir and an orchestra can be placed there.

Because of this, a small, one-manual console, coupled to the Brystværk, has been placed behind the base of the organ, and the Brystværk has doors which can be opened also at the rear toward the choir. The main organ and the Rygpositiv could then be erected at a suitable distance.

Sorø presented an interesting restoration problem. When the old organ had been dismantled at the time of the new construction in 1942, the back of the main façade revealed that this façade was of a much earlier origin than was previously assumed. As seen in Figure 48 B, the main façade, before the reconstruction, was thoroughly camouflaged with eighteenth-century ornaments of an inferior quality, and the outer pipe flats had been converted to angular towers. The base had been augmented to the entire breadth of the façade and thus there were rational grounds for believing that the façade dated from the rebuild at the close of the eighteenth century.

The only questionable features were actually the slender borders of the pipe flats and the strange four-sectional division of the intermediary flats, but these features might be the usual result of bungle in an old organ façade.

Since it was possible to determine from the back that the framework of the main façade was entirely intact and had not undergone changes in the course of time (apart from certain minor additions), there was no difficulty in arriving at the correct date and the original form. Scarcely more than the framework of the Gothic organ had been preserved, but due to an irregularity in the pipe flats (they were a little broader on the north side than on the south) and various traces of ornaments, pins, etc., the original pipe grouping was successfully reconstructed.

Anyone who sees the organ façade now (Fig. 48 A) will understand the temptation to reconstruct it, but the question was whether this could be accomplished in a justifiable manner. All of the Gothic ornaments had disappeared, the Gothic painting was also gone, the top-decorations had been removed, and the only remaining items were the Baroque figures over the side flats and the intermediary flats, as well as the two lions, which, according to the church records, were intended to support the Royal coat-of-arms. (These details were contemporary with the Rygpositiv, 1628.)

To undertake a reconstruction on this basis contradicted all of the established principles of restoration. It would have been more correct and honest to retain the eighteenth-century form and let the organ tell its story. But the Gothic façade was so beautiful and the story so pitiful that it was decided to ignore all of the good principles and risk the experiment.

With inspiration from the pipe flat ornaments of the Rygpositiv, which were evidently influenced by the original ornaments of the Gothic façade, Erik Pedersen, the painter and sculptor, composed the main organ ornaments, and made them join the entity in a completely natural way.

The problems concerning the instrument were less complicated. In the main organ the space for both Hovedværk and Pedal was satisfactory, and the Brystværk was located under these Werks in the base of the organ. The house of the Rygpositiv which had been emptied in 1846 did not cause much speculation.

The Brystværk was enclosed in a swell-box, but the swell shades have been put in two frames behind a grill that can be opened like doors. Thus the completely free sound can be heard when desired, and with the grill closed, the Brystværk is an ordinary swell-box without front pipes. The specification of the Sorø organ is:

Hovedværk	*Rygpositiv*	*Brystværk*	*Pedal*
Gedaktpommer 16′	Rørgedakt 8′	Trægedakt 8′	Principal 16′
Principal 8′	Quintatön 8′	Nathorn 4′	Subbas 16′
Spidsfløjte 8′	Principal 4′	Spidsgedakt 4′	Quint $10^2/_3$′
Gedakt 8′	Dækfløjte 4′	Dækfløjte 2′	Oktav 8′
Oktav 4′	Gemshorn 2′	Nasat $1^1/_3$′	Gedakt 8′
Rørfløjte 4′	Sesquialtera II	Cymbel II	Oktav 4′
Quint $2^2/_3$′	Scharf III	Regal 8′	Quintatön 4′
Oktav 2′	Dulcian 16′		Blokfløjte 2′
Mixtur V	Krumhorn 8′		Mixtur IV
Trompet 8′			Fagot 16′
			Trompet 8′

In spite of the ostensibly Baroque tonal structure, this instrument was designed for performance of the entire organ literature.

In one sense it is wasteful to build larger organs, but nevertheless, the decision was made to use eighty-five stops when the Danish State Radio organ was constructed, and the purpose was to obtain a historically accurate performance. There was no intention of copying various historical organ types and assembling them into one large second-hand store! Every detail must be incorporated in the whole and subordinated to it.

The organ was divided into four manual Werks and a Pedal: a 16′ Hovedværk, an 8′ Positiv, and an 8′ French-type Crescendo Werk (manual III), and finally an additional swell Werk (manual IV) whose variety of single mutations enabled it to act as a "timbre pharmacy".

The specification for the Danish State Radio organ in Copenhagen is:

I. manual	*II. manual*	*III. manual*	*IV. manual*	*Pedal*
Gedakt-pommer 16′	Træprincipal 8′	Principal 8′	Bordun 16′	Untersatz 32′
Principal 16′	Gedakt 8′	Nathorn 8′	Flute harm. 8′	Principal 16′
Principal 8′	Quintatön 8′	Salicet 8′	Gamba 8′	Spidsgedakt 16′
Spidsfløjte 8′	Oktav 4′	Gedakt 8′	Rørfløjte 8′	Subbas 16′
Spidsgambe 8′	Dækfløjte 8′	Unda maris 8′	Vox celeste 8′	Gedakt 16′
Bordun 8′	Oktav 2′	Oktav 4′	Quint $5^1/_3$′	Quint $10^2/_3$′
Oktav 4′	Spidsgedakt 2′	Gemshorn 4′	Principal 4′	Oktav 8′
Rørfløjte 4′	Oktav 1′	Spidsquint $2^2/_3$′	Gambetta 4′	Gedakt 8′
Quint $2^2/_3$′	Sesquialtera	Blokfløjte 2′	Flute oct. 4′	Oktav 4′
Oktav 2′	Scharf IV	Terz $1^3/_5$′	Piccolo 2′	Quintatön 4′
Valdfløjte 2′	Ranket 16′	Septim $1^1/_7$′	Cornet IV	Nathorn 2′
Rauschquint III	Krumhorn 8′	Sivfløjte 1′	Mixtur VII	Flute oct. 1′
Mixtur V–VII	Regal 4′	Mixtur V	Fagot 16′	Cornet IV
Trompet 16′		Cymbel II	Tromp. harm. 8′	Mixtur VI
Trompet 8′		Dulcian 16′	Obo 8′	Basun 32′
		Trompet 8′	Clairon 4′	Basun 16′
		Vox humana 8′		Fagot 16′
		Skalmeje 4′		Trompet 8′
				Zink 4′
				Cornet 2′

As pictured in Figure 111, the Hovedværk and the Positiv are at the centre in the piano-shaped cases, with the Principal 16′ placed outside the house as façade pipes for the Hovedværk, and similarly, the wooden pipes of the Principal 8′ in front of the Positiv. To the left of the Positiv, the Oktav 8′ of the Pedal may be seen, and behind it, the wooden pipes of the Untersatz 32′. To the right of the Positiv, the wooden pipes of the Quint $10^2/_3$′ are seen in the foreground; behind them, the Principal 16′ (Pedal); and behind this pedal stop, the top ends of the Spidsgedakt 16′ appear. At the extreme right, the Trompet 8′ of the Pedal is seen *en chamade*. The Basun 16′ has been mounted in the same way at the left. Under the Hovedværk, there is a Trompet 4′ *en chamade;* it also belongs to the Pedal and has been placed here together with the small pedal stops. The Crescendo Werk of manual III stands behind the grill at the left, and behind the grill at the right, the Crescendo Werk of manual IV.

For purely decorative reasons, the placement of the large pedal stops has been treated with a certain amount of freedom. They have been mounted without houses, and the pipes are spread out to cover the width. Here the principles had to yield a little in favour of the decorative idea, but only a little, because the large bass pipes are quite capable of standing alone and without a house.

The organ in Tranebjerg Church, Samsø (an island almost in the centre of the Danish kingdom), shows an interesting and convenient arrangement of the 8′ façade Principal, convenient because there is ample space in the organ case and because large and small pipes have been combined in an appropriate fashion (Fig. 112).

The first three decades of the Organ Reform Movement may rightfully be designated as a period of expansion. No unique and previously unknown tonal resources were discovered during this time, but all of the old, long-forgotten ideas were now being revived to us, and many well-known concepts were subjected to such a refreshing revaluation that they were no longer old. We have reached a point where additional innovations are not expected. A certain routine has been attained, and the stream of events has moved into the next phase: the exploitation of our new knowledge.

After saying that the period of expansion did not produce any completely new and sensational tonal resources, some comment must be added concerning one exception: the electronic organ. It did not become popular in Scandinavia, especially not in the churches. From an artistic point of view, it has never been of any importance and might be quietly ignored if the reason for its unpopularity was not of interest.

The Hammond organ came to Scandinavia in the beginning of the 1930's. At that time, many American churches had already been using it for some years, and to judge from the advertising, the days of the old pipe organ seemed to be numbered.

The technology of amplifiers, which was quite new then, made it possible to create music from electronic vibrations and to transform them into sound, with the aid of an amplifier and speaker. Totally new perspectives were disclosed.

This technology was most immediately applicable to some organ-type keyboard instruments, partly reproductive constructions, partly autonomous types. The light-organ (colour-organ) is an example of the reproductive type; it operates on the principle of sound films (with sound recordings of various instruments or with organ stops on rotating glass discs). The Hammond organ belongs to the autonomous constructions.

The basic idea is this: some small angular iron discs are placed on a spindle which rotates at a constant speed. Off each of these discs is a small electro-magnet; and while the edges of the iron disc are in rotation, they pass the core of the magnet. If an electric current is sent through the coil of the magnet, this current will be affected by the rotating edges of the iron discs, and thus electronic vibrations are produced.

Each manual key has an iron disc and a magnet, and the total of the edges on the iron discs is calculated (in correlation with the speed of rotation) to produce the frequency of vibration required by the respective pitches. The keys simply have contacts for connecting or disconnecting the current from the electro-magnets, and this current operates the amplifier and speaker. From every key there is a connection for both the fundamental and the pitches in the scale which correspond to the remaining partials (on C, for instance, c, g, c′, e′, g′, c″). These series of partials, including the fundamental, can function individually in eight different intensities. Furthermore, the intensity of the composite sound is regulated by a volume control.

This would indicate that a very well-stocked "tonal pharmacy" is at hand, and besides, Hammond organs are equipped with two manuals, each having the resources described, and a pedal board with a 16′ stop. The iron discs are designed to produce perfect sine-shaped vibrations, that is, the sound is entirely pure. The tuning is also mathematically pure (although tempered, of course), and the Hammond organ never goes out of tune. Its speech is absolutely precise and free of inharmonics. There are no difficulties with changes in temperature and humidity, and the installation problems are reduced to a minimum because the Hammond organ occupies no more space than a two-manual console. Speakers of the necessary size, partially or completely invisible, can be placed and distributed according to the acoustical conditions in the room. Finally, a Hammond organ costs only a fraction of the price of an ordinary, medium-sized pipe organ.

In brief, the Hammond organ has the perfection that the nineteenth century desired, together with the ability of invisible mounting that many twentieth-century architects desired after an understandable irritation with the profusion of ugly and unwieldy factory organs. If the Hammond organ had appeared twenty years earlier, there is no knowing what would have happened to organ building. But in the 1930's the organ had already taught us that "perfection" was not the ultimate goal, and when we were introduced to it in the Hammond organ, our conviction was intensified so much that the many technical, practical and economical advantages were entirely overshadowed by the essential factor: the sound.

Today we know that the Hammond organ can be greatly improved and various other ways of making electronic music have developed. Electronic instruments can be supplied with inharmonics, chiffing and other "imperfections". In fact, there are no limits to what can be done. Any curve on a piece of paper can become a sound. It is possible to design any sound desired.

In spite of all this, music is still being made with the same primitive materials which have been used for thousands of years: strings, flutes, reeds, etc., with the corresponding resonating bodies. This situation is unlikely to be changed, for in the last analysis, the old-fashioned musical instruments are a pleasure because they are not lifeless in our hands. They have their laws, and they can be obstinate, but they reward us with something beyond our own efforts or even our own capabilities. As we advance in our study of sound, it is increasingly evident that the government of certain tonal phenomena is a rather unpleasant task. But if we build electronic instruments we shall have to command these phenomena. The instruments offer nothing, they are tonally neutral, and they neither contribute nor require anything in the architectural sense.

Today, when seeking a point of view for the renovation and modernization of the organ, we must realize that progress may occur without fresh discoveries and that the means at hand are sufficient. More than sufficient. And we must remember that the primary influence on the formation of a style is not created by new inventions; this was not even the case in the transitional period between Gothic and Renaissance when the organ, as such, came into existence. Technique and methods of procedure have, admittedly, had great influence on forms and ways of expression, but the formation of a style requires completely different and more powerful forces. Cavaillé-Coll had "given birth" to his giant organ before he knew anything about the Barker lever, the practical condition which opened the door to reality. And we know far too well that the ensuing pneumatic and electrical period set a record for both the quantity of inventions and the lack of style.

If we ignore all of these late inventions (and we do) it must be confessed that organ building through the ages has produced an amazingly small number of innovations. Aside from the fact that the cast tin sheets used for pipes are now trimmed by machine and that common woodwork machines have also been put to use, organs today are built with exactly the same methods of production as three hundred years ago. In the future, these methods will undoubtedly be retained as they cannot be surpassed.

An entirely different matter is the question of whether electro-acoustics can help to clarify some of our tonal problems. For a number of years, one of the urgent questions before us has been the polyphonic clarity of the organ. At present there is a great demand for this quality, due to our desire to play the classical organ literature as well as the modern music that is being written.

More intensive and important work has been spent on this problem than at any previous time. The degree to which the formation of partials is dependent on the scales has been studied (Bibliography, Ingerslev), and tests and comparisons have been made of the remaining old instruments and some more recent ones (Bibliography, Klotz), but a far greater quantity of research material ought to be collected. Particularly close attention must be given to space acoustics because the reverberation period and the conditions relevant to the diffusion of sound (the location of the organ) are factors of great importance. The studies up to this time have given only cursory consideration to this, and for the most part, the theoretical work must be described as being at a truly preparatory level.

For the present, experience in daily work with the selection of stops, scaling sequences, and location has provided the best instruction. Organ builders can tell how individually the question must be treated because of space acoustics and location of the instrument.

In daily work the results have shown that polyphonic clarity is not an isolated phenomenon with an independent existence. The procedures which are beneficial to it also have other consequences, and on some occasions, clarity and tonal beauty are inversely proportional.

It is a well-known fact that we hear much more clearly in an acoustically dry room than in a room with a longer echo, and details are easier to distinguish when we are sitting quite near to the instrument. But the majority of listeners would surely prefer to renounce a small amount of clarity in order to sense the resonance of the room (as long as the echo does not prevent them in hearing what happens). The overblowing Gedackts, with their remarkable series of overtones, are well-suited to polyphonic music, and the same holds good for sevenths, ninths, sixths, and other unusual overtones. But such stops do not contribute to tonal beauty.

An appropriate deference to both qualities should be the ideal, and it is possible to attain both clarity and tonal beauty, excepting the case where the room is so large and the reverberation period so long that the sound is blurred.

Another problem applicable to an electronic-acoustical study is the question concerning the gradual mellowing of sound in musical instruments.

A third problem is, as stated earlier, space acoustics.

There are certainly enough problems of a purely technical nature, and no organ builder should be hesitant about the starting point for his work. From our present position, the problems are sufficient for at least two ambitious generations, and it will be like this as long as there are reflective and industrious organ builders.

It is not easy to forecast where the emphasis will be placed in future stylistic formation or whether this emphasis will be underscored by a limitation of resources. We have come into contact with a larger world (both in space and time), and we feel the importance of an original solution to every single assignment. For this reason, some people may think that we are on the road to a stylistic chaos, on the way to building organs in composite styles. But churches are far from uniform in terms of age, size, quality, and style.

Perhaps the danger of chaos would have been imminent if we had not learned that the components must be co-ordinated into a whole, or if we had failed to comprehend the need for selection, rejection, and change until the whole is simple, clear and natural. The result must look easy and obvious. This working procedure will doubtless preserve the personality and give direction to the development. It is encouraging to observe that the sense of simplicity and clarity has been restored after many years of confused, unnatural, and impressively complicated solutions.

When this is understood, we can spare ourselves a lengthy discussion of style, and much talk about the creation of a modern, contemporary style will be superfluous. We know very well that a style cannot be provoked. All attempts of this sort merely lead to preposterous curiosities having no inspiration beyond the sheerest vanity. We must realize that Style evolves in the course of calm daily work. This is one of the lessons of history.

Aside from the small, primitive instruments of Antiquity and the Middle Ages, the organ cannot claim a very long period of evolution, but its length is enough to reveal the sensitivity with which the instrument reacts to the intellect of changing times and places. As a "cultural barometer", there is scarcely a more delicate apparatus to be found; it registers many details. The organ reveals us as we are.

11

Maintenance - Rebuilding - New instruments

When an organ goes out of tune, the trouble is very seldom in the pipes. If the fluework is affected, dust may have collected on a languid, an insect may have decided to spend the winter in a pipe, a spider may have spun its web in front of a pipe mouth – all of these will upset the tuning and voicing. In metal or wooden pipes, the tension in the material can slightly change the position of the mouths and languids, but such things are rarities.

In most cases, the cause is to be found in decidedly external circumstances. A technical flaw may impede the wind supply to the pipes (for example, leaks, looseness in the mechanical action, a drawn stop not pulled all the way out), or the difficulty may be the resonating bodies' well-known and unavoidable dependence on the specific gravity of the air. With flue pipes, this means that the pitch will rise and fall with the temperature. For instance, a flue pipe tuned to chamber pitch a′ (435 c.) at 15°C. will have a pitch of approximately 440 cycles when the air is heated to 22°C., and the pitch will fall to 435 cycles when the air is cooled to 15°C.

Similarly, the reeds with proportionately shorter resonators are least affected by the temperature. This is due to the reduced influence of the resonating body on the reed tone. It is easily understood that changes in temperature can create multiple difficulties for the interrelation of fluework and reeds and the interaction of the various Werks. All organs–irrespective of their quality–are susceptible to these difficulties associated with certain external conditions.

From a purely technical consideration of tuning, the contemporary-classic placement of the Werks is admittedly unfortunate. It would be better to put all of the pipes on the same level, thereby equalizing the temperature as much as possible. But today, so much importance is attached to the tonal advantages derived from the Werk principle and the location of Werks at different levels, that technical imperfections in tuning are completely subordinate. In the same way, we would not dispense with the regals, although they are harder to keep in tune with the fluework than the long-resonator reeds.

Organists must be patient and adjust to the inevitability of these alterations in tuning caused by the temperature. The reeds must be tuned to the fluework with the same temperature as when they will be used (preferably just before playing). If the temperature is unstable, it may be necessary to tune quite often. For centuries, the organist has been obliged to tune his own reeds, just as the violinist must tune his own instrument.

But why tune the reeds when it is actually the pitch of the fluework that has changed? This is done for two reasons: first, it is much easier to tune the reeds than the fluework; and secondly, the reeds are more capable of withstanding frequent tuning. For the small flue pipes, it is a real punishment to be tuned with the tuning cone (or "horn"), and the durability of the tuning slots is limited when tuning is too frequent. However, repeated tuning of the fluework is really unnecessary. The pitch may rise or fall a little with the temperature, but this rise and fall will be proportional throughout all of the fluework–there are no reciprocal defects in tuning if the heat is evenly distributed. In a Werk where the pipes are standing close together in the same house, a fairly uniform temperature may be assumed. There will seldom be extensive pitch differences among the ranks in such a Werk (with the possible exception of the façade pipes which are exposed). Conversely, a difference in temperature between the Rückpositiv and the Hauptwerk may well occur, and this difference will vary from time to time, resulting in transient shiftings of the tuning balance between these Werks.

It would be foolish to become impatient with an organ whose tuning is temporarily unbalanced due to temperature fluctuations. This condition will correct itself when the normal temperature is restored. In such a situation, it is not only fruitless but also injurious to undertake large or small corrections in tuning, not to mention a complete tuning of the fluework. The organ ought to be tuned at a time when a uniform temperature prevails, that is, when the church heating is not on. The fluework should be tuned only once during the year, and even then, the organ builder should do no more than absolutely necessary.

When the tuning octave has to be corrected, it is particularly important that the fewest possible changes be made because the entire organ must be tuned to this octave. So many other seemingly small things demand consideration when tuning the fluework that this job should always be delegated to an expert. Over and above his ability to tune the organ, the good tuner must also "train" it to stay in tune, and for that reason, he occasionally must protest against requests for tuning "out of season."

The changes in temperature and tuning produced by winter heating may be harmful in various ways. When it is necessary to heat a cold church in a relatively short time, a difficult transitional period is inevitable while the heat is penetrating the organ and is being evenly distributed throughout all of the pipes. If the volume of the church auditorium is small in proportion to the number of listeners, a considerable increase in temperature will occur during a church service or a concert because each person produces a quantity of heat energy–breathing, for example, will do this. The effect can be so devastating that the reeds, which were carefully tuned before the service, may become increasingly unpleasant toward the end of the service. But why should anyone be hesitant about tuning a single reed stop in the middle of a concert? It can be done in a few minutes; an orchestra tunes frequently during a concert.

At this point, there is good reason to call attention to the somewhat exaggerated statement that an organ is "out of tune," simply because some very slow beats can be found here and there. Theoretically this is true of course, but beats are present in very minute tuning flaws, and they constitute an extremely precise test of tuning purity which may be utilized while tuning. If such a literal interpretation is applied, it would be impossible to tune a large organ with absolute purity because the pipes are greatly influenced by their surroundings. When two pipes have been tuned to the same third pipe, this does not prove that the first two pipes are in tune with each other because the pipes have a reciprocal effect while they are working–in professional terminology they "pull apart"–and sometimes this difference cannot be eliminated or equalized sufficiently to permit complete purity. A door that is closed after the tuning can destroy an otherwise correct result, and this makes it necessary to tune with just enough impurity that purity will be attained when the door is closed. This, however, is easier said than done. In a swell box, the tuning may be satisfactory when the swell is open and less satisfactory when it is closed. The tuner's own body is equally likely to upset the tuning. If a lamp is used inside the organ during the tuning, the tuner must be very careful that the pipes do not absorb radiant heat from the electric bulb. In such a case, the pitch will fall when the lamp is removed and the pipes are cool again.

Additional considerations of this type mean that even the most carefully tuned organ is not absolutely free of beats, and when temperature changes are also taken into account, it is obvious that the tuning of an organ can never represent theoretical perfection. The question is whether the beats are so fast that they constitute an actual irritation. At this moment, it is tempting to recall that the Baroque organs, with multiple-rank mixtures and inferior wind systems providing unsteady wind pressure, had a pronounced degree of impurity and irregularity in tuning, if judged in a theoretical sense. And in orchestras of our own time we can find equally large, or larger, deviations from mathematical purity. Every vibrato is, theoretically, a serious impurity, and the wind instruments are mainly dependent on whether they have been "warmed up." Here it should be remembered that the tempered system of tuning has fourths and fifths which are somewhat impure and thirds which are very impure. In addition, there are the clashes between the intervals of the scale and the pure tuning of the mutations. We have long since been content with a great deal of impurity in every interval except that of the octave. Furthermore, there is some doubt concerning our ability to enjoy an entirely pure tuning.

Patience is also required with the temperature problems of the fluework, if it is impossible to correct the cause of the imperfections, that is, to achieve a constant temperature. Fortunately, many of these problems can be modified if the registrational plan is adjusted to the circumstances. As a general comment, the Werks should be played separately in such conditions, with the coupling of two or more Werks being restricted to "plenum" registrations. The façade pipes should also be used with a certain amount of caution. While the church is being heated, the shutters and doors in the organ case should be opened so that the warmth may quickly penetrate the entire instrument. The lowest shutters, in particular, must not be overlooked because the warm air, after an initial rise, will descend, pressing the cold air downward and outward. This air circulation often creates a cold draught from the organ and may be mistaken for a leak in the instrument, but to clear up the matter, the organist can stop the organ blower to see if this will eliminate the draught. To maintain a check on these conditions, a thermometer may be installed in each Werk of the organ. These thermometers will reveal the temperature changes which may be responsible for faulty tuning, and the necessary adjustments can then be made.

With these considerations in mind, a constant winter temperature would seem to be the ideal solution to tuning problems, and a constant indoor temperature is relatively easy to maintain with present-day heating systems. In terms of economy, continuous heating is preferable because boilers and radiators are under much less strain with the regular, lighter load than when they are forced to heat a large, cold room for one day of the week. In a regularly heated room, chilliness and draughts from cold walls and arches are also eliminated, and again this means that the room temperature can be kept lower without it feeling cold. It has been asserted that fuel consumption, into the bargain, is decreased by continuous heating.

This type of heating has only one objectionable result, but unfortunately, it has serious implications for the woodwork. Uninterrupted heating causes the humidity to drop too much, particularly in dry periods with frosty weather when heavier heating is required.

At this point, a brief review of junior high-school physics may be useful. The atmosphere can absorb a certain amount of water if first the water is converted, by evaporation, into an invisible gas: water vapour. When the air has absorbed its maximum amount of water vapour, it is said to be saturated or that its percentage of humidity is 100. The warmer the air, the more water vapour it can hold; in other words, the degree of saturation or the humidity decreases when air is heated (presuming, of course, that no more water vapour is added to the air during the heating period). And conversely: when air is cooled, the humidity percentage rises until the point of saturation has been reached. And with further cooling, the water vapour will be precipitated in the form of fog, dew, or rain.

Because of this, the percentage of humidity does not show the amount of water contained in the air. It indicates only the degree of saturation, but when woodwork and organs are involved, this is precisely what must be known since this percentage expresses the capacity of the air to absorb moisture.

As winter approaches, the open air loses a good deal of its water content, and in freezing weather, the air contains very little moisture. Indoors, when the dry winter air is heated, the humidity drops sharply, and the woodwork standing in this dry, heated air surrenders some of its moisture. In relation to water vapour, wood and air have exactly the same characteristic: both absorb the available moisture to the best of their abilities. Wood may absorb moisture from the air or the air may absorb it from the wood, depending entirely on whether the wood or the air is drier. Wood retains this characteristic even after it is quite old and well-seasoned.

For wood, this process implies that while it is drying, the loss of moisture causes shrinkage in the direction across the grain, and the absorption of moisture causes swelling in the same direction. The dimensions of the wood can be altered as much as two percent. This fact must be carefully considered in organ construction. Even with the best of constructions, excessive swelling will cause warping, unless precautions are taken to allow for it. Well-constructed instruments can tolerate wide fluctuations in humidity without functional disturbances, but the joints in any instrument will be strained when the wood is swollen. It is highly desirable to prevent great fluctuations in humidity. This control is vital to both the life-time and the reliability of the organ.

The reaction of the old slider chests to changes in humidity has already been discussed (p. 96). We know of many instances where old organs, which had functioned excellently for many generations, suddenly became unmanageable–with reference to tuning and action–after the church had installed a new, modern heating system, thereby increasing the semi-annual variations in humidity.

Excessive humidity encourages mould, rot, attacks by woodborers, and a gradual dissolution of the glue used in many parts of the organ. But the semi-annual changes in humidity are much worse for the constitution of the organ. In Danish churches, this is rapidly becoming a serious problem. The difficulty may be partially attributed to the insular climate with its fairly high degree of humidity during the summer–80 % on the average. Another contributing factor is the growing tendency to heat the churches throughout the winter in an effort to maintain a temperature approximating that of an ordinary room. This means that the humidity index in the coldest months can drop to 40 % (the record low to date is 30 %), the equivalent of an ordinary apartment with central heating. The winter months prior to Christmas are not the worst because there is still some moisture in the air and the buildings. When freezing begins, after the New Year, trouble is to be expected, especially when a strong wind blows fresh, cold, dry air in through the large, loose church windows, and the verger does extra heating to keep up the temperature.

To those who know something about wood, the conclusion is evident: humidity control is far more important than temperature control. The ideal would be to keep both temperature and humidity constant, and this is possible with modern air-conditioning. Up to now, these installations have been very expensive, and Danish churches have not yet introduced them. Other methods must be used for the present.

Humidity has an amazing ability to spread, and there is virtually no way of reducing the humidity inside a building during the summer. The only effective antidote is heating, and it is impracticable in that season. The normal amount of summer humidity must be the basis for regulation, and the problem is to maintain this amount of humidity throughout the winter, either by using a humidifier to add moisture to the air indoors, or by holding the temperature down–possibly a combination of both.

The old method of placing large, flat, water-filled zinc trays inside the organ during the winter is still recommendable, but there should also be evaporation pans on every radiator in the room, and even this will be insufficient. A very fast increase in moisture can be accomplished with the excellent small sprayers which are now on the market. These would be more practical if the high chalk-salt content in the Danish subsoil water did not leave a residue of irritating dust.

Of course, every organ ought to have its hygrometer so that the organist, or the sexton, can keep a constant check on the humidity and then take the necessary precautions. A delicate, expensive instrument is not required; it should simply indicate whether the relative humidity is rising or falling. However, the hygrometer should be correctly adjusted, but this is easily done. For an hour, let the hygrometer remain in moisture-saturated surroundings, for instance, under a cheese-dish cover together with a wet cloth. The needle should then climb to 100 %, and if it fails to do this, it can be turned to the proper position by means of the small adjusting screw on the back of the instrument.

When the hygrometer is used in the church, it will show that the humidity index drops when the room is heated, and vice versa. No one intends that the summer hygrometer reading of 80 % must be retained throughout the winter. Fluctuations extending over a few days are of no importance because wood reacts slowly; nor is there any immediate danger if the relative humidity should drop to 60 % during some of the winter months. Quick heating on Sunday is not harmful to the wood (the same cannot be said of the tuning); the decisive factor is the average humidity for the week or the month.

Unfortunately, there is a widespread misunderstanding that an instrument is being well-treated when a constant temperature is maintained during the winter. This is not the case, however, unless a fairly even degree of humidity is also maintained.

Electrical heating has made steady gains in popularity, especially in small churches, and some discussion of it is surely appropriate. The advantages are obvious, and they have been discussed so often that further repetition is scarcely necessary. The disadvantages on the other hand are seldom reported, but with their specific effect on organs, they must be treated here.

The principle of electrical heating is to "envelop" the churchgoers–figuratively speaking–in a warm, ascending air current, protecting them from the chilliness emitted by the frigid walls and vaults. The warm air current can be started just before the church service and stopped immediately after it, with a minimal number of calories being used in making the building comfortable for the congregation. However, the heating of the walls and vaults is also minimal, and consequently the moist air exhaled by the members of the congregation will be condensed, with a part of this moisture clinging to the cold walls. The conditions in a humid church are worse when electrical heating has been installed; in many cases the result is catastrophic.

Excessive humidity in a church is not easily brought under control. Circulating air fans and ventilation do not always lead to the desired result. If the outside air is warmer than the air in the church, the moisture content of the outside air may be so high that some of it must be released when this air enters the cool church. The result, therefore, is the opposite of the intention. Circulating air fans are useful only in dry weather or when the outside air temperature is no higher than the temperature in the church.

In many cases, church moisture originates in the damp earth, the moisture of which is absorbed by the walls and penetrates the floor. This situation may be improved by draining the ground and by the installation of moisture-proof materials inside the floor and walls. Otherwise, heat is the most effective counter-agent.

Quick heating of the church auditorium produces a reaction in the organ tuning which has been described. The pronounced difficulties associated with electrical heating need no further explanation. It is fortunate that only small churches with small organs have used this type of heating, because the consequences would be absolutely incalculable in large organs with several Werks. Organ builders, of course, are far from enthusiastic about this "explosive" type of electrical heating, but it can be used in another way–this is simply expensive.

The best type of church heating–particularly where very high ceilings are concerned–is undoubtedly floor heat. Under the floor of the church, heating tubes are installed to given a low heat (15–16°C), and this heat is continuous during the entire heating season. A few individual radiators for counteracting cold draughts from windows, etc., are also provided, but the principle is to furnish a gentle, radiant heat from the floor underneath the church pews. The heat is concentrated in the part of the church where it is needed. This system is truly satisfactory. The temperature up under the vaults is lower than that on the floor, and there are remarkably small differences in temperature throughout the room. Of course this is quite ideal for organs, and the advantage of the system is the reduced circulation of air in the room–with the woodwork undergoing minimal drying.

Due to the countless effects of church heating on the prosperity of an organ, the organ builder should be consulted when the heating system of the church is installed, rebuilt, or renovated. One preliminary general statement can be made: without air conditioning, a church should never be heated to a temperature above 15°C. (59°F.). The next 3–5°C. will not only necessitate large quantities of expensive fuel, but if this heating is regular, it will often lead to costly organ repairs and annoying disturbances of the action. Fifteen degrees Centigrade should be adequate because a church service seldom lasts more than an hour and a half. The church-goers can keep their coats on!

It was quite interesting to see that organs in the cold churches of the war years stayed in better condition than they have in the post-war period with its bountiful supply of fuel and new boilers. In France, where the summer is drier than in Denmark and the cathedrals are only partially heated during the winter, the degree of humidity is more constant and permits a type of organ construction which would last only a few years in the Danish climate.

Humidity control for a room must be repeatedly emphasized as a cardinal point in organ maintenance, and there is every reason to say this again because it has been overlooked for a long time. Today's rapid church heating has made this a matter of acute necessity.

Only an expert can make satisfactory repairs of technical defects and the tuning of the fluework, but there are many small matters which the organist should be able to remedy, temporarily at least. Many churches are located far away from any organ builder, and calling an expert can be both difficult and expensive.

Once each year an organ should have an inspection and a thorough tuning, and this should be sufficient if nothing extraordinary happens. But no two organs are the same, and for this reason, it is advisable that the organ builder, in every instance, gives the organist the necessary instructions concerning his instrument and the things which must be checked regularly. The present discussion will deal with routine problems, as well as some directions for coping with them.

First some remarks concerning slider chests with entirely mechanical action, including mechanical stop action. There is just one pallet for each key. If one of these pallets is loose, escaping air will enter the groove, which means that all of the stops pulled in that Werk will receive "false" air. If there is a small leak, there may be just enough air to make one of the soft or high-pitched stops produce a sound, and when additional stops are pulled, the cipher stops because there is not enough air for two or more pipes. The mechanical connection (tracker) for this particular pallet may be a little too tight, thus pulling the pallet out of place. First, check to see if this is the case. Lift up on the tracker under the wind chest. If the cipher disappears, the regulating screw, situated next to the chest, can be loosened a little. If this does not help, the defect is in the pallet. Something may have fallen on it and is preventing it from closing tightly or the pallet may be warped and slightly crooked or leaky. In this event, the cover for the pallet chest must be removed, and the pallet must be opened and cleaned; or, if it is crooked, try pulling up on the edge of the leather. Then press the pallet firmly toward the pallet seat. Large leaks may be due to the following situations: the action is jammed at some point so that the pallet spring cannot return the pallet to rest position; or, one of the pallet's guide tacks has fallen out, causing the pallet to strike the side of the opening. The pallet may be caught on the guide tack or the pallet spring may be broken. The latter, however, occurs only rarely.

The various parts of the mechanical action are often hard to reach, with consequent difficult in finding the location of the defect, but the keyboard itself is always a good place to begin the search. If the key sticks when pressed down, there is every possibility that the trouble is in the keyboard. In damp churches, it is not uncommon for the felt to bulge or pinch at the first guide tack. If this happens, the situation usually can be corrected by working the key up and down while pushing it firmly from side to side–this flattens the felt. It is also possible that something has fallen down between the keys. Mouse droppings have just the right diameter for wedging between two keys, and they even have a certain adhesiveness which prevents them from falling all the way through. They are always very effective, but with a strip of stiff cardboard the situation can easily be corrected. There is no reason to send for the organ builder on such an occasion. If it is impossible to discover the defect of the action a piece of elastic can, as a last resort, be fastened at a suitable place under the wind chest. The elastic will assist the pallet spring in pulling the action back into position.

If a certain tone is silent in all stops, there is unquestionably a defect in the mechanical action, possibly a loosened regulating nut. When the action for an entire Werk becomes too loose and causes the key drop (and thereby the opening of the pallets) to be too shallow, the result will be insufficient wind in the channels for the simultaneous use of all stops. The opposite can also be imagined; that is, the action becomes so stiff that ciphers occur in various places (see pp. 100–4), particularly when only a single stop or a few stops have been drawn. If this kind of change occurs in the regulation, the organist must not start adjusting the regulation screws. Only the organ builder may assess and undertake the necessary changes in the suspension and the support of the action.

The completely mechanical stop action is so simple and uncomplicated that defects very rarely appear. If a stop fails to function, the trouble is often caused by a pin that has worked its way out of one of the joints. Such defects are not difficult to find or correct when they occur in an accessible place. Where pneumatic stop action is concerned, it is best to leave the repairs to an expert.

In the usual types of slider chest, many disturbances (as discussed on p. 94) are created by warping in the top boards. There is little that a layman can do in these circumstances. If a slider is jammed, he may try to loosen the screws in the top board. Then he must remember to tighten them again when the top board is restored to its original form. When working with the screws in the top board, the pipes must be treated with great care; if it is necessary to remove them, he must note carefully–in advance–the side toward which the mouth turns. The pipes must be remounted as before or they will go out of tune. Caution must be exercised to avoid shifting the tuning devices, especially the "hats" on stopped pipes. And lastly, the pipes must be reset firmly and vertically so that they fit tightly into the holes of the top board. If they are a little off centre, part of the wind will miss the foot holes, and the tone will be not only weaker and lower but also unsteady.

The use of the tuning springs is mandatory in tuning the reeds. Certain devices also regulate the tuning to a degree, but these are intended for voicing (equalizing, for example), and hence they must not be touched when tuning alone is concerned.

A silent reed pipe is not extraordinary. In the treble range, very few particles of dirt are enough to hinder the vibrations of the reed, but normally this is very easy to correct. There is a good possibility that pushing the tuning spring upward will free whatever is caught. If this is not successful, the organist must lift off the block (reed head) and try to remove the foreign element, but this must be done with caution to avoid altering the curvature in the tongue. Sometimes insects find their way into the shallot itself, and there may be considerable difficulty in removing them without damage to the tongue. The use of a vacuum cleaner is advisable in such instances. If a tone reacts slowly to the movements of the tuning spring, the reason is usually a loosening in the wedge which grips the tongue (see Fig. 25). This can happen easily if the wood is dry inside. The wedge must be refastened, and it is important that the tongue be replaced in the correct position. If it is too high, and its lower end fails to cover the opening, the tone will be weak or perhaps entirely mute; if the tongue is too far down, the tone will be weak or thin. When a change in the curvature of the tongue is necessary, the work must be delegated to an expert.

Unskilled persons may accidentally knock the tuning springs on the small, high-pitched pipes so far down that the springs slip out of the bottom of the shallot. This is evidenced by the tone suddenly becoming much deeper –irrespective of what is being done with the tuning spring. If this happens, do *not* push up on the tuning wire because this will certainly ruin the reed. The block has to be removed and the tuning spring reset–with the utmost care.

Should the whole instrument–or one of the Werks–abruptly go completely out of tune or become mute, the regulation of the wind is probably defective. A check must be made to see if the reservoir is standing properly. The regulating valve is not functioning if the reservoir is standing in raised position with expanded folds, if the upper surface is pressed against something, or if it has not been raised at all. Either the regulating valve does not close, which permits too much wind to enter the bellows and a consequent exaggeration in the wind pressure, or the valve does not open and no wind can enter. In the majority of cases, the problem is in the rope pulley leading from the top of the reservoir to the regulating valve. The rope is caught in some manner, or it may have slipped off one of the reels–it may even be broken. This condition is relatively easy to diagnose and also easy to repair. A long rope will be affected by dampness since rope contracts when moistened and expands while drying. If it expands, the regulating valve will not open sufficiently, and the result is too little wind for a large number of stops; if it contracts, the top of the reservoir may be elevated to such an extent that it presses against an obstacle, and then the wind pressure becomes too high. In both instances, the effect is drastic, but this fault is easily remedied. The fault, of course, may be in the regulating valve itself, but in that case, a professional man must correct it.

A pedal board is relatively easy to remove and this is desirable for cleaning purposes. Possibly it is anchored with a couple of screws in the floor, but otherwise it can be pulled straight out like a drawer. Putting it back into place is much more difficult since there are good chances of damaging the small rollers which are in touch with the pedal keys. When sliding the pedal board into place again, great care must be exercised so that none of the pedal keys is depressed or hanging down because these keys will strike the rollers instead of gliding over them. If force is used, the rollers may easily be broken. In general, never use force when an obstacle appears. Take time to find the reason.

The pneumatic or electro-pneumatic systems are so individualized and so complicated that the layman will always have difficulty in doing anything about functional disturbances–and it is equally difficult to furnish general directions. Here it is imperative–far more than in mechanical action instruments–that the organist must have his instructions from the organ builder.

First, an introductory statement of a general nature: the causes of a "general cipher" (a cipher in all stops of a Werk) and of a "general" mute note may be located either in the relay valve of the console (and in the switch system respectively) or in the relay of the wind chest. In the case of the general mute note, the trouble may be in the connection from the console to the wind chest.

A cipher in a single stop is always due to a defect in the wind chest. A layman's chance of making any repairs is limited to the cone chest–and he can of course also remove the pipe which is ciphering.

The membrane moulding of the pipe in question must be unscrewed. If the cipher disappears, the pallet pin was striking the very membrane which lifts it, and thus the pallet could not fall all the way down into the pallet seat to close tightly (see Fig. 34). The wooden nut on the pin must either be screwed up a little higher or a thickness of cardboard must be inserted between the membrane moulding and the wind chest. Perhaps loosening the screws of the membrane will be sufficient, and further action can be left to the organ builder.

If the tone in question continues to cipher after the membrane has been loosened, the flaw probably lies in the cone valves. A little dirt may be caught there. Try a firm downward pull on the pallet pin, thus pressing the pallet down into the pallet seat. Check to see if the pallet moves easily –it may be caught on the guide tacks. In this case, some "massage" is needed. Move the pallet up and down, then sideways until it moves easily enough to drop and close tightly by itself.

If a tone is mute, the pallet may be sticking in the pallet seat. This is easy to correct when the membrane moulding is unscrewed because the pallet can be raised from below. As a rule, however, the reason is a leak in the membrane, or–less frequently–the membrane is sticking together and cannot rise. A leaky membrane must be replaced, but a temporary repair can be made, for example, with a strip of adhesive tape.

Ciphers can be produced by drying in the top board (in some systems also the bottom of the wind chest) and this permits the wind from the channel to enter the borings. It is worthwhile to try tightening the screws in the top board, but increasing the degree of humidity is more satisfactory. The difficulty will disappear in a short time.

One category of ciphers remains for discussion, and they constitute an especially pernicious group because ciphers of this kind may occur with no stops being drawn. The pipes are not ciphering in this case although it often sounds that way. The sound comes from small cracks which appear when the woodwork dries, and localizing them is often very difficult because they come and go at random. If the organist is so fortunate as to find the crack when it is "whistling," it is easy to fill.

Many of the defects that appear in an organ during the winter months are due to drying of the wood, and these defects can be alleviated by increasing the moisture in the air. This is the best and must effective way of remedying such problems; at the same time, it is definitely the least expensive method. Wood, however, reacts slowly and a week or two may pass before an improvement is observed. The improvement depends on the extent of the drying as well as the amount of moisture that has been added to the air. Of course it is preferable to prevent such problems by maintaining a constant degree of humidity.

The variable Danish climate is undoubtedly one of the reasons why we have so few old organs in our churches. Beyond any doubt, many of the organs which have been discarded could have been saved and restored. They would have served several more generations if they had received proper care.

In reaching a decision concerning the disposal or retention of an organ, differing viewpoints will inevitably find expression, and these viewpoints admittedly have changed during the past 150 years. Still, certain points should make it possible to arrive at common principles for a reasonable and objective judgment, thereby eliminating the worst errors.

In very old mechanical-action organs, the wind chests and the tracker action are usually the first items to go out of order, but repairs are justified if the wood is sound. At the time of these repairs, there will be opportunities to improve the construction of the wind chests and their capacity to tolerate fluctuations of humidity. This should not be neglected.

Repairing the tracker action may soon become so large a job that a complete renovation can be made without appreciable increase in expense. Modern tracker actions are better than ever before, and in a renovation, there is an opportunity to utilize the newest ideas, which certainly justify the increase in expense. At the same time, there is a chance of correcting a poor location of the organ, and this can be a matter of far-reaching significance.

When an organ is infested with wood-worm that are alive and working, there are very few alternatives. The instrument can stand as long as it functions, but expenditures should be limited to those for minimal repairs. Liquid chemicals for killing wood-worm are available, but for a thorough eradication, the wooden parts of the organ must be soaked in this fluid for several days so that the wood is penetrated completely by it. This procedure may be impractical for several reasons: first, many organ parts are quite large; second, an organ simply cannot tolerate so much moisture; and third, impregnation fluids have a very unpleasant odour which will be highly annoying for a long time after the treatment. Treating the surface of the wood is practicable, but not too effective. At best, the final destruction will be somewhat retarded. Wood-worm can also be exterminated with the help of poison gas or by heating the pieces of wood to 200°C. for about twenty-four hours. These methods are excellent when working with small church furnishings (epitaphs, etc.), but when applied to organs, such procedures are just as unusable as the impregnation fluid bath.

If the attack is already in progress, we must acknowledge our helplessness with regard to wood-worm, but in the case of new organs, there is a definite alternative and a solution to the problem. Begin by selecting the kinds of wood which wood-worm do not molest, such as oak, teak, certain types of mahogany, Oregon pine, etc. Additional expense is involved at the time of purchase, but it is absolutely good economy to spend this money.

If the metal pipes are well-made at the outset, they will last for hundreds of years. There may be problems with the very large tin pipes because the lower part of the pipe foot collapses under the sheer weight of the pipe. Usually this is not difficult to repair.

On the other hand, a pipe metal which is too thin will cause the pipes to collapse as the metal softens. The tone production will suffer, and sooner or later the melting pot is the only alternative.

Technical matters are obviously not the sole consideration in making a decision about the retirement of an organ. Today historical values are widely respected, and there is good reason for this. The old organs have taught us a great deal that is new and useful, and beyond any doubt, every "historical" organ (this customarily refers to one which is more than 150 years old) has a contemporary value for the performance of the older organ literature and for practical use in the church service. The need for preserving and maintaining early organs-sixteenth, seventeenth, and eighteenth centuries–will scarcely cause any objection because few of them survived the nineteenth century. But problems do arise when these organs are to be restored.

Very few of them have been preserved in their truly original form. Passing epochs have left a mark on the specifications scale, scaling, voicing, placement or casework. The question is whether to let all changes remain to tell their story while providing a mere technical reconditioning–this is a good, time-honoured principle of restoration–or if the way should be cleared for reconstruction, with possible additions of something new.

This decision depends primarily on the use to be made of the organ. If its sole function is that of an historical monument without regular, practical duties, the organ builder would assume the "museum" viewpoint and restrict himself to the common principles of restoration. The idea of reconstructing the original form is tempting; today we have certain reasons for considering every change in a "classic" organ to be a deterioration.

Another question relates to the resources that will contribute to the reconstruction, how much is lacking from the original structure, and what clues are available for deducing these things. An acquaintance with the specification and unequal temperament will not suffice. To risk such an experiment, it is necessary to have information about the pipe scales, the composition of the mixtures, the technique of voicing, and various other matters. Still, this is a dubious undertaking because the "original" form –strictly speaking–is a thing of the past. Reconstruction is impossible even though the best and most complete clues are present. If all of the stops have been preserved, as in the Compenius organ, time and tonal patina have removed the original quality of sound, and no voicing skill would be adequate to recall it.

Today a literal application of the term "reconstruction" is not customary, but it should be clearly understood that reconstruction–in the true sense–is an impossibility.

Fortunately an organ seldom has to be regarded as a "museum piece." Most instruments are in service, and this lends an entirely different aspect to the problems. A requirement must be met and our obligation is to "write history." We have the authority to revise, improve and extend the work of the past, just as our successors must have the privilege of correcting our work.

To proceed in this fashion, the absolute condition is a recognition of our responsibility toward the artistic whole. Respect and caution must be demonstrated, but we know that new and old can thrive together. Stylistic agreement is not an absolute condition for artistic unity. Certainly no one will deny that Schnitger greated a genuine work of art in his rebuild of the Scherer organ at the Jakobikirche in Hamburg; and the two Jakobi organs in Lübeck, each a work of art (the large one with its casework and the small one with both case and Werks) whose integrity is unquestioned, even though they represent different stylistic periods.

In that era, it was quite natural to add something to an earlier structure; in this respect, we have a different attitude. For us, there is an innate rightness in the organs built prior to the first quarter of the nineteenth century, either restoration or enlargement is not difficult. But in the following period, an increasing number of details are encountered which cannot be reconciled with our conceptions of sound, architecture, etc. What shall we do with these organs?

Most of these instruments are so solidly constructed that only woodborers or careless heating could destroy them. On the other hand, they have such conspicuously objectionable qualities that it would be better to dispose of these organs. The most striking weakness is their purposeless expansion in the church auditorium. Beyond the casework, which occupies more space than necessary, the organs in that era required considerable space for a large, old-fashioned system of bellows, possibly replaced at a later date by a modern blower. The combination of casework and bellows required an organ gallery whose size, in too many instances, was overwhelming in relation to the church auditorium. Tonally, these organs are inadequate for meeting present-day requirements, with particular reference to polyphonic clarity, and the deficiencies are accentuated by any efforts to add something new (this is usually prohibited by a lack of space). Enlargements, in general, must be advised against because the gain would scarcely correspond with the expense. With certain types of scaling, a tonal improvement may be achieved by reworking and revoicing the stops, perhaps replacing some of them. This can be done with reasonable expense, and it may produce an essential improvement. For the sake of economy, it is of great importance that the technical arrangements (wind chests, action, wind channels, etc.) undergo a minimum of alteration because the large expenditures occur in these areas. If the organ builder and the Church Board are resigned to the customary appearance and dimensions of nineteenth-century organs, and if they can be content with a redisposition, and if the necessary precautions related to heating and humidity are exercised, the "organ problem" for several generations may be solved with an instrument from that era.

With the introduction of pneumatic action at the beginning of the twentieth century, the durability of the instrument received a mortal blow. The new mechanisms were afflicted with certain "childhood" diseases, and the numerous small parts in these actions required such fragile materials that their lifetime was destined to be relatively short. The inaccurate response of the action is too well-known, and the mention of it is merely routine. The typically nineteenth-century spatial demands were continued in these instruments, whose stop-lists steadily increased as the years passed.

The defects came to light after a quarter of a century because the thin materials lasted for that length of time. Today we are better informed, and as a result, a new instrument is often preferred to a major repair of a pneumatic organ, even though the expense is multiplied. If the necessary funds can be procured, this is better economy, and the additional advantages certainly do not need enumeration.

Admittedly pneumatic organs do have some good points. No one will deny that a pneumatic cone chest is extremely reliable, as well as simple and inexpensive to repair. If reliability is the sole criterion, this type of instrument may be quite satisfactory. But any enlargement is unmerited, and it would be false economy to undertake anything more than the necessary repairs and possibly a modest redisposition of such an organ.

In technical terms, pneumatic organs have made it far too easy to add a few stops at random. There are no specific principles of placement to consider; in working with stop channels, the wind chests may be located according to personal whims or the available space. The wind trunks or electric cables will find their way to the various stops.

These are dangerous alternatives, and unfortunately, they have been utilized on a large scale. Far too much money has been wasted on "improvements" of this kind, but the resulting patchwork and shoddiness have at least been here to teach us that a better survey of history and organ problems is necessary if our achievements are to have more than momentary significance and are to be worthy of our churches. Each period must admittedly have the right to leave an imprint on artistic matters, but not such hasty changes as those indicated by the pneumatic rebuilds. So short a lifetime simply reveals a lack of quality. The painstaking and genuine creations also bear the stamp of their era, but still they have an ageless quality which makes them serviceable for many generations. And this is more than respect.

Now there is clearly a desire for something more genuine, and thus the pneumatic organs will come tumbling down when there is hope of a new instrument. Probably some nineteenth-century organs will also be dismantled, for while they are not worn out and their gentle quality is recognizable, they are inadequate for the present assignment.

Many problems of a widely different nature awaited solutions after the decadence of the pneumatic era. Something has already been said about the procedures employed in the creation of a new organ, but there is good reason to speak about the method of choosing the organ builder. That area also reflects a certain amount of progress. In the past, it was customary to use a bidding system, "inviting tenders", frequently with a specification and a rather innocuous description of the work as the only basis. With the belief that the entrepreneurs were then bidding on the same thing and under the same terms, the price became the conclusive factor. The situation was not improved by the fact that many who acted as consultants and experts on such occasions were, to an appalling degree, lacking in the qualifications for being consultants or assuming any responsibility. The organ builder usually was regarded as a business man, and the whole system favoured the compliant organ builder who willingly built "as requested" in order to get contracts. If anything went wrong, he could place a major portion of the responsibility on the expert, a poor consolation to the buyer.

It is quite reasonable that the owner (or the Church Board) must have an expert advisor to represent his interests to the organ builder and to make certain that the builder fulfils his obligations. But if the organ is classified as something more than a machine, or perhaps even a work of art, the organ builder must be considered as an artist or craftsman, and it would be catastrophic to deprive him of his initiative and his responsibility. This responsibility cannot be taken over by others.

An organ builder ought to have the freedom of solving his problems according to his own convictions. Only then can he be judged as he deserves, by the instruments that he has built. This is the best opportunity for seeing (and especially for hearing) his ability and his artistic development. The owner will have definitely better information about organ builders if the latter can refer to one or more instruments and promise to deliver one of similar quality. By allowing extant instruments to settle the competitions, more responsibility will be placed on the organ builder, assuming that he makes his own specification and designs and is not compelled, by uninformed persons, to produce something contrary to his conviction.

The reckoning of the price is naturally not irrelevant in a competition. Knowing approximately how large the organ must be and the layout of the Werks, the organ builder can–without undue effort–give a fairly definite estimate of the cost. A bid must be made on an organ, and of course this bid must contain precise information about what will be delivered within the given economic limitations. There must also be good sketches of both the pipe arrangement and casework so that the buyer knows what the organ builder is doing. However, even a design of this kind is inadequate for a competition because the essentials in an organ are altogether indescribable on paper.

In other words, there is no reason to start several organ builders on the elaborate work of making designs in order to attain a basis of judgment for a competition. It is far safer to select the organ builder on the basis of his instruments and the approximate price that he can give in advance.

When he has been appointed, this is the time to make a design and a detailed bid. No organ builder wishes to hand over his ideas before knowing whether he will get the contract. His time is consumed in collecting and developing ideas, and instead of participating in a price war, he prefers to reserve adequate time for these preparations, thereby using his capabilities and strength for the projects which are definite. Competition will still be present.

Some persons may object that new workshops have no chance in such a competition, and this of course is true. In reply to this objection, we may say that the man starting a new business has presumably "won his spurs," earned the confidence and made the connections which are conditions for getting the first order. With the completion of this order, he has qualified for the competition. Quantity is not the decisive factor.

The results of a competition will always depend on the persons who select and evaluate. The buyer and his experts are not excluded, even though they are inclined to let the organ builder work freely and according to his own convictions. A number of organ builders are always available, and it would be strange if they did not represent different standards of taste, quality, and price.

And the delivery period–an inescapable point. This period is understandably long and difficult. The preparations for an organ, the discussions with the authorities, and the collection of a great deal of money require time. Much patience has been exercised before arriving at the reality. Even so, the buyer should not try to press the organ builder into a forced delivery (and the organ builder should not submit to pressure). It is far more important that the work be done properly than for it to be slightly accelerated. This is absurd in comparison to the length of time that the organ is going to be used. Naturally no organ builder will prolong the delivery period when he must deliver his instrument on the basis of a definitely stated price, and it is equally obvious that if he is induced to make a forced delivery, the buyer is making a bad bargain.

Organs can be delivered in widely varying qualities, for widely varying prices and delivery periods. These things depend on the extent of preparations. Today we can build organs with a long lifespan, and due to this, our responsibility is increased. This responsibility extends far into the future.

Bibliography

Adlung, Jakob: Anleitung zur musikalischen Gelahrtheit. Erfurt 1758.

– – Musica mechanica organoedi I. II. Berlin 1768. Christard Mahrenholz, Kassel 1931.

Andersen, Poul-Gerhard, Finn Viderø, Sybrand Zachariassen: Orgelbygge och orgelspel. Lund 1955.

Antegnati, Constanzo: L'arte organica. Brescia 1608.

Baake, Ferdinand: Beschreibung der grossen Orgeln zu Wismar und Halberstadt. Halberstadt 1846.

Bedos: Dom Bedos de Celles, L'art du facteur d'orgues. 1766–1778.

Bendeler, Johann Philipp: Organopoeia oder Unterweisung wie eine Orgel zu erbauen (1690–1735).

Bericht über die dritte Tagung für deutsche Orgelkunst in Freiberg. Kassel 1928.

Bericht über die Freiburger Tagung für deutsche Orgelkunst. Augsburg 1926.

Beyer, P. C., Frölich Hansen, K. G., Lauridsen, H., Mølgaard, H. T. & Petersen, Erik: Radioteknik og Elektroakustik. København 1948.

Biehle, Johannes: Die Tagung für Orgelbau in Berlin 1928.

– – Raumakustische, orgeltechnische und bauliturgische Probleme. Leipzig 1922.

Biermann, Johann Hermann: Organographia Hildesiensis. Hildesheim 1738. (Kassel 1930).

Bormann, Karl: Die gotische Orgel von Halberstadt. Berlin 1966.

Bouman, A.: Orgels in Nederland. Amsterdam 1949.

Burgemeister, Ludwig: Der Orgelbau in Schlesien: Studien zur deutschen Kunstgeschichte. Strassburg 1925.

de Caus, Salomon: Les raisons des forces mouvantes. Frankfurt 1615.

Cavaillé-Coll, Aristide: Etudes experimentales sur les tuyaux d'orgues. Paris 1868.

– – De l'orgue et de son architecture. Extrait de la Revue générales de l'architecture. Paris 1872.

Cellier, Alexandre: L'orgue, ses éléments – son histoire – son esthétique. Paris 1933.

Clutton, Cecil & Niland, Austin: The British organ. London 1963.

David, Werner: Johann Sebastian Bachs Orgeln. Berlin 1951.

Dähnert, Ulrich: Die Orgeln Gottfried Silbermanns in Mitteldeutschlands. Leipzig 1953.

Deimling, Ernst Ludwig: Beschreibung des Orgelbaues von D. L. E. Offenbach. 1792.

Diruta, Girolamo: Secunda parta del transilvano dialogo. Venice 1609.

Die Dresdener Handschrift. Orgeldispositionen. Paul Smets, Kassel 1931.

Dufourcq, Norbert: Esquisse d'une histoire de l'orgue en France du XIIIe au XVIIe siècle. Paris 1935.

Ellerhorst, Winfrid: Handbuch der Orgelkunde. Einsiedeln 1936.

Flade, Ernst: Der Orgelbauer Gottfried Silbermann. Leipzig 1926.
Friis, Niels: Diverse orgelmonografier.
– – Orgelbygning i Danmark. Renaissance, Barok og Rokoko. Copenhagen 1949.
Freeman, Andrew: English Organ Cases. London 1921.
– – Swedish Organs and Organ Builders 1200–1861. (The Organ Vol. IX, Nr. 37. London 1930).
Gastoué, A.: L'orgue en France. Paris 1921.
Hammerich, Angul: Et historisk orgel på Frederiksborg slot.
Hardouin, Pierre: Le Grand Orgue de Saint-Gervais à Paris. Paris 1949.
Hennerberg, C. F.: Die schwedischen Orgeln des Mittelalters. Vienna 1909.
– – Orglar i Norden under medeltiden. (Nordisk kultur XXV).
Hess, Joachim: Dispositien der merkwaardigsten Kerkorgelen. Gouda 1774.
– – Luister van het Orgel. Gouda 1772.
Hill, Arthur George: Organ Cases and Organs of the Middle Ages and Renaissance. London 1883.
– – Medieval Organ Cases in Spain.
Hopkins, Edward and *Rimbault, E. F.:* The Organ, its History and Construction. London 1877.
Hülphers, Abrah.: Kort Beskrivning över Orgwerken i Sverige. Westerås 1773.
Ingerslev, Fritz & Frobenius, Walther: Some Measurements of the End-Corrections and Acoustic Spectra of cylindrical open Flue Organ Pipes. A. T. S. Nr. 1. 1947.
Jahnn, Hans Henny: Die Orgel. Berlin 1925.
– – Entstehung und Beschreibung der Kurvenmensuren. Leipzig 1926.
Jeppesen, Knud: Die italienische Orgelmusik im Anfang des Cinquecentum.
Jeans, James: Musik og Fysik. Overs. ved Iver Gudme. Copenhagen 1947.
Kaufmann, Walter: Der Orgelprospekt. Mainz 1949.
Kircher, Athanasius: Musurgia universalis. Rome 1650.
Klotz, Hans: Über die Orgelkunst der Gotik, der Renaissance und des Barock. Kassel 1935.
Lottermoser, Werner: Warum akustische Messungen an Barockorgeln? Archiv für Musikwissenschaft Nr. 2. 1952.
Lunelli, Renato: Der Orgelbau in Italien in seinen Meisterwerken. Mainz 1956.
Løffler, Hans: J. S. Bachs Orgelprüfungen. Leipzig 1925.
Mahrenholz, Christard: Die Orgelregister, ihre Geschichte und ihr Bau. Kassel 1930.
– – Die Berechnung der Orgelpfeifen-Mensuren. Kassel 1938.
Merklin, Albert: Organologia. Madrid 1924.
– – Aus Spaniens altem Orgelbau.
Mersenne, Marin: Harmonie universelle 1636/37.
– – Harmonicorum libri XII. 1648.
Niedt, Friederich Erhardt: Musicalischer Handleitung II. Teil 2. Aufl. hrsg. von J. Mattheson. Hamburg 1721.
Pirro, André: L'orgue de Jean Sebastian Bach. Paris 1895.
Praetorius, Michael: Syntagma Musicum. Tomus secundus. De Organographia. Wolfenbüttel 1618. (Kassel 1929).

Praetorius, Michael & Compenius, Esaias: Orgeln Verdingnis. Kieler Beiträge zur Musikwissenschaft, Heft 4. Berlin 1936.
Raugel, Felix: Les orgues et les organistes de la cathédrale de Strasbourg. Paris 1948.
– – Les orgues de l'abbaye de Saint-Mihiel. 1919.
– – Recherches sur les maîtres de l'ancienne facture française d'orgues. 1925.
– – Les anciens buffets d'orgue du département de Seine-et-Oise. 1926.
– – Les grandes orgues des églises de Paris et du département de la Seine. 1927.
– – Les anciens buffets d'orgues du département de Seine-et-Marne. 1929.
– – Les maîtres français de l'orgue aux XVIIe et XVIIIe siècles.
– – Les grandes orgues de la cathédrale de Forcalquier. 1935.
Rheingold-Verlag: Div. Orgel-Monographien.
Rosenquist, Carl E.: Orgelkonst. Lund 1937.
Rupp, Emile: Die Entwicklungsgeschichte der Orgelbaukunst. Einsiedeln 1929.
Schlick, Arnold: Spiegel der Orgelmacher und Organisten. Heidelberg 1511. (Mainz 1932).
Schweitzer, Albert: Deutsche und französische Orgelbaukunst. Leipzig 1906.
Servières, George: La décoration artistique des buffets d'orgue. Paris et Bruxelles 1928.
Sorge, Georg Andreas: Der in der Rechen und Messkunst wohlerfahrene Orgelbaumeister. 1773. (Mainz 1932).
Sponsel, Johann Ulrich: Orgelhistorie. Nürnberg 1771. (Kassel 1931).
Stahl, Wilhelm: Geschichte der Kirchenmusik in Lübeck. Lübeck 1931.
– – Die Totentanzorgel der Marienkirche in Lübeck. Mainz 1932.
Sumner, W. L.: Father Henry Willis, London 1955.
– – The Organ.
Supper, Walter: Der Kleinorgelbrief.
– – Die Orgeldisposition.
– – Lesebuch für Orgelleute.
– – Wege zu neuem Orgelgestalten durch die Orgelbewegung.
Töpfer, Johann Gottlob: Die Orgelbaukunst nach einer neuen Theorie. 1833.
– – Erster Nachtrag zur Orgelbaukunst. 1834.
– – Lehrbuch der Orgelbaukunst. 4 Bd. mit Atlas. 1855.
– – (Allihn) Die theorie und Praxis des Orgelbaues. 1888.
Vente, M. A.: Bouwstoffen tot de Geschiedenis van het Nederlandse Orgel in de 16. Eeuw. Amsterdam 1942.
– – Die brabanter Orgel. Amsterdam 1958.
Walcker, Oscar: Zur Geschichte der Orgelmensuren. Augsburg 1926.
Wangemann, O.: Geschichte der Orgel und der Orgelbaukunst. 1881.
Werckmeister, Andreas: Erweiterte and verbesserte Orgelprobe. 1692. (Kassel 1928.)
Westblad, Gösta: Kyrkoorgeln. Stockholm 1941.
Wester, Bertil: Gotisk resning i svanska orglar. Stockholm 1936.
Wörsching, Joseph: Der Orgelbauer Karl Riepp. Mainz 1940.
– – Die Orgelbauerfamilie Silbermann in Strassburg i. E.
Zang, Johann Heinrich: Der vollkommene Orgelmacher oder Lehre von Orgel und Windprobe. 1804.

Plates

42. *Sion* (Sitten), Switzerland, c. 1400. Possibly war loot from Italy. See p. 270. (After drawing by Hill)
43. *Malmö,* Sweden; formerly Petri Church, now Malmö Museum (c. 1500). Rückpositiv new. See text p. 271. (Photo Almquist & Cöster, Hälsingborg.)
44. *Lübeck;* large organ of Marienkirche (1516). See text p. 271. Note the Renaissance positive below central tower of main front, added later. It was removed during restoration in the mid-nineteenth century, the front being used for the choir (pulpitum) organ. (After painting in St Annen Museum, Lübeck.)
45. *Kiedrich,* c. 1450. See text p. 271.
46. *Lübeck,* Marienkirche. Totentanzkapelle. Main organ 1477; rückpositiv 1557. See text p. 271.
47. *Lübeck,* small organ of Jacobi Church; main organ from end of fifteenth century, rückpositiv 1636. See text p. 271.

48 A. *Sorø* Abbey Church. Main organ c. 1500, partly altered in 1628 when the rückpositiv was added. See text pp. 271 and 314.

48 B. *Sorø* Abbey Church. Organ before reconstruction 1942; i. e., in the form given to it in the rebuilding at the end of the eighteenth century. At the reconstruction in 1942 is was restored to the form from 1628. (Photo National Museum, Copenhagen)

49. *Lübeck,* large organ of Jacobi Church. Main organ 1504, rückpositiv and pedal towers 1673. See text p. 272.
50. *Augsburg,* Annenkirche, Fuggerkapelle, 1512. See text p. 272. (After drawing by Hill)
51. *Rheims,* c. 1500. Front principal, 24′. See text p. 272. (After drawing by Jacques Celliers, 1583) (Photo Archives photografiques, Paris)
52. *Bologna,* St Petronio. The Gothic front, it seems, was not magnificent enough and so has been "improved" with a later frame.
53. *Bologna,* St Peronio. Console part. The stops are pushed down and hooked; i. e., the organ has spring-chests.
54. *Siena,* Santa Maria della Scala (1501). See text p. 274. (After drawing by Hill)
55. *Tirano.* See text p. 274.
56. *Strassbourg,* Münster (1492). See text p. 274.
57. *Harenkarspel,* now Rijksmuseum, Amsterdam (c. 1530). See text p. 274. (Photo Rijksmuseum, Amsterdam)
58. *Schemda,* now Rijksmuseum, Amsterdam (1526). See text p. 273. (Photo Rijksmuseum, Amsterdam)
59. *Schemda.* Note elaborate facets of front pipes.

60. *Utrecht,* St Nicolaas. Main organ 1478. Rugwerk 1580. See text p. 275. (Photo Piet Vreke, Middelburg)

61. *Utrecht,* St Nicolaas. Detail of main organ blockwerk soundboard. (Photo Rijksmuseum, Amsterdam)

62. *Haarlem,* St. Bavo. The large organ c. 1500. Below, right, is a smaller organ, built 1594. (After painting by Piter Saenredam) (Photo Rijksmuseum, Amsterdam)

63. *Alkmaar,* St. Laurens, choir organ (1511). See text pp. 276 and 278. (Photo Rijksdienst v/d Monumentenzorg)

64. *Roskilde Cathedral.* Rückpositiv c. 1555, main organ 1654. See text p. 276. (Photo National Museum, Copenhagen)

65. *Jutfaas* (1540), originally Nieuwe Zijdskapel, Amsterdam. See text p. 277. (After drawing by Hill)

66. *Amsterdam,* Nieuwe Kerk (1655). See text p. 277. (Photo Lichtbilden Instituut)

67. *Alkmaar,* St Laurens, large organ (1654). See text p. 278. (Photo Rijksdienst v/d Monumentenzorg)

68. *Herzogenbosch* (c. 1725). See text p. 278. (Photo Rijksdienst v/d Monumentenzorg)

69. *Haarlem,* St. Bavo. Müller organ 1738. An example of North German influence. The front has pedal towers with 32′ principal, bovenwerk and rugwerk with 8′ principal and hoofdwerk with 16′ principal.

70. *Flensburg,* St Nicolai (1605). The front, made by Henrik Ringeringk, woodcarver of Flensburg, is dominated in various ways by the decorative; e. g., several of the pipes in the three large panels of the main front have overlengths to fill out the panels, nor is the bipartition of the rückpositiv integral to the organ. Towers not used at all.

71. *Tønder* Church. An example of the "Hamburg" type, with detached pedal towers in the balustrade, great organ, brustwerk and rückpositiv. The front derives essentially from a reconstruction of the organ in 1630, though there appear to be traces of the church's first organ of 1590 in the rückpositiv. The brustwerk, which was partly built in front of the "stool", was added in 1685, and the very dominating acanthus decoration dates from 1701. (Photo Th. Frobenius)

72 A. *Haderslev* Cathedral after reconstruction in 1947. Also a front of Hamburg type. See text pp. 291 - 96 and 314. (Photo Kaj Ludolph, Haderslev, copyright)

72 B. *Haderslev* Cathedral before reconstruction. (Fig. 73 in text)

74. *Copenhagen,* Holmens Church (1740). Offshoots of the Hamburg line in Scandinavia preferred in most cases to site the pedal towers in the organ loft in connection with the great organ. Such was the practice in most of the large organs built by Carstens. (Photo Jonals C., Copenhagen)

75. *Copenhagen,* Vor Frelsers Church (1698). Here pedal organ and great organ have also joined, and further, there is no clear distinction between the two organs. The shapes in general are very decoratively determined, and – as at Flensburg, St Nicolai – decorative considerations have also occasioned the bi-

partition of the rückpositiv. Of the small pipe panels, only the bottom ones of each organ are sounding. The others have dummy pipes. (Photo Kunstakademiet, Copenhagen)

76. *Löfsta* Bruk Church (1728). Exceptionally, Cahmann has employed detached pedal parts in the balustrade, perhaps because of the church's immense width. The left side of the pedal is not included in the picture. The disposition is quite symmetrical. (Photo Bertil Wester)
77. *Kölingared* Church. Also a broad front in a wide church, but in a more normal style, for Cahmann, with the pedal parts built together with the main organ. (Photo Einar Erici)
78. *Hamburg,* Michaëliskirche (1768). Largest front pipe in middle 32′ C. Otherwise, the front a typical representative of the Casparini-Silbermann line's fronts, tending to false fronts, with sounding pipes, but without any organic connection between organ and front. See text p. 283. (After a photograph before the fire of 1906. The front was rebuilt as a copy of the old one)
79. *Växiö* Cathedral (1779). See text p. 284.
80. *Karlskrona,* Frederikskyrkan (1724). See text p. 284. (Photo Bertil Wester)
81. *Amiens* (orig. sixteenth century). See text p. 285.
82. *Chartres.* See text p. 285. (After drawing by Hill)
83. *La Ferté Bernard.* See text p. 286. (Photo archives photografiques, Paris)
84. *Moret.* See text p. 286.
85. *Versailles,* St. Louis. See text p. 286. (Photo Archives photografiques, Paris)
86. *Abbaye de Mondaye.* See text p. 286. (Photo Archives photografiques, Paris)
87. *Dom Bedos'* proposed front without pipes. See text p. 287.
88. *Paris,* St. Sulpice. See text p. 287.
89. *Perpignan* (1504). See text p. 288.
90. *Salamanca,* small organ (1380). See text p. 287. (After drawing by Hill)
91. *Zaragoza* (1473). See text p. 287. (After a drawing by Hill)
92. *Tarragona* (1563). See text p. 287. (After a drawing by Hill)
93. *Toledo,* Imperial organ (sixteenth century). See text p. 288. (Photo Metzler)
94. *Salamanca,* large organ (eighteenth century). Front facing chancel. (Photo Metzler)
95. *Salamanca,* large organ. Rear towards aisle. (Photo Victor Schlatter)
96. *Granada* (eighteenth century). Note the large dummy pipes in the outer panels and the many reed pipes. (Photo Metzler)
97. *Granada.* A view from the aisle showing the other choir organ from behind and a corner of the Gospel organ. (Photo Metzler)
98. *Toledo,* the Baroque organ (1758). See text pp. 159–60. (Photo Metzler)
99. *Toledo,* the Baroque organ. Detail of console part.
100. *Weingarten* (1750). See text p. 289.
101. *Ottobeuren* (1766). See text p. 289.
102. *Solothurn,* Switzerland. The eighteenth century could also employ simple means.
103. *Old Radnor,* St. Stephen's (c. 1500). Probably the oldest surviving English organ front.

104. *Cambridge,* King's College (1606). The pulpitum organ seen from the choir.
105. *Cambridge,* King's College. The same organ seen from the nave. See text p. 297.
107. *Jægersborg* Church (1844). See text pp. 309–12. (Photo Sv. Glensdal)
108. *Jægersborg* Church. Detail main organ. (Photo Sv. Glensdal)
109. *Copenhagen,* Gustavs Church (1947). See text p. 313. (Photo Jonals Co.)
110. *Copenhagen,* Grundtvigs Church (1940). See text p. 314. (Photo Jonals Co.)
111. *Copenhagen,* State Radio (1946). See text pp. 316–17. (Photo Jonals Co.)
112. *Tranebjerg* Church, Samsø (1954). See text p. 318. (Photo E. Frobenius)
113. *Østerlars* Church (1956). The famous round church on the Danish island of Bornholm is internally shaped like a barrel-vaulted room that has been bent into a ring. Here the organ has the Hauptwerk and Pedal on the same wind chest, in addition to a Brustwerk. The organ is mounted radially in the room, and both front and back of the organ are equipped with façade pipes. (Architect: Rolf Graae. Ornaments: Poul Høm)
114. *St. Peder,* Næstved (1957). The old Brebus organ from 1585 (originally built as a choir organ for the church) was moved to the west end of the nave during the nineteenth century, where it served as a "screen" for a pneumatic instrument. During the rebuilding in 1957, a Hauptwerk and Brustwerk were mounted in a new house, standing behind the old façade and adapted to it. Pedal towers and Rückpositiv in modern style were added, according to the wish of the National Museum. (Paintings: Viktor Steensgaard. Architect: the author)
115. *Our Lady,* Vordingborg (1958). The seventeenth-century organ loft had to be retained unchanged; further, a connection to the tower vault behind the loft was re-created by uncovering the earlier window above and the doorway below, which had been bricked up. The beautiful carved balustrade of the loft precluded a Rückpositiv, hence the organ was built with two central positives, one speaking towards the nave, the other towards the tower. The Hauptwerk and Pedal were mounted on common wind chests on both sides of these positives. (Pipe ornaments: Viktor Steensgaard. Architect: the author)
116. *Our Lady,* Skive, Denmark (1965). This small church needed a fairly large organ of 19 stops, and therefore the design had to be as compact as possible. The Principal 8′ of the Hauptwerk is mounted above in the centre of the front, excepting the six biggest pipes which have been placed together with the 8′ Principal of the Pedal, whose lowest octave fills up the side compartments. (Colours and ornaments: Poul Høm. Architect: the author)
117. *The Cathedral of Skara,* Sweden (1964). The large west window of the church required a low central part of the instrument, and here an 8′ Hauptwerk was placed. Behind it a Swell-box, and on both sides of it the Principal 16′ of the Pedal. The Rückpositiv is a 4′ Werk in order to keep the front as low as possible in the middle. (Paintings: Olle Hellström. Architect: the author)
118. *St. Nicolaas,* Utrecht (1956). The Romanesque window behind the organ was discovered during a restoration of the western part of the church. Hence the centre part of the organ had to be as low as possible. The organ has a 16′

Pedal, 8′ Hauptwerk, 4′ Rückpositiv and 2′ Brustwerk. (Pipe ornaments: Viktor Steensgaard. Architect: the author)

119. *Cathédrale de St. Pierre,* Geneva (1965). The organ has four manual Werks: a 16′ Hauptwerk, Crescendo Werk, a 4′ Brustwerk, and an 8′ Rückpositiv. The 16′ Principal of the Hauptwerk is mounted in the recessed central part above, covering the Crescendo Werk. The pipe compartments below contain the 8′ Principal of the Hauptwerk, and the 16′ Principal of the Pedal is mounted in the side towers. (Architect: the author)

120. *Copenhagen,* Christianschurch (1761). See text p. 299. (Photo Jonals Co.)

121. *Chartres.* See text p. 298. (Photo Archives photografiques, Paris)

122. *Amiens.* See text p. 299. (Photo Archives photografiques, Paris)

123. *Labial pipe forms,* from left to right: Hohlflöte, Principal, Principal, Viola da Gamba, Flûte harmonique, Flachflöte, Blockflöte, Gemshorn, Spitzgamba, Salicet, Koppelflöte, Rohrflöte, Gedackt, Gedackt, Quintatön, Spitzgedackt, Wooden Spitzgedackt. (Photo Jonals Co.)

Index

Personal names in italics are those of writers also included in the Bibliography. Numbers in bold type refer to Figs.
o. = organ *bdr.* = organ builder.

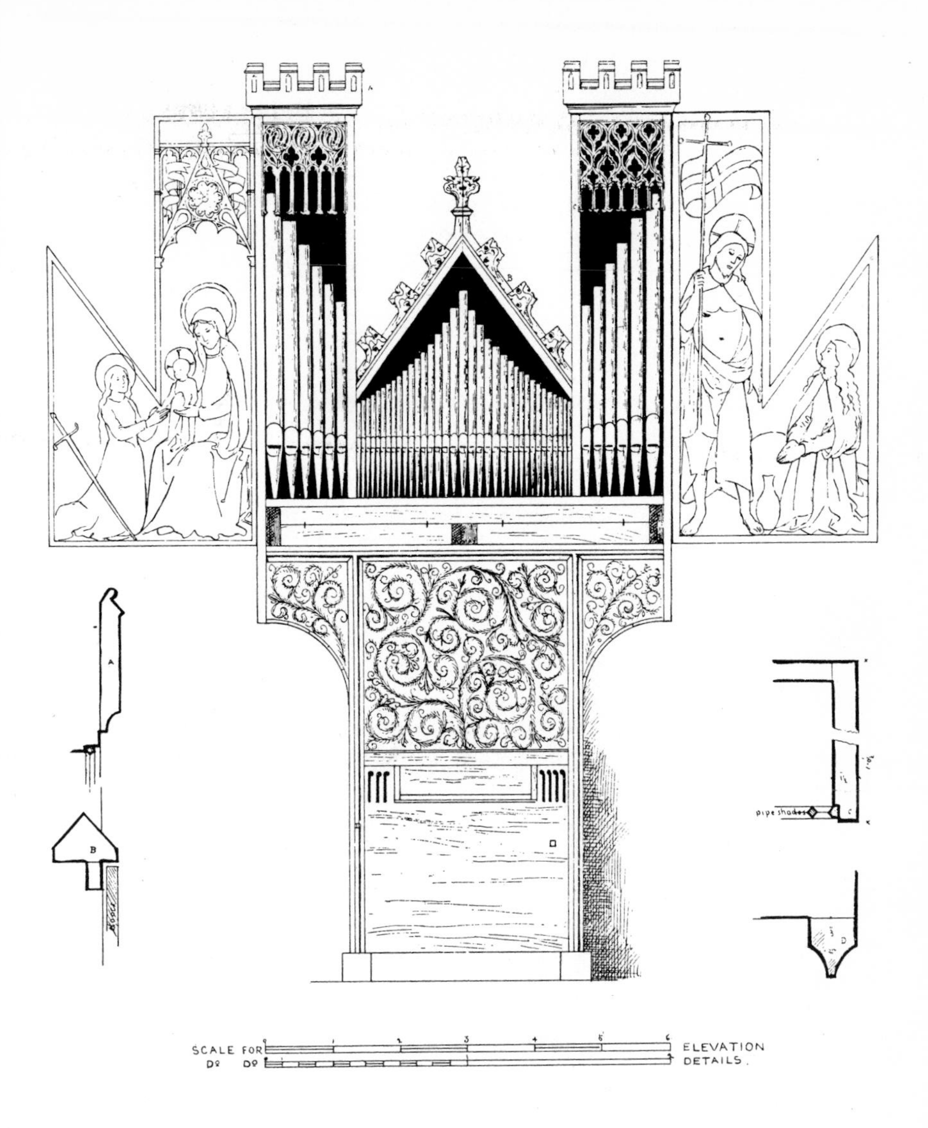

Fig. 42

Fig. 43

Fig. 44

Fig. 45

Fig. 46

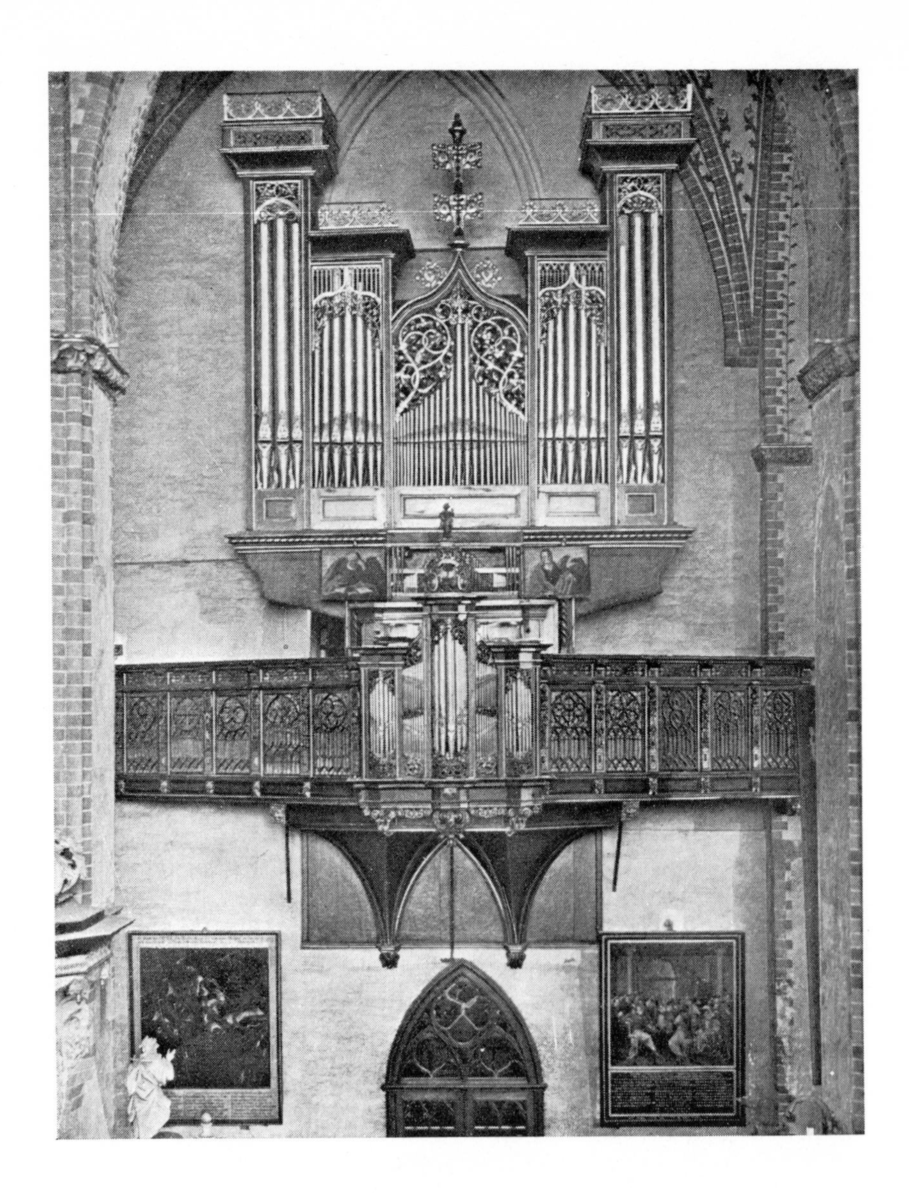

Fig. 47

Fig. 48A

Fig. 48B

Fig. 49

ORGEL MACHER IO HANN VON DORRN
Augsburg. Annenkirche.
A. G. Hill del.

Fig. 50

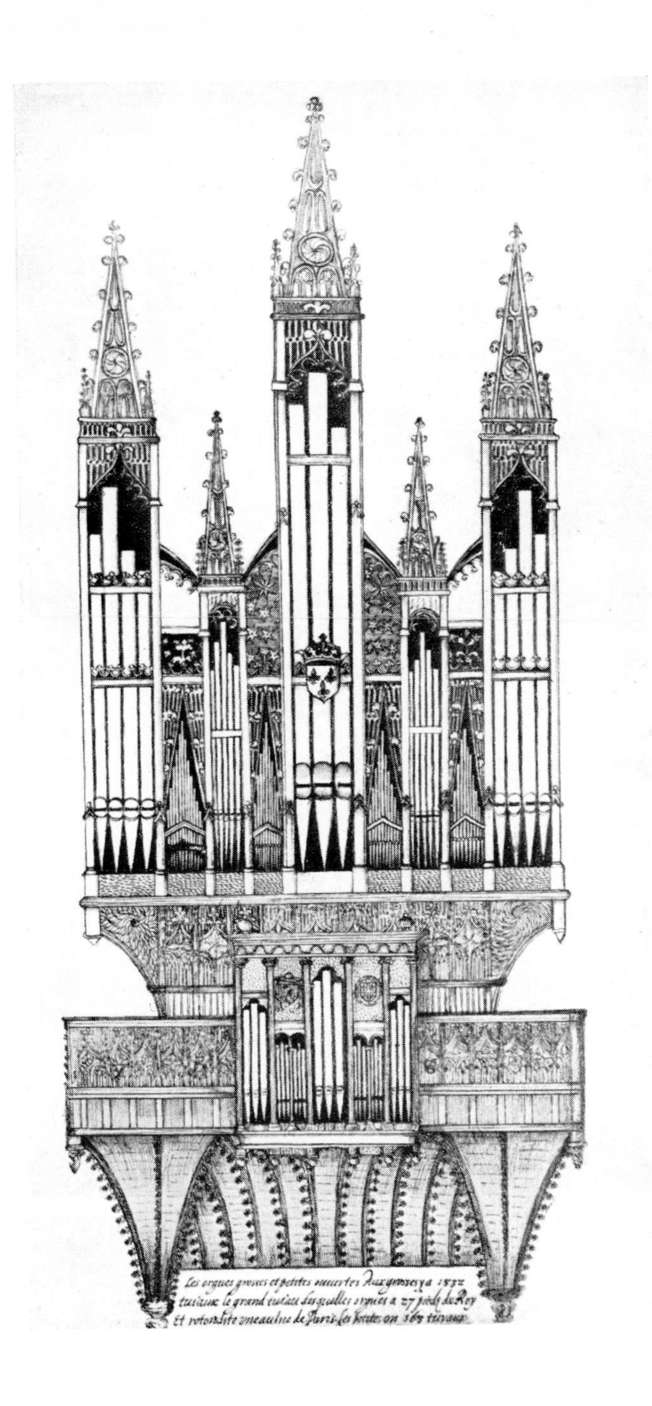

Fig. 51

Fig. 52

Fig. 53

HAEC MARIÆ SANCTAS PRIO RVMPVNT ORGANI LAVDES AT VOS
CEROS AMPLIFICATE LARES
A.G. Hill del:

Fig. 54

Fig. 55

Fig. 56

Fig. 57

Fig. 58

Fig. 59

Fig. 60

Fig. 61

Fig. 62

Fig. 63

Fig. 64

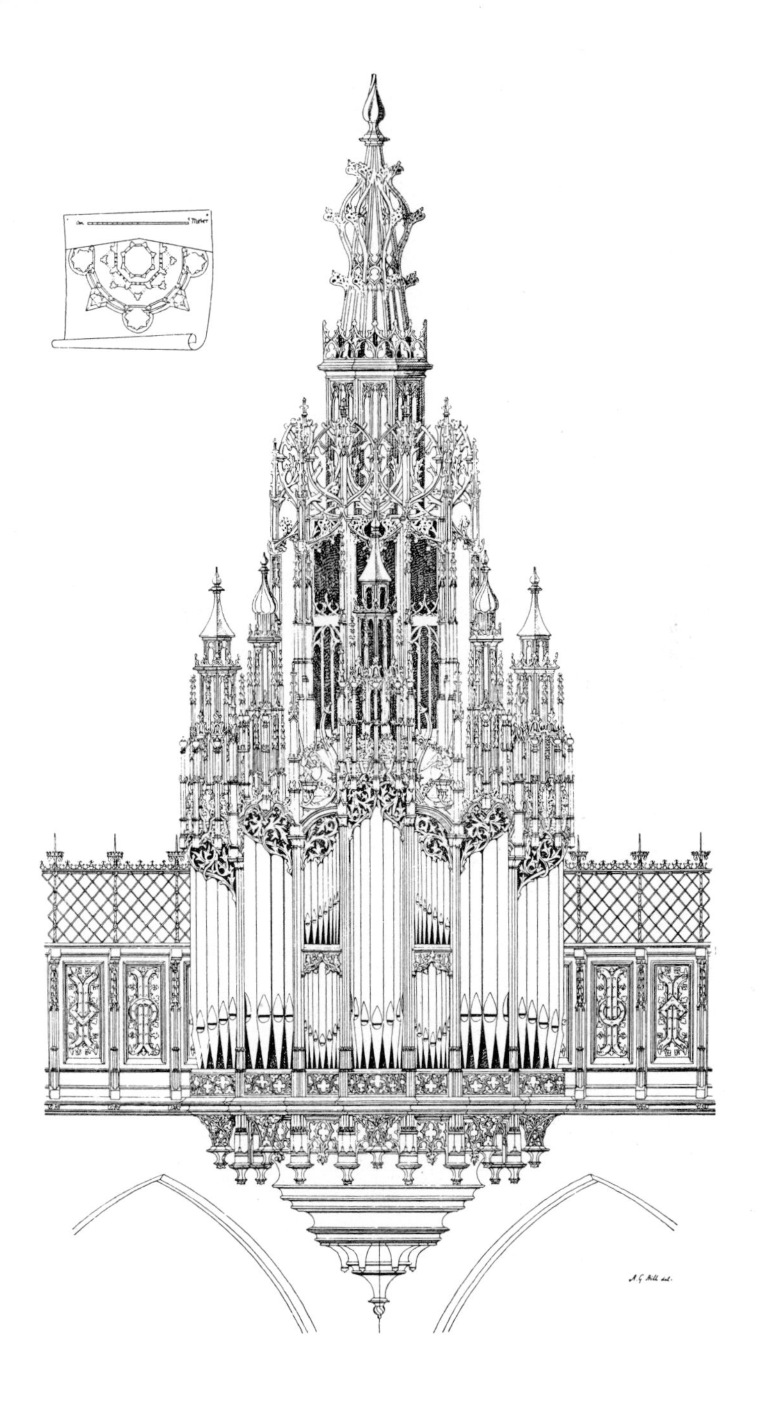

Fig. 65

Fig. 66

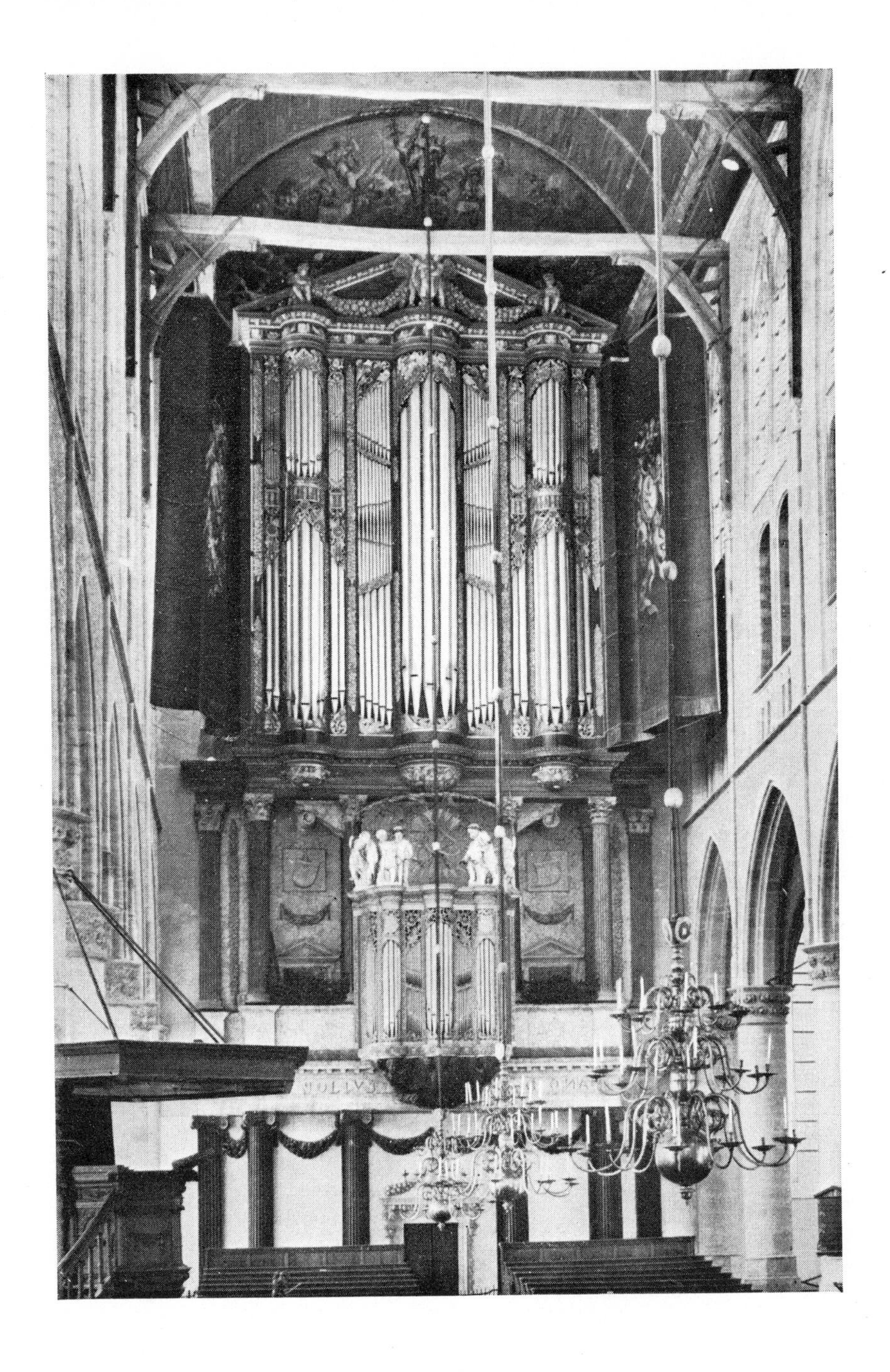

Fig. 67

Fig. 68

Fig. 69

Fig. 70

Fig. 71

Fig. 72A

Fig. 72B

Fig. 74

Fig. 75

Fig. 76

Fig. 77

Fig. 78

Fig. 79

Fig. 80

Fig. 81

Fig. 82

Fig. 83

Fig. 84

Fig. 85

Fig. 86

Fig. 87

Fig. 88

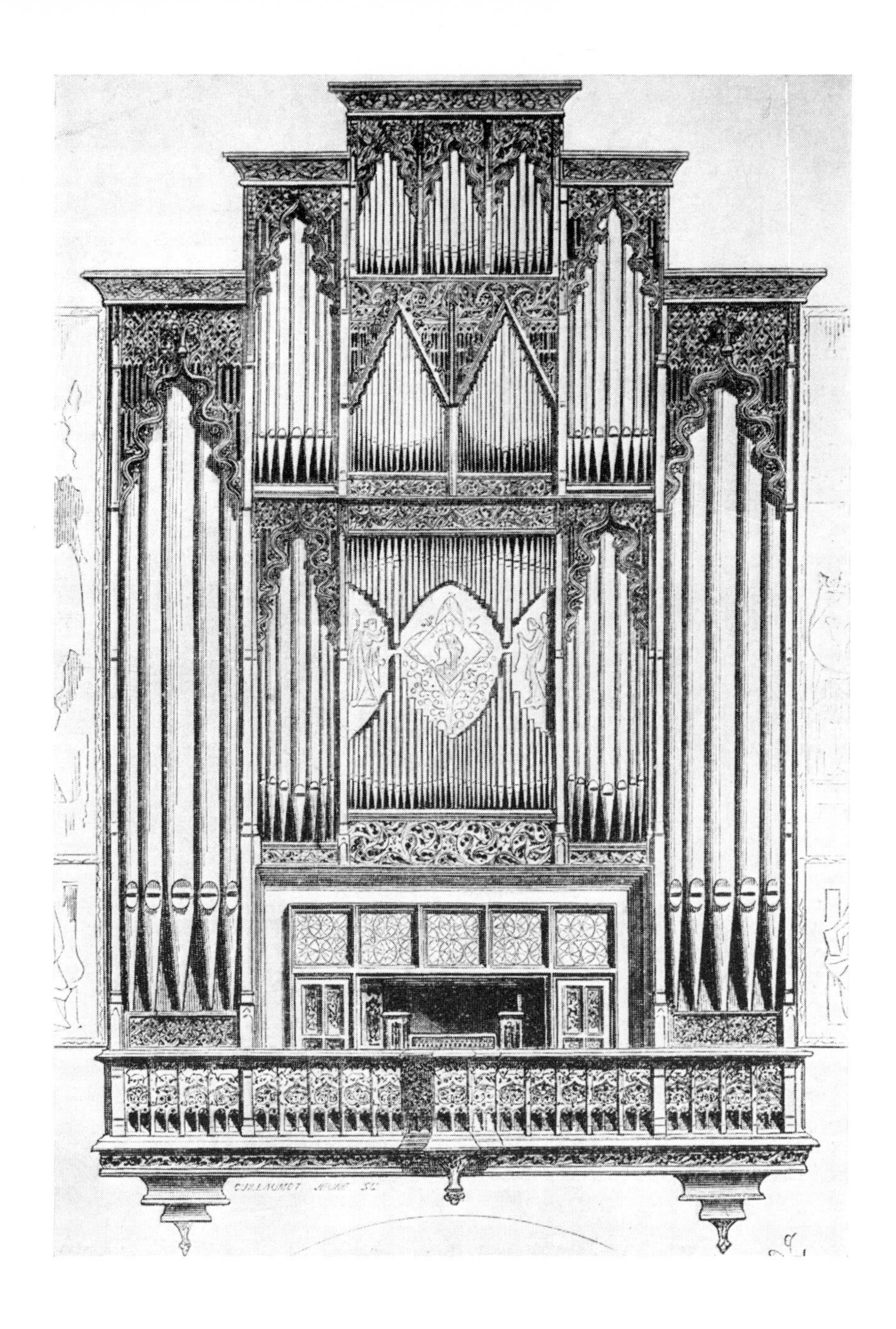

Fig. 89

Fig. 90

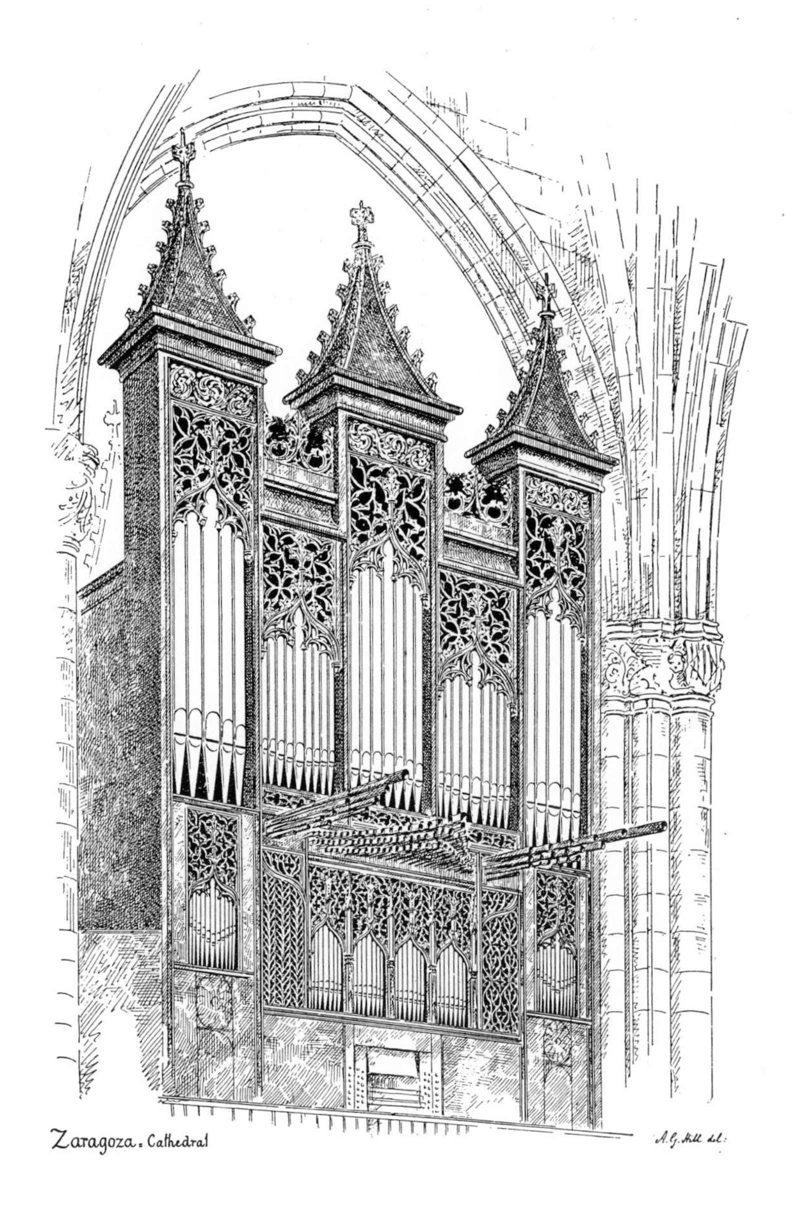

Fig. 91

Fig. 92

Fig. 93

Fig. 94

Fig. 95

Fig. 96

Fig. 97

Fig. 98

Fig. 99

Fig. 100

Fig. 101

Fig. 102

Fig. 103

Fig. 104

Fig. 105

Fig. 107

Fig. 108

Fig. 109

Fig. 110

Fig. 111

Fig. 112

Fig. 113

Fig. 114

Fig. 115

Fig. 116

Fig. 117

Fig. 118

Fig. 119

Fig. 120

Fig. 121

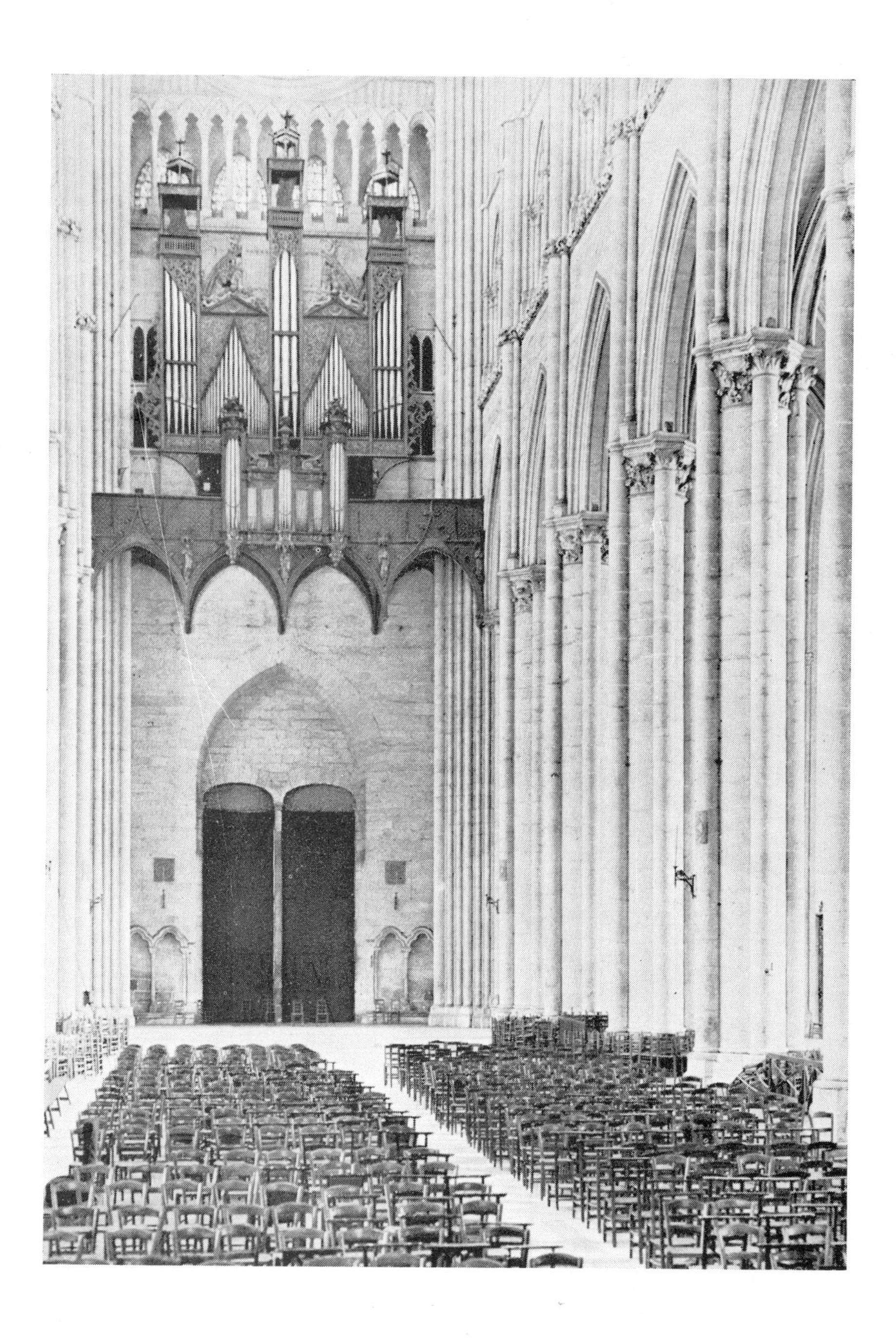

Fig. 122

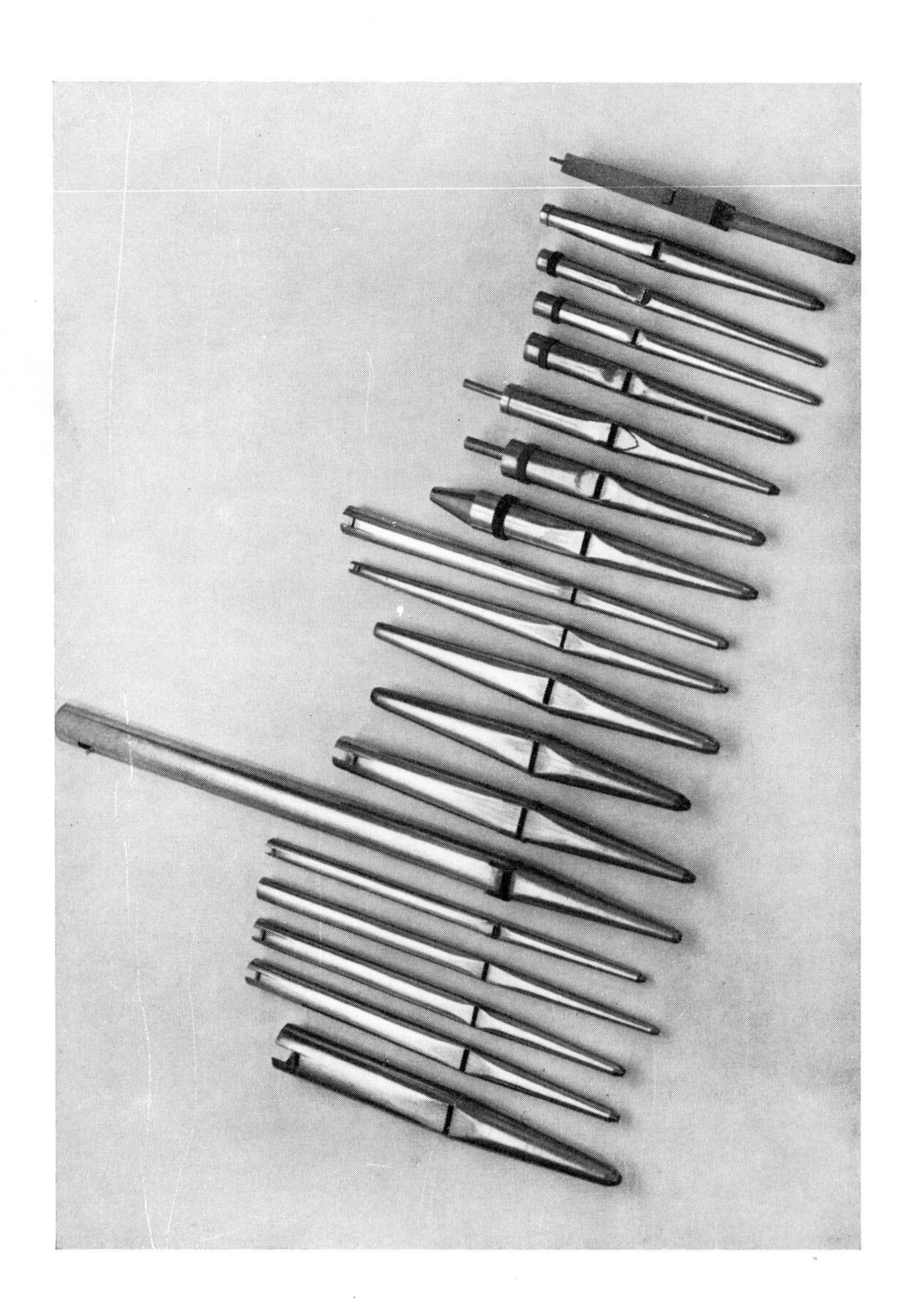

Fig. 123